The
Developmental
Psychologists

RESEARCH ADVENTURES
ACROSS THE LIFE SPAN

D1399685

McGRAW-HILL SERIES
IN DEVELOPMENTAL PSYCHOLOGY

CONSULTING EDITOR
ROSS A. THOMPSON

The
Developmental
Psychologists

RESEARCH ADVENTURES
ACROSS THE LIFE SPAN

❖

EDITED BY

Matthew R. Merrens

Gary G. Brannigan

State University of New York—Plattsburgh

The McGraw-Hill Companies, Inc.

New York   St. Louis   San Francisco   Auckland   Bogotá   Caracas   Lisbon
London   Madrid   Mexico City   Milan   Montreal   New Delhi   San Juan
Singapore   Sydney   Tokyo   Toronto

McGraw-Hill

A Division of The **McGraw-Hill** Companies

THE DEVELOPMENTAL PSYCHOLOGISTS
Research Adventures across the Life Span

This book is printed on acid-free paper.

1 2 3 4 5 6 7 8 9 0 DOC DOC 9 0 9 8 7 6 5

ISBN 0-07-007259-0

This book was set in Palatino by ComCom, Inc.
The editors were Michael Clark, Beth Kaufman, and Fred H. Burns;
the production supervisor was Richard A. Ausburn.
The cover was designed by Karen K. Quigley.
R. R. Donnelley & Sons Company was printer and binder.

Cover art: Felix Vallotton, LE BALLON (THE BALL), Musée d'Orsay, Paris; Giraudon/Art Resource, NY. Artist Copyright SPADEM/ARS.

Photo Credits: Page v, top and bottom: photos by Robin Brown; page 88: photo by News Bureau, Arizona State University.

Library of Congress Cataloging-in-Publication Data

The developmental psychologists : research adventures across the life
   span / edited by Matthew R. Merrens, Gary G. Brannigan.
      p.   cm. — (McGraw-Hill series in developmental psychology)
   Includes bibliographical references.
   ISBN 0-07-007259-0
   1. Developmental psychology—Research—Case studies.   I. Merrens,
Matthew R.   II. Brannigan, Gary G.   III. Series.
BF713.D463   1996
155—dc20   95-25520

About the Editors

Matthew R. Merrens (Ph.D., University of Montana) is Professor and Chairperson of the Department of Psychology at SUNY–Plattsburgh. His research has focused on personality assessment and behavior modification. He has coordinated a large innovative introductory psychology course and has authored several general psychology handbooks. He is the coeditor of *The Undaunted Psychologist: Adventures in Research* and *The Social Psychologists: Research Adventures*. Dr. Merrens received the SUNY Chancellor's Award for Excellence in Teaching. He and his family enjoy outdoor activities in the Lake Champlain–Adirondack region of New York.

Gary G. Brannigan (Ph.D., University of Delaware) is a Professor of Psychology at SUNY–Plattsburgh and a fellow of the Society for Personality Assessment. His research is primarily on psychological assessment and therapy with children. He served as Director of the Psychological Services Clinic at SUNY–Plattsburgh and is currently a consultant to the Clinton County Association for Retarded Citizens' Early Education Program. He is also serving on the editorial boards of three journals. In addition to coediting *The Undaunted Psychologist: Adventures in Research* and *The Social Psychologists: Research Adventures*, and editing *The Enlightened Educator: Research Adventures in the Schools*, he has published numerous articles, chapters, books, and tests, including (with A. Tolor) *Research and Clinical Applications of the Bender-Gestalt Test* and (with N. Brunner) *The Modified Version of the Bender-Gestalt Test*. His interests include sports, art, music, and fine dining.

To my grandson, Samuel Jeffrey Merrens, and his grandmother, Roberta
MRM

To my wife, Linda, and my sons, Marc and Michael
GGB

Contents

❖

Foreword

❖

Sometimes it can be tough being a developmental psychologist. Two years ago, I asked my oldest son what he wanted to be when he grew up. "A scientist," he replied. "Oh, you mean like me?" I naively asked. Scott made a face. "No, Dad. A *real* scientist!"

Scott's response revealed his views of what science is like, and what scientists are like. His nine-year-old portrayal of science consisted primarily of laboratory tests on chemicals, proteins, and other natural substances in test tubes. He imagined scientists to be men and women in lab coats who worked in those labs, carefully testing theoretically formulated hypotheses and examining the results. Although I have succeeded in broadening Scott's views about science and scientists during the past few years, it has occurred to me that his initial images of science mirror the way most people view the scientific enterprise. Even within psychology, for example, students are often presented with a very limited model of psychological science as an experimentally based, laboratory-oriented field of study. It is, but it is also much more.

Together with our vaunted (if somewhat narrow) portrayal of the rarefied scientific enterprise, we also tend to acquire vaunted (if somewhat narrow) images of research scientists themselves. These are the creators of new knowledge, the insightful thinkers and ingeneous researchers, who inspire our attention and admiration. What graduate student, attending her or his first professional meeting, has not experienced the momentary tongue-tiedness, self-consciousness, and mind-numbing awe when introduced to a senior scholar whose work has been read and admired during the preceding months? While such respect can be ego-enhancing to any scholar, it also reflects a somewhat limited appreciation of the qualities that contribute to scientific advance, and can pose an impediment to an appreciation of the humanity of the research enterprise.

It would be unfair to characterize the personal accounts of *The Developmental Psychologists: Research Adventures across the Life Span* as efforts to debunk the esteemed images of science and scientists that we often acquire from coursework and the popular culture. It is certainly true, however, that these first-person autobiographical accounts put a more human face on the study of developmental psychology. In describing how they became involved in developmental psychology, experienced a sudden or unexpected change in career orientation, developed their interests in a particular research topic, or struggled with a thorny theoretical problem, the senior scholars who contributed essays to this volume disclose how much the research enterprise is characterized by logical, careful deductive thinking and hard work—and also by elements of serendipity, surprises, and good (or sometimes bad) luck. They also reveal elements of the personal lives that, for every scientist, provide a context and catalyst for their research interests.

As you begin reading this volume, you will encounter remarkable people. You will meet a scientist who, as a boy, was a Jewish refugee from Nazi Germany, who worked as a printing apprentice in Shanghai, and eventually enrolled in psychology courses at a city college in San Francisco because they could be scheduled harmoniously with his job. You will encounter a leading researcher on genetics and development who was suspended from his Catholic school as a fourth-grader for bringing a book on evolution to class. You will discover an adolescent whose auto accident led to a long hospitalization in an orthopedic ward, where she took an introductory psychology course and observed first-hand the care provided to the older adults in her ward, leading to a provocative research career on aging. You will find a mother who, having sought the stimulation of coursework after raising young children, turned from studying the grooming behavior of insects to the movements of young babies. You will meet an insightful student of fatherhood who, in one of his first efforts to study men with their newborn infants, was asked by a nurse whether he had insurance in case one of the dads dropped their child! You will watch as an important program of research arose from a casual lunchtime conversation with a colleague about her adolescent daughter's search for an after-school job. You will encounter senior scientists whose interests in development were forged from their work as a summer lifeguard, or as a cook in a hamburger joint, or from the social and political unrest of the 1960's, or from a brief internship with emotionally disturbed children.

Above all, you will find considerable diversity in how careers develop and how research insights are attained. Many of these scientists succeeded because of their focused pursuit of research questions and interests in the course of straightforward career pathways. But as you will see, for others, the pathways were neither straightforward nor predictable, and research interests shifted according to unexpected discoveries, adaptation to circumstances, or taking advantage of opportunities that happened to have emerged. In many of these accounts, careers and research were forged not only from scientific controversies but also academic politics and the public debates that can cast a sharp spotlight on a researcher's work. For some women, careers were shaped also by their efforts to accommodate the constraints imposed by a partner's professional commitments, or child-rear-

ing demands, or the biases of the university environment. In all of these accounts, the lessons are multifaceted: hard work and good thinking often
(but not always) pay off; life is full of surprises; there are diverse avenues
to a successful research career; scientists are neat people.

As they have accomplished in two previous volumes of autobiographical profiles of prominent psychologists, Matthew Merrens and Gary
Brannigan have offered, for students of developmental psychology, a
provocative and insightful compilation of first-person accounts that put a
human face on science and scientists. As a human enterprise, developmental science benefits from the careful thought, hard work, personal reflection, and fortuitous circumstance that are part of human experience.
And the scientists who do this work are persons—not just "big names"—
whose careers are richly enlivened by the personal histories they bring to
it. We are indebted to these scholars for sharing these insights, and to Merrens and Brannigan for catalyzing and collecting them for us.

The *McGraw-Hill Series in Developmental Psychology*, of which this volume is a part, has been designed to enrich and expand our common knowledge of human development by providing a forum for theorists, researchers, and practitioners to present their insights to a broad audience.
As a rapidly expanding scientific field, developmental psychology has important applications to parents, educators, students, clinicians, policy-
makers, and others who are concerned with promoting human welfare
throughout the life course. Although the fruits of scholarly research into
human development can be found on the pages of research journals, and
students can become acquainted with this exciting field in introductory
textbooks, this series of specialized, topical books is intended to provide
insightful, in-depth examinations of selected issues in the field from which
undergraduates, graduate students, and academic colleagues can each benefit. As forums for highlighting important new ideas, research insights, theoretical syntheses, and applications of knowledge to practical problems, I
hope that these volumes will find many uses: as books that supplement
standard general textbooks in undergraduate or graduate courses, as one
of several specialized texts for advanced coursework, as tutorials for scholars interested in learning about current knowledge on a topic of interest,
and as sourcebooks for practitioners who wish to traverse the gap between
knowledge and application. The authors who contribute to this series are
committed to providing a state-of-the-art, accurate, and readable interpretation of current knowledge that will be interesting and accessible to a
broad audience with many different goals and interests. We hope, too, that
these volumes will inspire the efforts to improve the lives of children, adolescents, and adults through research and practice that are much needed
in our world.

Whether you are a senior scholar learning about the lives of your colleagues, a graduate student seeking inspiration for further progress on a

thesis, an undergraduate student wondering if developmental psychology is really for you, or a casual reader wondering about the lives of those who contribute to developmental knowledge, I hope you enjoy the unfolding life stories that follow.

Ross A. Thompson
Consulting Editor

Preface

❖

The Developmental Psychologists: Research Adventures across the Life Span follows
upon the success of *The Undaunted Psychologist: Adventures in Research* and
The Social Psychologists: Research Adventures. In *The Developmental Psychologists,* and in our previous books, we give the reader an "insider's" view on the
process of how psychological research takes place. To adapt comments by Ann
Weber (University of North Carolina–Asheville), who reviewed one of our earlier
books, personal narratives add the much needed human element to research as they
address many of the important questions that frequently go unanswered in textbooks and journals: Who are you? Where did you come from? Why and how did
you get involved in research? And how did you develop this particular research
interest? Can I identify with you? Do you have off days and ironic moments? What
keeps you excited about your work? What has your experience taught you? What
personal lessons can I carry away from your story? and so on. These in-depth, first-
person accounts of developmental psychology research are designed to complement
texts with either a chronological or a topical format, or to serve as primary readings in advanced courses. While each chapter has a different emphasis and "flavor,"
each contributor gives the reader a view of the researcher as a person dealing with
the planning, design, and methodology of scientific inquiry.

Developmental psychology is probably the most popular psychology course
after introductory psychology. Students are curious about where they came from
and where they are heading. They want to know and explore their own development from infancy to the present and are interested in what's coming next. They
want to prepare for their roles as parents and older adults and are very interested
in understanding the process of aging. We find that students are fascinated with
all the various factors and influences that impact upon the developmental process
and are keenly interested because they are so intimately involved in the process.
Developmental psychology traces the path from conception to death and focuses
on genetic, physical, cognitive, emotional, social, and other factors that impact us
along the way. The research in developmental psychology involves issues and circumstances that we encounter daily, read in the newspaper, see on TV, and talk
about with friends.

The Developmental Psychologists is a dynamic collection of personal adventures that will help bring to life and enrich the material presented in texts. Our contributors have provided lively accounts covering a broad range of topics that closely parallel texts in developmental psychology. They include:

Issues in the nature/nurture debate

Motor development in infancy

The development of receptive language

Issues surrounding parenting and child abuse

Attachment and emotional development

The development of prosocial behavior

Gender differences in development

Piagetian perspectives on cognitive development

Father-child relationships

Puberty

Moral development

Issues in adolescent employment

Adolescent temperament

Memory enhancement in Alzheimers patients

Longitudinal study of cognitive functioning

Interpersonal relationships across the life span

Stress and adaptation in adults

Dying and death

As you read the experiences of each contributor, you will begin to see how they encountered significant issues and developed research strategies to study them. You will also see the interaction between one's personal life and career and how the two are often woven together in an interesting and successful manner.

ACKNOWLEDGMENTS

The Developmental Psychologists: Research Adventures across the Life Span tells of the experiences of eighteen distinguished researchers. The chapters genuinely communicate the excitement and enthusiasm of their search for knowledge and understanding. We are very appreciative of their efforts and thank them for their commitment to this book.

We owe a significant debt of gratitude to Jane Vaicunas, Publisher at McGraw-Hill. Jane's guidance and support helped make this book a reality. We also very much appreciate the ongoing support and counsel of

Beth Kaufman and Mike Clark and their editorial analyses and recommendations. The reviewers of this book also provided many suggestions for clarifying and improving the chapters. We thank John Bonvillian, University of Virginia; Mary Gauvain, University of California, Riverside; Janis Jacobs, University of Nebraska, Lincoln; and Kenneth Kallio, State University of New York, Geneseo.

We are grateful to the State University of New York–Plattsburgh for providing the supportive environment that enabled us to pursue this project. The advice and help of our colleagues, especially Cindy Lightfoot, Taher Zandi, and Lary Shaffer were also invaluable. In addition, the assistance of the following students was very important to the final outcome: Amanda Jankowski, Lynn Mintz, Joshua Duntley, and Melynda Kraft. Their suggestions helped make this book more reader-focused and accessible.

Our secretary, Judy Dashnaw, is especially deserving of the highest commendation. Her superior editorial and word processing skills were absolutely vital to the timely and successful completion of this project.

Finally, we would like to thank our wives, Roberta Merrens and Linda Brannigan, for their efforts in reading and proofing the chapters in this book. Their comments, thoughts, and ongoing support contributed greatly to the quality of this volume.

Matthew R. Merrens
Gary G. Brannigan

Introduction

❖

*T*he Developmental Psychologists: Research Adventures across the Life Span is a collection of eighteen specially prepared chapters that describe exciting explorations in human development. Textbooks do a good job of conveying factual data, principles, theories, and, in general, "bottom line" findings. They do not give the student a view of how a developmental psychologist thinks, plans, and goes about engaging in the process of research. Scientific research is an active process, not just a set of results and statistical analyses. It is important for students to view this process with all its ups and downs, successes and failures, and joys and sadnesses. *The Developmental Psychologists* opens the door to allow readers an inside view of this exciting process. Students will learn by observing researchers confront problems, define methods, and initiate research to probe issues and answer questions. They will also gain insight into the developmental psychologist as an individual whose personal life and life circumstances often interact with his or her research career.

As editors, we have intentionally avoided imposing a uniform structure or style on the chapters. We believe strongly that the eighteen researchers have unique and different tales that should be told in their own manner. We want you to hear the unique voices and perspectives of the contributors as they relate their individual stories. In this way, we have eliminated the "middleman" so you can experience for yourself what developmental psychology research is all about. We hope that through reading these research adventures you will come to view the process of science in a new light. You will undoubtedly see that scientific inquiry is just the opposite of the sterile and bland view that one often sees in the terse style of journal reports or the summaries in conventional texts. You will also see how research careers develop, change, and are impacted by chance and the influence of colleagues, students, and the world in which we live.

We asked the contributors to tell how they encountered research issues that were especially interesting, unique, and/or problematic, and demanded some form of resolution or understanding. In the process, they provided an insider's view of developmental research by stressing the critical thinking and problem-solving aspects of research (e.g., generating ideas, developing methodology, conducting studies, applying results), as well as the personal and situational factors that influence decision making.

The use of personal narratives is not new. Our friend and colleague at SUNY–Plattsburgh, Phil DeVita, has used this approach in several anthropology books, and we have collaborated on several similar books in psychology. Reviewers of these projects are enamored with the approach. The following thoughts, based on input from David Myers of Hope College and Rosemary Hornack of Meredith College, are representative of their feedback.

> Since it's easy to be intimidated by brilliant people—who seem from a distance to easily come up with great ideas and execute them flawlessly—you will greatly appreciate the humanness of these personal stories. As they take you backstage to view their research careers, you will read stories of uncertain initial directions, of serendipity, of false starts, of self-doubts, of job insecurity, of the importance of supportive mentors, colleagues, and students. You will also see the passion that drives these people and the ideals that guide them, values such as lifelong learning; reading and study of published literature; benefits of hard work, trial and error, and perseverance; making the most of all that you know from any source of experience; turning misfortune into opportunity; careful observation; precision; and keeping an open mind.

In selecting topics for this book, we provide coverage across the life span and sample research in physical, emotional, social, and cognitive development. Contributors were chosen for the excellence of their contributions to developmental psychology and also for their ability to communicate to readers. Also, we have avoided chapter introductions and summaries in favor of letting the stories simply "unfold." We do, however, want to give you a taste of what's to come. We hope this sample of the research adventures will whet your appetite for more.

In our opening chapter, Robert Plomin brings clarity to the age-old nature-nurture question by exploring the emerging and exciting field of behavioral genetics. This perspective shows how the interaction of genetic and environmental variables creates a clearer view of the developing person. Then, Esther Thelen shows us how one's personal life can interact quite successfully with career interests, and how she creatively improvised to understand motor development in infants. Neil Bohannon gives us a candid glimpse of his professional development, and describes the diverse issues involved in the acquisition of language during childhood. The issue of child abuse and neglect confronts us daily in the media. Byron Egeland deals with this vital topic and presents some encouraging approaches to break the cycle of maltreatment that transcends generations. Ross Thompson's stimulating research focuses on infant-parent attachment and how youngsters develop emotionally. Out of his research come ideas for legal policy regarding child and family issues. Our society is often characterized as uncaring, cold, and callous. Through the research of Nancy Eisenberg, we explore how we develop prosocial behaviors such as helping, sharing, and offering comfort to others. Beverly Fagot describes the impact of gender in the developing child through a series of fascinating studies. David Elkind describes his exciting research and personal experiences in exploring cognitive development from a Piagetian framework. Through Ross Parke's efforts, we learn about a dynamic research odyssey exploring father-infant relationships. Jeanne Brooks-Gunn details her exciting explorations of puberty, highlighting the significant issues confronting adolescent girls. Lawrence Walker's chapter deals with research on moral development and the provocative question of whether one sex is morally superior. Have you ever wondered whether teen employment has a positive or negative effect on their development? Laurence Steinberg explores this relevant issue and provides some answers. How do we acquire the personality and temperamental characteristics that we possess as adults? Jacqueline Lerner describes her stimulating research on the role of temperament in child and adolescent development. Cameron Camp, as Sherlock Holmes, shares his interesting research on memory enhancement in Alzheimers patients. K. Warner Schaie, in his own life span autobiographical presentation, describes the history of a longitudinal study of cognitive functioning and how he came to be a gerontologist. Laura Carstensen focuses our attention on social and emotional behaviors in aging. Her research offers interesting and optimistic ideas about emotional issues and social relationships in later life. Stress is a common aspect of all our lives. David Chiriboga gives us valuable insights into the impact of stress and adaptation through a life span perspective. The very end of the life span, aging and death, is often the most ignored aspect of development. Robert Kastenbaum lets us know why it is vitally important for this terminal phase of life to be intensively explored and understood.

We hope the brief view of what's to come will spark your interest and get you excited for the journey ahead. We also hope that it lets you see the research process for what it is—an exciting adventure. Enjoy the trip.

The Developmental Psychologists

RESEARCH ADVENTURES ACROSS THE LIFE SPAN

*R*OBERT PLOMIN (Ph.D., University of Texas at Austin) is MRC Research Professor at the Institute of Psychiatry and Deputy Director of the Institute's Research Centre on Social, Genetic, and Developmental Psychiatry in London. Dr. Plomin has served as president of the international Behavior Genetics Association and his recent awards include the Fulbright Scholar Award and Fogarty Senior International Fellowship. He was also named the 1993 Distinguished Scientist Lecturer by the American Psychological Association. Dr. Plomin (pictured with the younger of his two sons) is married to the British developmental psychologist, Judy Dunn.

1

Nature and Nurture

❖

W hat images does the word *nature* bring to mind? Pastoral scenes of green fields, blue sky, and gurgling streams? What about the word *nurture*? A mother nursing her baby? These two words, each with its own warm connotations, have created more than a century of conflict in psychology when they are brought together in what is known as the nature-nurture controversy. I grew up as a scientist in the middle of the nature-nurture controversy because my career has focused on understanding the contributions of genetics (nature) and environment (nurture) to individual differences in developmental psychology. The purpose of this autobiographical account is to describe my nature and nurture as a scientist growing up in the eye of this storm. I hope this will personalize the issues and findings of this field of research known as behavioral genetics.

The nature and nurture provided by my family does not seem particularly relevant to my story, but I would like to mention two experiences that occurred early in my life. First, I believe that my stubborn nature, and especially the nurture of my family, gave me a strong dose of self-esteem that enabled me to take the heat that comes from studying taboo topics.

The second is an incident which in retrospect seems to have been a turning point in my life, although I must admit that I am somewhat skeptical about this kind of memory because I think it is easy to create meaningful myths when you look back on your life. I attended a Catholic elementary school in Chicago. It was a good education for the most part but the incident I remember involves the intrusion of religion in science. When I was in fourth grade, we were given a routine show-and-tell science assignment. By chance, I had been reading a beautifully illustrated popular book on evolution. I remember being impressed with the beauty of natural selection as an explanation of how species evolved. So, I stuck the book in my school bag the next morning. When my turn came in class, I had barely opened the book when the nun whisked me out of class and down to the principal's office. I

3

was suspended from school! This was the 1950s and for a Catholic to believe in evolution was a mortal sin (i.e., die and go straight to hell!). Evolution had never been mentioned before, so I had no way of knowing that the topic would cause such offense.

This incident marked the end of religion in my life (except that science is now like a religion to me). I remember thinking that if nuns and priests refused even to talk about something that seemed so reasonable and important as evolution then I should be skeptical about other things that they chose to talk about. The incident did not lead directly to my interest in genetics but I think it had some imprinting effect that lay dormant for fifteen years.

The story of my education might be relevant if only to give some hope to other late bloomers. I worked part-time from about the time of the evolution incident and nearly full-time during high school (a tough all-boys Catholic school). Toward the end of high school I was told that I could get paid to go to a Catholic commuter college (DePaul University) with which the high school was affiliated. As an inner-city kid, it sounded like a good scam, so I continued to work full-time and took classes as they fit into my work schedule. I took a hodgepodge of courses, from English to film to philosophy. However, the end of my philosophy career came during a class on a hot summer night. The philosophy department's strength was in an area known as phenomenology, which attempts to distinguish between the phenomenon and its essence. This was at least the third class in which the professor started talking about "deskness," the essence of a desk. I walked out of the class and never attended another philosophy class. I began to realize that I was interested in things that could be examined empirically, and I sensed that philosophers were primarily interested in things that could not be tested. This realization led me to focus on psychology during my last few semesters of college.

I was not a serious student. I was too busy making what was for me a lot of money. At age 15, I started to work at an educational association across the street from my family's apartment by shoveling snow from the sidewalks and taking out garbage. Then I started typing for them and rose in the ranks. By the time I was in college, I had become assistant to the research director of the association and traveled around the country helping organize conferences. Although I did not think about it much, I assumed that I would just continue working at the association when I finished college. However, I had a wonderful adviser, Bob Brewer, in the psychology department who encouraged me to apply to graduate school. I remember that I had no idea of what graduate school was all about. Brewer got application forms for me and said the magic words, "You might get paid to go to graduate school." In the autumn of my senior year, I applied to several of the schools that Brewer suggested and then forgot about it. In January, I received a telephone call from Arnold Buss in the Department of Psychology at the University of Texas at Austin. He also said the magic words about getting paid to be a graduate student. I accepted on the spot even though I still did not really know much about graduate school.

I had the strong feeling of waking up intellectually in graduate school. In part I was awakened by my mentor, Arnold Buss, who loved to argue; something I was not used to doing. Another contributing factor was the department's orientation that students should be taught to be generalists at a time when psychology, like other sciences, was pushing toward specialization. All new graduate students took a two-year series of "core" courses that covered the breadth of the department from perception and information processing to social and clinical psychology.

BEHAVIORAL GENETICS

In the second year of graduate school, one of these core courses was in behavioral genetics. In the late 1960s, the psychology department at Texas was one of the few places in the world that offered a course in behavioral genetics. No doubt it was the only place that required all psychology graduate students to take it. The department had more behavioral geneticists than nearly anywhere else, including animal researchers Jan Bruell, Marty Manosevitz, and Del Thiessen, and human researchers Joe Horn, John Loehlin, and Lee Willerman.

Inbred Strains

This concentration of behavioral geneticists was the result of efforts by Gardner Lindzey, who came to Texas in the mid-1960s, but who had been enticed into university administration by the time I arrived in Austin. Although most well-known for his work in personality and social psychology, Lindzey had also conducted pioneering work in the 1950s showing that genetic factors played an important role in classic learning experiments. He compared the learning performance of different strains of inbred mice. When animals are mated brother to sister for many generations, they become inbred, which means that all members of the inbred strain have the same genes, like identical twins. Because different inbred strains have different genes, the influence of genetic factors can be investigated by comparing the performance of different inbred strains. Lindzey and others found that different inbred strains of mice performed very differently in various learning conditions, a result that has been replicated in hundreds of subsequent studies. This means that genes make a difference in behavior.

The core course in behavioral genetics was team-taught by several of the faculty. It reviewed emerging research that found genetics to be important not only for animal behavior but also for human behavior. I was impressed by the strength of the findings and by the novel perspective they offered for understanding development. I had begun to worry that developmental psychology had a mountain of statistically significant results but only a molehill of socially significant results. Behavioral genetics research yielded some powerful results about the importance of genetics which had not been assimilated into developmental psychology.

Selection Studies

For example, in addition to studies of inbred strains, behavioral geneticists (and humankind since the beginning of recorded history) were able to select successfully for behavior. One such artificial selection study by Gerald McClearn involved selection for sensitivity to alcohol. McClearn started with a genetically diverse group of mice and tested them for how long they slept off an injected dose of alcohol. He took the mice that slept the longest and bred them together and he also bred the mice that slept the least. The offspring of the "long-sleep" mice slept longer than the original population and the offspring of the "short-sleep" mice slept less. The long-sleep and short-sleep mice continued to be bred for several generations (one generation only takes about three months in mice). After five generations of selection, the long-sleep mice slept twice as long on average as short-sleep mice. After ten generations of selection, there was essentially no overlap in the sleep times of the two selected lines of mice. That is, every mouse in the long-sleep line slept longer than any mouse in the short-sleep line. Statistics were not needed to see that genetics played a major role in this measure of sensitivity to alcohol. Selection studies have been successful for just about every behavior investigated, suggesting a widespread influence of genetics on animal behavior.

In the late 1960s, psychology as a whole was beginning to return to a more balanced view that recognized genetic (nature) as well as environmental (nurture) influences in development. In the 1950s, learning theory was the queen of psychology. Learning theory came with an environmentalism that assumed that all that we are psychologically is what we learned to be. The 1960s was a time of change in psychology as well as society and there were signs of growing disenchantment with an environmentalism that ignored biology.

Twin Studies

In psychiatry, one study singlehandedly turned things toward a more balanced view. For his dissertation research in the early 1960s, Len Heston decided to conduct an adoption study of schizophrenia. Twin studies that compared identical and fraternal twins had suggested a genetic influence. Identical twins are about 40 percent concordant for schizophrenia, whereas fraternal twins and other first-degree relatives are only about 10 percent concordant for schizophrenia. Concordance is simply the percentage of pairs in which both members are affected. You can think of it as a risk estimate. If you have no family members who are schizophrenic, your risk for being diagnosed as schizophrenic during your lifetime is almost 1 percent, the base rate for schizophrenia in the population. If you have a first-degree relative (parent or sibling) who is schizophrenic, your risk is about 10 percent rather than 1 percent. If you have an identical twin who is schizophrenic, your risk is about 40 percent. This finding implies a genetic influence because identical twins, who come from the same fertilized egg, are identical genetically, whereas fraternal twins are only 50 percent genetically similar because, like any brothers or sisters, they are derived from two separately fertilized eggs.

Adoption Studies

Heston wanted to test this hypothesis of genetic influence using the other major human behavioral genetic design, the adoption design. If genetic influence is important, children adopted at birth away from schizophrenic parents ought to have an increased risk for schizophrenia even though they were not reared by their schizophrenic parents. Heston compared the risk for schizophrenia for adoptees born to schizophrenic parents to the risk for a control group of adoptees. He tried three times to get money to support his research but to no avail because the prevailing view that schizophrenia is environmental in origin was so strong. Heston found a psychiatric institution in Oregon where three or more decades ago schizophrenic mothers who became pregnant gave up their children for adoption in the first few weeks of life. The control group consisted of adopted children from the same adoption agencies as the experimental group. Heston traced and interviewed the forty-seven now-adult adoptees in the experimental group and fifty adoptees in the control group. (Because he had no money to conduct the research, Heston had to travel all across the country to interview these adoptees by returning rental cars.) The results were dramatic: Five of the forty-seven adoptees in the experimental group were schizophrenic but no cases of schizophrenia were found among the fifty control subjects. Heston's results have since been replicated in other adoption studies.

FROM AUSTIN TO BOULDER

Inbred strains and selection studies of animal behavior and twin and adoption studies convinced me that genetics made a major contribution to behavioral development. I decided to learn more about behavioral genetics, especially as it relates to development. I began to work with Marty Manosevitz who was following up on some of Lindzey's early research concerning learning in inbred strains of mice. Manosevitz also encouraged me to develop my own research, and I became interested in combining behavioral genetics and evolution. Instead of studying inbred strains of mice that had been bred in the laboratory for decades, I wanted to study the behavioral development of wild mice trapped in ecologically different environments. I trapped mice at as high an altitude as possible in the Rocky Mountains of New Mexico and Colorado and in the desert and in temperate areas of Texas. Using a diverse set of laboratory measures of behavior such as activity, I found that mice on one side of a barn are as different behaviorally from mice on the other side of the barn as they are from mice in a very different ecology. This suggests that genetic differences among mouse populations are due more to founder effects than to selection for different ecologies. That is, the mouse who founds a new colony contributes its genes disproportionately to subsequent members of the colony.

During the summer when I was finishing the testing of these mice, I developed a severe allergy to mice, an occupational hazard that affects many mouse researchers. To finish the study, I had to wear a mask and limit my time with the critters in order to be able to breathe. Even now, twenty-five years later, I can tell if a piece of paper has been in a mouse lab because within a few seconds my eyes redden and I start to sneeze. My severe allergic reaction to mice put an end to my budding career as a mouse researcher.

In between sneezes, I talked with Arnold Buss about human temperament—early appearing biologically influenced dimensions of personality such as activity and emotionality. I was particularly interested in applying behavioral genetic strategies to personality development to find those aspects of personality that show the most genetic influence. Buss and I conducted a twin study of children using their parents' ratings of temperament. Our approach to temperament focused on four traits: emotionality (fear and anger), activity, sociability, and impulsivity. We used the acronym EASI to label our approach to temperament and, in 1975, wrote a book about it called *A Temperament Theory of Personality Development*.

This EASI approach to temperament was the topic of my Ph.D. dissertation in which I conducted a combined twin and parent-offspring study of the EASI dimensions using parental rating questionnaires. The children were 137 pairs of twins from 2 to 6 years old. Both parents rated both children on the EASI questionnaire. On an adult version of the same questionnaire, parents also rated themselves and their spouses. This combination of ratings made it possible to compare twin results when each parent rated both children, when one parent rated one twin and the other parent rated the other twin, and for average parent ratings. All these approaches suggested genetic influence in that identical twin correlations were greater than fraternal twin correlations. The design also made it possible to compare parent-offspring resemblance to the twin results. This, too, was consistent with the hypothesis of genetic influence. In addition, because both parents were included in the study, the extent of temperament similarity between spouses, known as assortative mating, could be investigated. Assortative mating affects estimates of genetic influence in twin studies. As other studies have shown, spouses scarcely correlate for temperament. Finally, because parents rated themselves as well as their children and their spouse, it was possible to explore the extent to which parents project their own personality into their ratings of their children and spouse. The answer was that they do not.

Something controversial had happened in the meantime, which I really only noticed as I switched from animal to human behavioral genetic research. As mentioned earlier, in the 1960s, psychology was shifting toward a more balanced view that recognized the importance of nature as well as nurture. However, this trend came to a screeching halt in 1969 with the publication of a *Harvard Educational Review* monograph on genetics and intelligence by Arthur Jensen. In a few pages in this lengthy monograph, Jensen raised the possibility that IQ differences between ethnic groups might be due in part to genetic differences. This created an explosion unlike any seen before in psychology and nearly killed the fledgling field of human behavioral genetics. It created a backlash against behavioral genetics that made it almost impossible to talk about genetic influence in psychology for several years.

This was brought home to me at my first major psychological conference, the Eastern Psychological Association conference in Boston in the early 1970s. A keynote address was given by Leon Kamin, who was leading the charge against behavioral genetics. Before an audience of thousands, Kamin decried the evils of behavioral genetics. He brought the crowd to its feet. The address, which became a 1974 book called *The Science and Politics of I.Q.*, was an ad hominem attack on behavioral geneticists and their political motives. I was shocked by what seemed emotional rabble-rousing and stunned by the welcome it received. During the past year, I have had a strong sense of déjà vu in much of the commentary concerning Murray and Herrnstein's book, *The Bell Curve*.

The issue of ethnic differences was being used to brand the whole field as racist, even though very few behavioral geneticists studied average differences between groups. In large part, ethnic differences were not studied because it is so difficult to pin down the causes of average differences between ethnic groups and, in part, because of the political explosiveness of the topic. These issues are explained well in a 1975 book *Race Differences in Intelligence* by John Loehlin, Gardner Lindzey, and James Spuhler. It is still the best book on the topic. The focus of behavioral genetics is on individual differences and the genetic and environmental sources of differences between individuals. We can use twin and adoption designs to address the causes of individual differences, not average differences between groups. It is most important to remember that the description and causes of individual differences *within* groups bear no relation to the description and causes of average differences between groups. That is, although genetics contributes to individual differences within ethnic groups, this does not necessarily imply that genetics is also responsible for average differences between ethnic groups.

A related concern about behavioral genetics often lurks in the shadows. Does the study of genetic influences on individual differences in development violate the fundamental belief that all persons are created equal? My answer is emphatically "No." By *equality*, philosophers and our founding fathers clearly meant political equality—equality in opportunity and equality before the law. They did not mean that people are identical. Individuality is a fact. It is also the foundation for the dignity of humankind: We are not interchangeable. The real danger lies in treating people on the basis of group membership—ethnic group, gender, age—when individual differences within these groups far exceed average differences between the groups.

During the early 1970s, the intense scrutiny of human behavioral genetics research, especially in relation to cognitive abilities, led to questions about whether some of the pioneering research in the field in Britain by Cyril Burt was fabricated or falsified. A biography of Burt published in 1978 by Lionel Hearnshaw seemed to clinch the case against Burt, but two recent books by Robert Joynson in 1989 and Ronald Fletcher in 1990 have reopened the case. Nonetheless, doubt was cast on the validity of some of the earlier research in human behavioral genetics. I saw this as an opportunity to start again with bigger and better studies.

I received my Ph.D. in 1974 and planned to stay on at Texas for another year, but in June a position opened up at the premier behavioral genetics institution in the world, the Institute for Behavioral Genetics at the University of Colorado at Boulder. By July, I was on my way to Boulder, having accepted a joint position in developmental psychology in the psychology department and in behavioral genetics at the institute. I stayed at the University of Colorado until 1986 when I moved to Pennsylvania State University. In 1994, I moved to London to join the faculty of the Institute of Psychiatry and to become deputy director of a new research unit called the Centre for Social, Genetic, and Developmental Psychiatry, which attempts to bring together research on nature and nurture in the investigation of development.

BEHAVIORAL GENETICS AND THE NATURE OF DEVELOPMENT

By the time I went to Boulder, I knew that I wanted to apply behavioral genetic strategies to the study of human development. What was needed was a long-term longitudinal adoption study of behavioral development.

For a few years, most of my weekends were spent driving to Denver and testing unwed mothers who were planning to relinquish their offspring for adoption. In the turbulent times of the mid-1970s, it took my colleague John DeFries and me several years to obtain funding for what is now known as the Colorado Adoption Project (CAP). The adoption design is particularly powerful in disentangling the influence of nature and nurture because it studies adopted children and their "genetic" parents (biological parents and their adopted-away children), "environmental" parents (adoptive parents and their adopted children), and "genetic-plus-environmental" parents (parents who rear their own biological children). Because about one-third of the adoptive parents adopted a second child, CAP was also able to study genetically unrelated children reared together and matched biological siblings. For nearly 250 adoptive families and 250 matched nonadoptive families, the CAP children were studied yearly on a broad battery of measures, including cognitive abilities, language, temperament, behavioral problems, motor development, and later, school achievement. The oldest children have now reached 16 years of age, at which time they are administered the same battery of psychological tests that their parents completed sixteen years earlier.

CAP results have been described in three books (1985 on infancy, 1988 on early childhood, and 1994 on middle childhood) and scores of research articles that show the important contributions made by nature as well as nurture in psychological development. For example, CAP shows genetic influence on objective ratings of temperament made by testers, on language as assessed by standard tests, on cognitive abilities, and, for the first time, on measures of self-esteem. CAP also led to discoveries such as evidence that genetic factors contribute to developmental change, not just continuity. Most surprisingly, as discussed later, CAP results suggested that measures of parenting, even videotaped observations during parent-child interaction, show genetic influence. Measures of parenting have, reasonably enough, been considered to be environmental measures. However, they can show genetic influence if parents respond to genetically influenced characteristics of their children. More on this later.

I also launched two other large-scale, longitudinal studies. In 1979, my colleagues and I began work in Sweden on a study of twins who had been separated early in life and who were then 50 years of age or older. We found several hundred such pairs of identical and fraternal twins and obtained matched pairs of twins who had been reared together. This study, called the Swedish Adoption/Twin Study of Aging (SATSA), is one of the first behavioral genetic studies that considers individual differences in the last half of the life span. The twins are studied every three years on a broad battery of behavioral and biomedical functioning that includes behavioral measures such as cognitive abilities, personality, and mental health, and health-related measures such as a physical examination, neurological functioning, blood pressure, spirometry, and blood and urine analyses. About sixty papers describe SATSA results showing genetic influence later in life for cognitive abilities, personality, and mental health; for physical health variables such as weight, serum lipid levels, and pulmonary function; and for the association between behavioral and biomedical functioning. A spin-off project studies all the twin pairs in Sweden over 80 years of age (about 300 pairs).

The other study is the MacArthur Longitudinal Twin Study (MALTS). Begun in 1986, MALTS consists of more than 300 pairs of twins whose emotional and temperament development is studied in their homes and in the laboratory during the transition from infancy to early childhood at 14, 20, 24, and 36 months of age. MALTS is exciting because it is a collaborative effort between behavioral geneticists and some of the top developmental psychologists including Joseph Campos, Robert Emde, Jerome Kagan, and Carolyn Zahn-Waxler. Although it is newer than the other studies, several papers have shown genetic influence for previously unstudied domains of development such as behavioral inhibition, empathy, and emotional expression as rated from videotapes.

These studies are large because reliable estimates of genetic and environmental influences require large samples. The studies are longitudinal because I am interested in genetic and environmental contributions to developmental change and continuity. For example, it is reasonable to assume that environmental influences become more important during the course of life as experiences, accidents, and illnesses increasingly contribute to differences between us. However, the results of behavioral genetic studies suggest that, to the contrary, genetic factors become increasingly important during development, especially in the area of cognitive abilities. In addition, longitudinal behavioral genetic data make it possible to study genetic contributions to developmental change from age to age. CAP and MALTS, for example, have been important in showing that genetic factors can contribute to change, not just to continuity, during early development. These ideas about genetics and development are summarized in my 1986 book, *Development, Genetics, and Psychology*.

Studies such as CAP, SATSA, and MALTS also have been important in showing that genetics plays an important role in normal psychological development such as the development of cognitive abilities and temperament. Although the 1970s was a tough time for behavioral genetics, the 1980s and especially the 1990s saw psychology become much more accepting of genetic influence. This switch from antipathy to acceptance of genetic influence in psychology can be seen in the increasing number of behavioral genetics articles in mainstream psychology journals and in research grant support. One symbol of this change was the 1992 centennial conference of the American Psychological Association. In preparation for the conference, a committee selected two themes that best represented the past, present, and future of psychology. One of the two themes chosen was behavioral genetics. A ten-hour series of symposia on behavioral genetics was organized for the centennial conference in an attempt to provide an overview of the past, a summary of the present, and a glimpse of the future of genetic research in psychology. This symposium series led to a 1993 book called *Nature, Nurture, and Psychology* which I edited with Gerald McClearn.

BEHAVIORAL GENETICS AND NURTURE

Research in behavioral genetics has contributed to our understanding of nurture, not just nature, because its methods address both nature and nurture rather than assuming that either one is all-important. I believe that some of the most interesting questions about genetics involve the environment and that some of the most interesting questions about the environment involve genetics. This body of research has made three contributions to understanding nurture.

Importance of Nongenetic Influence

First, nongenetic influence provides the best available evidence for the importance of environmental influence. Decades of environmentalism assumed but did not assess the importance of the environment. Now that the pendulum is swinging away from environmentalism I sometimes worry that the pendulum will swing too far in the other direction, toward a biological determinism. Consider schizophrenia. Twenty years ago, the message from behavioral genetics research was that genetics is important. Now genetics so completely dominates research on schizophrenia that it is important to emphasize that, although genetics is important, most of the reason why one person is diagnosed schizophrenic and another person is not is due to environmental factors. One piece of behavioral genetics data makes this point. Identical twins are about 40 percent concordant. This means that for 60 percent of such cases, genetically identical pairs of individuals are *discordant* for schizophrenia. There can be no genetic explanation for this.

Nonshared Environment

The second contribution of behavioral genetics to understanding nurture is what this research tells us about *how* the environment works during behavioral development. The research tells us that the way the environment works must be very different from the way it has been thought to work. Instead of making two children growing up in the same family similar to one another, which is what theories of socialization assume, it makes them different. We know this because genetically unrelated children growing up in the same adoptive family scarcely resemble each other for personality, psychopathology, and cognitive abilities (after adolescence). Other behavioral genetic results converge on this surprising conclusion that growing up in the same family does not make siblings similar for environmental reasons. Siblings are similar of course, but for genetic rather than environmental reasons. The environment is important, but environmental influences in behavioral development operate to make children in the same family different, not similar. It does not mean that family environment is unimportant. Rather, environmental influences in development are doled out on an individual-by-individual basis rather than on a family-by-family basis.

This topic is called nonshared environment because these environmental influences are not shared by children growing up in the same family. The key question is why children growing up in the same family are so different. Because developmental psychologists had seldom studied more than one child per family, little was known until recently about different experiences of children in the same family. Research so far suggests that children in the same family experience quite different environments. For example, if you ask adolescent siblings about differences in their parents' treatment of them, you get an earful! On the other hand, when you ask parents about it, they are less likely to indicate that they treat their two children differently, perhaps because of social norms against it. Most important, if you observe children interacting with their parents—as we have done in videotaped observations in infancy and early childhood—you find that parents do in fact behave quite differently to their two children. This is the rationale for the title of a 1990 book on this topic that I wrote with Judy Dunn: *Separate Lives: Why Siblings Are So Different*. This finding has sparked research in developmental psychology that studies more than one child per family and asks why they turn out so differently.

Several of these research projects are summarized in a 1994 book that Mavis Hetherington, David Reiss and I edited, *Separate Social Worlds of Siblings: The Impact of Nonshared Environment on Development*. The three of us are also working on a study called Nonshared Environment in Adolescent Development (NEAD) that attempts to identify specific sources of nonshared environment. NEAD is a nationwide study of more than 700 families with twins and nontwin same-sex siblings including full siblings, half siblings, and genetically unrelated siblings. Families are visited in their homes twice for two to three hours and they complete many questionnaires about family interactions as perceived from the perspective of the mother, father, and each child. An interesting feature of the study is the inclusion of videotape observations of each dyad (e.g., mother and one child), each triad (e.g., mother and father with one child), and the tetrad (mother, father, and both children). Each dyad, triad, or tetrad is left in a room for ten minutes with the videotape camera running on a tripod without an experimenter present while they discuss a list of problems that they had previously identified as important issues for that grouping of family members. Although papers describing NEAD results are just beginning to be published, the project has been influential in showing how siblings in the same family experience very different environments. The NEAD project has also shown that genetic factors contribute importantly to interactions and relationships among family members, which is discussed in the following section.

The Nature of Nurture

The third contribution of behavioral genetics to understanding nurture is a topic that has been called the *nature of nurture*. This is an example of the excitement that comes from looking at old issues in developmental psychology from the new perspective of behavioral genetics. Although it sounds paradoxical at first, behavioral genetic analyses of measures of the environment widely used in developmental psychology, such as measures of parenting, yield evidence for genetic influence in twin and adoption studies. Genetic analyses of environmental measures sound paradoxical because behaviorism has conditioned us to think of the environment as something "out there" independent of the individual. To the contrary, measures of the psychological environment almost always involve behavior.

In developmental psychology, a major class of environmental measures involves parenting. Parenting is parental behavior directed toward their children, such as parents' responsiveness, affection, and control toward their children. For example, consider an item often included in measures of parenting in studies of cognitive development: how often parents read to their children. Differences among parents in how often they read to their children could be affected by genetically influenced characteristics of parents, such as their cognitive ability. Parental behavior might also reflect genetically influenced characteristics of the children. For example, brighter children might ask their parents to read to them more often.

The hypothesis of genetic influence can be tested by analyzing environmental measures in twin and adoption studies. Are identical twins treated more similarly than fraternal twins? Are genetically unrelated "adoptive" siblings treated less similarly than genetically related siblings? A score of twin and adoption studies during the past decade consistently implicate a genetic contribution to measures of the environment widely used in research in developmental psychology.

For example, one such measure of the home environment often used in studies of cognitive development is called the Home Observation for Measurement of the Environment (HOME). The HOME is used during a home visit to rate observations of mother-infant interaction, such as mother's responsiveness to the child (e.g., mother responds to child's vocalizations) and mother's affectionateness (e.g., mother shows positive emotional responses). The HOME was included in the home visits of the CAP when each child was 1 year old and again at 2 years of age. For the nonadoptive and adoptive siblings in CAP, this meant that each home was visited when each child was 1 and 2 years old, with an average gap of about two years between the visits for the older and younger child. At 1 year of age, the correlation between HOME total scores for 105 pairs of nonadoptive siblings was .57. Because nonadoptive siblings are genetically related, it is possible that their mothers treated them similarly in part because the siblings are similar genetically. The critical test is whether the correlation is lower for adoptive siblings who are genetically unrelated. The answer was "Yes": The correlation between HOME scores for eighty-seven pairs of adoptive siblings was .35. Similar results were obtained at 2 years of age. The nonadoptive sibling correlation was .57 and the adoptive sibling correlation was .40.

Other observational twin and adoption studies, as well as studies using questionnaires, consistently yield evidence for genetic influence for measures of the family environment. Moreover, environmental measures outside the family also show genetic influence. For example, several studies have shown that measures of life events, used in literally thousands of studies as environmental measures, include genetic influence. The first report came from SATSA. A widely used measure of life events yielded identical twin correlations that were greater than fraternal twin correlations; moreover, identical twins reared apart were more similar than fraternal twins reared apart. Genetic influence was especially strong, as you might expect, for life events items for which we have some control (e.g., major conflict with family member) as compared to those items for which we have little control (e.g., major illness of family member).

One implication of such findings is that environmental measures cannot be assumed to be environmental just because they are called "environmental." Research to date suggests that it is safer to assume that ostensible measures of the environment include genetic influence. Another implication is that, if environmental measures as well as outcome measures show genetic influence, it seems reasonable to consider the possibility that prediction of outcomes from environmental measures may be mediated genetically. For example, as just discussed, the HOME is a widely used measure of the home environment that was developed in order to predict cognitive development in infancy and early childhood. Developmental research on such topics has been conducted in families in which parents and their children are related genetically as well as environmentally. However, developmentalists never considered the possibility that genetic factors might be involved in the HOME's prediction of children's cognitive development. An important discovery in recent research is that genetic factors account for about half the association between the HOME and cognitive development. One simple way to broach this topic is to investigate such associations in families in which parents are not genetically related to their children, that is, in adoptive families. If associations between environmental measures such as the HOME and developmental outcomes such as cognitive ability are truly environmental in origin, the associations should be just as strong when parents are not genetically related to their children. To the contrary, such environment-outcome associations are much diminished in adoptive families. This approach and others suggest that genetics contributes to associations between environmental measures and developmental outcomes.

Another key question is how measures of the environment come to show genetic influence. Experience itself—how we interact with our environments—may be influenced by genetic factors. Children actively select, modify, and create the environments they experience, in part for genetic reasons. Consideration of these active correlations between nature and nurture takes up the challenge of Anne Anastasi in her 1958 American Psychological Association presidential address to move beyond questions of how much variance is accounted for by genetic and environmental factors to the question of how genetic and environmental variables coact during development, the developmental duet in which genotypes become phenotypes. These issues are the topic of my 1994 book called *Genetics and Experience*.

*D*NA

During the past few years, I have returned to the nature side of nature-nurture research in an attempt to use new molecular genetic tools emerging from the human genome project to begin to identify specific genes responsible for the widespread genetic contribution to behavioral development both in mouse and man. These genetic advances include thousands of new genetic markers, many of which involve genes expressed in the brain. Prior to 1980, there were just fifty or so genetic markers such as the ABO blood system which refers to a gene with three forms (A, B, and O). People differ in this gene and can have any double combination of the three forms—for example, AA, AB, or AO. Blood types such as the ABO gene are detected by differences in biochemical reactions of the products of these genes. In contrast, the new genetic markers detect differences in DNA itself, that is, in the nucleotide bases that comprise the steps of the spiral staircase of the DNA double helix. Many thousands of such DNA markers are available and are being linked to map the human genome which consists of 3 billion nucleotide base pairs. The ultimate goal of the human genome project is to know the entire sequence of the 3 billion base pairs of DNA.

In the meantime, the thousands of new DNA markers can be used to ask whether any genes associated with these DNA markers are related to behavior. Especially valuable for psychologists are DNA markers for genes expressed in the brain—thousands of such DNA markers have been identified in recent years. We are at the dawn of a new era in which molecular genetic techniques will revolutionize genetic research on behavior by identifying specific genes that contribute to genetic variance, even for complex behavioral dimensions and disorders. At first, research of this type focused on single-gene disorders such as Huntington's disease. Now research is increasingly attempting to identify genes that contribute to more complicated disorders that involve many genes as well as environmental influence. Such disorders include common medical diseases such as hypertension as well as mental disorders such as schizophrenia and manic-depression. I am interested in using these new tools from molecular genetics to identify some of the many genes, each with small effect, that are responsible for the genetic contribution to variation in normal as well as abnormal psychological development.

The genetic quest is to find, not *the* gene for a behavior, but rather the multiple genes that affect the trait in a probabilistic rather than predetermined manner. The breathtaking pace of molecular genetics leads me to predict that by the turn of the century psychologists will use DNA markers as a tool in their research to identify relevant genetic differences among individuals. These DNA markers can be assessed inexpensively by DNA factories from just a drop of saliva or blood, thanks to a technique called polymerase chain reaction that amplifies DNA to make millions of copies of a particular sequence of DNA. If a set of DNA markers could be identified that together account for a reasonable portion of the genetic variance for a particular trait in developmental psychology, the set of DNA markers could be used as an index of genetic factors.

THE FUTURE

The momentum of these findings and methods will propel the field of behavioral genetics far into the next century. Another reason for optimism about the future of the field is that it is successfully being given away. For example, some leading developmental researchers have begun to incorporate genetic strategies in their research. I believe that the best behavioral genetics research in developmental psychology will be done by developmentalists who are *not* primarily behavioral geneticists. They will ask theory-driven questions and interpret their research findings in a way that will make the most sense for their fields. There is a lot more to do—we have just scratched the surface of behavioral genetics research in developmental psychology.

My hope for the future is that the next generation of developmental psychologists will wonder what the nature-nurture fuss was all about. I hope they will say, "Of course, we need to consider nature as well as nurture in understanding psychological development." The conjunction between nature and nature is truly *and*, not *versus*.

SUGGESTED READINGS

DUNN, J., & PLOMIN, R. (1990). *Separate lives: Why siblings are so different.* New York: Basic Books.

PLOMIN, R. (1986). *Development, genetics, and psychology.* Hillsdale, NJ: Erlbaum.

———— (1990). *Nature and nurture: An introduction to human behavioral genetics.* Pacific Grove, CA: Brooks/Cole.

———— (1994). *Genetics and experience.* Newbury Park, CA: Sage.

———— & McCLEARN, G. (Eds.). (1993). *Nature, nurture, and psychology.* Washington, DC: American Psychological Association.

*E*STHER *T*HELEN *(Ph.D., University of Missouri) is Professor of Psychology at Indiana University, Bloomington. She is the author, with Linda Smith, of* A Dynamic Systems Approach to the Development of Cognition and Action, *and* Dynamic Systems in Development: Applications, *as well as numerous papers and chapters. She has been honored with an early career award from the Developmental Psychology Division of the American Psychological Association, and is currently holding a Research Scientist Award from the National Institutes of Mental Health. She serves on the editorial boards of five journals. She enjoys music, gardening, travel, and nonviolent mystery novels.*

2

The Improvising Infant: Learning about Learning to Move

❖ ──────

I hope that readers will learn from this book not only how people conduct research but also something about how people conduct lives. I am sure that within the chapters of this book are stories of researchers whose lives have followed a singular vision, a burning question, or a straight path from college to graduate school to a position at a research university. I suspect that my story is equally represented—and probably even more likely among women. It is in some ways an unscripted story, because it did not follow the conventional ways of academic training and careers. But as I reflect on where my questions have led me, I also see a theme played out in my work.

I like the musical metaphor used by Mary Catherine Bateson in her book *Composing a Life*. In this book, she tells the stories of five women, of my generation and older, as they seek a coherent life in times when women's roles and expectations are rapidly changing. She likens their lives not so much to a structured musical score, where the notes and chords follow a planned and logical sequence, but to improvisation. The women in Bateson's book did not so much play out their lives according to the conventional scores of their age, gender, education, backgrounds, or even larger visions, but composed them from the opportunities and constraints of their daily situations and what they brought to those situations. As each personal victory or tragedy unfolded, the women opportunistically seized upon it and used it to build. The improvisational metaphor is especially apt; like good jazz, the notes and riffs of everyday life may seem unplanned, but from them comes a coherent structure. The secret seems to be the ability to improvise as circumstances change: to explore, select, and use what the situation affords us. (Later, I will argue that this metaphor applies just as well to infants learning motor skills; hence the title of this essay.)

In my scientific life, I see both the big themes and lots of improvisation. Every day seems a lot like improvisation, but the themes also come through, especially when writing an essay like this one, when one tries to make sense of the local encounters and chance events. Some themes of my scientific life are: (1) I like to describe behavior as it plays out through time, (2) I like to try and construct a "big picture" from data, and (3) I have enjoyed crossing disciplinary boundaries.

FROM BIOLOGY TO PSYCHOLOGY

I could not have identified these themes when I was an undergraduate biology major at the University of Wisconsin in the early 1960s; I had not yet composed them. But they—and the more compelling dynamics of family— must have fed my decision not to go to graduate school in molecular or cellular biology, exciting new areas in which I had done well as an undergraduate. Although I had enjoyed my classes and lab work, it just didn't feel right to continue. The questions were not right for me. I never thought much about psychology. I blush to admit that although I have now taught in a psychology department for over fifteen years, I never had an undergraduate psychology class! At the time, academic psychology was dominated by the behaviorists, and I knew enough about the work to be decidedly underwhelmed.

So instead of graduate training, I chose the more traditional path of supporting my husband's professional career (he is a historian), and soon after, of starting a family. What did get me back to science was a confluence of largely chance events. The first was the winter of 1970 in Madison, Wisconsin, one of the coldest and snowiest on record. My husband was a visiting professor and I was home with two preschoolers. To go out, it took an hour to bundle up the kids, and that was *if* I could start the car and shovel out the driveway. I resolved that when we returned to our home in Columbia, Missouri (which was a lot warmer!), I would "take a class" as a way of expanding my interests beyond jello cubes and *Sesame Street*. I have often reminded my children that they were entirely responsible for my career.

Well, what class was the bored housewife to take? The second chance event was the class I eventually chose, animal behavior, taught in the biology department at the University of Missouri, where my husband was on the faculty. I loved it! The class was taught by Fritz Walther, a classical ethologist trained by Konrad Lorenz himself. Professor Walther made me see the coherence of behavior and biology, and I immediately recognized that this was the level at which I had questions to ask. Ethologists carefully watched animals as they lived out their complex lives. They described behavior as their subjects sought food, avoided predators, found mates, and raised their young. Then the ethologists asked about what *caused* the animals to act in this way: What triggered behavior, how did it evolve, and how did it develop? These are the questions that motivate me to this day.

Although a theme was beginning to emerge from the notes, I cannot remember actually ever deciding to become a researcher and faculty member, and sometimes I am even sort of surprised at how I went from League of Women Voters meetings to addressing large audiences at scientific meetings. What happened was that one class led to another and I ended up in graduate school. I went to the University of Missouri because that was where we happened to be. Maybe if I had been more driven by the vision of career rather than just doing interesting things, I would have made different choices. But as it was, I tried to do the best I could with what circumstances offered.

My graduate training was an amalgam of biology and psychology. This was also unplanned. I was interested in behavior, and they taught more about behavior in the psychology department than in biology. These local decisions—to take this class or that, work on this problem or that, had both good and bad consequences. Because I was following my own interests and fashioning my own program, I fell between the mentoring cracks. I never belonged to a real "lab," or had an intense intellectual relationship with a close group of colleagues and mentors, although I had fine, supportive teachers. I did not feel especially deprived at the time. Now I can see that this situation allowed me much room for improvisation and discovery. Like sensitive parents, my professors provided help and facilitation but let me find my own way.

*F*ROM INSECTS TO BABIES?

The theme that emerged from that first course in animal behavior until the present is an overarching interest in patterns of behavior and their change over time. It all began in an unlikely species—a tiny, parasitic wasp. My professor, Donald Farish, was interested at the time in how patterns of behavior could reveal phylogenetic relationships; that is, how behavior rather than anatomical structure could tell about the evolution of species. The behavior was grooming. It turns out that, in the family Hymenoptera, the bees and wasps, you can describe an evolutionary "family tree" just as well on grooming patterns, the ways in which these creatures rub their antennae, legs, and bodies, as on fixed anatomical features.

For my master's thesis, however, I looked in detail at the structure of grooming movements in one species of wasp that lived by laying eggs on other insect larvae. The tiny critters went through a real grooming dance;

first they rubbed the antennae, then the head, then the front legs in a certain pattern, and so on. It looked like their nervous systems played a tape, and out came not just the pattern of a single type of movement, but also an elaborate sequence. Did the sequence come entirely from the tape inside the nervous system, or was there something about cleaning the antennae that triggered cleaning the head?

To test this, I did the logical experiment. I cut off the wasps' antennae. Sure enough, the insects waved their legs and cleaned the air where their antennae were supposed to be—it must be the tape. But no, when I looked really closely at the structure and sequencing of "air grooming," it was different from that of intact wasps. There must also be feedback from the groomed structures. This is a theme that has recurred over and over in looking at patterned behavior. Yes, there is internal structure, but no movements occur without information from the outside. But as for improvisation, insects don't do very much of it.

Although it may seem implausible to jump from some of the simplest animals to the most complex, it was a natural transition for me to go from insects to infants. I was taking and much enjoying a course in developmental psychology—another fortuitous event. As I read the famous developmental psychologist Jean Piaget's description of "circular reactions"—actions that infants repeat over and over again, I was reminded of the stereotyped movement sequences I was seeing in the little wasps. Do human infants do the same kind of repeated motor sequences? I wrote a paper on the topic for the class and discovered that, yes, people for a long time had noticed rhythmic movements in normal infants, but also in infants and children in institutions, as well as in people with mental retardation and other handicaps such as autism. There were explanations based on animal behavior, speculations coming from Freudian theory, and theories grounded in medical neurology, but really, not much was known.

Well, I reasoned, what a good topic for a dissertation! It would combine my background in behavioral biology with my newly emerging interest in developmental psychology. Since none of my professors objected, I forged ahead.

AN INFANT ETHOLOGIST

In many ways, my dissertation research set the direction of my research career. I began, as I still begin now, as a good ethologist. In order to understand behavior you have to know what it looks like. You need to see what form the behavior takes, how frequently and under what circumstances it is performed, and how it changes. So I undertook a longitudinal study of observing twenty normal infants in their homes every two weeks over their first year to chart these "rhythmic stereotypies" in their natural setting. It was a big job; my assistants and I would visit two homes every day, lugging a box of toys to keep the siblings happy, a Bayley test kit to keep track of the babies' developmental progress, and a heavy reel-to-reel video recorder and camera. We became like members of the families and shared many experiences, including one time, even being attacked by fleas deposited by the family pets! As we watched everyday family life, we detailed, both by a sampled frequency count and by a detailed narrative, the episodes of repetitive movements performed by the infants.

In addition to the pleasure of watching our little subjects grow and develop, I learned a great deal from this intensive period of observation. I did not enter into the observations with a theoretical bias, perhaps a benefit from not having a single, dominant mentor. I learned how to watch behavior very patiently and carefully. I completed the study having gained some understanding of infant rhythmicities. But, as in any good research, it also raised a lot more questions. I became convinced that the previous explanations of rhythmicities were insufficient, and that maybe accounts of other aspects of infant development were incomplete as well.

SHAKE, RATTLE, AND ROLL

What I found was that these perfectly normal infants spent a lot of time moving their limbs and bodies in rhythmic, stereotyped ways. They moved nearly every body part: We saw kicking, rocking, swaying, banging, waving, bouncing, and jumping movements. Some of these movements are pictured in Figure 2-1. All the babies did them, although some more than others. But what was most intriguing was that these movements were associated with distinct developmental periods. In particular, infants performed these oscillating movements when they had some emerging control of that body part or posture, but before they became really skilled. For instance, infants swayed back and forth just after they learned to sit, but not after they were sitting in a stable and comfortable manner. They rocked back and forth just after they could get up on their hands and knees but before they actually crawled well. They banged their arms and waved their toys after they could reach and grab, but before they had fine manipulation skills.

I saw these rhythmic movements like a window opening on the process of developing skills. At these points of transition, when control was just emerging, the system said "Do something"—try to crawl, find out about this interesting toy—but the infant's brain could not yet tell the muscles precisely when and how much to contract to actually get those arms and legs going right. So the system, given a general "go" signal, does what limbs and muscles can do—oscillates like a spring that has been pulled tight and released. When the baby has learned the right muscle settings, she or he now can do more interesting things than repeat a goalless movement, and the stereotyped behaviors normally stop.

But what makes an infant do a particular rhythmic movement at a particular time? When I looked at the real-life situations that were associated

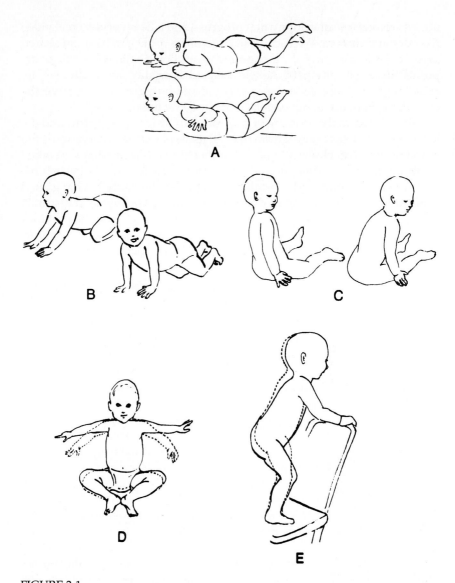

FIGURE 2-1
Infants performing rhythmic stereotypies of their legs, arms, and torsos in various postures.

with bouts of stereotyped movement, I saw that they were not randomly performed. Infants often did these movements when they were excited, or when they were drowsy. (Indeed, adults perform rhythmic movements under similar circumstances; some normal adults report rocking or head banging when drowsy, and many people jump up and down when they are really excited, or bang their fists when angry.) And although most of the movements seemed almost involuntary, frequently infants seemed to "take over" the movement for some seemingly intentional action. A little boy, for example, banged his hand against his tray and kicked his feet in between spoonfuls of food. He seemed to be communicating his impatience to his mother, who was feeding him.

Infants' abilities to take some action, adapt it to serve a new purpose, and then modify that action to better fit the new purpose is another developmental theme that came from my dissertation and has carried through my later research. Here, in fact, is the improvisation theme: Play a melody, explore how you can change it. As I will explain, this capacity to move bits and pieces of behavior around, so to speak, has important implications for understanding how the brain and the body work.

THE ORGANIZATION OF INFANT MOVEMENTS

When I finished my Ph.D. dissertation, I was not in a very good position to find a job. I was trained in a strange combination of fields, and I had no group of well-known mentors to recommend me. Luckily, and again, by chance, a few people in the psychology department and the administration of the University of Missouri liked what I had done as a student, and offered me a half-time faculty position. The only lab space available was a funny little house next to the main psychology building. Maybe the building's history explained why it was vacant: Many years ago, the psychology building housed the University of Missouri Medical School and my lab was the morgue, where the dissections were done. The tile walls, cement floors, and drains were not ideal for a baby lab, but with carpets and colorful posters, it would do. I was thrilled to be able to continue to do research. (I now have a beautiful watercolor painting of the little house hanging in my living room, a gift from a former student.)

As I said before, my dissertation raised many intriguing questions. The first thing I wanted to know was how infants actually did these movements. What did the movements look like in time and space? How were they controlled? I knew very little about motor control in general, and so in order to answer these questions I had to begin to learn about an entirely new field.

I started by looking at leg kicking because it was a very rhythmical behavior that infants did all the time, and about which I could find no previous studies. Videotape was just becoming easy to use in the lab; so, using an enormous Sony 3/4-inch video recorder, I devised a system to analyze infant leg movements. It was very primitive compared to the expensive computer-assisted devices I now have, just a plexifilm grid placed over the video monitor. As I advanced the videotape frame-by-frame, I could track the x,y coordinates of little squares of tape we put on the babies' legs. By knowing the position of the joint and the videoframe, I could reconstruct the path of the limb over time. (The fancy devices work on the very same principle.)

What my students and I discovered confirmed my earlier impression that common infant kicking was indeed very organized. Infants were not just flailing around. The movements were quite precisely timed—about one-third of a second to flex the leg toward the body, and a little longer to extend it back out, and the kicks occurred in rhythmic bouts, one kick after another. When infants kicked at a faster rate, the actual movement times did not change much, but the time *between* kicks became shorter. This is exactly what happens as people *walk* faster; the swing of their legs forward does not become much quicker at all, but the time between swings decreases. Maybe I had found the motor tape in young infants that later controlled locomotion! Perhaps there was a program inside the baby, just waiting to play out, like the tiny wasps' grooming.

THE MYSTERY DEEPENS

I did not hold onto the motor tape theory very long. My students and I looked more closely at these movements, into the actual muscle patterns controlling these kicks. We used tiny electrodes to sense the muscle contractions on infants' legs. (Electromyography, or EMG, detects muscle activity in the same way as an EKG records heart activity by detecting minute electrical changes in the body.) What we found was that although the patterns of leg movements were quite organized and even looked programmed, in comparison, the muscle patterns were very unspecific. When babies flexed their legs in a kick, all the muscles fired at the same time, including muscles that normally flex *and* those that normally extend the leg. Even more surprising, was when the infants extended their legs after the flexion, no muscles contracted at all. What could be going on? How could the movements have more organization than the patterns of muscle contraction that produced them? If there were a tape, it would not be a very precise one; nothing inside was apparently timing the movements.

This single discovery cascaded into a new way of thinking about motor development, and indeed, about thinking about development in general. Some other processes must be involved in producing leg movement patterns because they were *more* than just muscle contraction patterns. But it took another set of experiments to sharpen my theoretical focus.

THE CASE OF THE DISAPPEARING REFLEX

One of the long-held mysteries of early development is the Case of the Disappearing Reflex. If you hold newborn infants upright by supporting them under the armpits, and then lower their feet to the table, they will take "steps"—an alternating kind of march that is always quite surprising to see, because newborn infants normally are so uncoordinated. Within a month or two, however, this early reflex disappears and can no longer be elicited. Traditionally, psychologists and pediatricians have assumed that the reflex disappears because it is inhibited by other parts of the brain as the infants mature.

But as I looked at the hours of videotape of infants kicking their legs, infants ranging in age from 2 weeks to over 6 months, I was struck by an incongruity. Kicking looked a lot like stepping lying down. Or stepping looked a lot like kicking standing up. But babies never stopped kicking. It not only did not disappear, it increased in frequency.

When my graduate student, Donna Fisher, and I carefully compared the movement and EMG patterns in very young infants, we found no difference between those of kicking and of stepping. They were one and the same movement done in different postures. Yet as they got older, infants stopped the movements when we stood them up and resumed them when we lay them back down. How could the maturing brain exert this inhibitory influence in one posture and not another? It did not make sense.

THINKING ABOUT SPRINGS AND LEVERS

I tried to back off from the traditional neurological explanation and think about *all* the things that were going on in this puzzling story. What was happening to infants as they got older in addition to changes in their brains? One obvious change was that during the first few months of life, when the stepping reflex disappears, babies grow very rapidly. They get much heavier. With a bit of detective work in the literature, I discovered that most of this postnatal growth is in subcutaneous fat tissue, rather than in muscle. So the legs were getting heavier, but not proportionately stronger.

For the next piece of the puzzle, I consulted with a biomechanist, someone who studies the mechanical actions of the body. Yes, he confirmed, if you think of the leg segments as levers, it would be true that lifting legs when upright takes more strength than when lying down. This is because gravity helps to flex the leg when infants are supine, but only opposes movement when they are upright.

So it began to make sense. Before infants developed fat legs, they had no problem moving them from either position. But as their legs got fat and heavy faster than their muscle strength increased, infants could no longer lift them to step when upright. However, they had no trouble kicking when supine. The stepping reflex did not really disappear, it was just masked by the changes in other systems. This led to several simple predictions, which we tested by experiments.

My favorite is the fish tank experiment. Heavy legs should not pose a problem underwater, because limbs become buoyant. If leg mass inhibits movements, infants who no longer step "on land" should step fine when their legs are submerged. So we bought the largest fish tank we could afford. It was a bit tricky explaining to parents why we wanted to hold their 2-month-old infants in torso-deep warm water in a large fish tank, but they all agreed. And, as predicted, our wet and slippery subjects all stepped like crazy.

Thinking about legs acting like levers made me aware of theories that suggested that limbs also can behave like springs. Muscles can store energy when stretched, and then spring back and even oscillate when released, just like an ordinary spring. The spring model could help explain kicking and, in particular, why I found precisely timed flexions and extensions in the movements themselves, but no alternating patterns of muscle contractions. When a spring (or a pendulum) oscillates, it does so with a particular timed cycle; indeed springs and pendulums are used as timekeepers inside clocks. But there is no clock itself inside the spring. The timing comes from the physical characteristics of the spring; its degree of springiness and its damping characteristics, and the fact that it stores energy when it is stretched. Likewise, the timing of kicking may come, not from a clock inside the infant, but from the leg acting as a spring. All the infant needs to do is stretch the spring (add energy by contracting muscles) and the pattern emerges as the spring oscillates. Perhaps springs had something to do with all the rhythmic behaviors I had observed in my dissertation research; when infants do not have very good control over a limb or posture, adding energy to the system may reveal its natural oscillations.

Springs and levers may seem far removed from developmental psychology, but they opened my eyes to how multidetermined behavior and its change must be. Some contributions to development may not be immediately obvious—like body fat! So I began to look for a way to conceptualize development that gave equal status to all the contributing factors.

TOWARD A SYSTEMS APPROACH

In nearly every textbook of child development, the authors devote an early chapter to the physical growth of infants. Motor development is often included as part of physical growth. In some ways this distinction tells readers that while physical growth and motor skill are necessary for psychological growth, they are also separate from it. A common message is that motor skill development, like growth, *just happens* as time passes: As the brain gets bigger and better, it instructs the body to do more and more complicated things. Psychological growth, the traditional view holds, is more complex and interactive.

It was my confrontation with the reality of legs as springs and levers that made me think that this traditional view was wrong. First, the body could not just be waiting around to be told what to do. In fact, it is because limbs and bodies are physical things—levers and elastic springs that are subject to gravity, that generate forces and move through space and time— that the brain *cannot* know ahead of time what to tell the body. How can the brain know in advance how much force to exert in what direction to get a limb of a particular mass and elasticity to a particular place, especially when those properties are changing rapidly? The traditional view has got it backward, I thought: The body has to instruct the brain. Infants have to learn about their own bodies in particular situations in order to acquire such skills as sitting or walking or reaching for things.

Second, in development, *everything* counts! It is not enough to ascribe change to just the nervous system, because behavior emerges from inter-actions. There are times when infants move their legs when lying down, or when submerged, but not when held erect. Can we say that babies "have" upright stepping because they can step under some circumstances? It is the wrong question. What we can say is, the system product of a heavy 3-month-old held upright is no movement of the legs. Under water, the very same system reorganizes to produce stepping motions. The behavior re-sides not in the infant, nor in the fish tank, but in the entire baby-in-context situation. Behavior does not live in disembodied form. Rather, it organizes itself in the real circumstances from whatever capabilities are available in the organism in relation to a task and a set of physical constraints. I like to use a term coined by Peter Kugler and Michael Turvey—*soft-assembly*—meaning that the actions you see are never wired into the system in a rigid fashion, but tacked together at the moment out of available components. Sometimes the assembly is very stable and looks the same from time to time. Walking is a good example of a stable assembly. But even stable behaviors are never *exactly* the same. People can and do make frequent subtle ad-justments to meet different conditions as they walk, or even to express dif-ferent moods.

Thinking about behavior in this way profoundly changes the way we think about development. To return to my musical metaphor, the infant's first year is not so much the playing out of a previously written score, but an improvisation. At any point in time, the infant has certain abilities and particular needs and desires; for example, to put interesting things in her mouth, or to keep Mom talking and smiling at him. What babies do is as-semble the best they have at the time to attempt the task—an improvisa-tion—and then as they repeat and repeat the attempts, they learn. Over time the match between their attempts and the world gradually improves and we say they become skilled. And as they master one task, it opens up new tasks. For instance, learning to crawl tremendously increases the number of opportunities to learn about the world as infants can then move them-selves from one place to another. It is the challenge of the task that keeps development moving forward, not a little clock inside the baby.

DEVELOPMENTAL DYNAMICS

I came to articulate the account of development in the previous paragraphs because I could not find an existing theoretical framework that fit the data I was gathering in my lab. More formally, my thinking has been influenced greatly by theoretical advances in other fields, notably from a mathematical and physical theory of complexity called "dynamical systems" or "chaos" theory. I first heard of dynamical systems because a few researchers, notably Scott Kelso, Michael Turvey, and Peter Kugler, were applying dynamics to adult motor behavior. It was very difficult for me to understand at first, but as I learned more and more, I became increasingly excited, and convinced that it would be very useful for understanding baby movements as well.

Many readers will have read James Gleick's popular book, *Chaos*, or seen a *Nova* program on television proclaiming this "new science." Dynamical systems theories are a departure from conventional approaches because they seek to understand the overall behavior of a system, not by dissecting it into parts, but by asking how and under what circumstances the parts *cooperate* to produce a whole pattern.

There are many kinds of dynamical systems and many applications, from weather patterns to brain waves, but for human development, a few general principles are important. First is the importance of time—dynamic means changing over time, and dynamic systems are those that act over time. Second, is the notion of "self-organization," that is that patterns can emerge from complex systems without a blueprint existing beforehand. Good examples are the patterns in clouds, snowflakes, or water flowing over a stream bed. Likewise, biological systems may exhibit complex patterns over time without a little person inside telling the parts what to do. Recall infants' legs showing regular movements from their springlike behavior. The pattern is self-organized. And third is that these systems may be "nonlinear." A system is linear when the strength of a response is proportional to the strength of the stimulus: For every amount of x, there is a proportional change in y. Nonlinearity means that sometimes just a little change in the stimulus will lead to a disproportional response, or even a shift into an entirely new kind of response. When systems show these kinds of nonlinear responses, the component parts may reorganize to a new form: A simple example is freezing water. As the temperature of the air is lowered, liquid water gets colder. At 32 degrees Fahrenheit, a phase shift occurs and the water changes into ice.

The lesson from dynamical systems is that to understand how a complex system behaves, we must understand its dynamics, that is, how it behaves over time and under different conditions. When is it stable and when does it change? In development, we are especially interested in phase shifts, or when the infant acquires new skills, skills like reaching and walking or learning words, that were not there before. When we see this transition, we then want to understand why and how the system reorganized. It is obviously more complex than lowering the temperature! But this way of thinking about systems and how they are organized is very useful.

Much of my work since moving to Indiana University in 1985 has been inspired by dynamical systems thinking. It is a very powerful metaphor. Once I began to look at things "dynamically" I could not go back to the more traditional approaches. Students and colleagues have told me the same thing, that seeing behavior as fluid and time-based changes their interpretations of phenomena they are studying. Dynamic systems thinking also affects the way you conduct developmental studies, because it naturally leads to longitudinal experiments where subjects are followed intensively to track behavioral changes over time. (I realized only recently that I had been conducting dynamic systems studies all along, beginning with my dissertation. I just did not know it!)

USING DYNAMICS: BABIES ON TREADMILLS

One of the most fun series of studies coming from this dynamic inspiration has been with babies on treadmills. I can't remember exactly why I thought it might be interesting to put a baby on a treadmill. I think I was looking for a way to restore the lost stepping reflex. I had no idea whether it would work and there is no way of testing the effect of a treadmill without a treadmill. So we designed and built a baby-scaled treadmill that could sit on a table top. We recruited our first subject; I don't know what we said to convince the parents and the Human Subjects Committee that it was perfectly safe. You can imagine our excitement and delight when the baby who was about 7 months old and, who didn't move a muscle when held upright without the treadmill, responded immediately to the treadmill with beautifully coordinated and alternating steps! With my colleague Beverly Ulrich, who has collaborated on most of these studies, I have tested many dozens of infants ranging from 1 month to 1 year of age, and nearly every one steps on a treadmill. It is quite remarkable to see because the infants don't seem to be intentionally "walking," yet their movements are quite mature-looking. Like adults, infants take more steps when you speed up the treadmill and even are able to coordinate their steps when each foot is on a separate treadmill belt going at different speeds. Figure 2-2 is an illustration of a baby on a treadmill.

The treadmill studies were important theoretically because they demonstrated again the principle of soft-assembly. Obviously infants were not designed to have treadmill stepping. Possibly no infants in human history ever faced a treadmill before. Yet, given this environmental context—stretch legs back on a moving belt—infants improvise a new and very coordinated behavior. What they do have in place are neuromuscular pathways that respond to this task, but the behavior resides in the combination of the infant and the treadmill—it self-organizes in this situation. In fact, what Beverly Ulrich and I later found was that many components contribute to treadmill stepping, including having legs with the right amount of "springiness" to benefit from the action of the treadmill.

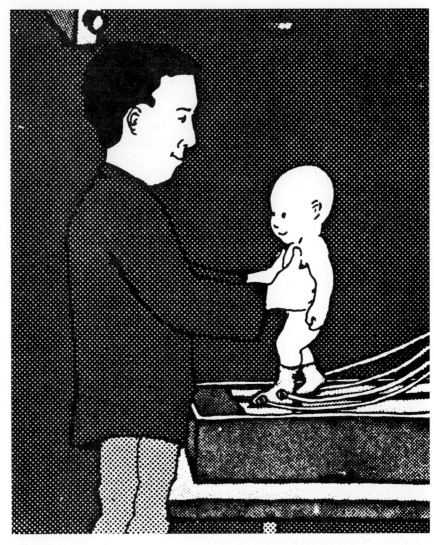

FIGURE 2-2
Infant being tested on the treadmill. The wires are connected to devices that help track the movements in time and space.

*I*MPROVISING LIVES

My current research follows the same overall pattern of first describing the developmental dynamics of an infant motor skill, and then trying to uncover what causes a new behavior to appear and become more skilled. My students and I have just completed a longitudinal study of how infants learn to reach. As we watched babies struggle hard to gain control of their arms, it was again clear how much of this is a problem-solving exercise, a problem each infant has to solve for himself or herself. This leads to more questions about how they discover a solution, and then how they remember it, and generalize it to other, similar situations.

In all this, however, I have come to appreciate more and more the value of improvisation not only for infants as they learn new skills, but for all of us as we live our lives. This is not to say we should not plan our futures and save our money, but rather that part of life should be taking advantage of opportunities that come along. One of the great joys of a research career is the freedom to follow silly ideas like putting babies in tanks of water or on treadmills on the chance they may do something interesting. Sometimes nothing will happen. However, I always teach my students to look just as carefully at the things that don't work out as at the experiments that work perfectly well because we can learn just as much. Improvisation means risk. Experiments might not work, and often infants try to walk and fall down. But improvisation also is our only means of discovery.

SUGGESTED READINGS

The August 1993 issue of *Child Development* has a special section entitled "Developmental Biodynamics: Brain, Body, Behavior Connections," edited by Esther Thelen and Jeffrey Lockman. The twelve articles and commentary are a good place to see the range of work now being conducted in early perceptual-motor development, and the implications for the field of child development in general.

Also:

GIBSON, E. J. (1988). Exploratory behavior in the development of perceiving, acting, and the acquiring of knowledge. *Annual Review of Psychology, 39,* 1–41.

OYAMA, S. (1985). *The Ontogeny of information: Development systems and evolution.* New York: Cambridge University Press.

THELEN, E. (1992). Development as a dynamic system. *Current Directions in Psychological Science, 1,* 189–193.

——— (1994). *A dynamic systems approach to the development of cognition and action.* Cambridge, MA: MIT Press/Bradford Books.

JOHN NEIL BOHANNON III (Ph.D. State University of New York–Stony Brook) is the Wesley A. Dunn Distinguished Professor of Psychology and Head of the Department of Psychology at Butler University. He has published articles and chapters in the fields of language development, language functions in nonhuman species, emotional autobiographical memories, and learning functions in the classroom. However, he is most proud of his satirical contributions to the Worm Runner's Digest and the Journal of Irreproducible Results. He served for eight years on the NIMH Small Grants review panel and as a reviewer for almost a dozen journals. He has received various awards for teaching and research, and when not in the classroom, working with students, or habitually avoiding his administrative duties, he usually can be found swimming his mile a day so that he doesn't turn into a zeppelin.

3

In Pursuit of Receptive Language

❖

IN THE BEGINNING

Every once in a while my parents would ask me what I wanted to do once I got out of college. They said this in hopes that I might look ahead and see the consequences of doing poorly at my studies. In fact, there was some serious doubt whether or not Fairfield University would grant me a baccalaureate degree with all the "rights and privileges thereunto appertaining." The problem partially lay with a series of required courses in theology and philosophy, enough to constitute a second major for all graduates of this small Jesuit institution. Although I did fairly well in my psychology courses, my performance in the less scientific requirements was abysmal. The chair of the department, Father McGrath, shared my parents' worry and informed me that should I graduate, a career in the Navy might suit me. To him, my struggles with Plato and de Chardin proved my lack of discipline and depth. I admit that up to that time, I had little idea what I wanted to do once I left college. However, being informed that graduate school was "out of the question" was enough to set me on a path of unlikely circumstance with, at the time, the least predicted result.

I could have been amused at the irony of Father McGrath's recommendation. After all, not having enough intelligence and discipline to pursue studies in psychology at the graduate level surely meant that I should go into the Navy and possibly control the deployment and use of tactical nuclear devices (this exact thought may have been the reason other professors wrote such good recommendations for me). Instead, I was angry that I had been condemned to leave psychology for other careers. A resolution formed in me to get my Ph.D., no matter how long it took. I had done quite well in physiological psychology and experimental courses. I, therefore, concluded that physiological psychology was the area to enter. However, in the early seventies, what little research money existed in physiological graduate programs was concentrated in high-powered universities, exactly the kinds of places that would never consider me as a viable graduate student. Thus it was that I entered a master's program at the University of Hartford at exactly the same time that an accomplished developmental psychologist, Bernard Z. Freidlander, was offered a professorship. The coincidence was fortuitous because he had a large grant to study language listening in children and he needed graduate research assistants (even to the point of admitting and hiring otherwise marginal candidates like myself).

My training in experimental psychology at Hartford was first rate and I assisted in several projects with both elementary school children and infants. Interestingly, there were no courses in developmental psychology offered at the graduate level. Bernard was too busy administering his grant, which allowed him time off from teaching. My course load and duties in the developmental lab demanded most of my time and although I completed two animal studies on my own, the lure of actual money channeled my efforts away from animal work. Although I applied to both experimental/physiological and developmental programs for my Ph.D., it was the new developmental program at SUNY at Stony Brook that accepted me. Again, my luck held because my future adviser, Frank Palmer, was just stepping down from an administrative post and agreed to sponsor "the graduate student no one else wanted." Frank was supportive and brilliant in helping me understand the nature of individual differences in the course of children's development, but he knew little about language development per se. These unlikely circumstances allowed me to do my own research in receptive language, get my doctorate in three years, and get a job as a language development specialist without ever having a single course in linguistics or language development. This may have been another fortuitous circumstance because it allowed me to look at problems in language development from the perspective of an experimental psychologist without the theoretical and paradigmatic baggage of established approaches.

The downside to all this luck continues to this day. Whenever I returned to Fairfield to give colloquia about my research, I have had to suffer through stories about my undergraduate struggles, usually ending with the punch line that I "proved that there is hope for everybody." I have also had trouble escaping the feeling that I never did get out of college nor have I really managed to grow up in the sense my dad (or Father McGrath) intended. Further, my parents still ask me what I want to do with myself when I finally do. However, I have had too much fun exploring problems I find fascinating, talking with and doing intellectual battle with some of the smartest people on the planet, to ever grow up and get a "real job."

The rest of this chapter reports my research forays into children's language environment and how language comprehension in children affects their course of development. As a graduate student, I investigated children's awareness and ability to use word order or syntax in language comprehension. The next section covers how children's capacity to comprehend determines the nature of the language more mature speakers use when addressing them. Finally, the most critical issue in language development is assessed: Do people correct children for language errors?

LISTENING NOT TALKING

Language developmental research was barely ten years old when I entered the fray. At Harvard, Roger Brown and his students were exploring the grammatical nature of children's speech. The nature of the rules children used to produce language and how they developed was the focus of most of Brown's early work. The regularities of the course of children's development in speaking compelled most researchers to adopt innatist positions to account for the phenomenon. How could children's early speech be so similar despite differences in social class, intelligence, and even languages without the trajectory of development being biologically preprogrammed? It was said that children were essentially mature speakers of their home language by the ages of 4 to 5. Of course, a lot of the mystery about the mechanics of children's emerging speech evolved because almost no one examined the nature of the language environment within which children were developing. Nor did the researchers of the time seem concerned with which parts of that environment children attended to. Fortunately, I was employed in a lab that was examining that very issue.

As a novice research assistant, I helped Kitty Rileigh do a selective listening study of elementary school children. She allowed children to choose between two versions of the same story, one with normal syntax (Josh was a dragon whose hobby was collecting pebbles of an unusual shape and color) and one with scrambled syntax (Dragon was hobby color whose Josh pebbles unusual an was a of shape and collecting). The children could hear one or the other version by moving a lever to one side or the other. After fifteen seconds of listening, the story would stop and they had to make another choice. She found that five- and six-year-old children did not seem to care which version they listened to; both were narrated in a bright female voice with virtually the same duration. Since I ran all sixty children in the study and questioned them afterward, I was convinced that they could not tell the difference. The children even recognized that it was the same story. A later study by Kitty showed that these same children readily chose a bright and lively intonation style over the same story narrated in a flat monotone when both versions consisted of normal word order. Therefore, it could not have been the case that the children were overwhelmed by the complexities of the task. They could make a choice using the technique, but they simply did not do so when the only difference between the versions was word order and meaning.

The possibility that 5- or 6-year-old children did not pursue meaning and correct syntax went against virtually all emerging tenets of developmental psycholinguistics. Children were supposed to be language sophisticates by the age of 4, not indiscriminately listening to any old language garbage. As I recall, this was the very issue that made publishing these findings difficult. Bernard and Kitty decided to focus on the intonation aspect of the work and finally got the data to see the light of print, whereupon they moved on to other problems. I, however, thought there was more to it.

I thought there were two mechanisms responsible for the children's unusual behavior. First, the similarities in the voicing of the normal and scrambled versions may have led the children to decide that it was the same story and either side would be just as interesting. Second, kindergarten children may not have been as sophisticated in language comprehension as their productive speech led us to believe. In other words, the normal and scrambled versions of the same story yielded roughly equivalent comprehension for the younger children. After a lot of argument with Bernard, a third study was performed using the selective story listening technique. Here the children were given a choice between correct syntax narrated in a monotone or a scrambled word order version spoken in a bright and lively tone. The performance of the 5- to 6-year-olds significantly improved. They chose the meaningful but monotonic version. On the other hand, it still boggled my mind that supposedly sophisticated language users seemed to require intonation differences before they would choose a meaningful narrative over verbal garbage.

Over the next three years, I performed a series of studies on elementary school children which assessed more directly their ability to discern the difference between normal and scrambled syntax and related that performance to more accepted measures of language skill. I examined children's ability to discriminate normal from scrambled word order in sentences they heard. The task was a simple one. I recorded forty-eight sentences on tape, half in normal word order and half in scrambled word order. The different versions of each sentence were matched for duration and intonation and the order of presentation was randomized. I introduced the task as a listening and guessing game. I asked the children (first through fifth graders) if they knew that people spoke differently, using different words and sentences to say the same thing. I also told them that I had two friends, Norman and Ralph, who spoke differently, and I had written down some of the things they had said and recorded them on tape (pointing to the cassette recorder). To make the game easier, I would let them listen to something Norman had said, whereupon I played the sentence "Mother told you to wash your hands." Then I told them that Ralph tried to say the same thing and played the sentence "Told mother you hands to your wash." "See?" I said, "That is how Ralph would say that." I asked if any of the children wanted to hear the examples again and did so for several of them. Once the game began the children were asked to tell me whether Norman or Ralph was speaking. I told them whether or not their guesses were correct. After the guessing game, the children were asked to imitate a number of sentences presented in either normal or scrambled word order. The last task of sentence memory was relatively well accepted as an estimate of language ability.

My first pass at the data analysis showed some moderate correlation between the number of correct guesses on the discrimination task and accuracy in imitation of the correct grammar sentences but the statistical predictions were nothing to write home about, let alone try to publish. My adviser, Frank Palmer, asked to see the raw data from the discrimination task to help me puzzle out the developmental trends. After about ten minutes, he started laughing. My heart sank. I thought that I had screwed up in some atrocious fashion. Seeing my dismay, he simply asked me to find a single child in the study that attained criterion performance of eight successive correct choices in the *last half of the discrimination task.* There were none. In fact, if the children did not start their criterion run in four sentences, they would respond randomly for the entire task! He showed me that there were essentially two groups of children, one group "got it" and hardly made any errors, responding "Norman" for the normal word order sentences and "Ralph" to the randomized sentences. The other group seemed to have no clue and responded randomly even though they were corrected after wrong guesses. The proportion of children who seemed to know it instantly increased over the ages studied. About half the first graders and all but one of the fifth graders seemed to "know" it from the very beginning. Frank then asked me to examine the sentence imitation data with this new grouping scheme of "discriminator" verses "nondiscriminator" children.

The results were rather startling. If the children could readily detect normal from scrambled syntax in the discrimination task, there were virtually no differences in their ability to imitate normal syntax sentences regardless of their age. However, the age differences remained in their capacity to repeat random word strings. In the first-grade children, where half of them failed to discriminate word order, the only differences occurred in imitation of the normal sentences. In other words, I had found a simple listening task that predicted whopping differences in children's capacity to process and produce normal speech. The reviews of the submitted report called the results "brilliant." Needless to say, this was heady stuff for a second-year graduate student.

For my dissertation, I followed up the first report by concentrating on early elementary school children, kindergarten through second grade. I also gave the children a standardized vocabulary test and a comprehension test along with the sentence imitation task. The results across 150 children were just as powerful as the first study. If children detected the differences in the discrimination task, they had a significant advantage in comprehending and producing normal syntax sentences. More important, there were no differences between the children on the vocabulary test. This meant that what we were seeing in the discrimination task was probably not due to differences in simple verbal intelligence but some sort of basic changes in language processing that occurred around the age of 6. A later, longitudinal study followed up 5 to 7-year-olds one year later. My word order discrimination task also predicted children's reading scores on several standardized achievement tests. The effect was so powerful that "discriminator" children were reading over one year ahead of their "nondiscriminator" age-mates even though there was no difference in vocabulary intelligence between the groups. Despite the power of these anomalous results, mainstream language development theory ignored them.

This early work taught several valuable lessons about language development. First, any description of development would be at least 50 percent inaccurate if it did not include what children could comprehend. Second, emerging explanations for how children develop productive language ("Golly! It's innate") seemed so underspecified and naive that anomalous results like my early work in syntax discrimination had to be ignored for the theories to survive. Even in my relative unsophistication, it seemed to me that the most important step in language development theory was specifying the connection between what children listened to (usually from their mothers) and their emerging language skill (see Figure 3-1). Recording the changes in children's productive speech is only the final result of learning mechanisms operating in the first step. Rather than being disheartened by the lack of attention to my discrimination research, I decided that there was a need in the field for linguistically untutored experimentalists like myself.

SPEECH ADDRESSED TO CHILDREN

The first course in language development that I taught at Emory University was a real turning point in my research. There were no appropriate textbooks available for undergraduates at the time and I used a general edited volume. Of twelve chapters on various aspects of how children learned to speak, there was but a single chapter on children's language environment. As part of the course, I had all the students travel to the home of another faculty member to talk to his 2-year-old son, Nat. The exercise was successful in that the regularities of Nat's productive speech were predicted very well by extant theories. However, the speech of these thirteen different undergraduates when addressing Nat was just as regular. This striking difference in the nature of the students' speech to Nat's mom and their speech to Nat started me inquiring into the role of this difference in language development. My early work examined what children would listen to when given the choice, assuming children had a widely variable sam-

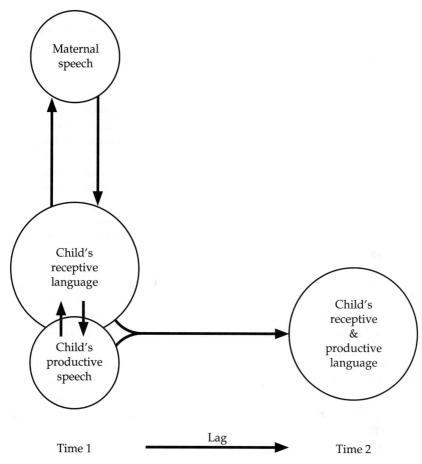

FIGURE 3-1

Hypothetical model of children's language environment and its effects on the child's developing language.

ple from which to choose. But what if that was not the case? What if there was a mechanism that limited the nature of the speech addressed to children? Then the process could be enormously simplified because we would not have to worry about how children choose things to listen to at all. Using the transcripts of the students' speech to Nat, I began to study the nature of the speech addressed to children.

Young children are limited in their ability to understand the full range of language when compared to adults or even older, school-age children. Anyone speaking to a young child seemed to automatically simplify and adapt his or her speech to the target child. This special subset of language behaviors has been called "motherese" because it typifies mothers' speech to children, "baby talk" because it often contains phonological simplifications ("mama" for "mother") or more broadly, just "child-directed speech" (CDS) since children are the most frequent recipients of this language register. By whatever name (CDS henceforth), this special speech register is characterized by short, simple, grammatically correct, and highly repetitive sentences composed of concrete words that usually describe something in the child's immediate environment. CDS is also composed of more questions, declarative sentences, and attention-getting devices than adult-directed speech. The prosodic features of CDS include a higher and more variable fundamental frequency, more variable intensity, a slower rate, and significantly longer pauses between the major syntactic constituents. Many of these features, such as short, simple sentences (measured in mean length of utterance or MLU) and tuning the content of conversation to the child's immediate environment, are consistent over the fourteen languages studied to date. Furthermore, several studies have found that children preferred listening to speech containing features of CDS rather than the speech more typical of adult conversations.

The first wave of reports concerning CDS focused on the specific situations in which the features of CDS occurred. CDS has been observed in diverse contexts ranging from mothers' and fathers' speech to their own and other children, to any adults' speech to children, to children's speech to other children, to speech to foreigners, adult retardates, the elderly, dolls, pictures of children, and dogs. Why features of CDS should emerge in all these contexts was curious. Some have argued that features of CDS have nothing to do with the desire to teach language or even to be understood, but with the need to gain a potential listener's attention, to express affection, or to demonstrate the speaker's social superiority. An alternative explanation is that speakers will "fine-tune" the length and complexity of their speech to the perceived or actual comprehension capacities of the listener. It was argued that if speakers fine-tune their speech to children, then evidence is required for three factors:

1. A method to determine the optimum simplicity of one's speech;
2. A method to determine the sophistication of the listener being addressed;
3. The "machinery" for the rapid implementation of factors 1 and 2 in ongoing conversation.

In a series of articles and theoretical papers, I outlined a fine-tuning mechanism that appeared to function in the following manner. Adults tend to use short and simple sentences (CDS) with children, and the length and complexity of those sentences tend to increase as the children grow more linguistically mature. The most likely influence on this pattern is a feedback system that operates within normal conversation, and depends upon cues from the listener. Children who are linguistically immature (as well as foreigners) tend to understand short and simple sentences, and signal their comprehension success to speakers using such sentences. Longer (and probably more conceptually and grammatically complex) sentences tend to result in comprehension difficulty for these children, and these comprehension problems are also communicated to their conversational partners. Thus, the ability to fine-tune one's speech would be aided by or dependent upon feedback from the listener indicative of the success or failure of the prior communication.

My student, Amye Warren, and I have shown that grammatical complexity and MLU are controlled on a moment-to-moment basis by feedback indicative of the listener's ability to understand. Children are less likely to answer questions and requests appropriately, and are more likely to fail to carry out commands and respond with "What?" or "Huh?" (i.e., contingent queries) when the sentences carrying these functions are relatively long and complex. When children of different ages are matched on their ability to comprehend language, there are no differences in the syntax of the maternal speech addressed to those children.

The feedback effect is so pervasive that we wondered how early it appeared. Did children also respond to comprehension cues by simplifying their speech? In prior work we used experimental confederates who were trained to respond with natural-seeming cues of comprehension success (Yeah, Uh-huh, Sure, etc.) or failure (What? Huh?). However, we wanted to test how 3- and 4-year-olds responded to these cues, and if an older listener might have a different effect from a listener who appeared younger than the target subject. We therefore built a "Chatty Kathy" doll with a wireless microphone and a speaker in her chest. The doll was about two feet in height and appeared to be about 2 years old, if she were real. Our equipment allowed Chatty to carry on conversations with children by having an adult in another room (using a high squeaky voice) speak for the doll.

We recorded 3- and 4-year-old children speaking separately with an adult and the doll, Chatty. During half of each conversation, the confederate adult and doll signaled comprehension success. During the other half of each conversation, the confederate signaled comprehension difficulty. The results revealed that even the youngest children simplified their speech with shorter MLU's when the doll showed signs of comprehension failure. However, little change occurred in the children's speech when the adult signaled failure. The children merely repeated their last utterances. This seemed almost automatic in the kids because even after eight or more repetitions (e.g., Child: "I gotta big ball." Adult: "What?" Child: "I gotta big ball."), the children seemed content to continue. Clearly, if adults signal comprehension difficulty, children's strategy is to merely repeat the exact same utterance. It was also interesting how the children treated the doll that could really talk. The kids acted as if the doll was a real child even to the extent of trying to throw a ball to the doll (which the experimenters encouraged, "Sure, I'll catch it," said the doll), and acting upset when the doll proved to be a dismal failure (Child: "Chatty, you're not trying hard!" Doll: "Maybe I'm not old enough to play catch").

In summary, CDS is the linguistic product of those communicative interchanges in which more adept speakers of a language attempt to talk to less adept language users. Effective communication demands that the one with the superior language skills adapt his or her speech to the abilities of the listener. The resulting effect is that most speakers' utterances will be consistent and lack variability when addressing the same child. Notice that this places an added burden on the immature language learner. The child is the source of the controlling signals that tailor the complexity of the linguistic environment. Hence, ineffective or misleading cues could cause excessive variability in the complexity of the utterances addressed to the child, which may in turn affect language development. Clearly, children differentially signal communicative success depending upon the length and complexity of utterances addressed to them (factor 2 above). Communicative failure results in the simplification of following utterances (factor 1), and both of these occur on a moment-to-moment basis within conversation (factor 3). There can be little doubt that the normal demands of communication result in a simple mechanism whose primary product is the simplified CDS register. Moreover, this mechanism is independent of an adult's intentions in the communicative interchange. Whether or not adults are consciously trying to "teach" language is irrelevant to the system, as long as there is a minimum interest in the passage of information between the conversational partners.

Unfortunately, by the mid-1980s, new arguments were being held up by linguists in order to further support innate mechanisms as the primary explanatory principles behind language development. I had submitted several grants to investigate the connection between CDS and language development, but all were turned down because I had not addressed the "negative evidence" issue (see below). I found myself searching for new factors in children's language environment to investigate.

*A*RE CHILDREN'S ERRORS CORRECTED BY OTHERS?

In 1985, I attended a conference at Carnegie-Mellon University on the newest set of explanations for language development. Theorists and researchers from all over the world attended to hear about the most promising mechanisms proposed to account for how children learn to talk. As I listened to each speaker, it struck me that all of them cited the same study and issue within the first five minutes of their respective reports. The problem that was so central to all of those theories has come to be called the "negative evidence" issue. In short, negative evidence was an axiomatic assertion that children were never informed about the distinction between grammatical and ungrammatical sentences. They all assumed that adults never make explicit comparisons between permissible and nonpermissible sentences nor are children's productive language errors corrected. If this assumption accurately prototyped the language learning situation, then children cannot learn language without considerable prior (i.e., innate) knowledge about the nature of language. On the other hand, if children's conversational partners provided some form of corrective feedback (i.e., negative evidence), then many of the innate linguistic constraints proposed at that conference would have become unnecessary. I began to wonder, "What if they are wrong?" If I could find negative evidence in speech to children, then the entire field would have to change.

The initial negative evidence data was reported by Roger Brown and Camille Hanlon in 1970. They found that their three children received no explicit correction (i.e., negative evidence) during an intermediate stage of syntactic development when the children were producing both correct and incorrect forms of the same construction. The importance of this finding is supported by the fact that it is the single most cited study in all of linguistics and language development research. The problem is so basic it can be illustrated as follows. Imagine a concept formation game where there are a series of stimulus sets. Each stimulus in the set of three is unique and varies from each other on several perceptual dimensions: size (small, medium, or large); color (red, blue, or white); shape (circle, square, or triangle); and any other aspect with at least three values. The task requires that everyone who plays ends up with the same answer; let's say "blue" is always correct regardless of the size or shape of the stimulus. If the subjects are never told whether their choices are right or wrong then convergence on the same answer is impossible. Some subjects will end up choosing "triangle," whereas others might choose the "large" one all the time. The only way people could end up with the same answers without being told "right" or "wrong" during play would be if they all "cheated" and knew the right answer before they started. In the same way, if children are never corrected for making language mistakes, then they should all end up speaking different versions of English, Spanish, etc. Clearly they do not do so in real life; therefore, many have assumed that children "cheat" by innately knowing a heck of a lot about language before they ever start the learning process.

As an experimental psychologist, I began to wonder about the Brown and Hanlon study. They observed only three children, narrowly defined what qualified as language corrections ("Hey kid! You said that wrong"), and only looked at a single language rule out of possible thousands. I could not think of any other phenomena in all of psychology where such an important theoretical issue rested on so little evidence. Some of my friends began to think in the same direction and questioned the Brown and Hanlon conclusions. Kathy Hirsh-Pasek and her associates found that parents repeated their young child's language errors significantly more often than the child's well-formed sentences. Catherine Snow and her students also observed that parents broke their conversational "flow" with children, using more questions and repetitions following a syntactical error than following an errorless utterance.

My students and I also examined adult responses to children's well- and ill-formed speech. The data came from two sources. One set of data consisted of naturalistic conversations between fourteen adults and a single child (aged 2:8) and, four months later, five more adults with the same child (aged 3:0). These transcripts allowed the comparison of one child's differential error rates and adult responses to those errors across a variety of listeners and estimates of short-range developmental change. The second data set consisted of transcribed conversations between ten children (aged 1:8 to 3:1) and both their parents. These data provided confirmation of some of the basic relations found with the single child, and a broader developmental scope (some of the children were still only using one-word sentences). Both sets of transcripts (about 4,000 adult and 3,000 child utterances) were coded for language errors in the child. Four types of errors were independently coded: pragmatic (Mother: "What color is that?" Child: "Vroom!"), semantic (calling a "sofa" a "cat"), syntactic (Is that a dog?) and in phonological (I wanna banama) errors.

Adult responses to well- or ill-formed child utterances were examined in two ways. The first centered on the probability of adult repetition following both well- and ill-formed utterances. Although almost any differential response would serve the informational requirements of negative evidence, repetition might provide additional information on the correct form of language. Data from the first set of transcripts revealed that adults tended to differentially use repetition after a syntax (well = 18 percent, ill = 27 percent) or phonology (well = 13 percent, ill = 29 percent) error. Moreover, this effect was modified by the length of the child's utterance with little differential adult responding (and also fewer child errors) in sentences less than four words in length. In contrast, when the child's sentences were five or more words in length the rate of adult repetition grew to over 40 percent while the rate of repetition of well-formed utterances shrank to 10 percent. It seemed that adults were both focusing on pronunciation errors and correcting the child's productions that were at the edge of the child's linguistic ability.

A second examination of adult responses was conducted on the second data set of mothers and fathers with their children. Here children's errors were coded for the number of syntax and phonological errors that occurred in each sentence. Moreover, the adult responses were examined for corrections of the exact error that occurred in the preceding child utterance (e.g., Child: "I goed there." Adult: "You went where?"). Analysis of the probability of adult corrective repetitions revealed that the parents significantly corrected single errors (41 percent, more often than multiple errors (20 percent). In addition, the adults were differentially sensitive to errors of different types. They almost always corrected semantic errors (88 percent) while providing negative evidence about syntactic (32 percent, and phonological (34 percent) errors much less often. In terms of learning, if children can only process a limited amount of information, then it may be that they can only use negative information in limited contexts. That is, children may only be able to process a single correction at a time.

What remained to be determined was whether or not children made use of the negative and specific evidence provided to them. One may argue that the reported rates of differential feedback are too low to account for children's development. On the other hand, the reported rates come from relatively short conversations, and the cumulative effect over a child's entire language learning career would contain millions of such corrective interchanges. There is some recent evidence that children were sensitive to the types of adult responses we examined. Jeff Farrar found that children were more likely to imitate a morpheme contained in an adult recast than the same morpheme contained in a nonrepetitious, adult utterance. We found that children were not likely to imitate just any repetitious adult utterance. Children imitated adult recasts and expansions (26.6 percent) of child errors six times more often than adult exact repetitions (3.6 percent) of correct child utterances. This suggests that children may indeed be sensitive to the differential adult behaviors that follow language errors. Moreover, the provision of negative evidence possibly occurs in just those contexts wherein the feedback is likely to be salient and useful (i.e., when children make solitary errors).

In summary, we found that all adults (not just the child's parents) tended to repeat and correct children's language errors. Further, children were very sensitive to these corrections, often imitating them in ongoing conversation. Thus, the language learning mechanism may not need to be so powerful or have so much innate knowledge that it can learn language without correction. To remain viable, innate language learning theories must now replicate the "pharaoh's experiment" of a child isolated from other language users. Legend has it that a pharaoh performed the first language development experiment. He had a child locked in a cage in the wilderness and attended by a mute. The purpose was to see if the child spoke some form of ancient Egyptian without instruction to prove that the pharaoh's language was the mother of all tongues. Unfortunately for the pharaoh, the cage was located near a trade route and the few words the child did use at the time of the test were Phrygian. Innatist theorists are faced with a similar conundrum. They must show that a child making language errors is capable of subsequently correcting those errors without exposure to feedback of any sort from any source—an almost impossible task.

CONCLUSIONS AND NEW DIRECTIONS

No one, including me, doubts that there are special language learning mechanisms in humans. After all, only human children come to speak and no other species actually speaks as humans do, even if laboriously taught. However, merely pronouncing the language learning mechanism as hereditary is very unsatisfying for an experimental psychologist. It does not specify which language behaviors will be learned or in what order the innate learning mechanism will interact with the environment to produce the exact developmental pattern we see in children. Only by understanding how children are exposed to language, how they come to understand it, and how more mature language users react to this emerging child skill, will we have a complete developmental theory.

Perhaps we should investigate some of the more puzzling problems children show in language learning. Some children show language delay even though they have normal hearing and intelligence. It is possible that a breakdown in the mechanisms of CDS or negative evidence in their language environments was the culprit and not some brain anomaly in the children themselves. Application of the findings reported above would, if successful, make an actual contribution to children's lives over and above the contribution to language development theory.

Yet again, there is a downside to my research. When my mom asks me what my work has shown, I tell her that I found out that people speak simply to children because kids do not understand complex sentences, and that adults correct children's language errors. She looks at me in disbelief and says, "You get paid for this?" My dad just rolls his eyes, convinced that I haven't yet grown up. However, specifying appropriate forms of intervention for language-delayed children seems different. Now that is a worthy goal of which even my dad would approve.

Acknowledgments

The author would like to thank all the students who worked on this research: Amye Warren, Liz Lotz Stine, Nancy Hepler, Angela Marquis, Laura Stanowicz, Victoria Symons, and Sherry Schnacke. I would also like to acknowledge the help of my friends and colleagues whose brilliance and advice have helped me over the years: Jean Berko Gleason, Brian MacWhinney, Kathy Hirsh-Pasek, Catherine Snow, Liz Bates, and Keith Nelson. Correspondence should be addressed to: J. N. Bohannon III, Head, Department of Psychology, Butler University, Indianapolis, IN 46208.

SUGGESTED READINGS

BOHANNON, J. (1976). Normal and scrambled grammar in discrimination, imitation, and comprehension. *Child Development, 47,* 669–681.

———— (1988). Children's control of adult speech in Spanish. *Acta Paedologica, 2*(1), 351–359.

———— (1992). Theoretical approaches to language acquisition. In J. B. Gleason (Ed.), *The development of language* (3d ed.). Columbus, OH: Merrill.

———— & HIRSH-PASEK, K. (1984). Do children say as they are told? A new perspective on motherese. In L. Feagans, C. Garvey, & R. Golinkoff (Eds.), *The origins and growth of communication* (pp. 176–195). New York: Ablex.

———— MACWHINNEY, B., & SNOW, C. E. (1990). Negative evidence revisited: Beyond learnability or who has to prove what to whom? *Developmental Psychology, 26,* 221–226.

———— & STANOWICZ, L. (1988). Adult responses to children's language errors: The issue of negative evidence. *Developmental Psychology, 24,* 684–689.

———— & STANOWICZ, L. (1989). Bi-directional effects of imitation: A synthesis within a cognitive model. In K. E. Nelson & G. Speidel (Eds.), *A new look at imitation in language acquisition* (pp. 122–150). Norwood, NJ: Ablex.

———— & WARREN-LEUBECKER, A. (1988). Recent developments in child-directed speech: You've come a long way, baby-talk. *Language Science, 10*(1), 89–110.

———— WARREN-LEUBECKER, A., & HELPER, N. (1984). Word order awareness and early reading. *Child Development, 55,* 1541–1548.

BROWN, R. & HANLON, C. (1970). Derivational complexity and the order of acquisition in child speech. In R. Brown (Ed.), *Psycholinguistics* (pp. 155–207). New York: Free Press.

DEMETRAS, M., POST, K., & SNOW, C. (1986). Feedback to first language learners: The role of repetitions and clarification questions. *Journal of Child Language, 13,* 275–292.

HIRSH-PASEK, K., TREIMAN, R., & SCHNEIDERMAN, M. (1984). Brown and Hanlon revisited: Mothers' sensitivity to ungrammatical forms. *Journal of Child Language, 11,* 81–88.

MACWHINNEY, B. (Ed.). (1987). *Mechanisms of language acquisition.* Hillsdale, NJ: Erlbaum.

BYRON EGELAND (Ph.D., University of Iowa) is the Irving B. Harris Professor of Child Development at the University of Minnesota. He is the Principal Investigator of the Mother-Child Project, a nineteen-year longitudinal
study of high-risk children and their families, and Project STEEP, an intervention
program for high-risk mothers and their infants. He has published a number of articles in the area of child maltreatment, high-risk children, and developmental psychopathology. He is a fellow in the American Psychological Association, American
Psychological Society, and American Association of Applied and Preventive Psychology. He served on the National Academy of Science Panel for the Study of Child
Abuse and is currently on the boards of the National Committee for the Prevention
of Child Abuse, American Humane Association, and the Youth Advisory Board of
the Boy Scouts of America.

4

Looking Backward and Forward for the Causes and Consequences of Child Maltreatment

❖

In looking back, I am amazed at how matter-of-fact events can have a profound influence on one's career and for that matter one's life. Shortly after I moved to the University of Minnesota in 1973, I was asked to give a talk on screening for school readiness to the staff at the Minneapolis Public Health Clinic. As I received my reimbursement for this presentation, coffee and a roll, I had a casual conversation with Dr. Amos Deinard, a pediatrician for the University of Minnesota Hospital, who worked part-time at the clinic, and Dr. Ellen Elken, the clinic director. They were talking about child abuse, and even though I knew nothing about it, I made the comment that it was time for someone to conduct a prospective longitudinal study of families at risk for child abuse and neglect. We discussed the idea for a short time and decided that we should be the "someone." Along with Dr. Deinard and some graduate students, we worked very hard on a research grant proposal to the federal government for funds to conduct such a study. After much hassle, which included canceling my winter vacation to work on the proposal, it was rejected by the granting agencies. A short time later, in 1975, we applied to the National Center on Child Abuse and Neglect and were funded. We received money to study a large sample of women who were pregnant for the first time and who were at risk for maltreating their children. Our basic research question was: Why do some high-risk mothers maltreat their children and others provide good quality care?

I hoped that the answer to the question of why some high-risk mothers maltreat their children would provide useful information for developing prevention and intervention programs. Much of my research prior to this time involved developing interventions for children with learning disabilities and a program for children who were impulsive, distractible, and lacking in social skills. Even though I did not know the child maltreatment literature, I was aware that maltreated children typically had serious social, emotional, behavioral, and academic problems as the following case study illustrates.

Eric's mother was typical of the parents placed in the psychologically unavailable maltreatment group. Starting at an early age she was only interested in interacting with her child when necessary. She fed, bathed, and provided for his basic needs, but she rarely interacted with him in an emotionally responsive and loving fashion. At six months of age Eric was a healthy, robust baby who was observed to smile and gaze at his mother in an attempt to elicit a social response and establish a social interaction. When he cried, his mother did not attempt to respond to his distress or needs but instead ignored his cries or showed him who's boss by isolating him in his room. As Eric learned to walk he would attempt to interact by being in close proximity to his mother but she usually ignored him. As he learned to talk he attempted to interact verbally but typically his mother was not interested. At age 2 Eric and his mother were observed in our laboratory in a problem solving situation. As he successfully solved the easier problems he would look to his mother for positive reinforcement and acknowledgement of his success but she provided none. On the difficult problems she did not provide him with any help or assistance, instead the few directions she provided were harsh and impatient commands. During most of the problem solving situations Eric's mother would sit with her arms folded and ignore Eric. His response was to cry and tug persistently on his mother's leg in a futile attempt to get her help.

At each assessment during the infant, toddler, and preschool periods Eric's mother was asked a series of questions about parenting and caring for her child. She would answer most questions by saying, "don't know." She seemed to have no knowledge of, or interest in what was important for her child's healthy development and well being.

As is typical of boys raised by parents who are psychologically unavailable, Eric began to show signs of serious behavior problems at an early age. At 42 months, in a laboratory teaching task situation Eric was aggressive, angry, easily frustrated, and noncompliant with his mother. At age 4 he attended nursery school for only a few weeks. His aggressive, noncompliant behavior was highly disruptive and led to his expulsion. His behavior continued to get worse. In first grade he began to receive special education services for his aggressive, noncompliant behavior and by third grade he was in a special class for emotionally disturbed children. During this time Eric's mother continued to show little interest in him. She did not visit his school when asked and she was not involved with any aspect of his education. His mother did not monitor his behavior at home nor did she attempt to manage his defiant behavior. His educational problems continued and shortly after his sixteenth birthday he dropped out of school. He moved out of his mother's home and has lived with various friends. He has been arrested for shoplifting and intoxication, and has only worked part-time since dropping out of school.

My interest in child maltreatment was to learn more about its causes and consequences and ultimately use this information to develop prevention and intervention programs for maltreating families.

Prior to 1975, all the research on the causes of child abuse and neglect had been retrospective in design. That is, the maltreating families were studied *after* the maltreatment had occurred. The typical retrospective design involved comparing maltreating parents to nonmaltreating control groups. Differences that were found were thought to be causal. While differences between maltreating and control families have been found in a variety of retrospective studies on a number of variables (e.g., socioeconomic variables, life stress and social support, personality characteristics of the parents, a history of having been abused as a child, and a "difficult" child), it cannot be concluded that these differences caused the maltreatment. To illustrate the difficulty in distinguishing cause from consequence in retrospective research, one needs only to look at the theory that young children with "difficult temperaments" cause their own abuse. From this perspective, the irritable, fussy, difficult-to-care-for infant is thought to stress the parents to the point that the parents abuse the child. Indeed, studies have found that maltreated infants are more irritable and fussy than nonmaltreated infants. This finding, however, may be interpreted to mean that a difficult temperament causes the abuse or it may mean that the maltreatment causes the young child to be fussy, irritable, and difficult to care for. As a matter of fact, Brian Vaughn and I found the latter to be the case. Infants who were maltreated were found to be irritable, fussy, and difficult to care for by 12 months of age. At birth and shortly after, they did not display these characteristics, indicating that difficult temperament did not cause the abuse, but instead the abuse caused the irritability and fussiness.

Starting with abusive families and looking backward leads to findings that often are misleading. For example, retrospective studies of the socioeconomic status of maltreating parents find a higher proportion of maltreating parents to be poor. Does this mean that all poor people maltreat their children? Clearly, the answer is no. Retrospective studies of the socioeconomic status of maltreating parents show a high proportion of poor parents in the maltreatment group; however, the results of a prospective study (i.e., looking forward) would tell a different story. Prospectively, the majority of poor people do not maltreat their children. I was interested in a prospective study that would answer the question, Why do the majority of poor parents provide adequate care for their children? What are the variables that differentiate poor parents who maltreat their children from poor parents who provide good quality care? Poverty may be considered a risk factor for child maltreatment, which means that the incidence of maltreatment is higher in a poverty sample than in a middle- or upper-class sample. By following a risk sample prospectively, I hoped to determine the true rate of maltreatment in the risk population and, more important, to determine why some high-risk individuals maltreat their children and others provide adequate care. This is the question that we have attempted to answer with our longitudinal study of first-time mothers who were at risk for maltreatment because of low-income status.

THE MINNESOTA MOTHER-CHILD PROJECT

In 1975, we enrolled 267 low-income mothers who were approximately six months pregnant in the Mother-Child Project. The mothers were recruited from public health clinics and were considered to be at risk for parenting difficulties because of poverty and a number of associated risk factors. Many of our mothers were teens. The average age of the mothers at the time of the birth of their children was 19; the youngest mother was 12 and the oldest was 34. Most mothers were not married, many were high school dropouts, and a number were not prepared for the arrival of a new baby. After the birth of their children, these mothers experienced high stress, lacked emotional support from husbands and other family members, and many lived in overcrowded, chaotic, and disorganized environments. All these risk factors increase the likelihood of child maltreatment.

In order to understand why some high-risk mothers maltreated their children while others provided good quality care, we administered a comprehensive battery of tests and interviews to all mothers, beginning at the sixth month of pregnancy and continuing at regular intervals up to the child's age of 19. During the first year, data was gathered when the infant was 2, 3, 4, 6, 9, and 12 months of age. We gathered extensive data on characteristics of the mother, including personality traits, IQ, and psychopathology, as well as parental attributions, expectations, and understanding of children. In order to assess the effects of the family's social environment on the quality of care the child received, we assessed the level of family life stress, the mother's relationship status with her husband or boyfriend, and level of social support available to the family. To determine the effect of the infant/child on the quality of care he or she received, we assessed such child characteristics as temperament, IQ, and developmental status. All these variables were used to predict good and poor quality of parenting. In addition to the above data, the mother-child relationship was observed in a number of naturalistic settings (e.g., feeding of baby and play situations) and semistructured laboratory situations.

These data were used as measures of quality of caregiving. In addition to attempting to determine the "causes" of good and poor parenting in a high-risk sample, we were interested in studying the consequences of abuse, neglect, and other forms of maltreatment and poor quality caregiving. From our sample of high-risk families, we identified forty-four cases of maltreatment which included physical abuse and neglect, sexual abuse (all investigated by child protection services), and a form of emotional abuse that we labeled psychologically unavailable parenting. Mothers in the psychologically unavailable group were emotionally unresponsive to their young children and, in many cases, passively rejected them. These mothers appeared detached and disinterested in their children, interacting with them only when necessary. Within the subsample, we found considerable overlap among the four types of maltreatment.

The rate of maltreatment in our high-risk sample is much higher than the rate in the general population. In the most recent (1993) annual survey of child protection records from each state, the National Committee for the Prevention of Child Abuse found a maltreatment rate of 0.45 percent of the children in the United States. These data are based on reported cases to child protection services which is a conservative estimate of the true rate. Survey studies of the prevalence of maltreatment indicated a rate as high as 15 percent which is similar to the rate we found in our high-risk sample. We and others who have studied high-risk families find that child maltreatment occurs with much greater frequency than is indicated by the number of cases reported to child protection services. In general, child maltreatment occurs with greater frequency in a high-risk sample such as our poverty sample, and it is underreported across the general population.

FINDINGS REGARDING ETIOLOGICAL FACTORS IN CHILD MALTREATMENT

The majority of investigations of the etiology of child maltreatment have focused on the role of parental characteristics in causing the abuse. Many early researchers in the field thought that maltreating parents were psychologically disturbed or were deviant on certain dimensions of personality. To test this hypothesis, mothers were given a battery of tests during the last trimester and a modified battery was given at later assessments as well. In our study, we found that most of the measures of personality traits (e.g., impulsivity, aggressiveness), psychopathology (e.g., anxiety, depression), or understanding and expectations of the child were not good predictors of the quality of parenting. In comparing the forty-four maltreatment cases to the remainder of the high-risk sample that provided adequate care, there were few differences on the personality or psychopathology measures. One exception was related to the Maternal Attitude Scale, a measure of a mother's understanding of the "psychological complexity" of her child and her relationship to her child. Maltreating mothers tended to score low on this measure. These mothers tended to see their children and caregiving as all good or all bad, not recognizing the complexity of the situation and the positive and negative feelings that accompany caregiving. For example, a mother scoring low on this scale would likely personalize her interpretation of a baby's cry (e.g., the baby is crying because I am a bad mother or he is a bad baby). Mothers scoring high on the test would interpret the cry as a signal that the baby is upset and distressed; she would be sensitive to the meaning of the child's behavior and developmental milestones, recognizing that infants are totally dependent on others for their basic needs but, at the same time, are independent beings with their own needs and desires. Mothers scoring high understand that, as the dependent children get older, a major developmental issue is to become more autonomous and independent. They recognize that they can influence their children's behavior and development, and that the children can influence the parents' feelings and attitudes.

A number of researchers in this area, particularly those with a sociological perspective, believed that the social context of the family was important to consider in determining the cause of child maltreatment. I looked at the life circumstances and social environment of the family, particularly the life stress experienced by the family, mother's relationship with her husband/boyfriend, and overall emotional support available to the mother. Our life stress scale consisted of a list of thirty-nine events (e.g., events included losing job, evicted from apartment, being arrested, sickness of a family member, physical fight with neighbor or friend, etc.). Mothers were asked to endorse events they had experienced since the last assessment. I found that the higher the stressful life events score, the greater the likelihood of the parents abusing their children, although this relation was only moderate. Many highly stressed families provided good quality care, and some families that experienced very little stress maltreated their children. I attempted to sort this out and found that high-stressed families that maltreated their children had mothers who scored high on measures of aggression, hostility, and impulsivity compared to high-stressed mothers who provided adequate care. The combination of stress, anger, and an inability to cope with frustration increased the likelihood of maltreatment occurring. Stress alone or anger and the inability to cope alone were not good predictors of maltreatment.

I examined a number of family relationship status variables for the purpose of identifying both risk and protective factors for maltreatment. A mother's relationship status (e.g., single or married) was not related to quality of parenting, although chaotic relationships (defined as boyfriend moving in or out on a regular basis, or a mother having a new live-in boyfriend every few months) were often associated with maltreatment, especially sexual abuse. If the mother's relationship to her husband/boyfriend was tense and much conflict existed, the likelihood of maltreatment increased. Certain relationship variables also serve as a protective factor which means that they reduce the chances of maltreatment occurring. For example, if a mother felt satisfied and supported in her relationship to her husband/boyfriend, the chances of maltreatment decreased. Support from a grandmother or other family members was also a protective factor.

A history of having been abused proved to be the single most signifi-cant risk factor for maltreatment among our sample, greatly increasing the likelihood that mothers would maltreat the next generation. All our moth-ers were asked about the quality of care they received as children. Forty-seven mothers reported having been physically or sexually abused and/or neglected. We examined how these mothers cared for their children and found that 40 percent of mothers who were maltreated as children were maltreating their children. Our rate of transmission of 40 percent is con-sistent with Joan Kaufman and Ed Zigler's estimate of 34 percent based on prospective findings from other investigators.

Even though the rate of transmission of maltreatment across genera-tions is high, the majority of individuals who were maltreated as children do not maltreat their children. This finding raised an important question, why were some parents who were maltreated as children able to break the cycle of abuse? To answer this question, we compared our mothers who broke the cycle of abuse with those who were maltreated and were found to maltreat their own children. We found that mothers who broke the cycle of maltreatment had participated in long-term, intensive psychotherapy as adolescents or young adults, or had received nurturant caregiving as chil-dren from someone other than the abusing parent. We explained these find-ings using contemporary attachment theory as described by John Bowlby. From this perspective, mothers who experienced abuse as children and who abused their own children, are thought to have developed represen-tational models or understandings of relationships as unsatisfying—an ex-pectation that one is likely to be rejected and not have one's needs met in close relationships. Mothers who were able to break the cycle of abuse are thought to have developed more positive "models" of relationships based on the positive experience of therapy and/or alternative caregivers; they come to view relationships as satisfying, not rejecting and abusive.

A second major finding in our study of how individuals break the cycle of abuse has to do with how maltreated children process the traumatic experience. We found that others who broke the cycle of abuse were able to integrate this experience into a coherent view of self, whereas mothers who were maltreated and who maltreated their own children seemed to have split off the abusive experience through the process of dissociation. Those who dissociated could only recall fractions of their childhood abuse or, alternatively, denied the abusive experience and idealized their parents. Those who idealized parental figures described their parents in a very pos-itive manner, although they could not recall any incidents or experiences to support this positive view. In every case, mothers who had not been able to break the cycle of maltreatment dissociated the abuse experience and did not resolve it or integrate it into their view of self.

In summary, the major conclusion from our prospective study is that there is no single cause of child maltreatment. The causes are complex and consist of a combination of risk factors that interact in different ways from one individual to the next. Variables such as poverty, unemployment, life stress, parents' poor understanding of their child, and a history of having been abused are not by themselves likely to cause child maltreatment. If parents have one of these characteristics they may be at greater risk for maltreating their children, but it is important to keep in mind that the majority of parents with one or a few risk factors do not maltreat their children. The greater the number of risk factors, the greater the likelihood that maltreatment will occur, but a large number of risk factors will not automatically lead to maltreatment, particularly if protective factors are present. The combination of risk and protective factors that cause child maltreatment may vary from family to family. The effects of this combination of risk factors for a particular family can only be understood by knowing the family, the family's history, the social environment in which the family lives, and the protective factors available to the family. The causes of maltreatment can only be determined by understanding the interaction of risk and protective factors within the broad social context of the family.

THE CONSEQUENCES OF MALTREATMENT

Another major goal of our research has been to examine the effects of different patterns of maltreatment on children's developmental adaptation across time. I was interested in determining whether the effects of maltreatment were temporary or long-lasting, and I hoped to identify protective factors that may have made maltreated children less vulnerable to the negative consequences of maltreatment. An important decision in studying development across time is the selection of particular outcomes and the procedures for measuring them at each developmental stage. Since I did not have expertise in the infancy and toddler period, I recruited Dr. Alan Sroufe to assist in the selection of developmental outcomes and procedures for this period. He is a faculty member in child development at the University of Minnesota and an expert in early development, particularly parent-infant relationships and attachment. We chose to assess mother-infant attachment through an observational procedure called the Strange Situation.

At each age we defined adaptation in terms of the salient developmental issue of that period, then we selected measurement procedures that we thought best assessed this outcome. Following the assessment of attachment in infancy, a task was designed to assess the developmental issues of autonomy and the awareness of self during the toddler period. In preschool, we were interested in the issues of self-control, coping with frustration, social skills, and interest in mastering the environment; and during the school years, we have obtained information on school adjustment, work habits and initiative, peer competence, and academic success. At each of these ages, we have obtained information on the children's adaptation from a variety of different sources, including videotaped observations in the home and in semistructured laboratory situations, as well as interviews with the children, parents, and children's teachers.

We assumed that using different measures and multiple sources of information would provide the most accurate picture of each child's typical behaviors and adjustment. We also assumed that observation of the child in his or her natural environment would provide the most typical representative sample of behavior. An example of observational data consisted of going into the child's classroom, in an unobtrusive fashion, and rating the child on a seven-point scale on such dimensions as compliance, attending to task, working independently, and peer acceptance. This observation data proved to be very valuable and ecologically valid, even though the ratings were quite subjective. Despite going to great lengths to train our observers, there are times when I worry that the data are not precise and reliable. How serious is it when a child has to be told to return to a seat three times before the child complies? Is this as serious as an incident where the child complies with the teacher's directions, but shows other forms of defiance such as mocking the teacher? It is important that coders agree on the seriousness of each of these incidents along the continuum of complying to noncomplying. A lack of agreement among coders results in a rating that is not an accurate reflection of the behavior being observed. Over the years we have developed procedures for assuring reliability and objectivity. My Ph.D. is from the University of Iowa and my training involved a heavy dose of statistics, measurement theory, and experimental psychology, which included an emphasis on precise measurement of the variable being studied. Even though complex behaviors such as parent-child relationship variables or child classroom behavior are difficult to measure in a precise fashion, they provide valuable information about the child's overall behavior and adjustment.

CONSEQUENCES OF PHYSICAL ABUSE

In infancy (18 months), physically abused children were more likely to be anxiously attached compared to the control group. Their problems became more apparent at age 2 when they were observed in a problem-solving situation with their mothers. This task comprised four problems of increasing difficulty; the simplest problem involved using a stick to get a prize from a plexiglas tube and the most difficult involved weighting down the end of a lever with a block to raise a prize through a hole in a plexiglas box. The toddler was expected to turn to mother for help in solving the most difficult problems. Physically abused children were rated as more angry, frustrated, and noncompliant with their mothers and they exhibited less enthusiasm for the task. It appeared that these children did not have confidence in their mothers' help and support and as a consequence they quickly became frustrated and angry. One 2-year-old boy was so frustrated with his mother for not helping him that he threw the wood block at her.

Two-year-olds are typically interested in mastering their environment, but without the help of a caring and supportive caregiver frustration results. For many maltreated children their approach to dealing with frustration is an angry outburst.

This pattern was even more apparent at 42 months when children were observed with an experimenter and with their mothers in a teaching task situation (e.g., child is asked to sort objects on the basis of size, color, and shape). The physically abused children were angry, avoidant of their mothers, and noncompliant to their mothers' directives in the teaching task situation. It appeared that these children did not trust that their mothers would be available for help and support, which resulted in anger and frustration. Some children would become angry at their mothers; many maltreated children by this age withdrew and were not interested in mastering their environment.

Children were also observed at 42 months in a barrier box task, which consisted of a plexiglas box filled with interesting toys. The box had a lock that was difficult to open and the children were told that they could play with the toys inside the locked box. Physically abused children had difficulty coping with the frustration of not being able to get into the box. They did not persist in attempting to open the box and they lacked self-control, expressed much negative affect, and showed little creativity and flexibility in their approach to the problem.

Many maltreated children had difficulty making the transition to school. They lacked the confidence to succeed and the skills to cope with social and academic demands. Anger, defiance, and negative affect characterized the physically abused children's behavior in the early school years. They were rated by their teachers on the Child Behavior Checklist as inattentive, unpopular, aggressive, and self-destructive. All but one of the physically abused children were referred for special education services. Differences were found between boys and girls who had been physically abused. The physically abused boys received significantly lower scores on the Peabody Individual Achievement Test compared to the boys in the control group. Physically abused boys and girls had more behavior problems compared to the control group; however, the abused girls exhibited more internalizing problems (e.g., anxiety and depression) while the abused boys showed more externalizing types of problems (e.g., defiance and aggression).

CONSEQUENCES OF NEGLECT

The effects of early neglect on development were observed at an early age and, as the children got older, were observed across a wide area of functioning. In the problem-solving task at age 2, neglected children lacked enthusiasm, were easily frustrated, and displayed more negative affect than nonmaltreated children. At 42 months, children who had early experiences of neglect had difficulty coping. In the barrier box task, they were judged to have low self-esteem; they were distractible and withdrew from the task without much of an attempt to solve the problem. In the teaching task, the neglected children differed from the control group on every variable. They showed little persistence or enthusiasm. They were angry and noncompliant toward their mothers, but they were also highly reliant on their mothers for help and support. In preschool and early elementary school, they were dependent on their teachers. They were more interested in the teachers' emotional support than attending to school work or playing with friends. Neglected children received significantly lower scores on all achievement subtests. On the Devereux Elementary School Behavior Rating Scale, they were rated by their teachers as extremely inattentive, uninvolved, reliant on teacher, and lacking creative initiative. In general the neglected children were doing poorly in school in almost every area; they had poor work habits and were dependent and isolated from peers.

CONSEQUENCES OF PSYCHOLOGICAL UNAVAILABILITY

Despite much interest in emotional maltreatment, there has been relatively little research in this area. Most states include emotional maltreatment in their child protection laws; however, the definitions are vague and highly varied from state to state. Marla Brassard, Stewart Hart and Robert Germain, in their book on emotional maltreatment, list rejecting, terrorizing, isolating, degrading, exploiting, missocializing, and corrupting as examples of emotional maltreatment. We added emotional neglect to this list and called this form of maltreatment, psychologically unavailable parenting. I became interested in emotional neglect as a graduate student reading about infants raised in institutions. Even though they were well cared for physically, the lack of emotional care resulted in extreme apathy, lack of interest in social interaction, and poor physical development, including in some instances extreme failure to thrive and death. My interest in attachment theory, which emphasizes the importance of parental emotional responsiveness for establishing secure attachment relationships, also served as a guide for defining emotional neglect as a form of maltreatment. Because infants are dependent on a primary caregiver for their survival and communicate their needs by crying, smiling, grasping, and gazing, it is important that primary caregivers be available to respond to infant needs and communications. The quality of the relationship formed between parents and infants, in part, depends on the parents' sensitivity and emotional responsiveness to the baby's needs. Parents who are emotionally responsive, supportive, and available are likely to have infants who feel secure in the relationship. The relationship provides a secure base from which the toddler may begin to gain confidence and independence to master his or her environment. I viewed a lack of emotional support, responsiveness, and availability as a form of psychological maltreatment and hypothesized that children experiencing this form of maltreatment would display negative consequences at later stages of development.

The staff classified parents as psychologically unavailable on the basis of observations of mothers and infants in a feeding and play situation at 6 months, play at 12 and 18 months, and a tool-use situation at 24 months. The nineteen mothers classified as psychologically and emotionally unavailable were unresponsive to their children's needs and unavailable for emotional support. Most attempts by the infant to elicit interaction by the parent were ignored. The parent was not available to comfort the distressed child or interested in sharing the child's feelings of success and accomplishment at mastering problems or skills at age 2.

One possible explanation for emotional unresponsiveness is that the children may not have attempted to elicit interactions from the parents. In an effort to determine if these children were unresponsive, we compared infants in the psychologically unavailable group to those in the control group and found no difference on the various measures of temperament or in the feeding situation at 3 months of age. The infants in the psychologically unavailable group did attempt to interact with their mothers early on, but mothers of these infants typically did not respond. These findings suggest that the infants do not "cause" mothers to be emotionally unresponsive.

The consequences of psychologically unavailable caregiving were striking. At 18 months, 71 percent of the children in this group were insecurely attached. Most were classified as anxious-avoidant, which suggests that these children coped with an unresponsive parent by denying the need for a close relationship with a caregiver. They appeared to be totally disinterested in their mothers. At 24 months, these children were angry, noncompliant, extremely frustrated, and experienced little positive affect. One dramatic finding was a forty-point decline in performance on the Bayley Scales of Infant Development from 9 to 24 months. At 42 months, children in the psychologically unavailable group were disinterested in tasks and in their mothers. In preschool and the early school years, they showed many signs of developing psychopathology. In summary, psychologically unavailable parenting has devastating consequences on the development of young children. The effects of this form of maltreatment are at least equal to or perhaps even greater than the effects of physical abuse and neglect.

INVULNERABLE AND RESILIENT CHILDREN

Our examination of the effects of maltreatment clearly indicate that these children as a group suffered severe consequences when compared to the nonmaltreated children from the same high-risk sample. We have also been interested, however, in invulnerable and resilient children in the maltreatment groups who were functioning in a competent fashion. We found that the term *invulnerable* did not apply to any of our maltreated children since all of them showed at least some negative consequences. In addition, while there was a range of outcomes in our maltreated sample, none of the children were functioning in a competent fashion. Some maltreated children were more resilient than others, but none of the children were immune or invulnerable to the effects of maltreatment.

We attempted to account for the relatively more positive outcomes within the sample of maltreated children by identifying protective factors within the child, family, or environment that were associated with more resilient functioning. We defined resilience as children falling in the average or competent cluster groupings based on the results of a hierarchical cluster analysis at each child assessment. Cluster analysis is a statistical procedure used to form groups of individuals that are similar. Within our study, there were only four to five maltreated children falling in the average or competent cluster groups at each assessment. None of the maltreated children fell in resilient groups from infancy to the early school years.

Despite the small samples, we were able to identify some protective factors that were associated with resilience within the maltreated sample. First, the highest functioning maltreated children had a history of secure attachment. Secure attachment seemed to provide the children with a good foundation. Second, maltreated children who were functioning in a more competent fashion in preschool had experienced major changes in their lives either in the form of a more stable home environment, foster home placement, or enrollment in a good quality day care center. A stable home environment consisted of living in the same place for at least a year, a male living in the home on a stable basis who provides support to mother and child, and no overcrowding. Unfortunately, in many of the most unstable homes there were a number of adults moving in and out of the home, creating considerable chaos and disruption.

As I indicated in the previous section, few of the children in the psychologically unavailable group were ever functioning in a competent fashion. Clearly the lack of emotional support had devastating consequences on the child's development. On the other side of the coin, for children who were physically abused or neglected, emotional support and responsiveness from a parent or someone outside the immediate family was a major protective factor.

CONCLUSION

I have presented a rather dismal picture of the effects of maltreatment; however, I believe that the poor developmental outcomes are often reversible. The tentative findings from the study of the highest functioning maltreated children indicate that children do respond in predictable ways to environmental change. We also found that environmental change in the form of a supportive relationship and/or intensive psychotherapy was related to breaking the cycle of abuse across generations. We have used the findings from our prospective study of the "causes" and consequences of maltreatment to develop a preventive intervention program for high-risk mothers and their infants. This program was called STEEP (Steps Toward Effective, Enjoyable Parenting) and it consisted of home visits and group sessions starting during the sixth month of pregnancy and continuing through the first year of the baby's life. An important goal of this program was to promote a secure mother-infant attachment by assisting mothers to be more sensitive and responsive to their infants. A secure attachment seems to be a protective factor in the face of later adversity and it is important for the child in negotiating other significant developmental issues at later ages. Another goal of STEEP was to promote the mother's understanding and awareness of her relationship with her infant, empowering her to manage her life in an often chaotic environment. In an evaluation of STEEP, using a sample similar to the risk sample used in our prospective longitudinal study, we found a more stable home environment and a number of positive parenting outcomes for mothers in STEEP compared to those in the control group.

It has been most gratifying to apply findings from our longitudinal study of the causes and consequences of maltreatment to the development of the STEEP program. Some of the adolescents in our sample are having babies. I'm very interested in following the total sample for at least five more years to determine quality of parenting and attachment in the next generation. From those children in our sample who were maltreated, I hope to learn more about the transmission of maltreatment across generations and identify the reasons why some are able to break the cycle of maltreatment. As we continue to follow our high-risk sample, including the maltreated children, through adolescence and early adulthood, we hope our findings will have further implications for theory, clinical practice, intervention, and prevention.

SUGGESTED READINGS

BOWLBY, J. (1980). *Attachment and loss: Vol. 3. Loss, sadness and depression.* New York: Basic Books.

BRASSARD, M., HART, S., & GERMAIN, R. (Eds.). (1987). *Psychological maltreatment of children and youth.* New York: Pergamon Press.

BRUNNQUELL, D., CRICHTON, L., & EGELAND, B. (1981). Maternal personality and attitude in disturbances of child-rearing. *American Journal of Orthopsychiatry,* 51(4), 680–691.

EGELAND, B. (1988). Intergenerational continuity of parental maltreatment of children. In K. D. Browne, C. Davies, & P. Stratton (Eds.), *Early prediction and prevention of child abuse* (pp. 87–102). New York: Wiley.

———— BREITENBUCHER, M., & ROSENBERG, D. (1980). A prospective study of the significance of life stress in the etiology of child abuse. *Journal of Clinical and Consulting Psychology, 48*, 195–205.

———— & BRUNNQUELL, D. (1979). An at-risk approach to the study of child abuse: Some preliminary findings. *Journal of the American Academy of Child Psychiatry, 18*, 219–235.

———— CARLSON, E., & SROUFE, L. A. (1993). Resilience as process. *Development and Psychopathology, 5*, 517–528.

———— & ERICKSON, M. F. (1987). Psychologically unavailable caregiving: The effects on development of young children and the implications for intervention. In M. Brassard, S. Hart, & B. Germain (Eds.), *Psychological maltreatment of children and youth* (pp. 110–120). New York: Pergamon Press.

———— & ERICKSON, M. F. (1990). Rising above the past: Strategies for helping new mothers break the cycle of abuse and neglect. *Zero to Three, 11*(2), 29–35.

———— JACOBVITZ, D., & SROUFE, L. A. (1988). Breaking the cycle of abuse. *Child Development, 59*(4), 1080–1088.

———— & SROUFE, L. A. (1981). Attachment and early maltreatment. *Child Development, 52*, 44–52.

———— SROUFE, L. A., & ERICKSON, M. (1983). The developmental consequences of different patterns of maltreatment. *International Journal of Child Abuse and Neglect, 7*, 459–469.

———— & VAUGHN, B. (1981). Failure of bond formation as a cause of abuse, neglect, and maltreatment. *American Journal of Orthopsychiatry, 51*, 78–84.

ERICKSON, M. F., EGELAND, B., & PIANTA, R. (1989). The effects of maltreatment on the development of young children. In D. Cicchetti & V. Carlson (Eds.), *Child maltreatment: Theory and research on the causes and consequences of child abuse and neglect* (pp. 647–684). Cambridge: Harvard University Press.

FARBER, E. & EGELAND, B. (1987). Abused children: Can they be invulnerable? In J. Anthony & B. Cohler (Eds.), *The invulnerable child* (pp. 253–288). New York: Guilford Press.

KAUFMAN, J., & ZIGLER, E. (1987). Do abused children become abusive parents? *American Journal of Orthopsychiatry, 57*, 186–192.

PIANTA, R. C., EGELAND, B., & ERICKSON, M. F. (1989). The antecedents of child maltreatment: The results of the Mother-Child Interaction Research Project. In D. Cicchetti & V. Carlson (Eds.), *Child maltreatment: Theory and research on the causes and consequences of child abuse and neglect* (pp. 203–253). Cambridge: Harvard University Press.

SROUFE, L. A. (1979). Socioeconomical development. In J. Osofsky (Ed.), *Handbook of infant development* (pp. 100–122). New York: Wiley.

STRAUS, M. A., & GELLES, R. J. (1986). Societal change and change in family violence from 1975 to 1985 as revealed by two national surveys. *Journal of Marriage and the Family, 48*, 465–479.

❖

*R*oss A. Thompson *(Ph.D., University of Michigan) is Professor of Psychology at the University of Nebraska—Lincoln, where he also has an appointment in the College of Law. His research on early attachment and emotional growth, and his policy studies concerning children and families, have yielded
more than 100 scholarly articles, including the books* Infant-Mother Attachment
(with Lamb, Gardner, and Charnov), Socioemotional Development *(as editor of
presentations from the Nebraska Symposium on Motivation), and* Preventing
Child Maltreatment Through Social Support. *He is Associate Editor of* Child
Development *and received an early career award from the Developmental Psychology Division of the American Psychological Association. He rounds out his life
experience by listening to classical music and jazz, running, reading theology—
and developing his skills as a soccer coach for his two sons and their buddies.*

❖

5

$\mathcal{A}$ttachment and $\mathcal{E}$motional $\mathcal{D}$evelopment: $\mathcal{F}$rom Clinic to $\mathcal{R}$esearch to $\mathcal{P}$olicy

❖

Psychologists "do research" in various ways. For some, research is a methodical, step-by-step procedure for carefully testing theoretical hypotheses. For others, research is a matter of demonstrating, in a laboratory or field setting, some phenomenon that the scientist believes noteworthy. For still others, research is a process of exploring uncharted terrain in some field of interest. There is no best way of "doing research." These alternative approaches are well-suited to different topics, and sometimes the best research strategy depends on whether the topic is new or has been studied extensively. But understanding how particular psychologists do research reveals much about why, and how, they think about research problems, and the meaning that research has to their scholarship.

To me, research is *discovery:* an odyssey of surprises, confirmations, and unexpected twists and turns that contribute to the excitement of a research career. Although I encourage my students to propose thoughtful hypotheses as they begin their work, I urge them not to take their expectations too seriously because research results often defy the most carefully formulated hypotheses. The excitement of a research career is that the story told by the data is always more interesting than the one you had expected to confirm. In this sense, human behavior is far more interesting and provocative than even the most thoughtful theories allow, and this means that the scientist must be instructed by the lessons revealed by unexpected research findings—while maintaining humility about her or his capacity to predict the next turn in the road.

Careers are like that, too. Viewed midcourse or in retrospect, people sometimes discover that they have followed career pathways that could never have been anticipated when agonized decisions were first being made about college, graduate school, the first academic appointment, or the choice of early research questions. If one is lucky, these pathways have been far more exciting than those that were planned and initiated long ago. Such a view of career development is in sharp contrast to the view that most people embrace at entry: that careers are formed through one's steady progression through well-defined and carefully considered choices at critical stages of professional growth. By contrast, if I could have read the story that follows when I was an undergraduate, I would have been pleased, but surprised.

UNEXPECTED CATALYSTS

I'm not sure when I first decided to become a developmental psychologist, but I suspect that it was shortly after I had devoted a semester to volunteer work at a therapeutic classroom for emotionally disturbed children during my junior year of college. By contrast with the passionless and logical reasoning of the law—which is where I had thought I would go—these preschoolers had compelling emotional needs, and had lacked the reliable, secure relationships in which those needs could be satisfied. I began considering graduate school as an avenue for exploring how emotional growth unfolds in the context of close relationships, and how children who are deprived of these human connections can be assisted.

I arrived at the University of Michigan fresh out of undergraduate school in 1976. I had sought admission to the graduate program in developmental psychology at Michigan because I wanted to study with Martin Hoffman, whose work on empathy I had long admired (and still do). I wanted to study empathy because it is an emotion that underlies compassion and care, and thus helps to define the emotional connections people share with each other. Most of my first year was devoted to fulfilling my undergraduate dream of working closely with a skilled scientist in course work and directed reading, but I was especially excited about starting my own research, under Hoffman's direction, on empathy in grade school children. Life seemed on course, until the unexpected happened. Hoffman announced at the end of my first year that he would be leaving Michigan soon to assume a faculty position in New York. My plans for working closely with him would have to be set aside, at least for the time being, and I would have to find another faculty mentor to work with. But as I was preparing to do so, something else also unexpectedly appeared on the horizon.

At the suggestion of another graduate student, I secured a research assistant position at the Child Development Project, an intervention program designed by a team of clinical researchers to assist troubled families and their young children. The purpose of the project was to apply the newest research about parent-infant attachment, and the insights offered by current theories about parenting, to the treatment of young families at risk for parenting disorders. The families who were treated by project staff were multiproblem families: They included single, teenage mothers for whom the conflicting needs to nurture a dependent child and to be nurtured themselves contributed to their neglect of offspring; parents whose psychological and emotional turmoil interfered with their capacity to support their babies' emotional well-being; and adults whose coping with financial need, legal problems, relational conflicts, and other stresses left little energy, or devotion, to the care of infant offspring. Their young children revealed the results of their parents' inadequacy: Many were far below norms for their age in weight, height, and other signs of good health; many received below-normal scores on standardized tests of cognitive development; many showed signs of emotional dysfunction, including persistent, plaintive crying, or a blunted, emotionless demeanor, or an inability to respond with animation and joy even to social play. They reminded me of some of the children I had seen in the therapeutic classroom several years earlier.

To the clinical team who worked with these families, parents carry the legacy of an earlier parent-infant relationship—the one by which they were nurtured years ago—in their care of offspring. We nurture, in a sense, as we were nurtured long ago. When their own childhood care was deficient, however, sometimes these "ghosts in the nursery" must be exorcised to enable parents to develop healthy emotional ties to their offspring. By offering informal therapeutic assistance—often in the kitchen, living room, or day care center, rather than a clinic—and guidance concerning the needs of young children, clinical researchers like Selma Fraiberg, Edna Adelson, and others who formed the core staff of the Child Development Project hoped to enable parents to provide better care and, at the same time, learn more about the psychological processes underlying parents' capacities to nurture their children.

At that time, I had little knowledge of parent-infant bonding, knew even less about infant mental health and, quite frankly, my motives for becoming a research assistant were mixed (it was better than being a teaching assistant). I learned, however, that my job was to apply current research knowledge to an evaluation of whether children benefited from the therapeutic interventions that their parents received. Based on case files, the outcomes of standardized developmental assessments, conversations with the therapists, videotapes of parent-infant interaction, and other information gathered during the course of therapeutic intervention, my task was to assess changes in each child's functioning. In some cases, this meant determining whether a baby who had been referred because of life-threatening weight loss had been restored to adequate physical and emotional health. In other cases, it meant determining whether a young infant who had been falling behind cognitively had begun to show age-appropriate achievements by the close of therapy. My contributions to the developmental assessments of offspring were incorporated into case discussions in which the entire staff participated, and which included evaluations of the progress of parents as well as their children.

Through this work, I began to see that one of the most important markers of growing physical and psychosocial well-being is change in the child's emotional life. A baby who mirrored a parent's depression in his or her shallow, listless emotional demeanor at the start of therapy would begin to exhibit the bright, animated exuberance of a typical child at the same time that other physical and social needs were being satisfied. A maltreated toddler's agitated caution in the presence of the parent slowly changed to a demeanor of positive, calm reassurance as therapeutic insights enabled the parent to become a more sensitive, reliable caregiver. I learned, in short, that the "emotional dynamics" of the child's behavior with the parent and other partners are often a crucial clue to the growth of psychosocial well-being that I was trying to understand. Since these emotional dynamics— such as the vitality, animation, range, breadth, and intensity of emotional responses—had been little studied at the time, I wondered whether it was possible to understand their development in typical as well as atypical infants.

ATTACHMENT AND EARLY PSYCHOLOGICAL GROWTH

The work of the Child Development Project was provocative also because it built upon important advances that were occurring in the study of parent-infant attachment. The growth of the mother-infant bond is, of course, one of the classic interests of psychology. Freud called this relationship "unique, without parallel, established unalterably for a whole lifetime as . . . the prototype of all later love relations" and argued that the expectations, emotions, and self-awareness arising from this relationship last a lifetime. Erik Erikson sounded a similar theme in arguing that infancy is when the first developmental crisis of "basic trust" is resolved, and believed that whether an infant can establish a sense of confidence in a caregiver determines whether the child will perceive the world as supportive and trustworthy or, instead, as full of dangers and threats. Not only within psychological theory but also in the popular literature of child rearing, the importance of sensitive, responsive parental care as the foundation for a baby's emotional well-being has been underscored in the writings of Benjamin Spock and others. Certainly anybody who observes an infant's shadowlike pursuit of her mother around their home, or who watches the baby's distress at his mother's departure turn quickly into smiles and "pick-me-up" gestures upon her return, can see the importance of this attachment to an infant's emotional well-being.

These diverse popular and professional views coalesced in the 1970s in a new theory of parent-infant attachment proposed by John Bowlby, an English psychoanalyst with a strong interest in the origins of security and trust in his adult clients. Bowlby believed that infants seek security in their caregivers not only because these adults satisfy their needs, but also because of motives that are deeply rooted in human evolution. Bowlby reasoned that throughout evolution, vulnerable and defenseless young offspring who stayed close to their caregivers were more likely to be protected and nurtured, and less likely to become lost or abandoned, than were infants who wandered away. He believed that emotional attachments evolved to provide the motivational system by which infants seek to stay close to protective adults and thus survive to maturity. Bowlby argued, therefore, that infants are innately predisposed to respond positively to their caregivers because of motivational processes that are deeply rooted in human evolution which contribute, by the end of the first year, to the establishment of an emotional bond between infant and parent—and to the growth of the child's sense of security that Bowlby (like Freud) believed could have life-long consequences.

These were provocative ideas, but they were destined to remain so until they could be tested empirically. Fortunately, at the same time that Bowlby's theory was becoming known among developmental scientists in the United States, a colleague of Bowlby who was on the faculty of Johns Hopkins University was devising a procedure for studying attachment relationships between parents and infants. Mary Ainsworth had observed infants and mothers in Uganda, Baltimore, and other settings, and she used these observations to create a laboratory procedure called the Strange Situation to reveal the security, or insecurity, of a baby's attachment to a caregiver. The Strange Situation is a deceptively simple procedure: It consists of a series of seven three-minute episodes occurring in a brightly decorated laboratory playroom that is equipped with toys for the baby and one-way observation windows, behind which researchers can monitor and videotape the baby's behavior. But it includes two separation episodes to create moderately escalating stress for the baby to heighten the child's need for the parent's assistance over the course of the procedure. In a sense, much as adults seek their own supportive "attachment figures" when they experience stress, worry, or feel threatened, so also infants seek their caregivers most when they are stressed or alarmed, and when they are reunited with their caregivers after separation, infants reveal the security they derive from the caregiver's companionship. This is consistent, of course, with Bowlby's views of how the baby's attachment provided protection as well as nurturance over the long course of human evolution.

FIGURE 5-1

The first episode of the Strange Situation is often characterized by exchanges of smiles and glances between mother and infant while the child plays with toys on the playroom floor.

The episodes of the Strange Situation proceed as follows (see Figures 5-1 through 5-7). In episode 1, the child and parent are alone together. A female stranger's entrance marks the beginning of episode 2, during which she converses with the parent after sitting quietly for a minute, and finally approaches to play with the baby. The parent's departure marks the transition to episode 3, during which the stranger provides comfort if the baby becomes distressed, but otherwise is quietly responsive. The parent calls the baby's name before returning at the beginning of episode 4, and during their reunion the stranger quietly leaves at an opportune moment. The parent's departure again marks a transition to a new episode, and for episode 5 the baby is entirely alone. The stranger returns to inaugurate episode 6 and, as before, either comforts the baby or remains quiet if the child is doing fine. Finally, episode 7 begins with the parent's return, and the stranger's unobtrusive departure, and the reunion of infant and parent is again observed.

On the basis of her early studies, Ainsworth distinguished three groups of infants. Infants who are "securely attached" greet the parent positively during their reunions, either by smiling, vocalizing, or showing a toy, or by approaching the parent and seeking contact. In either case, their un-

FIGURE 5-2
Infants vary considerably in whether the stranger's initiatives, during the second episode, elicit caution or sociability.

equivocal pleasure at the parent's return indicates confidence in the parent's helpfulness and assistance after a stressful separation. By contrast, infants who are "insecure-avoidant" may conspicuously avoid the parent during reunions or, more commonly, ignore or rebuff the parent (such as looking away for a while before responding to the parent's return). They look precociously independent, but their behavior suggests a lack of confidence in the parent's availability or helpfulness. Last, infants who are "insecure-resistant" are often very distressed by the separations, but their efforts to be held and comforted during reunion are combined with angry behavior, such as pushing away, rejecting toys the adult offers, or even hitting the parent. It seems as if these infants are never capable of reestablishing a sense of security, even after the parent has returned.

The interest of developmental scientists in Bowlby's attachment theory and in Ainsworth's Strange Situation procedure grew in tandem during the 1970s because both offered new ways of thinking about the meaning and significance of parent-infant attachment. Rather than regarding their emotional bond merely as the outgrowth of the caregiver's association with food, warmth, and nurturance—as earlier theories had proposed—attachment theorists argued that infants have an innate motivation to develop close relationships with those who care for them, and the secu-

FIGURE 5-3
During the third episode, infants may be more wary of the stranger without the
mother's supportive presence.

rity they derive from those relationships can have long-term implications
for psychological growth. Moreover, Ainsworth's pioneering studies using
the Strange Situation suggested that the large majority of infants are typically securely attached, and that the sensitivity and responsiveness of
parental care during the first year provides the basis for a secure attachment. Just as Freud and Erikson had argued, it appeared that the security
derived from the parent's sensitivity during infancy forms an important
cornerstone for psychosocial growth.

STABILITY IN STRANGE SITUATION BEHAVIOR

I witnessed these exciting discoveries from the vantage point of my work
at the Child Development Project, where ideas concerning the security of
attachment and the importance of parental sensitivity guided the therapeutic work with troubled parents and their young offspring. But the
"buzz" about attachment theory also infiltrated the seminar discussions
and colloquium presentations that enlivened graduate life at Michigan. As
developmental researchers around the country began using the Strange Sit-

FIGURE 5-4
Attachment researchers devote particular attention to the nature of the baby's reunion responses to the parent during episode 4.

uation to elucidate the origins and later consequences of a secure attachment in infancy, research journals began to publish studies of attachment
that provoked animated, sometimes heated, discussion among developmental scientists.

   Besides Ainsworth's pioneering research, one of the important studies
of the security of attachment concerned its consistency over time. Although
many developmental theories argue that the security or trust derived from
the parent-child relationship tends to persist over time, in the late 1970s,
developmental researchers were having considerable difficulty devising reliable measures of infant-parent interaction that yielded consistent individual differences. Whether they counted the frequency of infant smiles,
the amount of time the infant spent in close proximity to the parent, the
amount of distress during periods of separation, or other indicators of their
relationship, scientists found that these measures were notoriously inconsistent. Infants might smile frequently to the parent during one observation and rarely the next; they might seek close proximity in certain situations and not in others; sometimes they were inconsistent in their behavior
toward the parent *within* a single observational session! Obviously, it was
hard to study infant-parent relationships when the measures used to describe these relationships were themselves so erratic and inconsistent, be-

FIGURE 5-5
The fifth episode of the Strange Situation usually elicits the greatest distress, which is why it is often shortened.

cause it is unlikely that the quality of the infant-parent relationship shifts so frequently and unpredictably.

Imagine, then, the excitement created by a paper published in 1978 by Everett Waters, who was then completing his graduate work at the University of Minnesota. Waters observed fifty infants twice each in the Strange Situation: once when they were 12 months old, and again when they were 18 months of age. When he counted the baby's smiles or looks to the mother each time, he found (as had earlier researchers) that infant behavior was inconsistent across the six-month period: Infants who smiled frequently at 12 months did not necessarily do so at 18 months, for example. Waters argued, however, that when researchers focus, as Ainsworth did, on the overall *organization* of infant behavior—that is, on the general security of the infant's attachment to the parent, whether it is reflected in smiling, looking, proximity-seeking, or in other ways—greater consistency might be revealed. And this is precisely what he found: Of the fifty infants observed at 12 and 18 months, all but two obtained the same classification (i.e., securely attached, insecure-avoidant, or insecure-resistant) each time.

Although this may not seem very impressive (after all, you and I act in a fairly consistent manner over even longer spans of time!), it is important to remember how significantly the baby is changing over this six-

FIGURE 5-6
Sociability toward the stranger is curtailed during the sixth episode by the infant's
concern about the parent's whereabouts.

month period: The 18-month-old is beginning to represent the world conceptually, use the first words to communicate, recognize the self, and understand others' social and emotional signals in a manner that the 12-
month-old cannot fathom. One-third of an 18-month-old's lifetime occurs
after the first birthday, and this is a period of flourishing individuality. In
light of previous dismal efforts to find consistent measures of infant-parent relationships, the news of Waters' findings hit the field of developmental psychology like a bombshell. I attended a colloquium by Waters at
Michigan during the same year that his study was published, and by contrast with the usual caution and skepticism with which academics greet
new scientific discoveries, the excitement generated by his research was pal-
pable. In the minds of many scientists, attachment researchers had finally
provided the breakthrough that was needed to understand the formative
significance of early infant-parent relationships. By focusing on the security of attachment as it is measured in the Strange Situation, they had succeeded in devising a measure of these relationships that was meaningfully
linked to the sensitivity of parental care, and in which individual differences were consistent over time, just as predicted.

I was interested in Waters' study for a somewhat different reason.
When I watched securely attached and insecurely attached infants in the

FIGURE 5-7
Reunion responses during the seventh episode of the Strange Situation are particularly informative of the security of attachment.

Strange Situation, I noticed that these infants differed not only in their responses to parents, but also in the "emotional dynamics" that had intrigued me since my work at the Child Development Project. In a manner that complemented their avoidant independence, for example, insecure-avoidant infants were also emotionally subdued or shallow: Many were not distressed by the separation episodes nor did they show pleasure during reunions, nor was there any wariness of the stranger. It was as if these infants were controlling their emotional reactions, resulting in diminished lability, blunted range, and limited emotional intensity. On the other hand, insecure-resistant infants seemed to *lack* emotional self-control: they often became distressed early in the Strange Situation (when they were alone with the mother), and were usually intensely distressed during separation episodes but, contrary to securely attached infants, they were incapable of calming even after the mother returned. If insecure-avoidant infants seemed emotionally overregulated, insecure-resistant infants seemed to be emotionally underregulated by comparison with securely attached infants. Could these apparent differences in emotional dynamics be confirmed, and better understood, in my own research? If so, could they contribute to a broader appreciation of the emotional dynamics inherent in the security of attachment?

EXPLAINING CHANGE IN PARENT-INFANT RELATIONSHIPS

By this time, a new faculty member had arrived at Michigan to become another catalyst to my interest in these issues. Michael Lamb had worked with Ainsworth when he was a student at Johns Hopkins University, and had also studied infant-father and sibling relationships. Michael arrived at Michigan during my third year of graduate study, and together we planned a research project (which later turned into my doctoral dissertation) to examine the emotional dynamics of infants in different attachment groups.

Our study was modeled along Waters' research. We, too, observed infants in the Strange Situation on two occasions during the second year: at 12 1/2 months and again at 19 1/2 months. From videotapes of their behavior, we classified the infants as securely attached, insecure-avoidant, or insecure-resistant. In addition, we made detailed ratings of their emotional behavior. From careful, time-sampled ratings of babies' facial expressions and vocal expressions throughout the procedure, for example, we calculated measures of their emotional range, intensity, lability, and other emotional dynamics. We wanted to see whether individual differences in the emotional dynamics of infant behavior would change, or remain consistent, over this seven-month period. If (as we expected) these differences in emotionality remained consistent—paralleling stability in the security of attachment—were they due to underlying patterns of temperamental individuality, or were they perhaps part of the organization of attachment behavior in the Strange Situation? This research project would help us begin to uncover the answers.

When the Strange Situation observations were completed, our first step was to identify infants as secure, avoidant, or resistant, and then compare their classifications at each age to confirm that infants remained consistent over time. When we compared each baby's attachment classification at 12 1/2 and 19 1/2 months, however, we were stunned. Of the forty-three infants we studied at each age, twenty-three of them *changed* between the two ages! We carefully reviewed the videotapes to ensure that this was not due to classification errors, but the outcome held. Some babies who had earlier been exemplary securely attached infants were later classified avoidant or resistant on follow-up; equally remarkable, some infants who had been deemed insecurely attached at 12 1/2 months were unmistakably secure at 19 1/2 months. Inconsistency, rather than consistency, was the rule.

We were astonished to find this. To be sure, it was not *completely* unprecedented. A study published in 1979 by Brian Vaughn and his colleagues reported that in 100 families, only 62 of the infants had the same attachment classification at 12 and 18 months. But in this socioeconomically disadvantaged sample, changes in attachment were associated with severe stresses in family life, and stress was particularly apparent in families with infants who changed in their attachment security. Thus when a family had to move because they were evicted, or a parent was seriously ill or had been jailed when the infant was between 12 and 18 months old, the child was more likely to change from securely to insecurely attached. Our sample was middle class, by contrast, and experienced very few of the legal, financial, medical, and ecological problems that were more common among Vaughn's lower-income sample. Even so, we also found that changes in attachment were associated with changes in family circumstances. In our families, however, these were not major stresses, but rather milder transitions in family life that might affect mother-infant interaction, such as a change in the mother's employment status or a shift in day care arrangements. Even these common transitional experiences could change the security of attachment, it appeared, by altering familiar patterns of mother-infant interaction. There was another difference between the Vaughn findings and our own. While stressful events precipitated changes from secure to insecurely attached in Vaughn's study, the changes in family circumstances in our study resulted in bidirectional shifts in attachment. That is, some infants changed from secure to insecurely attached, while other infants moved in the opposite direction, from insecure to securely attached. Flexibility, rather than consistency, in attachment was clearly apparent.

The publication of our results in 1982 provoked a strong response. One commentator argued that since the consistency of attachment security was such a well-replicated result in previous studies, our failure to find it was probably due to errors in our use of the Strange Situation procedure. We defended our research, and pointed out that existing studies (by Vaughn, and now by us) had yielded highly variable estimates of consistency in attachment over time. Subsequent research has borne this out: No one has replicated the high level of consistency reported by Waters (nor, for that matter, the low level of our study); rather, the proportion of infants obtaining the same attachment classification in repeated Strange Situation assessments has varied considerably. It seems, in other words, that it is normal for infants to change in the security of attachment over time for reasons associated with consistency and change in their caregiving arrangements. Other critics noted that our findings were difficult to reconcile with long-standing theoretical views that, once they develop, infant attachments should remain consistent over time because of their formative influence on early psychosocial growth. They had a good point.

How *could* we explain these findings? If the mother-infant bond is, in Freud's terms, the "prototype of all later love relations," how could it exert its formative influence if the security of this relationship might be changing for the baby? After pondering this question, Michael and I concluded that parent-child relationships are important because of their *cumulative* impact on a developing child. In infancy, parental sensitivity and responsiveness is crucial to the growth of security and trust; at later ages, the same sensitivity may contribute to the growth of other positive psychosocial qualities like empathy, sociability, and cooperativeness. The personalities of offspring are guided, in other words, by the continuing influences of caregivers that are manifested in a secure (or insecure) attachment in infancy, and in other psychological characteristics in later years. But relationships can change for many reasons: Family stress or changing circumstances, the child's developmental achievements, and variations in marital harmony, job demands, and other features of parental life are among the many catalysts for change that may occur in many families. Changing life circumstances present opportunities, as well as challenges, to parents and children to renegotiate new patterns of interaction that can continue to foster the child's security, sociability, and self-confidence in a developmentally appropriate fashion. Some changes—such as the therapeutic assistance provided by my colleagues at the Child Development Project—can enable insecurely attached infants to develop secure relationships with their parents by aiding parents with their personal struggles. Other changes, such as the stresses experienced by Vaughn's lower-income families, might undermine the early growth of a secure attachment. In each case, the security of attachment provides a momentary window into a parent-child relationship that is important, not just because of its earliest influences in infancy, but because it is part of the continuing, cumulative effects that parents have on the psychological growth of offspring.

In the years that followed, Michael and I coauthored a book and published several papers developing this new view of infant-parent attachment. Together with the work of other researchers, it has contributed to a more dynamic portrayal of early psychological growth; one that regards the security of attachment not as an important foundation for early psychological growth, but a provisional foundation that may be altered by the effects of subsequent experiences in close relationships at home, with peers, and with other partners throughout life. This view has now become part of attachment theory.

Meanwhile, the dissertation on the emotional dynamics of attachment was completed, revealing that securely and insecurely attached infants varied in their emotionality just as I had expected, and in a manner that (we later learned) might also reveal the role of temperamental individuality. During this time I got married, and discovered that my wife, Janet—who is a preschool educator—was also commenting on the same kinds of dynamic individuality in the emotions displayed by her 3- to 5-year-olds. Janet has influenced my thinking in other ways also, especially by reminding me how much the actual behavior of children in real-life settings confounds as well as confirms the expectations of scientists, like myself, who tend to study children in carefully designed laboratory experiments! As a consequence, I soon began studying attachment and emotional processes in naturalistic settings (like day care) as well as the laboratory.

FROM RESEARCH TO POLICY

As Michael and I were pondering the dilemmas caused by our surprising research results, a tall, bearded fellow appeared one morning at the office door. His name was David Chambers, a law professor at the University of Michigan who had heard about attachment theory and research. David had earned the esteem of his legal colleagues throughout the country for his incisive thinking in family law, including penetrating studies of the enforcement of child support orders from reluctant fathers. Now he was thinking about how courts should decide about the custody of children when parents divorce, and whether developmental research could provide judges with new guidelines for considering whether the child's "best interests" dictated custody to mother, to father, or jointly after divorce.

David asked us whether the Strange Situation procedure could be used by courts to decide to which parent a young child had the strongest, or most secure, attachment. If so, perhaps this would provide one basis for a custody decision. After thinking about his question, Michael and I realized that the Strange Situation might be especially *un*informative for custody decisions. After all, if stressful events can alter the security of attachment, then a Strange Situation that occurs while a family is in the midst of the turmoil of separation and divorce proceedings is likely to yield misleading conclusions. But together, the three of us wondered what other implications attachment research might have for judicial decisions pertaining to custody.

Attachment theory emphasizes the importance of adults who assume a psychologically significant role in the child's life. Contrary to a long legal tradition of favoring the mother in custody disputes—especially for young children who are in their "tender years"—attachment theorists argue that regardless of gender or biological ties, preserving the child's relationship with the adult who assumes a caregiving role that inspires the child's trust and confidence should be most important. At times, this means that a nonparental caregiver should be preferred over a biological parent when the former has assumed exclusive and continuing care for the child. When parents divorce, however, *each* adult is likely to be psychologically important to the child, in which case a custody decision might be based on which parent has assumed the most significant caregiving role—while simultaneously seeking to ensure the child's continuing contact with *each* parent after divorce. By emphasizing the psychological ties that bind the child to significant caregivers, and by underscoring the importance to the child of maintaining these relationships, attachment theory provides a way of thinking about "the best interests of the child" that contrasts with the traditional legal focus on parental gender or proprietary rights.

The three of us mulled over these psycholegal issues for more than a year during weekly lunchtime meetings at an Ann Arbor health food cafe. While Michael and I sought to educate David about current issues within attachment theory, he and his student assistants provided us with an education in legal analysis that helped us understand the need for thoughtful, well-reasoned guidelines that could be implemented by judges encountering a wide variety of child custody disputes. The tangible result of these meetings was an influential article that David contributed to the *Michigan Law Review* in 1984, which advocated that judges use a "primary caretaker preference" in determining child custody awards, especially when young children were concerned. This article, along with the contributions of other legal scholars, has had an important influence on rethinking child custody standards in recent years. The intangible result of these meetings was another surprise for me: the realization that I was becoming deeply interested not only in creating new knowledge about infant attachment and its emotional dimensions, but also in thoughtfully applying this emerging knowledge to child and family policy problems. I was returning, unexpectedly, to the legal interests I thought I had abandoned in college. As a consequence, I became involved in the Bush Program in Child Development and Social Policy, a newly inaugurated program for advanced graduate students in the social sciences at Michigan that was designed to enhance their understanding of, and contributions to, policy analysis on topics concerning children and families. And I began "talking policy" with a broad range of faculty and students from a wide variety of disciplines, united by our common interest in advancing children's "best interests" in a variety of policy areas.

BACK TO THE FUTURE

These heady but surprising graduate school experiences set my professional course. At the University of Nebraska, I teach graduate and undergraduate courses in developmental psychology. I also teach at the College of Law, where my course on children and the law includes third- and fourth-year law students as well as advanced doctoral students in psychology. Together, we test the legal assumptions underlying child and family policy against current findings from psychological research and ask, in turn, whether useful legal guidelines can be derived from research studies, and whether they address the range of difficult issues that judges, lawyers, and other legal actors must sometimes consider. As the associate director of the Center on Children, Families, and the Law at the University of Nebraska, and as a member of our department's Law-Psychology Program, I work with students who are obtaining degrees in various academic disciplines relevant to child development and family policy. My own writing includes policy papers on topics concerning the applications of research to policy, including infant day care, grandparent visitation rights, divorce and custody, child maltreatment, and ethical practice in psychology.

My psycholegal work is supplemented by continuing studies of the emotional dynamics of infancy. The dissertation research revealed that these emotional dynamics play a very important role in the baby's attachment behavior, and more recent research has explored the dynamics of emotion in various clinical groups of infants, ranging from maltreated toddlers to premature infants to children with Down syndrome. My students and I have also explored the development of these emotional dynamics in typical infant samples. In one study, we observed infants of three ages in a variety of emotion-eliciting circumstances and discovered that the period of 6 to 12 months of age is marked by increasing emotional "vitality." In other words, with increasing age infants display greater exuberance, speed, persistence, and intensity in their emotional responding, whether they are showing pleasure at peek-a-boo or distress at being separated from mother. We believe that this heightened emotional vitality contributes to the growth of attachment because many of these early emotional experiences—whether positive or negative in emotional tone—are social in nature. Caregivers are involved, for example, in exuberant social play, in the relief of distress, and in a myriad of other shared emotional experiences in the first year of life. A baby's caregivers thus become the emergent focus of the full range of dynamic emotional experiences that help create, for the child, expectations of security, confidence, and trust in the parents' helpfulness and nurturance. My students and I are now studying parents' interpretations of infant crying as one way of understanding how these dynamics of emotion develop over time, and the growth of empathy in parents and offspring.

Understanding the growth of attachment relationships, and their later consequences for psychological development, also remains a central interest to me because of the provocative questions raised by unexpected research findings in graduate school. In many respects, the theory and research on attachment have provided developmental researchers with an unparalleled opportunity to explore questions of classic interest in psychology pertaining to the formative influence of early experience, the qualities of parenting that are important to young offspring, and the long-term consequences of early security and insecurity. These questions will continue to captivate psychologists as well as practitioners because they articulate the needs of young children who cannot speak on their own behalf, and the obligations of adults who care for these children. And I look forward to being surprised by the lessons taught by my own research findings, and those of others, knowing that the lessons taught by the data are always more interesting than those I might have expected to find.

SUGGESTED READINGS

BOWLBY, J. (1969). *Attachment and loss: Vol. 1. Attachment.* New York: Basic Books.

FRAIBERG, S. (Ed.). (1980). *Clinical studies in infant mental health: The first year of life.* New York: Basic Books.

KAREN, R. (1994). *Becoming attached.* New York: Warner Books.

LAMB, M. E., THOMPSON, R. A., GARDNER, W., & CHARNOV, E. L. (1985). *Infant-mother attachment: The origins and developmental significance of individual differences in Strange Situation behavior.* Hillsdale, NJ: Erlbaum.

THOMPSON, R. A. (Ed.). (1990). *Socioemotional development. Nebraska Symposium on Motivation* (Vol. 36). Lincoln: University of Nebraska Press.

———— (1993). Socioemotional development: Enduring issues and new challenges. *Developmental Review, 13,* 372–402.

———— (1994). Fathers and divorce. *The Future of Children, 4,* 210–235.

*N*ANCY EISENBERG *(Ph.D., University of California, Berkeley) is Regents' Professor of Psychology in the Department of Psychology at Arizona State University. Dr. Eisenberg is President-Elect of the Western Psychological Association and is a member of the governing council of the Society for Research in Child Development. She currently is the recipient of a Research Scientist Development Award from the National Institute of Mental Health. Nancy Eisenberg is married to Jerry Harris, an academic school psychologist. They both work at Arizona State University and spend their summers working and playing by the ocean in Yachats, Oregon.*

6

In Search of the Good Heart

❖

I have always been fascinated by social behavior and its origins. As an example, when I was about 12 or 13, I baby-sat a few times for a psychologist who had whiskers and hair that were longer than was the norm in the early 1960s. I recall wondering whether this man—who, coincidently, later hired me for my first post–Ph.D. job—had long hair because he was a psychologist, or whether some other factor (such as his social attitudes) accounted both for his being a psychologist and for his hair.

Despite this early interest in people's behavior and my early intuitive understanding of correlational relations (a must when studying social development), I never considered a career in the field of psychology. Indeed, I was only vaguely aware of what psychologists did. When I applied to the University of Michigan, my stated goal was to become a medical technician. This choice reflected the advice of a psychologist who tested me for vocational aptitude and suggested that medical technology was a good field for a woman with an aptitude for science—a medical technologist could work part-time while rearing her children. By the time I started my freshman year at Ann Arbor, I had changed my intended major to microbiology; somehow I concluded that the routine that I imagined to be central to a laboratory technician's job would not capture my interest.

I had done well in high school because I was expected to, not because I was intrinsically interested in any of my courses. Thus, my initial choices of a college major were based on factors other than interest. Imagine my surprise and pleasure, then, when I took my first psychology course in college and found it fascinating.

A colleague and friend of mine has asserted that academics have a great job because they are paid to study topics in which they have real interest. I agree. My re-

89

search program over the years reflects my own personal interests, and the ensuing questions that have arisen as a consequence of pursuing these interests. In research, the results of specific studies sometimes lead to more questions than answers and may take the researcher down new and interesting paths.

My particular research interests have changed somewhat over the years; however, there is continuity in the topics I have addressed. My early research interests were influenced by the social zeitgeist in the United States during my adolescence and early adulthood. In 1964, when I was entering adolescence, President Lyndon Johnson declared war on poverty in the United States. A major goal of the administration's proposed policies was to eradicate poverty and its negative consequences on the poor. Thus, there was a strong humanitarian component to Johnson's proposed domestic policy. Then during the 1960s and early 1970s, the Vietnam war and civil rights movement emerged as issues that polarized the nation. Discussion of these issues frequently focused on concepts of justice, human rights, and the welfare of individuals. As a college student involved to some degree in the political unrest of the time, I became concerned about the development of humanitarian political attitudes.

I moved on to the University of California at Berkeley for graduate work, and it was my good fortune that my graduate adviser, Paul Mussen, was also interested in the development of humanitarian political attitudes. As a consequence, much of the research I conducted in graduate school pertained, at least in part, to this issue. However, during my first semester, when writing a term paper on the development of humanitarian political attitudes, it became clear that to understand such attitudes, I would have to study the development and origins of other-oriented, prosocial behaviors and cognitions—behaviors such as helping, sharing, and comforting others and their roots. This is the direction in which much of my individual research effort focused in the years that followed.

PROSOCIAL MORAL REASONING

In my master's thesis and doctoral dissertation, I examined a variety of aspects of prosocial development, including reasoning about prosocial issues, helping behavior, and emotional reactions that are conceptually linked to prosocial functioning (e.g., empathy and sympathy). However, the primary focus in my early work was on the cognitive aspect of prosocial functioning—specifically, prosocial moral reasoning.

In my research, I defined prosocial behavior as voluntary behavior intended to benefit another—for example, sharing objects, providing assistance with tasks, donating money to charities, and working on projects that benefit others. Thus, prosocial moral reasoning is people's *reasoning* about dilemmas in which an individual has an opportunity to assist others, but at a personal cost. To assess prosocial moral reasoning, I present children with illustrated hypothetical stories in which the story protagonist can help another person, but at a cost. The child is then questioned regarding his or her choice of action and the reasons for the choice. A typical dilemma is one in which a child has an opportunity to assist a same-sex child who is being pushed by a bully when doing so might incur the bully's wrath.

This work was based on Lawrence Kohlberg's well-known research on moral reasoning. However, I believed that Kohlberg's conception of moral reasoning was prohibition-oriented rather than prosocially oriented. In Kohlberg's moral dilemmas, the focus is on wrongdoing such as killing, stealing, lying, or breaking a promise. Often dilemmas pit one prohibition against another; for example, in the famous Heinz dilemma, respondents must reason about the choice between stealing a drug to save one's wife and allowing one's wife to die of cancer, both of which are behaviors viewed as negative in our society. Based on dilemmas of this sort, Kohlberg delineated six stages of moral reasoning which were viewed as reflecting developmental (age-related) changes in individuals' moral reasoning. He viewed his stages as invariant in sequence (that is, development always proceeds in the same order) and universal across cultures. Each stage is viewed as representing a totally new way of thinking, and individuals do not revert to using reasoning at a much lower level. Although Kohlberg assumed that his stages of reasoning were applicable to the entire range of moral issues, this assumption had not been adequately tested.

I hypothesized that although there might be similarities between prohibition and prosocial moral reasoning, there also might be differences. For example, one might expect other-oriented reasoning involving perspective taking and sympathy to be particularly prominent in prosocial moral reasoning. Further, although Kohlberg viewed other-oriented reasoning as emerging relatively late, I expected it to emerge by the preschool years. Based on the existing research literature, I concluded that younger children may recognize aspects of another's perspective and needs, feel empathy or sympathy, and assist as a consequence. In addition, I hypothesized that authority- and punishment-oriented reasoning, Kohlberg's stage 1, would be infrequent in prosocial moral reasoning because children seldom are punished for not acting in a prosocial manner, whereas they frequently are punished for wrongdoing.

Based on a series of studies in which I interviewed children of different ages and followed a group of children from ages 4 to 5 to early adulthood, I have delineated age-related changes in prosocial moral judgment. The age-related levels that my colleagues, students, and I have found are presented in Table 6-1.

As can be seen in this table, my students and I have found that young

TABLE 6-1 LEVELS OF PROSOCIAL REASONING

Level 1.   Hedonistic, self-focused orientation: The individual is concerned with self-oriented consequences rather than moral considerations. Reasons for assisting or not assisting another include consideration of direct gain to the self, future reciprocity, and concern for others because one needs and/or likes the other (because of the affectional tie). (Predominant mode primarily for preschoolers and younger elementary school children.)

Level 2.   Needs-oriented orientation: The individual expresses concern for the physical, material, and psychological needs of others even though the other's needs conflict with one's own needs. This concern is expressed in the simplest terms, without clear evidence of self-reflective role taking, verbal expressions of sympathy, or reference to internalized affect such as guilt. (Predominant mode for many preschoolers and many elementary school children.)

Level 3.   Approval and interpersonal orientation and/or stereotyped orientation: Stereotyped images of good and bad persons and behaviors and/or considerations of others' approval and acceptance are used in justifying prosocial or nonhelping behaviors. (Predominant mode for some elementary and high school students.)

Level 4a. Self-reflective empathic orientation: The individual's judgments include evidence of self-reflective sympathetic responding or role taking, concern with the other's humanness, and/or guilt or positive effect related to the consequences of one's actions. (Predominant mode for a few older elementary school children and many high school students.)

Level 4b. Transitional level: The individual's justifications for helping or not helping involve internalized values, norms, duties, or responsibilities, concern for the condition of the larger society, or refer to the necessity of protecting the rights and dignity of other persons; these ideas, however, are not clearly and strongly stated. (Predominant mode for a minority of people high school age or older.)

Level 5.   Strongly internalized stage: Justifications for helping or not helping are based on internalized values, norms, or responsibilities, with the desire to maintain individual and societal contractual obligations or improve the condition of society, the belief in the dignity, rights, and equality of all individuals. Positive or negative affect related to the maintenance of self-respect for living up to one's own values and accepted norms also characterizes this stage. (Predominant mode for only a small minority of high school students and no elementary school children.)

SOURCE: N. Eisenberg, 1986, *Altruistic emotion, cognition, and behavior.* Reprinted with the permission of Erlbaum Publishers.

children tend to use primarily self-oriented, hedonistic reasoning (e.g., "He shouldn't help because he might get picked on") or needs-oriented (primitive empathic) prosocial reasoning (e.g., "She should help because the girl's leg is bleeding and she needs to go to the doctor"). In elementary school, children's reasoning begins to reflect concern with approval and en-hancing interpersonal relationships (e.g., "Her family would think she did the right thing") as well as the desire to behave in stereotypically "good" ways (e.g., like a "nice" girl or boy), although such reasoning appears to decrease in use somewhat in high school. Beginning in late elementary school or thereafter, children begin to explicitly state that they would take the other's perspective or sympathize; they also begin to verbalize abstract moral principles and internalize affective reactions such as guilt.

Several very interesting conclusions could be drawn from these find-ings. First, as predicted, children virtually never said they would help in order to avoid punishment or because of blind obedience to authorities such as adults. This finding differs greatly from what had been found for prohibition-oriented moral reasoning. In addition, even 4- to 5-year-olds appeared to frequently orient to others' needs and exhibit what often seemed to be primitive empathy. Again, this finding would not be ex-pected from earlier work on conceptions of moral reasoning, although it is consistent with some research on empathy in young children. Third, ref-erences to empathy-related processes such as taking the other's perspec-tive and sympathizing were particularly common in prosocial moral rea-soning. Finally, like James Rest and some other researchers examining prohibition-oriented moral reasoning, and contrary to Kohlberg's asser-tions, I found that even individuals who typically used higher-level rea-soning occasionally reverted to using lower-level reasoning (such as ego-istic, hedonistic reasoning), especially when they chose not to assist the needy other.

The use of lower-level reasoning by people capable of higher-level rea-soning suggests the influence of situational variables when people use the various levels of moral reasoning in their repertoire. Consistent with this notion, in cross-cultural research, we found some minor differences in the reasoning of children from different cultures—differences that seemed to reflect concerns that were salient in their own cultures. For example, chil-dren who lived in communally oriented kibbutzim in Israel were particu-larly likely to emphasize reciprocity between people, whereas city children from both Israel and the United States were more likely to be concerned with costs to themselves for engaging in helping behavior. This research was conducted with colleagues in Israel (Rachel Hertz-Lazarowitz and Ina Fuchs), one of whom I initially met at a conference on prosocial behavior in Warsaw, Poland, in 1980.

If individuals' moral reasoning differs somewhat across situations, then one would expect, at best, a modest relation between people's typical moral reasoning and their tendencies to actually behave in prosocial ways. In fact, that is what my students and I have found. Children with relatively high-level moral reasoning and empathic-type reasoning seem more likely to help or share than other children. In contrast, children who are relatively high in hedonistic, self-oriented reasoning (that is, reasoning in which they focus on the costs to the self for helping) are relatively unlikely to act in a prosocial manner. Thus, prosocial moral reasoning does seem to influence prosocial behavior to some degree. However, because the magnitude of the relation between moral reasoning and behavior is not large, factors in addition to moral reasoning must influence whether or not people behave prosocially.

After a few years of studying primarily prosocial moral reasoning, I knew I needed to expand my research horizons in order to achieve a better understanding of prosocial development. Most of us believe that logic and rational cognitions are not the sole influences on our behavior. One factor that seemed to be neglected in the study of prosocial behavior—and, at the time, in psychology in general—was the role of emotion in social behavior. My work on prosocial moral reasoning suggested that children's orientation to others' needs and their consequent emotional reactions affected prosocial responding; moreover, contemporaneous work on empathy by people such as Martin Hoffman, Marian Radke-Yarrow, and Carolyn Zahn-Waxler suggested that responding emotionally to others' feelings and needs frequently motivates comforting, helping, and sharing behaviors, even in very young children. Thus, increasingly I turned my attention to the role of emotion in prosocial responding, and changed from a focus primarily on cognition to one that emphasized emotion.

EMPATHY: HOW TO CONCEPTUALIZE AND MEASURE AN INTERNAL AND COMPLEX PHENOMENON

Although I was eager to study the role of empathy in prosocial development, I found that this was not an easy task. First, in the research literature, there was a lack of clarity about what empathy was, and whether all types of empathic responding would be expected to enhance prosocial behavior. And second, as I started work on empathy, it became increasingly clear that the usual methods used to measure empathy were not adequate.

With regard to the conceptual ambiguities, the term *empathy* often had been used to refer to most, if not all, emotional reactions that one might have when exposed to a person in need or distress. Yet one may feel a variety of responses to others' needs, including sadness, concern, anxiety, or even happiness. At the time I became interested in assessing empathy, C. Daniel Batson, a social psychologist, had started to discuss an important distinction among empathic responses that seemed critical to understanding prosocial behavior. He differentiated between what he calls empathy (and

I will call sympathy henceforth) and personal distress. Sympathy is an other-oriented response to another's distress or need, such as feelings of concern. In contrast, personal distress is a self-oriented, egoistic response to another's need or distress—such as feelings of discomfort or anxiety when confronted with another's negative state.

This distinction is important because people who experience concern for another person would be motivated to try to improve the other's condition, whereas people who experience personal distress would be expected to try to reduce their own aversive, negative feelings. We all can think of times when viewing a distressed person (for example, a car accident, famine, or war victim) was so aversive that we wanted to avoid further exposure to the person. Some people seem to have a hard time even listening to others' problems because to do so arouses too much negative emotion. These are examples of personal distress. Sometimes personal distress leads to prosocial actions, but primarily because helping the distressed person might be the quickest way to reduce one's own distress if there is no easy way to escape dealing with the distressed individual. But when it is easy to avoid the distressed individual, people who are experiencing personal distress might be expected to avoid rather than help the distressed person.

Batson's initial research on sympathy and personal distress suggested that the distinction between sympathy and personal distress was critical to an understanding of altruistic behavior (prosocial behavior that was motivated by sympathy rather than concrete rewards or social approval). He found that people who experienced sympathy when exposed to a distressed individual tended to assist even if it was easy to escape contact with the person. In contrast, people experiencing personal distress tended not to help if they could easily avoid doing so and if others were unlikely to know that they did not help. However, all Batson's research had been conducted with adults. It was unclear whether the distinction between personal distress and sympathy was meaningful among children and whether it predicted their prosocial behavior.

Thus, my goal was to assess children's various emotional reactions to others in distress or need, and to relate these reactions to children's willingness to assist others. However, I quickly found that it was very difficult to assess children's emotional responses, even if one did not try to distinguish between sympathy and personal distress. In most of the prior work on children's empathy, empathy was assessed with a picture story procedure. With this procedure, children are told brief stories (sometimes illustrated with pictures) about others in emotionally evocative contexts (e.g., when a child loses his or her dog). Emotion words are not used in the stories. Then children are asked, "How do you feel?" (or a similar question). If children say they felt an emotion similar to that which the story protagonist would be expected to experience (e.g., sadness in the lost dog story), they are viewed as empathizing. If not, they receive a low score on empathy.

In our early studies using this type of method, we obtained some disturbing data. We (Randy Lennon and I) found that the degree to which children provided "empathic" responses was influenced by whether or not the experimenter was the same sex as the child. We came across this finding by chance; because Randy is male and was an experimenter in a couple of studies, we obtained data that differed in regard to sex differences from studies conducted by women. Specifically, we found that children received higher scores when interviewed by same-sex experimenters, perhaps because they were more motivated to provide the socially desirable, "correct" response to the experimenter. Even lengthening the stories to increase the likelihood of their having an emotional impact did not help; indeed, children who gave empathic responses to longer stories were relatively unlikely to spontaneously help or share in real-life interactions with others at preschool (although they were somewhat more likely to comply with requests for helping or sharing). In a review of the existing literature, we found no real association between empathy as assessed with picture story methods and prosocial behavior, despite the long-standing theoretical assumption that people who feel another's distress or experience concern for another will be motivated to help.

In the same review, we found that children's self-reports of their emotional reactions in experimental situations in which they were exposed to enactments or films of needy or distressed others also were unrelated to their prosocial behavior. Thus, we had to question the efficacy of any self-report measure of empathic emotion for children. It could be that children frequently have difficulty determining what they are feeling; in addition, young children simply may find it hard to put into words what they feel.

This left us in a quandary. Empathy-related reactions are internal, yet we believed that children's self-reports of their internal emotional experience were insufficient. We needed to find a way to assess children's emotional reactions to others that did not involve self-reports.

In an effort to deal with this problem, we turned to two different methodologies. First, we assessed children's facial reactions while they were exposed to empathy-inducing stimuli (e.g., films of needy or distressed people). Coding of facial expressions was not a new technique; however, it had seldom been used to assess empathy. Further, no one had tried to differentiate between sympathy and personal distress using facial expressions. Thus, we had to develop ways of coding markers of other-oriented attention versus self-focused, distress reactions to others.

The second methodology that we turned to was psychophysiology. This was a daunting task because I knew nothing about psychophysiology or the equipment involved (nor did my colleague, Richard Fabes, who has been a collaborator in nearly all my research on this topic). And psychophysiological equipment is expensive, but researchers cannot obtain grant money to buy such equipment until they have demonstrated competence in using physiological methods.

Luckily, in a closet in the home economics department, we found old equipment for collecting heart rate data—so old that it was no longer manufactured. What's more, it did not work and we were told that it could not be fixed. However, a bright and generous colleague of mine, Dennis Glantzman, was able to repair it so that we could try to collect some initial data. And when we had problems with that equipment, a colleague at another university, Joseph Campos, generously loaned us his equipment (and also spent hours on the phone answering our many questions about psychophysiology).

Our troubles were far from over, though. At that time in Arizona, there was much concern about child molestation. As a consequence, the director of a school in which we were to conduct research did not want us to go beneath children's clothing to attach the electrodes (small circular, bandagelike pieces) on the children. This was a problem because heart rate electrodes are usually attached on the ribs or back. Thus, we had to try to find an electrode placement that was not beneath clothing. Because children are active and movement undermines the quality of the heart rate data, finding a suitable location was a difficult task.

The answer to our problem came from an unexpected source, a paramedic who was an acquaintance of a graduate student working with us. The paramedic said that in serious accidents, they often attached electrodes above the sternum on the flat area near the clavicle (just under the shoulder). We found that this placement worked reasonably well if we were careful about where we put the electrodes (more recently, we use the rib placement but hook up children in the presence of one of their parents).

Yet another problem remained. We needed to reduce the anxiety that young children might have in regard to our equipment. We did this in a variety of ways, including putting colored stars on the electrodes and telling children that athletes and astronauts sometimes wear equipment like ours.

We then turned our attention to other less pragmatic conceptual issues. To our knowledge, no one had ever tried to use physiological measures to differentiate between sympathy and personal distress. Nonetheless, based on the limited relevant psychophysiological research and theory, we came up with a hypothesis regarding how heart rate patterns might differ when people experience sympathy versus personal distress. Specifically, we hypothesized that sympathy, which involves an other-oriented focus of attention, would be associated with intake of information concerning the needy other, interest in the other, and outward attention. These types of information processing had been associated in prior psychophysiological research with heart rate deceleration.

In contrast, when vicarious emotional responding results in an aversive reaction such as apprehension, anxiety, or discomfort (i.e., personal distress), it would be expected to be associated with the processing of information relevant to one's own situation. Cognitive elaboration, anxiety, and active coping had been associated with heart rate acceleration across a variety of studies; thus, it seemed reasonable to hypothesize that a self-focused, personal distress reaction would be associated with heart rate acceleration.

At a somewhat later point in our research, we also used skin conductance (previously called GSR or galvanic skin response) as a physiological marker to distinguish between personal distress and sympathy. Skin conductance measures sweat and is used in lie detector tests. By this time we had hypothesized that people who are feeling personal distress are experiencing a relatively high level of empathic emotional arousal that they cannot sufficiently modulate (i.e., regulate and bring down to a more tolerable level). Their arousal is so high that it is experienced as aversive; consequently, the person focuses on his or her own distress rather than that of the needy other. If this analysis were accurate, one would expect feelings of personal distress to be associated with high levels of skin conductance because skin conductance has been found to tap (among other things) emotional arousal.

Our ideas about facial and physiological markers of sympathy and personal distress were new. Thus, before we could examine the relation of facial and physiological measures to prosocial responding, we had to provide some evidence for the validity of these measures. To this end, we conducted a series of studies in which we put people in situations likely to induce either sympathy or personal distress, and then examined whether our facial and physiological measures differed across these conditions. For example, preschool and elementary school children or adults were exposed to films about others that were likely to elicit either concern for another (e.g., a film about a child with spina bifida) or personal distress (e.g., a film about people in a frightening situation). Alternatively, children and adults were asked to recall and tell us about real events when they felt no emotion, concern for another, or concern about their own welfare.

In general (although not always for all measures), the results of these studies confirmed the usefulness of our measures. For example, we examined change in subjects' heart rate over a short period of time (e.g., six seconds) right after they had seen a particularly evocative portion of the film. We tended to get heart rate acceleration in situations that we expected to evoke distress and heart rate deceleration in response to sympathy-inducing stimuli. Moreover, heart rate generally was higher when people talked about distressing rather than sympathy-inducing events. Similarly, in studies of this sort, skin conductance tended to be higher while people watched distress-inducing as opposed to sympathy-inducing films, although this finding was stronger for older elementary children and adults than for children in early elementary school.

We also found that facial expressions associated with distress (e.g., nervous moving of the mouth, biting lips) and those associated with concerned attention (a marker of sympathy, including intense attention, with the eyebrows over the nose pulled together and down, often accompanied by tilting the head forward) differed across the films in the predicted manner. Generally children exhibited more concerned attention as well as sadness in the sympathy-inducing situations and more distress in the distressing contexts. Adults, in comparison to children, exhibited less facial affect in our experimental situations, so our findings for them were weaker.

Luckily, when asked to tell us how the films or mood-induction procedures made them feel, both children and adults in our studies have tended to report the expected emotions—distress in the distressing conditions and sadness and sympathy in the sympathy-inducing ones. This finding bolstered our confidence that we had picked appropriate stimuli to test our various measures of sympathy and personal distress.

All of this initial work was merely to verify that our new facial and physiological markers (i.e., imperfect indicators) of sympathy and personal distress were valid measures. It took more than two years to conduct and analyze the first study; luckily I already had tenure! The next step was to use these measures to examine the relation between empathy-related responding and prosocial behavior.

THE RELATION BETWEEN PROSOCIAL BEHAVIOR AND EMPATHY-RELATED EMOTIONAL RESPONSES

The typical procedure that we (my colleague Richard Fabes, our students, and I) have used to test the relation between prosocial behavior and our various markers of vicarious emotional responding is to expose subjects (children or adults) to someone in need or distress by means of films, and then provide them an opportunity to assist the other person. Assistance in various studies has taken many forms—for example, donating money for physical therapy or a charity that helps people like those in the film, helping to package play materials for children in the hospital rather than playing with attractive toys, giving up recess time to get together homework materials for a child in the hospital, or adults' donating time to do household tasks for a single mother whose children are in the hospital due to an accident. Of course, we have tried to match the helping tasks to the capacities of the children or adults in the studies.

To make the distressed people seem real, we used educational films about children who have a disability or have been injured; sometimes these films were presented as pilot shows for the local university-based public television news program (subjects thought they were evaluating the films in terms of how interesting they were). Typically, study participants viewed the empathy-inducing film while we took physiological and facial data, and then were asked to rate a number of adjectives to indicate how the film made them feel. A short time later, subjects were provided an opportunity to help the person in the film, but to help as anonymously as possible. For example, people could help or donate when no one else was in the room, and the situation was such that the experimenter could not readily see if the person helped. Alternatively, the subject indicated whether or not he or she was willing to assist by filling out a form that went to someone other than the experimenter. In this manner, we tried to reduce the possibility of people helping merely to gain social approval or to avoid disapproval. Running studies such as these is a tricky affair because study participants cannot know that we are trying to measure their prosocial behavior. Indeed, conducting these studies is similar to directing a play.

Much to our delight, the data from these studies usually provided at least partial support for our hypotheses. In a number of studies, we found that children and adults who exhibited heart rate acceleration and higher skin conductance during the empathy-inducing parts of the films were less likely to assist the needy or distressed person than were other people. In contrast, individuals who exhibited heart rate deceleration during the initial evocative parts of the films tended to act prosocially. Further, in these studies, facial expressions indicating concerned attention and/or sadness (viewed as an index of empathic sadness that often leads to concern) frequently were associated with higher levels of helping, whereas facial distress was correlated with low levels of helping. The findings for the facial measures were more consistent for children than adults, probably because adults mask their facial responses quite well. Further, the facial findings have been obtained more often for boys than girls; we are not yet sure why this is so. In contrast to the findings for physiological and facial measures, children's self-reported reactions to the films infrequently predicted helping, although self-reports more often predict behavior for older children and adults.

The results of these studies were exciting for several reasons. First, they provided evidence that children, like adults, experience both sympathy and personal distress. Second, we obtained clearer evidence than was previously available that emotional responding in reaction to another's plight does influence whether children and adults assist other people. Third, consistent with Batson's work with adults, we found that whether or not people help others is a function of the *type* of emotional response (sympathy or personal distress), and not merely if a person responds emotionally in empathy-inducing situations. These findings suggested to us that empathy-related responding is a very important component in prosocial development and merits yet closer attention.

SOCIALIZATION OF EMPATHY-RELATED RESPONDING

As might be expected in studies of empathy-related responding, there are differences among people in the degree to which they exhibit and report sympathy and personal distress. Consequently, we have become interested in factors that influence whether individuals tend to respond with sympathy versus personal distress when dealing with others' need or distress. Clearly, some people are more sympathetic than others. We wanted to know why.

One factor that immediately comes to mind when considering individual differences is children's socialization. Although there is evidence that some of the individual variation in empathy-related responding is genetic in origin, it seemed likely to us that children's experiences in the home and other social settings influence their emotional reactions to others. Parents' socialization practices may, to some degree, reflect their unique genetic makeup, a genetic makeup that is passed on to offspring and may affect children's capacity for empathy. However, children's interactions with socializers probably contribute to individual differences in empathy and sympathy above and beyond any contribution due to genetic inheritance.

We hypothesized that variations among children in their tendencies to experience sympathy and personal distress would be related to differences in both the characteristics of their parents and in the practices their parents use when dealing with their offspring in emotionally evocative contexts. Based on prior work indicating that warm, supportive parents tend to have prosocial children, it seemed likely that parents who are prone to sympathy rather than personal distress would rear sympathetic children. Our reasoning was that sympathetic parents are likely both to model sympathetic reactions for their children to imitate and to instill a positive attitude toward, and interest in, other people. In addition, sympathetic parents may tend to use reasoning as a disciplinary technique, which seems to enhance concern for others.

To examine this issue, in several studies we obtained parents' reports of their own tendencies to respond with sympathy and personal distress, and also assessed children's empathic tendencies in the laboratory. Generally we have found that sympathetic parents tend to have same-sex children who are sympathetic and/or unlikely to experience personal distress when exposed to others in need. Specifically, sympathetic mothers tend to have daughters who are relatively sympathetic or low in personal distress when exposed to another person who is distressed, whereas sympathetic fathers tend to have sympathetic sons. In another study, mother and child watched an empathy-inducing film together. We found that mothers who tended to exhibit facial distress and heart rate acceleration during the film had children who did likewise. Thus, in general, we have found that individual differences in parents' empathy-related responding are associated with corresponding differences in children's responding. Unfortunately, due to the correlational nature of the data, we cannot be sure whether individual differences in parents' responding cause differences in children's responses. At present, we can only speculate in regard to the processes that mediate the similarity between parent and child.

We also have found that the ways in which families deal with the expression of emotion are associated with children's vicariously induced emotional responding. In a study with adults, we asked people about the degree to which positive emotions (e.g., happiness), dominant negative emotions (e.g., anger, hostility), and gentle negative emotions (e.g., apologizing, expressing a sense of loss) were expressed in their home backgrounds. We found that women (but not men) who reported that they came from homes in which positive and gentle negative emotions frequently were expressed also reported relatively high levels of vicarious emotions (e.g., sadness, sympathy, and distress) in reaction to viewing sympathy-inducing and distressing films. Among elementary school-age children, the expression of gentle negative emotions in the home has been correlated with girls' sympathy. In contrast, boys and girls from homes in which hostile negative emotion is common seem to be prone to personal distress.

We also have found that parents' explicit reactions to children's emotional displays are associated with children's sympathetic reactions. For example, parents' reports of restrictiveness in response to children's expression of their own negative emotion have been associated with elementary school children's tendencies to experience personal distress rather than sympathy, particularly for boys. In one study, maternal emphasis on controlling emotions that were unlikely to injure another (e.g., one's own sadness and anxiety) was associated with boys' facial and physiological signs of distress when viewing a sympathy-inducing film, accompanied by self-reports of low distress in reaction to the film. Thus, these boys seemed prone to experience distress when confronted with others' distress, but did not want others to know what they were feeling. Boys whose parents stress control of emotions such as anxiety and sadness probably have difficulty dealing with these emotions in social settings.

Our studies also suggest that a variety of other emotion-related parental practices and teachings affect children's empathic responding.

For example, initial findings indicate that boys whose parents encourage them to deal instrumentally with situations causing their own sadness or anxiety (e.g., to try to make the situation better) are likely to experience sympathy rather than personal distress in empathy-inducing contexts. Parents who teach sons to instrumentally deal with negative emotions and situations may be less likely to become overaroused when experiencing vicariously induced negative emotion and more likely to experience sympathy. In addition, reinforcing girls for being sympathetic and prosocial appears to promote girls' sympathy. Moreover, mothers who are warm, but also direct their children's attention toward others when discussing empathy-inducing situations tend to have elementary school children who are sympathetic and helpful. Findings such as these support the view that children's tendencies to respond with sympathy versus personal distress are in part learned, although the relevant socialization processes are likely to be complex and may involve genetic factors.

Information concerning factors in the environment that influence the development of sympathy and personal distress is important not only for furthering our understanding of prosocial development, but for practical reasons. Programs for fostering sympathetic and prosocial development have now been introduced in a number of schools, and information from research is critical for designing these programs. I have helped design some of these programs and, thus far, the results are promising. For example, an intervention project in the San Francisco Bay area of California seems to have enhanced cooperative and prosocial behavior in students. In addition, information concerning practices related to prosocial development filters down (often slowly) to the public by means of newspaper and magazine articles and "how-to" books on raising a caring or moral child. Thus, research on empathy and prosocial development may, in a small way, help to foster positive interactions and caring among people—a badly needed commodity in today's world.

RECENT DIRECTIONS

In recent work, we are studying personality and temperamental characteristics that are associated with sympathy and personal distress. We wanted to know what is different about people who are prone to sympathy versus personal distress. It seemed to us that one important difference was how people deal with the experience of emotional arousal. Consistent with this idea, we have initial evidence that people who are capable of regulating their emotions and their emotionally driven behavior (e.g., aggression) are prone to sympathy, whereas people who are emotionally intense and have difficulty regulating themselves are prone to personal distress. This work has led us to explore the roles of emotional reactivity and regulation processes in a wider range of social behaviors than we have previously examined, including the development of children's socially appropriate behavior, popularity with peers, and constructive versus nonconstructive coping with anger. We now view prosocial behavior and sympathy as examples of socially competent responses and are trying to apply what we have learned about them to other aspects of social competence.

So it goes: One question leads to the next. But that is what keeps the job exciting. I am paid to satisfy my curiosity by means of research (and to train others to do so). For someone who is naturally curious, it is a great job.

Acknowledgments

Writing of this chapter was supported by a Research Scientist Development Award from the National Institute of Mental Health (K02 MH00903). Much of the research discussed was supported by the National Science Foundation, as well as the Institute of Child Health and Human Development.

SUGGESTED READINGS

BATSON, C. D. (1991). *The altruism question: Toward a social-psychological answer.* Hillsdale, NJ: Erlbaum.

CLARK, M. S. (1991). *Prosocial behavior: Vol. 12. Review of personality and social psychology.* Newbury Park, CA: Sage.

EISENBERG, N. (1986). *Altruistic emotion, cognition, and behavior.* Hillsdale, NJ: Erlbaum.

—— (1992). *The caring child.* Cambridge, MA: Harvard University Press.

—— & FABES, R. A. (1991). Prosocial behavior and empathy: A multimethod, developmental perspective. In P. Clark (Ed.), *Review of personality and social psychology* (Vol. 12, pp. 34–61). Newbury Park, CA: Sage.

—— FABES, R. A., SCHALLER, M., CARLO, G., & MILLER, P. A. (1991). The relations of parental characteristics and practices to children's vicarious emotional responding. *Child Development, 62,* 1393–1408.

—— MILLER, P. A., SHELL, R., MCNALLEY, S., & SHEA, C. (1991). Prosocial development in adolescence: A longitudinal study. *Developmental Psychology, 27,* 849–857.

—— & MUSSEN, P. (1989). *The roots of prosocial behavior in children.* Cambridge, England: Cambridge University Press.

—— & STRAYER, J. (1987). *Empathy and its development.* New York: Cambridge University Press. (Being translated into Spanish.)

OLINER, S. P., & OLINER, P. M. (1988). *The altruistic personality: Rescuers of Jews in Nazi Europe.* New York: Free Press.

BEVERLY I. F*AGOT* (*Ph.D., University of Oregon*) *is Professor of Psychology at the University of Oregon and Research Scientist at Oregon Social Learning Center in Eugene. Dr. Fagot is on the editorial boards of* Child Development *and* Developmental Review. *She is a fellow in the American Psychological Association and the American Psychological Society and a member of the Society for Research in Child Development, the International Society for Infant Studies, the International Society for Behavioral Development, and the Society for Research in Child and Adolescent Psychopathology. She is the author of over eighty publications in gender-role development and family processes. Dr. Fagot is married, has two grown sons, a daughter-in-law, and one granddaughter. She enjoys outdoor activities, including hiking and river running.*

7

Falling into Gender-Role Research

❖

ow does anyone get into his or her life's work? Sometimes when reading
scientific autobiographies, it all sounds so planned. Perhaps so for some
people, but in my case I sort of fell into studying gender-role development.
In fact, I feel that I sort of fell into developmental psychology.

I began my undergraduate years as a chemistry major and never considered
psychology; in fact, I probably didn't even know what it was. I had completed a
traditional college preparation course during high school, which in the 1950s certainly did not include a subject as esoteric as psychology.

While in college, I had a summer job for four years as a lifeguard in south
Phoenix, which had a large, diverse, low-income population. I spent part of the long,
hot days talking with adolescents who were bright and articulate and utterly alienated from school. The other part of the day was spent at the wading pool watching
large numbers of toddlers and preschoolers play. Those summer days shaped my
interests in two ways. First, I became fascinated with the development of young
children. To this day, I am captivated by children from 1 to 5 years of age, especially the way they think and play. Second, I was overwhelmed by the injustice of
our society, at the way these children were discarded by the school system and society in general. By my junior year, I had switched my major to psychology with
the goal of becoming a child clinical psychologist.

So off I went to graduate school with this goal in mind. I never thought of developmental psychology as a major area, perhaps because I had never taken a
course in it and certainly had never encountered research in the field. My introduction to clinical psychology was fairly typical of the early 1960s. The first year, I
did some play therapy with a young middle-class boy who was having difficulty

with peers at school. One night a week for the entire year, we met in a play-room and I attempted to apply play therapy guidelines to his behavior. Believe me, Dibs he was not, nor was I Virginia Axline, but we struggled through. I expect that these nightly meetings did him no harm, or much good either, but for me it was a frustrating experience. What did this have to do with those children I had worked with for four summers in Phoenix?

My second attempt at therapy was quite different. I worked with a 6-year-old boy who did not speak and had been diagnosed as autistic. We were attempting to teach him to pronounce words, and had developed an m&m machine that would give him an m&m when he pointed to the right picture and said the word. He was a very sweet little boy and quickly talked me into buying him an ice cream cone after each session, so I suppose he learned something from our six months together. I learned two things. The first was learned by the end of our initial encounter: Never work with children with hard leather shoes for they hurt when they kick. The second thing was actually taught to me by my own son, then 16 months old. I brought him into the lab and was going through the teaching routine where he received an m&m for saying the word and pointing to the picture. He put up with this for about three minutes, looked carefully at the machine, and ran around to the back where he scooped out several dozen m&m's. End of lesson. He brought home to me just how different autism was from the normal developmental path and that my real love in psychology was in child development. I finished my first year in graduate school rather discouraged. I loved much of the academic work, but was not really very taken with clinical work.

A year's clinical internship working at a VA hospital completed my disenchantment with clinical psychology. I found myself thinking that many of the patients were saner than many of the staff and certainly a lot more interesting to talk to. Of course, I wasn't the first to notice this. Ken Kesey used his sojourn as an aide at the same hospital more profitably by writing *One Flew Over the Cuckoo's Nest*. But I am forever grateful that, at that time, internships were done early in one's graduate career rather than at the end as is done now.

I came back from the internship wondering why I was in psychology and thinking I should have stayed in chemistry. Meantime, I was extremely fortunate to begin work with Gerald Patterson just at the time when he began to do the observational work with families that was to lead to his theory of the coercive cycle in the development of aggression. This was my first real exposure to research, as I had spent one year of graduate school attempting to learn different types of therapy with children and a second year learning to give Rorschachs to chronic schizophrenics. During the next three years, as I worked with Jerry's research group, I changed from clinical to developmental psychology and learned how to do observation in natural settings.

At that time, psychology was dominated by behavioral approaches, and Jerry Patterson was interested in how parent reinforcement would control children's behavior. He developed two tasks to study this: The marble box and the light gun. In each task there were two options (i.e., the children were presented with an apparatus with two holes and told to drop marbles in the holes, or they were shown pictures of two dinosaurs and told they could shoot at the pictures with their beam of light). The children were allowed to freely respond for a baseline period, so that we gained some notion of how often they preferred one hole in the marble box or one side of the picture. We used an old machine called an Esterline Angus, which responded with a little movement to the left or right each time a choice was made. The apparatus had a pen attached so that we had a written record of the preference pattern. We then calculated side preference using the pen-and-ink pattern produced by the movement, and the parent or a peer was told through a bug in the ear when to verbally reinforce the nonpreferred side. These studies were an attempt to get beyond self-report measures to study the social responsiveness of children.

When I first began working with Jerry, he was still relying very heavily on interviews to gather information about parenting. All of us felt that this was a poor way to understand child rearing, as we felt that parents often were "faking good" or didn't really know how they were responding in many situations. My own distrust of interviews was reinforced during data collection over and over again, but one mother and her 9-year-old son stand out in my mind. We were asking the mother questions about discipline styles, and her son who had finished his portion of the interview came over and sat down beside her. He was fidgeting and kicking the side of the bench they were both sitting on. She kept telling him to stop, but he was bored and simply kept squirming around and interrupting. We asked her if she ever used physical punishment and she quickly said no, she didn't believe in it, but in the same breath she backhanded her son across the chest and told him if he continued to interrupt, he was really going to get it. Numerous such examples moved the research group into the uncharted, real-world waters of observational research (see Figure 7-1).

We had already entered the real world; that is, we were conducting our studies in the field, either in schools or outside our families' homes. Jerry had two mobile labs, one a truck and trailer and one a large remodeled school bus, in which we ran our marble box and gun studies and interviewed the mothers. Neither vehicle had very good brakes and Eugene is a hilly town, so we all grew experienced at braking by hitting curbs, at knowing the routes with the least steep hills, and at closing our eyes and hoping no one would cross our path. In one two-week period, another graduate student and I managed to get the school bus stuck on a particularly tight, hilly turn, and twice a tow truck had to get us out.

The next week another graduate student and I blew out the electricity for a whole school when we plugged our bus in to get electricity for the marble box and gun studies (see Figure 7-2).Despite all this, we still felt that our best research strategy was to move into the real world using observa-

FIGURE 7-1
Nothing deters the dedicated observer.

tional techniques. While the marble box and gun studies did suggest that
children's social responsiveness was related to parent reports of parenting
style, we still felt we would get a better measure of the parenting process
through direct observation.

It is difficult to recapture the confusion we felt and the problems we
faced while attempting to do observational research before the development of the technology we now take for granted. Observational research
today depends very heavily on handheld computers, camcorders, and computers with lots of memory capable of crunching thousands and thousands
of entries. When we began observational work in the mid-1960s, none of
these tools was available. In fact, there were no set rules for either family
or school observations. Many of the people working with Patterson in
those early years helped define both observational methodology and statistical analyses. Our first attempts to collect data used what the anthro-
pologists call an "ad lib" approach; that is, picking a behavior of interest,
such as aggression, and coding every incident of that behavior during a
given time period (see Figure 7-3). That first attempt resulted in a major

FIGURE 7-2
We blew out the electricity for a whole school when we plugged in our bus to get electricity for the mobile lab.

publication in 1967 by Patterson, Richard Littman, and William Bricker that has been widely cited, but today none of us in observational research would use this technique for anything except code development. The difficulty with ad lib coding is that the most salient events and the most exciting kids capture your attention, so that certain types of behaviors, such as physical aggression, are overrepresented, and more subtle forms of behavior are underrepresented. I was particularly worried about sex differences in styles of aggression and thought that the behavior of girls was being consistently overlooked by using this observational approach.

Consequently, when I began my dissertation project, I decided to look at sex differences in preschool children and the reactions of others to their behaviors. As I look back on it, this was a ridiculous project for a dissertation. I was in totally uncharted waters; I had no idea what observation methods to use, had never trained observers, and was completely in the dark in terms of data analysis. At that time, observational work in psychology was mostly single-subject design, and I was proposing to examine two groups of preschoolers. In addition, I planned a longitudinal pro-

FIGURE 7-3
An observational researcher can handle a little chaos.

ject lasting over the period of one year. However, Jerry Patterson was supportive as always and excited about the problem, and anyway none of us knew what we were getting into. At about the same time, another one of Jerry's students, John Reid, was getting himself into a similar morass attempting to do home observations. All three of us survived, and I believe that our efforts have been very influential in shaping the observational field.

In addition to taking on this major project, like most graduate students, I was extremely naive about how long it would take to solve a problem. I thought that I was taking on a two-year project for my dissertation, which would give me clear-cut results that I would publish and then move on to a new area. It is now twenty some odd years later, and I am still working on why gender (somehow the name of the area got changed along the way) is such a critically important variable in a child's development.

However, back to the nursery school. After a good deal of reading, mostly in the anthropology primate literature, I decided on an observation schedule in which the behavior of each child in the group was recorded once during a five-minute interval in a predetermined order. The reaction from any other group member, either peer or teacher, to the child's behavior was also coded. In the computerized present this would be a very simple code, but then a code consisting of twenty-eight behaviors and ten reactions was a major undertaking. Child behaviors included such things as *paint at easel, play with trucks,* and *hit another child,* and reactions included *positive verbal response, associative play,* etc. I then trained two coders on-line, as this was prior to portable videos, and after three months of hard work during one summer, we were ready to go. The hard work was not just training for agreement but figuring out how to compute statistics demonstrating such agreement. For nine months we observed children during the free play period of two nursery schools, obtaining twelve code sequences on each child in the group each day. Each sequence included the child's behavior and the group member's reaction to that behavior.

Now I was faced with what in the world to do with these data. There were no real text books available for analyses of this type of data. Was it categorical? Yes, of course, because each individual observation represented one category. An amazing number of experts suggested using chi square, which was, of course, totally inappropriate with multiple observations on each child. We finally decided to create proportion scores and, as the main purpose of the study was to study sex differences, we used two tests to examine differences in the proportions of boys' and girls' activities. For teacher and peer responses, we simply reported the raw number of times teachers responded to boys' and girls' male-preferred behaviors (such as rough-and-tumble play) and female-preferred behaviors (such as coloring) and the number of times boy and girl peers responded to the target child's male- and female-preferred behaviors.

By today's standards, these analyses were incredibly simple and straightforward. Despite this simplicity, the major findings—that 3-year-olds show consistent preferences for sex-stereotyped activities, that the preferences are stable over the nursery school year, that teachers give more reinforcement for feminine-preferred behaviors, and that boys and girls react more to their own sex—have been replicated over and over again in numerous countries. In fact, it is hard to remember that the findings were somewhat of a surprise, as previous studies of sex typing had found that 3-year-olds were not strongly sex-typed. But then, most of those studies had used a procedure requiring more verbal skills than most 3-year-olds possess. Like most good dissertations, this one posed many more interesting questions, and I was launched into the field with lots of questions, a technique that did not require a massive laboratory, and some understanding of how to proceed in the area of observational measurement of children's behavior.

It was good that I had these questions and these skills. As a rather typical 1960s female graduate student, I was married, had a family, and was place bound. Therefore, for the next ten years, my career did not follow what might be considered a typical academic track. Instead, my main job was running the university's undergraduate advising program, doing some adjunct teaching, and doing observational studies.

Some very clear questions emerged from my dissertation. What happened in the house to children prior to the age of 3? Would preschool children differ in their behavior with male and female teachers? Would male teachers respond differently from female teachers? What would happen to children who showed consistent cross-sex preferences? Did the strength of parents' and teachers' sex stereotypes influence the way they behaved? For the next ten years, I spent time conducting observational studies to answer some of these questions.

As I look back upon my career, I now consider it fortunate that I was not on a normal academic six-year tenure track, as observational work takes a long time. One study that I published on sex-typed reactions of parents to toddlers took a year and half to complete and, with the technology of the day, another half year to analyze the data. I do not think I would have been able to do this type of research with a typical academic job. Sometimes what seems like adversity or unfairness can have unexpected benefits.

However, with the advent of affirmative action and with the pressure for the university to add female faculty, in 1977 I moved into a regular tenure-track psychology job at the University of Oregon. The psychology department had recently moved into a new building with a laboratory that could be used for observational research. For the next few years, I ran numerous research playgrounds there, which was a real advantage over observing in regular preschools. For the first time, we could really hear, as there was a microphone system; we could control toys and activities; we could control the number, type, and age of children in each playgroup; and we could train the teachers.

Another advantage of moving into the department was that for the first time I had graduate students. (Parenthetically, it is interesting to note how graduate students' interests help shape one's own interests.) My first group of graduate students (Sandra Kronsberg, Rick Hagan, Mary Leinbach, and Tony Hoffman) and I spent many profitable hours in these playgroup studies, and we were able to do studies that examined much more carefully the patterns of reactions received by boys and girls in infant and toddler playgroups.

This was also an exciting time as video technology was finally starting to have an impact on the field, and we began to realize that this new tool had real possibilities for stripping some of the contextual effects from people's judgments of the importance of the child's sex. Sandra Kronsberg embarked on a dissertation attempting to control for the actual sex of the child in determining parental reactions to children's risky and irritating behaviors. What seemed like a simple question turned out to be fraught with methodological problems. We first had to determine if we could find children judged as gender neutral. For weeks we filmed our laboratory children walking and running up and down the hall, and then we presented the tapes to undergraduates to judge the children as male or female. Even with toddlers, we found very few children dressed in their usual clothes who could pass as both a boy and a girl. Back to the hall, this time with children in identical turtle-necks and pull-on jogging pants with ski caps on their heads (see Figure 7-4). Another group of undergraduates rated the children, and this time we collected a group of young children who were not obviously sex-typed.

The next step was to develop a videotape of children engaged in a variety of risky behaviors. The parents in our labs joined the project with great enthusiasm, and after five months we had a tape of children engaged in all kinds of risky or irritating behaviors, from pulling garbage out of a wastebasket to riding a tricycle into the street. The next step was to bring parents into the laboratory to look at each video clip and tell us when they would intervene, either verbally or physically. The parents recorded their responses on an old prime computer. As this study was run right before the widespread availability of personal computers, we had to run the subjects in the university's cognitive lab. The cognitive lab had never before been invaded by real, live families, and it was quite honestly a meeting of two different cultures. Despite many complaints about the noise (parents often brought their children), computer failures, broken appointments, etc., 128

FIGURE 7-4
The unisex toddler outfit.

mothers and fathers completed the task; the dissertation was completed and published; and we came away with many questions about the differences between real-world observation of children and video observation. We saw fewer differences in the mothers' and fathers' reactions to the videotape than we had seen in home observations, and we saw fewer differences in reactions to the stated sex of the child on the videotape than we had seen in home observations. We sensed that parents perceived the video task as requiring them to respond as they thought they *should* respond. The demand characteristics of coming into a formal laboratory situation and sitting down before a computer appeared to restrict the range of responses.

We began to realize that there were many dangers in video technology, as the camera simply does not have the capacity to take in information that the human eye and brain do. So for the next few years, Rick Hagan and I began a series of methodological studies examining differences between findings when observed by videotape versus on-line, and trying to understand how observers affected observational findings. We needed to know when it was appropriate to use video cameras and when human eyes did a better job. Many hours were spent in small, crowded observation rooms training groups of observers and working out complicated plans for ensuring that each session would be both videotaped and recorded on-line. In 1980–1982, we were still working with clumsy, heavy cameras attached to even heavier, clumsier video recorders. These studies would be much easier to do today with the smaller, lighter, better quality video equipment available. We learned how to sequence information so that observers could learn codes faster and to space training sessions to maximize memory and recall. We also learned a great deal about preparing appropriate materials for teaching observation systems. The time spent working on observational methodological problems was time well worth it, both for our understanding of the process and also in terms of practical training. For his dissertation, Rick trained several groups of coders on a very complicated computerized code, and training time went down from over 250 hours to about 150 hours.

Psychology was changing rapidly in the 1980s and was now dominated by cognitive theory. One of my group of graduate students, Mary Leinbach, was extremely interested in the child's cognitive understanding of gender (by this time, *gender* was a widely used term). Her dissertation examined the very early stages of gender understanding, namely the child's ability to label his or her own and others' gender. We developed stimuli using pictures of very traditionally stereotyped men and women and boys and girls, and presented the children with a very simple choice, to point to the mommy or daddy or the boy or girl. Mary's dissertation showed that children understand adult gender labels first, and that understanding of child labels trailed by almost eight months. Almost all children understood adult labels within two to three months of each other, but the understanding of child labels showed a much wider age distribution, with some children as young as 20 months understanding child labels, while others did not understand them until well past their third birthday.

This very simple gender-labeling task was then used as the basis of a set of studies that Mary and I completed while she remained a research associate in my laboratory. We found that more traditional families had children who learned gender labels earlier and who continued to know more about sex typing even at the age of 4. We found that gender labels appeared to serve as an organizer for adoption of gender-role behaviors. Children who knew gender labels showed increases in sex-typed behaviors, played more with same-sex peers, and the girls showed a decrease in aggression. We have replicated these findings in two home studies and in two laboratory studies. Additionally, in a study with another graduate student, Cherie O'Boyle, children who knew gender labels showed a greater understanding of gender stereotypes than children who did not.

This line of research with Mary continued to hold my interest. We were joined by another student, Barbara Hort, and embarked on trying to understand the metaphorical aspects of gender knowledge. The study of gender labeling had been very informative, but we were also interested in how children fill in their gender schema; that is, how does gender come to have the sprawling network of associations described by Sandra Bem? Bem suggests that all kinds of information enters into gender schema—information that has little to do with biological sex but comes to be called masculine or feminine. Her description of her daughter coming home from kindergarten explaining that thumbs were boys and fingers were girls is a favorite of mine. We have begun to explore how gender categories are constructed and just how early gender knowledge comes to have meaning beyond simple preferences for activities and toys.

Gender schema must also include dimensions of meaning that underlie the concepts of masculinity and femininity. In our laboratory, we found suggestions of such dimensions in preschoolers' choice of picture stamps on their hands after the gender-labeling tasks. We tested a group of 4-year-olds using a set of cards depicting animals and plants. The children were asked to sort the cards into one box for girls and another box for boys. The 4-year-olds assigned bears, fire, and fir trees to boys and men, while butterflies, hearts, and flowers were for women and girls. We strongly doubt that such notions are taught directly. True, children may observe women, more often than men, with or wearing flowers, but do they see men in the company of bears or women with butterflies? It is at least plausible that these youngsters have begun to associate qualities such as strength or dangerousness with males, and gentler qualities with females, whether or not they can name the attributes involved. The recent surge of interest in metaphor as a cognitive process makes this suggestion somewhat less outlandish than it would have seemed a few years ago.

To attempt to understand just what dimensions underlie masculinity and femininity, we went back to the always-present undergraduate subject pool. We first had 100 undergraduates rate dozens of items such as bear, butterfly, clouds, needle and thread as masculine, feminine, or neutral. We then had 4- to 7-year-olds sort the same items as to whether they belonged to boys or girls. Once that was done, we then chose a list of adjectives, some associated with masculinity, some associated with femininity and some more neutral (the adjectives were all common words such as hot, cold, dark, mad, etc.) and had an additional 200 undergraduates rate the eight most masculine, the eight most feminine, and the eight most neutral items on this list of adjectives. We found clear differences in the ways that masculine and feminine items were described, with feminine items being described as soft, small, clean, etc., and masculine items described as dark, mad, angular, etc.

Now that we were able to find agreement among adults on a variety of masculine and feminine stimuli, we went back to the children. We developed animal families in which we paired the masculine and feminine attributes from our adult studies, and then asked each young child to tell us which was the mommy or daddy (see Figure 7-5). We found that, by the age of 5, all the children could differentiate male from female solely on the defined attribute, and even 3-year-olds effectively used most of them. We have tested children in five different cultures and have found amazing agreement on some attributes (such as happy versus mad, rough versus smooth) and cultural differences on others (such as hair length).

At the present time, we are presenting a group of young children with toys that have been altered according to these attributes, and pairing the metaphor of gender against the content of the toy. For instance, everyone agrees that tea sets are for girls, but what about black, spiky tea sets? It turns out that the metaphor is stronger than the content, and that boys say they would like to play with that toy.

Gender research continues to be of great interest to me, and the work can be amusing. Children consistently amaze us with their responses to laboratory questions. Recently we were presenting a little boy with the animal family task and asking which one was a mommy or daddy and his response was to drop his pants and announce his lack of underwear (see Figure 7-6). Somehow he understood that our underlying interest was how biological sex shapes one's life.

FIGURE 7-5
Which is the mommy and which is the daddy?

Going back to the early 1980s, my student Tony Hoffman was in clinical psychology and much more interested in applications to clinical problems. While in the graduate program, he started a play group for abused children and gave us another milieu in which to observe. More important for my future research interests, he became interested in the relation of behavioral codes to qualitative judgments of the meaning of the code. For instance, did parents agree that our clusters of negative behaviors were negative? At this point, my old mentor, Jerry Patterson, and my former fellow graduate student, John Reid, were continuing to work away at Oregon Social Learning Center (OSLC) on the problem of aggressive families. Tony established contact with them and had the behavioral code categories rated by parents of nonclinical children (from "very pleasant" to "very annoying"). The parent ratings were then used to create new positive, negative, and neutral clusters of behavioral codes. The clusters distinguished treatment from control boys. One important finding was that using the parent cluster of positive behaviors allowed us to test differences between families using many more behaviors. If we looked only at negative behaviors,

FIGURE 7-6
A 3-year-old boy's response to the gender-labeling task was, "Look, I don't have on any underwear."

many families could not be included in our statistical analyses because they never did anything negative during the observation. However, all families used some positive behaviors, so all families could be included.

However, for me, the importance of this dissertation was the reestablishment of contact with the OSLC group and a return to my early interest in the problem of family aggression. Consequently, in 1983 I returned to OSLC to try to understand how the family process influences the development of problem behaviors.

We embarked upon a major project with 180 families who had 18-month-old children. We did observations of these families in their homes and in the lab using Ainsworth's Strange Situation, and we saw the children for at least six months in our play groups. Parents filled out questionnaires and rated their children on temperament measures. When the project first started, I planned to see the children for five years, but somehow we have continued with this group of families right up until the present. Currently, the 11-year-old children are doing laboratory tasks with friends.

Lest one think that this work with families has been an abandonment of interest in gender, I see it as just the opposite. We know too little about how family processes and gender-role development interact to form differences in adjustment and maladjustment and in competencies. At this point, I see my work on gender contributing to a better understanding of these complexities. Just as my first group of graduate students and their interests influenced mine, I find that my present students have led me into new areas, so that self-regulation, temperament, empathy, and family structure variables have all become a part of my work.

We are now looking at young children's assignment of different emotions to males and females. One of our most consistent findings is that, for young boys, aggressive items and activities are consistently included in the male stereotype. In our metaphor work, we have been surprised to find how consistently *powerful, rough, dark,* and *angry* define *male.* We are using a set of animals, identical except for facial expression, and asking 3- and 4-year-olds to tell us which is the mommy or daddy (see Figure 7-7). So far, we have looked at anger, happiness, and sadness compared to neutral, and

FIGURE 7-7
We are looking at young children's assignment of different emotions to males and females.

found the most consistent rating is that anger defines male, sadness defines female, and happiness is equally divided. We find this an interesting parallel to the clinical literature in which males tend to have problems with anger and lack of control and females with depression.

One nice thing about a research career is that it often leads you back to asking the same old questions in different ways. At this point, I find myself pretty much back to where I was early in my career, asking why some children have so much difficulty growing up and why boys and girls are so different.

Acknowledgments

Over the years, Dr. Fagot's research has been supported by grants from the National Institute of Mental Health, the National Institute of Child Health and Development, and the National Science Foundation. Thanks go to the many students and research staff members and to the parents and children who have made the research possible. For their illustrations for this chapter, special thanks are due to Jerry Patterson and Margaret McKean.

SUGGESTED READINGS

Axline, V. M. (1964). *Dibs: In search of self.* New York: Ballantine Books.

Bem, S. L. (1993). *The lenses of gender: Transforming the debate on sexual inequality.* New Haven, CT: Yale University Press.

Carter, D. B. (Ed.). (1987). *Current conceptions of sex roles and sex typing.* New York: Praeger.

Fagot, B. I., & Hagan, R. (1988). Is what we see what we get? Comparisons of taped and live observations. *Behavioral Assessment, 10,* 367–374.

———— Hagan, R., Leinbach, M. D., & Kronsberg, S. (1985). Differential reactions to assertive and communicative acts of toddler boys and girls. *Child Development, 56,* 1499–1505.

———— & Leinbach, M. D. (1993). Gender-role development in young children: From discrimination to labeling. *Developmental Review, 13,* 203–224.

———— & Patterson, G. R. (1969). An in vivo analysis of reinforcing contingencies for sex-role behaviors in the preschool child. *Developmental Psychology, 1,* 563–568.

Maccoby, E. E. (1988). Gender as a social category. *Developmental Psychology, 24*(6), 755–765.

Patterson, G. R., Littman, R. A., & Bricker, W. (1967). Assertive behavior in children: A step toward a theory of aggression. *Monographs of the Society for Research in Child Development, 32* (5, Serial No. 113).

———— & Reid, J. B. (1970). Reciprocity and coercion: Two facets of social systems. In J. Michaels & C. Neuringer (Eds.), *Behavior modification and clinical psychology.* New York: Appleton-Century-Crofts.

DAVID ELKIND *(Ph.D., UCLA) is Professor of Child Study at Tufts University in Medford, Massachusetts and has served as president of the National Association for the Education of Young Children. His awards include an honorary degree from the University of Rhode Island, The Nicholas Hobbs Award from the American Psychological Association (Community Psychology Division), and he was a G. Stanley Hall Lecturer for the APA. Dr. Elkind and his wife Debbie spend the academic year in Boston and the summers at their home in Sandwich on Cape Cod.*

8

The Uses of Academic Conflict

❖

As a graduate student at UCLA in the early 1950s, I led a rather conflicted life. Fortunately, this disturbance did not originate in my own troubled psyche, but rather was a reflection of a personality schism within the psychology department itself. At that time the faculty was split (reflecting a division in psychology as a whole that has continued to widen) between the experimentalists on the one hand and the clinicians on the other. Neither had much respect for, nor much good to say about, the other. We, the students, were caught in the middle.

One semester, to illustrate, I had a morning course in experimental methodology. Our highly regarded professor made a point of demonstrating, with elaborate statistical proofs, that projective tests in general, and the Rorschach inkblot test in particular, were unscientific. He contended that using such tests was akin to employing a crystal ball and was hardly different from relying upon astrological signs to predict behavior. In the afternoon of the same term, I took a course with Bruno Klopfer, the grand old man of Rorschach. Klopfer interpreted patients' responses to the inkblots so well that he was able to diagnose brain tumors months before they showed up on neurological measures. Without ever seeing their Rorschach records, Klopfer had his own diagnosis for the experimentalists.

The departmental conflict presented serious problems when I was ready to do my doctoral research. I was attending graduate school thanks to the Veterans Administration Clinical Training Program. As part of that training, I spent several days a week in a mental hospital doing testing and therapy. Nonetheless, I was also being indoctrinated into the values of positivistic science. While my clinical heart was very tempted to do a Rorschach investigation, as many of my fellow clinical students were doing, my experimental conscience directed me to attempt something a little more scientifically rigorous. I ended up conducting a rat study which I thought might build a bridge between the two warring camps within the department. From a theoretical position, it seemed to me that both the Freudians and the Hullians (the dominant learning theory of the time) would predict that learning that produced a variety of need satisfactions (reinforcements) would be more effective than learning which satisfied only a single need.

For my dissertation, I designed an experiment in which the maze running times of rats deprived of both food *and* water were compared to the maze running times of rats deprived of food *or* water. As predicted, the rats deprived of both food and water ran the maze faster than either the food-only or water-only deprived animals. While the results were gratifying, my experience running rats was not. As a species, they are rather nasty beasts—particularly when they have been deprived of food or water and, more especially, when they have been deprived of both. To this day I have scars on my hands where those ungrateful wretches—I did clean their cages after all—bit me.

In addition to teaching me everything I didn't want to know about rats, my first experience running an experiment did afford another important lesson. I discovered that, in the actual learning situation, there were many more variables in play than I had anticipated. For example, one variable that I had not even thought about was *crowding*. After running the rats a few times, I noticed that animals housed four to a cage (because I had run out of scrounged cages) ran faster than animals housed two to a cage. The crowding variable seemed to operate independently of the need-deprivation variable and thus did not affect the experiment. While crowding made sense as an empirical variable, it wasn't dreamed of in either the Freudian or the Hullian paradigms. This experience taught me to be conscious of the multiplicity of factors operating in any actual situation and to be suspicious of excessively "clean" experimental findings.

After graduation, and completion of the clinical psychology training program, I applied for a postdoctoral research fellowship with David Rappaport at the Austen Riggs Center in Stockbridge, Massachusetts. Rappaport was a noted Freudian scholar and Austen Riggs was an outstanding residential treatment center for troubled youth. Erik Erikson was there at that time. Rappaport chose me as his research assistant and I was elated at the opportunity to study with him. To my surprise, however, before I traveled to Stockbridge I began receiving shipments of books from Rappaport. But they were not, as I had expected, volumes by or about Freud. Rather they were books written by someone whom my college textbooks had described as a quaint Swiss gentleman who interviewed children on the banks of Lake Geneva. His name was Jean Piaget.

When I arrived at Austen Riggs, Rappaport devoted our regular weekly meetings to a discussion of one of Piaget's books, namely, *The Child's Conception of Number*. We sometimes spent an entire hour on a single page of the book and I learned to read in a way that I had never done before. Rappaport approached a text in what today would be called the "hermeneutic" tradition. That is, he took a great deal of time to interpret each sentence and paragraph in its social, historical, and scientific context. This method of reading gave me a true appreciation of the breadth and depth of Piaget's (not to mention Rappaport's) knowledge in many fields quite outside of psychology.

Nonetheless, as I read Piaget's experiments, particularly the number investigations, I was quite skeptical. From a methodological standpoint—methodology was my strong point—his studies were very weak indeed. To begin with he did not describe his samples or his sampling procedures. Excerpts from the examination of children at different age levels were offered but there was no further description of the children in terms of sex, socioeconomic status, etc. Nor was there any indication of how many children were examined and by whom. Piaget provided no quantitative data to support his conclusions about age differences in children's performance. Finally, his procedures were not standardized and there was no concern with validity or reliability of his interview procedure.

I then designed several replication studies in order to check Piaget's findings in a more systematic and "scientific" way. First of all I standardized the procedure by always asking the same questions in the same order. Second, I selected a sample of children in local schools, all of whom were from comparable homes in terms of socioeconomic level, race, and ethnicity. I pretested the procedures by repeating them at weekly intervals with the same children to test for reliability. The most difficult task was to devise a scoring scheme. What I came up with was assigning a number to each of Piaget's substages. For example, a child who said that a row of pennies spread out was more than a row in which they were close together—and that this would remain true even if the crowded pennies were spread apart—received a score of 1. A child who said the longer row was more, but that they would be the same if returned to the starting point, was given a score of 2. Those children who said the longer row had the same number of pennies as did the shorter row were given a score of 3.

I tested at least thirty children at each age level from 4 to 7 years (at the Austen Riggs Nursery School and at a local elementary school) with Piaget's number conservation task and then analyzed the results using the analysis of variance procedure. We did not have computers then, and I had to calculate the statistics on what was, at that time, considered a state-of-the-art machine that would automatically calculate square roots! I had a fairly good idea of what the results would be before doing the calculations. From their distinctly different responses to the number conservation task, I was quite sure that there would be statistically significant differences among the age groups. There were indeed. But another of my assumptions proved to be wrong; there were no sex differences.

My experience in testing children with the Piagetian procedures had given rise to two revelations. First of all, I found that when I examined children using Piagetian procedures, children at different age levels performed much as he had said they would. That was a turning point in my young career. From a critic I became an advocate. In Piaget, I discovered a way of resolving the conflict that I had suffered with throughout my graduate training. Piaget's work offered a way to satisfy my clinical desire to deal with issues of substance (children's concepts of number, space, time, geometry, causality, and so on). At the same time, as a result of my first investigations, I was convinced that these studies could be done quantitatively and with rigor and thus could also satisfy my scientific sensibility.

The second revelation was that I enjoyed working with children much more than I did with adults, and certainly a great deal more than I did running rats. Consequently, although I had been trained as an adult clinician, I decided I would really like to work with troubled children. After I left Austen Riggs, I went to the Beth Israel Hospital in Boston to gain clinical training with children and adolescents. Clinical work with children, I soon learned, is not just a "size smaller" version of adult clinical work. It is a discipline unto itself.

At the same time, I just kept up with my Piagetian investigations. Inasmuch as I had no grant monies, I did all of the interviews myself. In this endeavor, my clinical training in diagnostic testing and therapy was important preparation, but I still had to learn how to talk to children. Working with children reinforced the lesson I had learned from my dissertation; namely, that in any given concrete situation many variables are in play that are not taken into account by the theory.

An amusing example may help to illustrate this point. While examining children with the conservation of liquids (comparing two equal amounts of colored liquids first in identical containers and then when one quantity is poured into another container that is taller and thinner), I found that some children did respond in accord with Piaget's descriptions, but others did not. Indeed some children appeared to be more Freudian than Piagetian. That is to say, these children would say that their container had more, even though it perceptually appeared to have less. One young man of this stripe told me that his container had more because, "I want more."

In these early investigations I had a twofold aim. On the one hand, I was training myself to do the Piagetian interviews because there was nowhere to go to get such training. Second, by publishing my replications of Piaget's experiments, using a standard experimental paradigm, controls, and statistical analysis of results, I hoped to make his work more acceptable to my experimentally oriented colleagues in this country. I was not alone in this effort and psychology in general was rediscovering its mind. The publication of John Flavell's (1963) book, *The Developmental Psychology of Jean Piaget* effected a quantum leap in the awareness of Piaget's research and theory for American investigators.

At this point, I would like to say something parenthetical about replication studies. When I first proposed my replications of Piaget's number conservation experiments to David Rappaport, he agreed to let me do them. But he also said it was not the kind of experiment that he himself would have undertaken. He was expressing what was, and probably still is, a widely held prejudice in psychology against replication studies. Although not original, my replication studies taught me the interview skills I needed and also suggested many of the nonreplication investigations that I carried out thereafter. Replication is commonplace in the physical sciences and I believe should be utilized much more in psychology.

After finishing my training at Beth Israel, I took a teaching job at Wheaton College in Norton, Massachusetts. There I taught child psychology, continued my replication studies, and began my studies of children's conceptions of their religious denomination. As I have already suggested, for me research always begins with some conceptual issue. I am sure researchers, like fiction writers, begin in different ways. Some fiction writers begin with a character, others with a plot, and still others with a moral or specific intriguing incident. In the same way, I expect some researchers begin with an observation, others with a methodology, and still others, like myself, with a conceptual issue. We all end up doing experiments but our problem finding starts from different places.

Here I want to make a comment about problem finding that may not sit well with everyone. I believe that successful researchers have a particular talent or ability that probably cannot be, at least not entirely, learned. For example, I do not know how I come upon problems to investigate, but they are always there. Yet many students come to me with no clue as to how to find a research project. Early on in my academic career, I gave up taking on doctoral students for just this reason. Since the requirement was that students come up with their own problems, I did not want to be tempted to hand them one of the many issues I saw waiting to be addressed. Nor did I have any wish to clone graduate students in my own image. Piaget used to say, "To the extent that there are Piagetians, to that extent I have failed." On the other hand, I have always welcomed graduate students who have come to me with their own research agendas and just wanted help with methodology.

After completing a half dozen replication studies, I decided to do some more original research. Although not a deeply religious person myself, it seemed to me that since about the turn of the century, with a few notable exceptions, psychology had largely ignored religion. This was probably due to two intellectual doctrines that were dominant during the first half of the century, namely those of Freud and Marx. Freud argued that religion was an illusion, a kind of projection of the father image. Marx, in equally disparaging tones, dismissed religion as the "opiate of the proletariat." Moreover, science was often depicted as being in conflict with religion, particularly over the Darwinian concept of evolution that was a direct contradiction to the biblical view of creationism.

These matters didn't trouble me. Having immersed myself in Piaget, I appreciated that there were various ways of viewing the world which were not right or wrong, but simply different. What did bother me was the fact that religion played a significant part in many people's lives, yet was being ignored as a legitimate subject for psychological investigation. Moreover, although Piaget had addressed religious issues in a few early papers, it was absent from his later systematic investigations. Religion thus provided both a relatively virgin subject for original research and a way of testing out Piaget's stages in a domain that he himself had not explored.

I proceeded to design an interview study to assess the stages of children's understanding of their religious denomination. Piaget had written that to reveal the child's spontaneous convictions—his or her own way of viewing the world—one has to ask children questions that they do not expect and to which they have no memorized answers. Accordingly, I constructed questions that I believed children had not been asked, such as "Can a dog or a cat be a Protestant or a Catholic or a Jew?" I also asked, "How can you tell a person is a . . .?" Still another question in the interview was "If you are a . . . can you change and become something else?" Armed with these and a few other definitional questions, I arranged to interview Protestant, Catholic, and Jewish children spanning the age range from preschool to junior high.

Again, lacking funds and students, I did all the interviewing myself and talked to well over 700 children. In analyzing the results, I combined Piaget's qualitative analysis with a quantitative one. As I expected, I found that children's spontaneous understanding of their religious denomination followed the sequence of stages laid down by Piaget. Young children, ages 4 to 6, had a global, undifferentiated conception of their religious denomination and did not distinguish religious from other global designations such as nationality. They believed that a dog or a cat could be Protestant, Catholic, or Jewish, because they regarded these as global categories applying to pets as well as to people.

Beginning at the age of 6 or 7, children began to display a concrete differentiated concept of their denomination. They understood religion as a unique category but differentiated among religious groups on the basis of concrete activities. "Protestants go to a Protestant church, Catholics go to a Catholic church." Children at this age were ambivalent about whether their pets could be said to have a religious denomination. When they thought of their pets as members of the family they said, "the pet could be Protestant . . . because we (the family) are." On the other hand, if they thought of the pet attending church or synagogue they gave a different kind of answer, "Well, no because the minister (priest, rabbi) wouldn't let him in and he might bark and stuff."

Finally, at the early adolescent stage, young people defined their religious denomination in terms of belief or understanding. "A Protestant is someone who believes in Christ but does not believe in the Pope" or "A Jew believes that there is only one God." Animals cannot really have a religious denomination because they "do not think," "lack intelligence," "don't have any understanding of things like that." By early adolescence, religious denomination is clearly conceptual rather than concrete and behavioral. In reporting these studies, as in reporting the replication experiments, I included qualitative descriptions to enliven the quantitative results.

I did a couple of other studies in this area, one on prayer and another on the varieties of religious experience in young adolescents. During this time I continued to read Piaget. Since only a few of his books had been translated, I began to read him in French even though I had not taken French in college. Because there were many cognates, I could make some things out and with the aid of a dictionary I was soon reading Piaget in French with some fluency. One book I encountered made a great impression; it was Piaget's book on perception. Unlike many of his other studies, those on perception were quite methodologically sophisticated and quantitative, perhaps because these were done with a Vietnamese colleague, Vignh Bang, who had extensive experimental training.

What intrigued me about Piaget's perceptual investigations was that they were done with relatively meaningless materials, such as shapes and line lengths. Whereas Piaget had always appealed to me because of his engagement with meaningful concepts and issues, his perceptual work was the exception. Would Piaget's theories regarding perceptual development hold for more meaningful perceptual materials? It was a question that initiated my most systematic, cohesive, and extensive research program, that on the perceptual development of children. It was a program that lasted over fifteen years.

After two years, I left Wheaton College for a position on the adolescent ward at the Neuropsychiatric Institute at UCLA (conflict again, I wanted to get back to clinical work and also my family was in California). During the year I spent there, I continued my studies of perceptual development that I began at Wheaton College. One of the first of these investigations was concerned with age changes in children's abilities to reverse figure and ground. Piaget's theory predicted that children's ability to see both images in an ambiguous figure should improve as they attained concrete operations. One of my students drew several cards with original ambiguous figures such as a duck in the white space created by the shape of a black tree trunk.

In administering the test, I called upon my clinical training with the Rorschach and the TAT (Thematic Apperception Test). Children were told "I am going to show you some cards with pictures on them. Different children see different things so there are no right or wrong answers. Just tell me what you see, what it looks like to you." Scoring was simple, the child was given a score of one for each figure that he or she correctly identified. We presented the cards (seven of them) to thirty children at each age level between 4 and 7 years. A second comparable set of figures was drawn to test for reliability and validity. The results were clear-cut. As predicted, older children were able to reverse figure and ground significantly more often than was true for younger children.

From Piaget's point of view, what happened was that children were developing what he called "perceptual regulations" that were analogous but not the same as the operations of intelligence. Young children, lacking perceptual regulations, were "centered" in their perception—caught and held by the dominant "Gestalt" features of the perceptual array. Piaget called these natural features such as good form and closure, "field effects." With increasing age, children were increasingly better able to overcome these field effects and explore the visual configuration in more flexible and systematic ways. The ability to reverse figure and ground, to illustrate, came about because children were able to grasp that one and the same contour line could, when added to some areas and subtracted from others, lead to new configurations.

We then conducted a study to see if training would affect children's performance on this task. The training procedures involved providing children with three progressively more directive prompts. The first was verbal; we asked children if they could see anything other than that which they first reported. If this did not elicit an additional response we named the hidden figure (e.g., duck) for them and asked whether they could see it in the figure. If the children could not see the figure with these prompts, we covered the dominant figure so as to make the ground image (e.g., duck) become a figure. While children at all age levels were helped by training, the oldest children made the most progress with the fewest, and least directive, prompts.

Although I did not appreciate it at the time, this finding was perhaps more in keeping with the work of Russian psychologist Lev Vygotsky than it was with Piaget's developmental theory. Piaget assumed that children spontaneously maximize their intellectual abilities without direct adult intervention. The task of the adult is to create an environment conducive to facilitating the child's intellectual development. In this respect, Piaget reflected, to some extent, the influence of Maria Montessori. The school at Piaget's Institute in Geneva (Maison de Petits) had a Montessori orientation.

In contrast, Vygotsky argued that learning about the world was, in part at least, mediated by adults by their modeling of psychological tools. The most important tool that adults modeled was language. Adult modeling, in Vygotsky's view, was necessary for children to realize their full potential. He posited a "zone of proximal development"—the difference between a child's spontaneous level of development and the level the child could achieve with adult mediation. The fact that all our subjects made progress as a result of training did indeed suggest that they had not spontaneously maximized their abilities and could be helped to do so with adult intervention. At the same time, both Piaget and Vygotsky agree that even with training the child cannot be accelerated beyond his or her developmental limits.

The last perceptual task we constructed was designed to assess children's ability to decenter across a temporal sequence. We showed children at different age levels four series of pictures in which one animal was progressively transformed into another (e.g., from a bird to a fish). The child's task was to name each figure. We wanted to see how far into the series we had to go before the child would change and see the other animal that was becoming increasingly more prominent. Older children routinely decentered earlier than the younger children and thus demonstrated that perceptual response sets were more easily overcome by children with more advanced mental development.

The perceptual studies derived from a central theory of development and not only provided confirmation of the Piagetian position, but also provided negative evidence against that of the Gestalt psychologists. According to Gestalt theory, boundaries become more fixed in development and therefore, say, figure-ground reversals should be less easy for adults than for children. The perceptual studies were well received. The figure-ground training study was published in *Science* and the tree with the duck in the white space was on the cover of the issue in which the article appeared. I was also asked to summarize this body of research in a comprehensive article for the *American Scientist.*

While at the Neuropsychiatric Institute, I received an offer to go to the University of Denver to head their Child Study Center and to start a child clinical training program. It sounded like a wonderful opportunity to at last combine my clinical and academic interests (the solution to my lingering ambivalence). At the University of Denver, I succeeded in getting a graduate training program in child clinical psychology. The program was set up to train students in child development–oriented evaluation and treatment.

In addition to my administrative, teaching, and clinical responsibilities, I continued with my work on perceptual development. At this point I began having students assist me in running experiments. But I found undergraduates much easier to work with than graduate students, so many of my studies were coauthored with college seniors. We did studies of perceptual exploration and found that with age children could increasingly explore disordered arrays of familiar objects in a systematic way without making errors of either omission or commission. As children attained perceptual regulations they were also able to see part-whole figures at the same time (a man made out of fruit) whereas young children could see only parts and not the whole. In addition, older children could make correct size comparisons across wider distances than younger children thanks to their enhanced ability to decenter and not overestimate the centered figure.

At this point it might be well to say something about writing. As a child I had always wanted to be a writer and even after moving to Boston and pursuing my clinical and research activities, I wrote for several hours early every morning, a practice I continue today when my schedule allows and during the summers when I write books. Learning to write took a great deal of time and practice and I often, as an exercise, rewrote the opening paragraphs of articles in the *Reader's Digest* and other magazines. One summer I even attended the Breadloaf Writer's Conference. In addition to my scientific writing, I wrote and published children's stories and articles in various popular magazines—but not before receiving my share of rejection letters.

To me, writing presents some of the same challenges as experimentation. Saying things clearly and concisely, in a logical order and with little ambiguity, is not easy. Good writing is always rewriting. I did, and do, take great pleasure in molding a piece of writing into a shape, finding the ideas, organizing them, and presenting them so that they make sense to others. Finishing a piece of writing is a little bit like getting results well beyond the .05 significance level.

During the period I was doing replication studies, I sent the published reprints to Piaget without receiving a reply. One day, the second year that I was at the University of Denver, I did indeed get a letter from Piaget. It was the most thrilling letter I have ever received. In it, Piaget wrote—in French of course—that he had read my work, liked it, and asked whether I would like to spend a year in Geneva at his Centre d'Epistemologie Genetique. Would I! Although he had some funds, they were not enough to support myself and family. I applied for and received a National Science Foundation Senior Postdoctoral Fellowship to study with Piaget. That summer, with a-year-old son in tow and pet dachshund properly boxed, we left for Switzerland.

Meeting Piaget was quite an event. There was a reception for all of the year's participants. My French was not very good and Piaget said he only knew a few words in English. Later when I became fluent in French, he told me that he had planned to go to England to learn English, but the First World War intervened and he never made the trip. In addition to attending Piaget's seminar and his large lecture class, I also conducted several experiments in the international school. I wanted to see whether children's ability to overcome illusions would be related to the attainment of concrete operations. Indeed, they were and children who had concrete operations were not taken in by the Mueller-Lyer illusion that was drawn in front of them while preoperational children were.

It was while in Geneva that I began to question some aspects of Piagetian theory. The conservation experiment had bothered me for a long time because although it was always described as dealing with a single quantity, in fact two quantities were always compared. I eventually distinguished between *identity* conservation (the transformation of a single quantity) and *equivalence* conservation (the comparison of the two quantities, one of which is transformed). Another study revealed, as the distinction between the two forms of conservation predicted, that identity conservation preceded equivalence conservation.

One evening, after dinner at Piaget's house, he invited me into his study to allow me to ask the questions that most troubled me. One of these had to do with his concept of "reflective abstraction." In my mind the term "abstraction" had always been associated with the empiricist school of psychology, nothing in the mind that was not first in the senses, to which

Piaget was completely opposed. Although he argued that the child was abstracting from his self-created "experiences" the notion of abstraction still seemed foreign to Piaget's position that knowledge is always constructed out of the child's cognitive abilities acting on material from the environment. Toward the end of his career, Piaget began to write about forms of abstraction that did not involve construction.

When I returned to Denver, I wanted to combine a developmental training program with the clinical training program. This was not, for political reasons, possible. At this time John Flavell had left the University of Rochester for Minnesota, and I was offered his position as head of the developmental psychology training program. Once again I had to take off my clinical hat and don an academic one. Fortunately, while in Rochester I was able to serve as a consultant to the family court and so continue my clinical work.

Because I had done so much work in the schools over the years, I became increasingly interested in education. Moreover, my research on perceptual development led me to look at the relationship between perceptual development and reading. So, in addition to continuing the studies of perceptual development, we began looking at reading as well. In several studies, we explored the conceptual development of early readers in comparison with the conceptual development of readers who started at the usual age. In general we found that early readers tended to be more advanced cognitively than nonearly readers. But we also found that early readers had someone in their family who took a special interest in them and read to them, took them to the library, and so on. Early reading is multidetermined.

While at the University of Rochester I began a small school for what I called, "curriculum disabled" children. These were children of average ability who were nonetheless functioning below the academic norm. The school served a dual purpose. In addition to providing a remedial program for the public school children who came to our school for a year, it also provided a laboratory experience for undergraduate students who took this program for course credit. I believe strongly that child development, like chemistry or biology, should come with a laboratory experience. The Mt. Hope School provided that experience.

During this period I continued my research on perceptual development but also undertook other studies. Work on conceptual orientation shifts demonstrated that adolescents were more flexible than children in shifting from one conceptual orientation to another. We also did a study of moral development that demonstrated that at all age levels, children regard personal injury as more serious than property damage. Finally, toward the end of my stay at Rochester we constructed a scale to measure a concept I had written about years earlier, we called it "The Imaginary Audience Scale." Basically, the idea is that in early adolescence young people are able, for the first time, to conceptualize their own thinking. However, they routinely make a common error. They confuse what they are thinking about with what others are thinking about. And since they are thinking mostly about themselves, they assume that others are doing the same thing. This gives rise to an imaginary audience, and makes them sense that they are always being observed and on display. The Imaginary Audience Scale involves items such as "You have been invited to a party and have been looking forward to it for a month. Just as you enter the room you discover a large grease spot on your jeans or skirt. What should you do?" While elementary school children and senior high school young people are little troubled, young adolescents suggest holding their hand over the spot, spilling something on it, or going home for new clothes. This scale is now widely used in studies of adolescence.

After twelve years at the University of Rochester, the grants for my school ran out and the university would not underwrite it until I could get more funds. I felt so strongly about the laboratory experience that I decided to leave Rochester. At that time the chairmanship of the Eliot Pearson Department of Child Study was open. I applied for the position and was accepted. What appealed to me about Eliot Pearson was that there was a children's school, a day care center and even a curriculum lab. In addition the department had people trained in education as well as people trained in child development. It was another setting in which I could combine my academic and applied interests. When I arrived in Boston, I tried to continue my research in the schools, but found that they were saturated with investigators from all the universities in the community. In addition, administrative activities were taking up a lot of my time. I was also becoming increasingly concerned about what was happening to the children in our society. I had been writing about the academic pressures on young children for a number of years, but in educational journals. In 1979, *Psychology Today* asked me to write a piece for them on the topic of pressures on children. An editor at Addison-Wesley saw the article and asked me to do a book on the topic. Although I had already written a number of books for my academic colleagues, I had not written any books for a wider audience.

After a couple of versions that were simply too dry and academic, I suddenly decided to write in a freer way and to use nonacademic materials like newspapers and magazine articles, personal experiences, and the like. For eight weeks I wrote a chapter a week. The result was *The Hurried Child: Growing Up Too Fast Too Soon*. It was an immediate success, and I suddenly was doing media interviews and lecturing extensively across the United States, Canada, and abroad. I quite abruptly moved away from the traditional research paradigm. It seemed to me that we could not study children as if the world was not changing and they were not in jeopardy (my clinical side dies hard).

So beginning in the early 1980s I began a different kind of research. As I traveled, I listened to parents, met with groups of children, read local newspapers, and visited various child settings and schools. In this way, I had a sense of what was happening around the country and published my observations in two additional books, *All Grown Up and No Place to Go* and *Miseducation: Preschoolers at Risk.* I also began to write a monthly column for *Parent's* magazine and continued to publish conceptual articles in the academic field as well as additional books.

After about ten years away from traditional research, I feel the need to collect data. We have designed and are field testing a new scale to assess another concept that I introduced years ago, namely, the personal fable. The new scale has subscales for speciality (positive and negative), invulnerability (positive and negative), and risk taking (positive and negative). Preliminary results are in the right direction and we find that the sense of invulnerability and speciality are greatest in early adolescence and that boys have a more positive sense of speciality and invulnerability than is true for girls.

Finally, in the fall of 1994, Harvard University Press published the most ambitious book that I have ever attempted, *Ties That Stress: The New Family Imbalance.* In that book I try to provide a new discourse for describing the family and the changes that have created a new imbalance such that children and youth are more at risk than they were during the modern era. Children and youth are not well served in contemporary society and we need to work hard to redress the imbalance so that the needs of children and youth are weighted equally with those of parents and adults. I am currently at work trying to apply postmodern concepts to educational reform.

In writing this chapter I have come to appreciate more clearly than ever before, how much the conflict between my theoretical and research drives on the one hand and my commitment to applied issues on the other, has colored my career. I realize, perhaps more fully now than in the past, that I have tried to cross these domains and attempted to translate theory into practice (as in my perceptual studies) and to some extent translate practice into theory (my work on egocentrism). For me, at any rate, this conflict has been a stimulus to my writing, research, and teaching. It has also provided wonderful variety and a great deal of fun to my life as an academic.

*S*UGGESTED READINGS

ELKIND, D. (1967). Egocentrism in adolescence. *Child Development, 38,* 1025–1034.

——— (1975). Perceptual development in children. *American Scientist, 63*(5), 535–541.

——— (1979). *The hurried child: Growing up too fast too soon.* Reading, MA: Addison-Wesley.

——— (1986). Formal education and early childhood education: An essential difference. *Phi Delta Kappan, 67,* 631–636.

——— (1994). *Ties that stress: The new family imbalance,* Cambridge, MA: Harvard University Press.

PIAGET, J., & SZEMINSKA, A. (1952). *The child's conception of number.* New York: Humanities Press.

ROSS D. PARKE (Ph.D., University of Waterloo) is a Professor of Psychology and Director of the Center for Family Studies at the University of California, Riverside. Parke was educated in Canada and previously was affiliated with the universities of Wisconsin and Illinois and the Fels Research Institute. He is a past president of the Developmental Psychology Division of the American Psychological Association. He has been editor of Developmental Psychology and associate editor of Child Development. Professor Parke is author of Fathers and coauthor of Child Psychology (with E. M. Hetherington), now in its fourth edition, and editor of The Family, Review of Child Development Research, Volume 7, and most recently is coeditor of Family-Peer Relationships: Modes of Linkage with Gary Ladd, and Children in Time and Place with Glen Elder and John Modell. His research has focused on early social relationships in infancy and childhood. He is well-known for his early work on the effects of punishment, aggression, and child abuse and for his work on the father's role in infancy and early childhood. His current work focuses on the links between family and peer social systems. He enjoys travel, swimming, art museums, and collecting contemporary prints.

9

Fathers, Play, and Emotion: A Research Odyssey

❖

People differ in how they select research topics. In selecting the topic of the father-infant relationship, I considered several factors. The topic was theoretically important since it would provide a corrective to the field's long-standing focus on the mother-infant relationship as the basis for later social development. In addition, I was attracted to the topic because I viewed it as an issue of social as well as scientific relevance. In the early 1970s there were beginning to be serious reexaminations and reevaluations of women's and men's roles in both the family and the workplace. I hoped that this debate could be placed on a firmer empirical foundation through systematic investigation of the father's role in infancy and early childhood. Moreover, I am attracted to topics that have been neglected or ignored by previous researchers or approached in ways that still leave plenty of room for making a contribution. My assessment of the field in the late 1960s was that the study of fathers was a topic waiting to be addressed in a convincing and useful way. Most of the current research on early social development involved only mothers. To a large degree, the study of fatherhood was assessed indirectly, mainly by the examination of the effects of father absence.

It was more than limitations in prior approaches that led to my interest in the father's role in infancy. The most critical turning point was the shift in theoretical paradigms for the study of early social development. Up until the late 1950s or early 1960s the most influential paradigm had been psychoanalysis, which emphasizes

137

the feeding situation as the critical context for the development of social responsiveness and the mother as the primary object of infant attachment. Although the influence of the original theory waned, the translation of psychoanalytic theory into the drive-reduction language of learning theory extended the life of the assumption of the centrality of both the feeding situation and the mother for early social development. According to this revised view, the mother, as a result of being paired with drive-reducing feeding activity, acquires positive secondary reinforcement properties and consequently is valued by the infant in her own right. Because the father was typically less involved in feeding activities, his role in infant development was minimized. Although the assumptions of drive-reduction theory were replaced by an ethological-evolutionary analysis, John Bowlby similarly presented an attachment theory of early social development that, like his predecessors, stressed the primary role of the mother in the development of social responsiveness. In fact, much of the research in infancy in the 1960s focused on the development of the mother-infant interaction system and specifically on the ways in which the infant's attachment to the mother develops.

The stage was set for a reemergence of the father's role in infancy by the general decline of secondary drive theory. Specifically, Harry Harlow's classic demonstration via surrogate mother experiments that the feeding situation was not the critical context for attachment development, combined with the emerging evidence that social and sensory stimulatory activities were important determinants of infant social development, led to a revival of interest in the role of noncaretaking socializing agents—including fathers. Another landmark event was Rudolph Schaffer and Peggy Emerson's demonstration that human infants showed "attachment" to individuals, such as fathers, who never participated in routine caretaking activities. They found that the amount of social stimulation and responsiveness of the social agent to the infant's behaviors were important determinants of attachment. Fathers, of course, are just as capable of providing these important ingredients for early social development as mothers. Therefore, by the mid-1960s, theoretical shifts finally legitimized the active investigation of the father's role in early infant social development. This revised view of social development was summarized in my earliest writing on infancy when Richard Walters and I wrote a paper on the role of the distance receptors in the development of social responsiveness. These theoretical shifts and the priming of my interest in infant social development through this early writing laid the groundwork for my first excursions into the study of fathers and infants.

EARLY WORK: FATHER-NEWBORN INTERACTION

I began this work when I was at the University of Wisconsin, my first academic job. The observational strategy that we adopted in our earliest studies of fathers and their newborn infants represented a radical departure from the favored experimental approach of the social learning tradition in which I had been trained as a student of Richard Walters. In our first attempt to study fathers and infants, we examined fathers' reactions to baby signals during the first few days of hospital stay after the birth of the baby. I tried an experimental approach initially but it was a disaster. We designed a device which we called the "infant behavior monitor" or IBM. This allowed us to provide fathers and mothers with information about the state of their newborn babies in the nursery. Different colored lights signaled that the baby was fussy, sleeping, or awake and happy. We hoped to examine the eliciting impact of these baby cues on fathers' and mother's wishes to interact with the baby. It didn't work—there were too many people and activities that interfered with the "experiment" and we wisely gave up on our experimental efforts. Moreover, by the early 1970s there were signs of dissatisfaction with the main methodological strategies that characterized the experimental approach. There was an increasing concern about the limited ecological validity of the laboratory paradigm, the sine qua non of the social learning theorist. I was particularly influenced by Alfred Baldwin, who accused child development researchers, particularly social learning theorists, of building a "mythology of childhood" in which a set of effects obtained in the laboratory is assumed to actually take place in naturalistic socialization contexts and be an accurate account of how the child is socialized. As a result there was confusion between necessary and sufficient causality: The laboratory experiments may tell us only that certain variables are potential contributors to the child's development. However, the extent to which these processes are, in fact, necessary or are actual contributors to socialization is left unanswered. In an effort to take these concerns about ecological validity seriously, I embarked on a series of studies that differed in terms of method and design from the previous experimental laboratory work that I had done. My assessment of our knowledge of father behavior with infants indicated that a good deal of descriptive work was a necessary first step before any more process-oriented experimental work was undertaken. This led to my earliest studies of fathers and infants. This work can be characterized in three ways that contrast with the earlier orientation: (1) direct observation, (2) naturalistic context, and (3) nonexperimental approach.

Observations of Fathers and Newborn Infants

A series of observational studies by my associates and me at the University of Wisconsin was conducted in order to describe—in behavioral terms—the nature of the father's interaction with his newborn infant. In the first study we observed the behavior of fathers in the family triad of mother, father, and infant for a ten-minute period in the hospital during the first three days following delivery. This focus on the triad was driven, in part, by necessity. Hospitals in the late 1960s often didn't allow fathers to be alone with their newborns. In fact, it was commonly assumed that fathers were uninterested in babies and incompetent to care for them. A nurse once asked me whether I had insurance in case one of the fathers dropped the baby. Another inquired about our drop rate data for dads. Some things have changed over the past twenty years as men are routinely permitted access to the labor and delivery rooms and contact with their infants.

To the surprise of many people in the late 1960s, the results indicated that fathers were just as involved and nurturant as mothers and that mothers and fathers did not differ on the majority of the measures. For example, in the first study with Sandra O'Leary and Steve West, they touched, looked, vocalized, and kissed their newborn offspring just as often as mothers did. In the second study with Sandra O'Leary, an even more striking picture emerged with the father showing more nurturant behavior in the triadic context than the mother and only slightly less when alone with the baby. There was only a single nurturant behavior—smiling—in which the mother surpassed the father. In fact, fathers tended to hold the infant more than mothers and rock the infant in their arms more than mothers. Fathers, in short, in a context where participation was voluntary, were just as involved as mothers in interaction with their infants.

However, there are a variety of questions that I raised about this study that limited its generality. First, the context was unique, since the mother and father were together, and possibly the higher degree of father-infant interaction observed was due to the supporting presence of the mother. Moreover, the sample of fathers was unique in ways that may have contributed to their high degree of interaction with their infants. Over half the fathers had attended Lamaze childbirth classes, and with one exception, all fathers were present during the delivery of the child. Both of these factors may have increased the fathers' later involvement with their infants. Finally, these fathers were well-educated and middle class, and their high degree of involvement may be more common in middle-class groups. It was simply unclear whether lower-class fathers would show similar degrees of interest and involvement.

To overcome the limitations of the original study, a group of lower-class fathers who neither participated in childbirth classes nor were present during delivery were observed in two contexts: (1) alone with their infant (dyad) and (2) in the presence of the mother (triad). This opportunity arose when I moved to the Fels Research Institute, which was affiliated with the University of Cincinnati College of Medicine, and Cincinatti General Hospital, which served a poor urban population. This study permitted a much more stringent test of father-infant involvement and permitted wider generalization of the previous findings. Moreover, we were becoming aware of the potential importance of contextual factors and this gave us the opportunity to compare father behavior in two settings: dyadic and triadic. As in the earlier study, the father was a very interested and active participant. In fact, in the family triad, the father was more likely to hold and visually attend to the infant than the mother. Nor was the mother's presence necessary for the father's active involvement; the father was an active interactor in both settings—alone and with his wife. However, we discovered that context was a significant modifier of parental behavior. Mothers and, to a lesser extent, fathers reduced the rate of occurrence for most categories of behavior directed toward the baby when they were with their spouses in the family triad as compared to when they were alone with the infants in the dyad. Parental behaviors such as touching, holding, rocking, imitating, and vocalizing decreased when a second adult was present. This reduction of activity in a triadic rather than a dyadic context was later termed a *second-order effect* by Urie Bronfenbrenner.

Let's return to our original story of our early studies of fathers and their newborns. More recently—twenty years later—I have returned to this issue of how parents affect each other's relationship with their infants. With Ashley Bietel, one of my students at Illinois, I examined the impact of maternal gatekeeping on fathers' involvement. Mothers who viewed fathers as biologically less prepared and less interested and skilled did, in fact, have husbands who were less involved in the care of their 3-month-old babies. Our interpretation is that mothers who hold more traditional views of gender roles may subtly put up barriers that may limit further involvement. Although there were few differences in the nurturant and stimulatory activities of the parents, fathers did play a less active role in caretaking activities than mothers. Fathers fed significantly less than mothers when they were alone with the baby. These findings suggest that parental role allocation begins in the earliest days of life.

In Search of Competence

I felt that the lesser degree of father involvement in feeding did not imply that fathers were less competent than mothers to care for newborn infants. Competence can be measured in a variety of ways, but our approach was to measure each parent's sensitivity to infant cues in the feeding context. Our decision to define competence in this way stemmed from our view that feeding was a social as well as an instrumental task and, therefore, it was important to measure the interactive features of feeding. Our thinking was clearly shaped by earlier analyses of feeding that focused on the social and stimulatory functions in contrast to the psychoanalytic and Hullian views of feeding as principally a biologically based drive-reduction system. Success in caretaking, to a large degree, is dependent on the parents' ability to correctly "read" or interpret the infant's behavior so that their own behavior can be regulated in order to achieve some interaction goal. To illustrate, in the feeding context, the aim of the parent is to facilitate the food intake of the infant. The infant, in turn, by a variety of behaviors, such as sucking or coughing, provides the caretaker with feedback concerning the effectiveness and/or ineffectiveness of the parent's current behavior in maintaining the food intake process. In this context, one approach to the competence issue involves an examination of the degree to which the caretaker modifies his or her behavior in response to infant cues. Douglas Swain and I found that the fathers' sensitivity to an auditory distress signal in the feeding context—sneeze, spit up, cough—was just as marked as the mothers'. Fathers, like mothers, adjusted their behavior by momentarily ceasing their feeding activity, looking more closely to check on the infant, and vocalizing to their infant.

Moreover, fathers are just as responsive as mothers to other infant cues, such as vocalizations and mouth movements. Both mothers and fathers increased their rate of positive vocalizations following an infant vocal sound; in addition, both parents touched and looked more closely at the infant after hearing infant vocalizations. These data indicate that fathers and mothers both react to the newborn infant's cues in a contingent and functional manner even though they differ in their specific response patterns.

Further, the amount of milk consumed by the infants with their mothers and fathers was very similar (1.3 versus 1.2 ounces with mothers and fathers, respectively). In short, fathers and mothers are not only similar in their sensitivity but are equally successful in feeding the infant based on the amount of milk consumed by the infant. Invoking a competence/performance distinction, fathers may not necessarily be frequent contributors to infant feeding, but when called upon, they have the competence to execute these tasks effectively.

FROM CAREGIVING TO PLAY: DISTINCTIVE ROLES FOR FATHERS AND MOTHERS

As this early work reveals, fathers and mothers play different roles in the family. Even in our newborn baby studies mothers engaged in caregiving more than fathers. Our subsequent work confirmed the common folklore of our culture; namely, that fathers function largely in the playmate role. Moreover, the styles of play that mothers and fathers engage in differ as well. Here is one example of an early study that documented these stylistic differences.

In collaboration with Thomas Power, a graduate student at Illinois in the early 1980s, I conducted a series of descriptive play studies in both the lab and home settings. Briefly, these studies involved 8- to 13-month-old infants interacting either in a lab playroom or at home with their mothers and fathers. In the lab studies, parents were told that we were "interested in the ways in which mothers and fathers played with their infants"; they were provided with toys and were instructed to use these toys in play with their infants. In the home studies, natural interchanges between parents and infants were videotaped. To illustrate, I will discuss a study in which we observed 8-month-old infants and their parents in our lab playroom.

In addition to our search for mother-father differences in play style, we were also interested in exploring different ways of coding play interaction that would help illuminate the ongoing debate in our own laboratory, as well as in other labs, concerning the choice between molecular and molar levels of coding. By molecular we mean moment-to-moment changes in behavior such as smiling and vocalizing. Molar coding refers to larger units such as play bouts that encompass a variety of molecular exchanges into a coherent whole (e.g., a peek-a-boo game). It was our view that multiple levels of analysis (molar and molecular) are often necessary to describe interaction patterns adequately. Therefore, a primary purpose of this phase of our work was to develop an observational system that could codify molar units of parent-infant play interaction while also providing a detailed description of the context and structure of these interactions. This kind of analysis was employed because of our belief that units of social interaction corresponding to extended sequences of social behaviors might be more meaningful in describing the nature of social interaction than would discrete, molecular units that correspond to the occurrence of individual social behaviors. Without the use of molar units, it is often impossible to specify the behavioral context in which a given behavior occurs. This is important, as the behavioral context often gives the molecular behavior its meaning.

These examples clearly illustrate why larger units are often necessary to capture the meaning of various social interchanges. Therefore, a central problem in coding social interaction is the relationship between levels of analysis; specifically, this requires the articulation of how molecular behaviors relate to specific molar units.

In this study, two units or levels were utilized. Specifically, molar units which we termed *play bouts* were identified; these corresponded to extended sequences of parent and infant behaviors that occurred frequently during the play interactions. In addition, molecular behaviors such as "smile," "touch," and "vocalize" served as the smaller units within these molar bouts and were coded. Thus, through simultaneous use of both molar and molecular units, the structure of the parent-infant play interactions could be described more adequately.

Two sets of findings merit comment. First, we were able to identify several distinctive types of parent-infant interaction bouts. These account for 88 percent of the play interactions observed. Comparison of the structure of the bouts indicated that they fell into three general categories of bouts in which the parent attempted to: (1) focus or otherwise manipulate the infant's attention or level of affective arousal (attention/arousal-regulating bouts), (2) influence or direct the infant's motor exploration of a toy (exploratory bouts), or (3) engage the infant in face-to-face social interaction (communicative bouts).

Moreover, as we had anticipated, the types of bouts revealed sex of parent differences as well. Fathers spent more time in toy touching bouts in which they physically stimulated their infants with the toy. In addition, fathers, especially fathers of boys, spent more time engaged in lifting bouts, which involves lifting, tossing, and shaking the baby. Mothers, on the other hand, engaged in more distance-receptor–oriented activities such as watching bouts. In this type of play bout the parent presents a toy, and makes it salient for the baby by moving or making a noise with the toy. These stylistic differences between mothers and fathers are commonly found.

However, not all fathers show this pattern of robust physical play. Fathers differ in age when they become fathers. Some become fathers in their early to mid-twenties, while others become fathers later in life. Life span theorists stress that the timing of entry into different family roles alters the way these roles are enacted. Recently, Brian Neville, another graduate student at Illinois in the late 1980s, and I explored the impact of timing of the onset of fatherhood on fathers' play style. Rather than being a style that characterizes men at all points in the life span, it was mainly the younger dads who were physically playful. The older fathers—in their thirties—were more likely to stimulate their children verbally and less likely to engage in the tickle and toss routines that are common in younger fathers. As fathers age, they begin to look more like mothers!

What functions do different types of play activities serve? Thomas Power and I suggested that:

> The fact that father-infant play was more physical than mother-infant play (especially for fathers of boys) indicates that fathers may play an important role in their infants' social development. This is suggested because the descriptive analysis of the physical bouts (especially the lifting bouts) showed that these bouts often serve as contexts for a wide range of communicative and affectively charged social interactions between parents and their infants. Therefore, through such interactions fathers may play an important role in facilitating the development of communicative skills and the formation of social relationships. (1982, p. 160)

In short, children are gaining the opportunity to learn to regulate their emotions in the context of play, especially physical play with the father.

Another implication of the physical play between fathers and their infants is suggested by the earlier work of Harry Harlow and his colleagues.

In this research, infant monkeys who were deprived of opportunities for physical interaction with either peer or adult monkeys showed serious deficits in their ability to regulate physical social exchanges, particularly aggression. Therefore, we might expect that early physical play may be important both as an antecedent of later peer-peer play and in the regulation of agonistic and aggressive interactions.

These observational analyses were useful in our research program not only for revealing differences in maternal and paternal interactional styles, but in generating further hypotheses that, in turn, could be evaluated directly.

THE IMPLICATIONS OF PHYSICAL PLAY FOR CHILDREN'S SOCIAL AND EMOTIONAL DEVELOPMENT

The next step in our research program was to address the issue of the impact of these variations in mother and father play styles on children's social behavior. As a developmental psychologist, I talk to parent groups about children's development. And they keep my research on track by asking the tough but important questions. In my case "What difference do fathers make to children's development?" At the time, Kevin Mac-Donald who had studied play in wolves joined me at Illinois as a postdoctoral fellow and we began a series of studies on the effects of father play on children's social and emotional development. To achieve this we set out to explore some of the links between play interaction in the family and social relationships with peers. We moved up the developmental ladder from infancy to preschool-age children in order to be able to adequately capture the nature of children's peer competence. Our first step was to determine whether the stylistic differences in play that we found in infancy were still present between preschoolers and their parents. Unless it was clear that these differences were still evident, this age choice would have been unwise. To find out, we deviated from our usual observational strategy and used a telephone survey approach. The decision to use a telephone survey reflected our conviction that different methodological strategies are useful at different stages of a research project. The survey provided a relatively economical way of evaluating the wisdom of our decision to move up to the preschool-age period. This served as a guide concerning the wisdom of investing the time and resources necessary to carry out an observational study. From our point of view it is not a substitute for doing the actual observational work. We telephoned 390 randomly selected intact families and asked the parents to report the frequency of physical play with their children of different ages (1 year to early adolescence) over the last twenty-four-hour period. Our findings yielded two insights: (1) mothers and fathers continued to differ in expected ways in their frequencies of physical play across age with fathers being more physically playful than mothers, and (2) physical play was still relatively common between parents and their children in the preschool period. This gave us greater confidence in our choice of the preschool-age period as the time period for testing our hypothesis concerning the possible implications of parent-child play for children's social development. Next we conducted a series of observational studies aimed at evaluating this general hypothesis.

Parent-Child Play as a Context for the Development of Peer-Peer Competence

The goal of this research was to provide a detailed description of the ways in which parent-child interaction patterns relate to children's peer-group interaction. It is based on the assumption that face-to-face interaction may provide opportunities to learn, rehearse, and refine social skills that are common to successful social interaction.

This research employed a two-step paradigm. In the first phase, mothers and fathers on separate occasions were videotaped interacting with their 3- to 5-year-old children. In all studies, a ten-minute period in which parents were specifically instructed to play physically with their children is included. Parents were given examples such as tickling, tumbling, or wrestling. Often this physical play period was preceded by a brief free play period in which parents could play *as they normally do*. In the second phase, measures of peer interactive competence were secured. These have varied across studies and include (1) teacher assessments, (2) sociometric ratings, and (3) observations of peer-peer interaction.

In our initial study Kevin and I observed 3- to 5-year-old boys and girls interacting during free and physical play with their mothers and fathers in their homes. A variety of measures of verbal and physical behavior were derived from videotapes of these play interactions, including: number of ten-second periods of parent-child physical play, verbal interchanges, directive statements, and ratings of children's positive affect. As a measure of peer status, teacher rankings of children's popularity were secured.

Our results indicate that popular boys have mothers and fathers who are engaging and elicit positive affect during play, mothers who are verbally stimulating, and fathers who are low in directiveness but physically playful. Girls whose teachers rated them as popular have physically playful and affect-eliciting, but nondirective, fathers and directive mothers.

We followed up this study with another one with Virginia Burks and James Carson, two of my graduate students at Illinois. We utilized a molecular coding strategy and measures of sociometric status which con-

firmed our earlier work and extended our understanding of familial antecedents of peer interactive competence. Popular and rejected 3- to 5-year-
old boys and girls were observed interacting with their mothers and fathers on separate occasions for a ten-minute physical play session in a lab
playroom. Dyads of popular children and their parents had more sus-
tained play bouts and played for a larger proportion of the time than
dyads of rejected children and their parents. Initiation strategies varied by
sociometric status. Popular parent-child dyads used noncoercive initiation
tactics, such as questions, while dyads involving rejected children and their
parents used more coercive tactics such as suggestions and directives.
Similarly, responses to initiations differed across the status groups. Dyads
involving rejected children were more likely to respond negatively than
popular dyads.

Many of the patterns found in parent-child play are similar to patterns
of peer interactions. Peer interactions with popular children generally involve more engaged activities which are of longer duration than interactions involving rejected children. Similarly, popular children tend to be less
controlling and more willing to adapt to the activities of the group, while
rejected children tend to be assertive and directive when they interact with
peers.

From Play to Emotion

In addition to the lessons learned about the appropriate style of initiating
a social interaction, children learn other lessons during playful interaction
with their parents, especially their fathers. They learn two lessons about
emotions. First, they learn to express particular emotions and, second, they
learn a set of emotional skills such as reading and producing emotions that
may be important for regulating social interactions.

Across a number of studies we have found that the quality of affect exhibited during the interaction of popular children and their parents differs
from the quality of affect displayed during the interactions of rejected children and their parents. Consistently, higher levels of positive affect were
found for children in the popular dyads than in the rejected dyads. This is
evident not only for the children, but for the parents as well. In these studies, ratings of positive and negative affect were made by observers either
for the entire period or for selected time-sampled intervals. Little information is available from these studies concerning specific types of emotional displays beyond their negative or positive valence.

In an effort to learn more about the nature of the specific emotional
cues exhibited by children of differing sociometric status and their parents,
James Carson and I recently examined the frequency with which parents
and children use different categories of emotional expression during

parent-child play. To achieve this goal, a new play paradigm was required, because naturally occurring physical play does not permit detailed video-taping of the emotional expressions of the partners. A hand game was developed that was physically arousing and stimulating but required the participants to remain seated during the course of the game. The game required one partner to "grab" the outstretched hands of the other player before the person withdrew his or her hands. Participants were told that they may switch "grabber" and "grabbee" roles at any time. This game is physically stimulating and has been found to be affect-eliciting in previous work done in our lab. Because children and parents remain seated in their chairs, it is possible to obtain high-quality videotape records of their facial expressions through the interaction. To permit face-to-face interaction, the child was placed on an elevated stool, while the parent was seated on a normal-size chair. Data have revealed status differences in the frequency with which some types of emotional cues are displayed during the course of parent-child physical play. Popular children were found to show more happiness and laughter, whereas rejected children showed more neutral affect. Parents of rejected children showed more anger as well as more neutral affect. In addition, the level of anger shown by fathers and their rejected children was positively correlated, which suggested that father and child may be engaged in reciprocal displays of anger. This pattern of positive correlations between anger and either popular or rejected children's anger was not evident for mothers, nor did fathers show this pattern with their popular offspring. Subsequent sequential analyses revealed that fathers and rejected boys were more likely to reciprocate anger during their interactions.

Similar evidence based on home observations of a relationship between peer acceptance and the type of affective expressions exhibited during the course of parent-child interaction comes from a recent study by one of my students, Lisa Boyum. In this work, kindergarten children of varying levels of peer acceptance—as indexed by sociometric ratings by their classmates—and their parents were videotaped at home during a family dinnertime. The affective expressions of mothers, fathers, and children were scored during thirty-second intervals throughout the dinnertime period. Lisa found negative correlations between the level of variety of fathers' negative affect expressions, including anger, disgust, and anxiety, and their kindergarten children's sociometric status. There were no significant correlations found for mothers. Just as James Carson found in laboratory parent-child interaction, paternal negative affect is associated with lower levels of peer acceptance.

These findings concerning the heightened degree of negative affect on the part of parents of less socially accepted children suggest that children may transfer some of the negative affect that is learned in the course of parent-child interaction to interactions with peers; in turn, this may account for the higher level of negative affect and aggression found among some rejected children. Children may be learning to display *specific patterns of emotions* during parent-child interaction that, in turn, may be utilized during peer-peer interaction.

Other evidence also implicates affect as an important factor in the links between family interaction and peer outcomes. Jude Cassidy, Laura Butovsky, Julia Braungart, and I, for example, recently found that parental emotional expressiveness in home contexts—as assessed by Amy Halberstadt's family expressiveness index—is positively associated with children's greater competence with peers as assessed by sociometric and behavior measures. Learning to express emotions, especially in a socially appropriate fashion, may be an important ingredient of emerging social competence. Together these studies underscore the important role of affect in the family-peer relationship.

One set of possible skills that is of relevance to successful peer-peer interaction and may, in part, be acquired in the context of parent-child play especially affectively arousing physical play is the ability to decode others' emotional states and to clearly encode their own emotional signals. In other words, *through physically playful interaction with their parents, especially fathers, children may be learning the social communicative value of their own affective displays as well as how to use these emotional signals to regulate the social behavior of others. In addition, they may learn to accurately decode the social and affective signals of other social partners.*

This speculation has led us to examine a variety of issues concerning the role of emotion in social interaction with others. Our studies suggest that the abilities to recognize and produce emotions and understand the causes and consequences of emotion are important ingredients for social relationships. Our argument is that fathers play a central role in teaching children about these skills, which in turn, may improve their social relationships.

Together, our findings provide support for the importance of parent-child play, especially play with fathers, as a potential context for learning and/or for refining and rehearsing emotional encoding and decoding skills—a set of skills that, in turn, appears to play a role in the successful management of peer social relationships.

REMAINING ISSUES

To sum up, our work began with the father's role in the family and has led us to the exploration of the role of affect and nonverbal communication in social interaction in families and the implications for children's relationships with peers. In recent work Tasha Howe and I are extending our model to explore the role of emotional understanding in abused children's social relationships. That is a new and unfolding story that is just beginning. Like most scientific enterprises you are never sure where you are going to end up, but that sense of discovery is after all what makes the "work" of science so much fun. And my personal journey is far from over as we continue our explorations of how emotions are socialized in family contexts.

Acknowledgments

This research program has been supported by grants from a variety of agencies including the National Institute for Child Health and Human Development, the MacArthur Foundation, and the Spencer Foundation. My most recent work has been supported by the National Science Foundation Grants BNS 8919391 and SBR 9308941. Thanks to many students and collaborators who have contributed so much to this enterprise. Finally my warm appreciation to my wife and colleague, Barbara Tinsley for her insight, support, and caring.

SUGGESTED READINGS

CASSIDY, J., PARKE, R. D., BUTKOVSKY, L., & BRAUNGART, J. M. (1992). Family-peer connections: The role of emotional expressiveness within the family and children's understanding of emotions. *Child Development, 63,* 603–618.

MACDONALD, K., & PARKE, R. D. (1984). Bridging the gap: Parent-child play and peer interactive competence. *Child Development, 55,* 1265–1277.

PARKE, R. D. (1994). Progress, paradigms and unresolved problems: A commentary on recent advances in our understanding of children's emotions. *Merrill Palmer Quarterly, 40,* 157–169.

——— (1996). *Fathers* (rev. ed.). Cambridge, MA: Harvard University Press.

——— (in press). Fathers' role in the family: Determinants and consequences. In M. H. Bornstein (Ed.), *Handbook of parenting* (Vol. 3). Hillsdale, NJ: Erlbaum.

——— BURKS, V. M., CARSON, J. L., & CASSIDY, J. (1992). Family contributions to peer relationships among young children. In R. D. Parke & G. Ladd (Eds.), *Family-peer relationships: Modes of linkage* (pp. 107–134). Hillsdale, NJ: Erlbaum.

——— & LADD, G. (Eds.). (1992). *Family-peer relationships: Modes of linkage.* Hillsdale, NJ: Erlbaum.

——— & TINSLEY, B. R. (1984). Historical and contemporary perspectives on fathering. In K. A. McCluskey & H. W. Reese (Eds.), *Life-span development psychology: Historical and generational effects in life-span human development* (pp. 203–248). New York: Academic Press.

POWER, T. G., & PARKE, R. D. (1982). Play as a context for learning: Lab and home analyses. In L. M. Laosa & I. E. Sigel (Eds.), *Families as learning environments for children* (pp. 147–178). New York: Plenum.

*J*EANNE *B*ROOKS-*G*UNN *(Ph.D., University of Pennsylvania) is the Virginia and Leonard Marx Professor of Child Development at Teachers College, Columbia University. In addition, she directs the Center for Children and Families at Teachers College. She also codirects the Adolescent Study Program at Teachers College and the College of Physicians and Surgeons at Columbia University. She is the President of the Society for Research on Adolescence and is a fellow in the American Psychological Association and the American Psychological Society. She has published 250 articles and 8 books on a variety of topics based on her policy-oriented research on family and community influences upon child and adolescent development, intervention aimed at ameliorating the developmental problems often associated with poverty, and long-term studies of risk and resilience in children and families. She has also conducted extensive research on girls' experiences of the adolescent and young adulthood years.*

10

Unexpected Opportunities: Confessions of an Eclectic Developmentalist

---------- ❖ ----------

E ver since I was a teenager, I liked to do several things at a time. It was not exactly a persistence problem—I could concentrate on something of interest for hours. But, after a while, I needed to think about something else. Often in the middle of one task my thoughts would abruptly switch to another seemingly disparate line. Perhaps it is just an attention span deficit, if the predilection for multitask processing could be subsumed under this rubric. Even now, I use classical music or, on Saturday afternoons, the drone of football games and family members talking as a way to focus on the task at hand—such as writing a research grant. Having an auditory distraction actually helps me focus on one task. The only exception is that hearing my young son's voice breaks all concentration, as I switch into my parental mode. Unfortunately, he now watches college football with my husband, forever ruining all pretense of my being with the family while actually writing.

Perhaps the other characteristic shaping my life as a developmental psychologist is a lifelong struggle with choosing how to allocate my time. My husband teases me that while I can narrow down my choices on a Chinese menu, I still want several selections from column A and column B. Many ideas in developmental psychology so excite me that when certain opportunities have arisen, it has seemed impossible to turn them down. I want to know the answer to a question, or am intrigued about a research paradigm that I have never used, or always wondered how scholars from other disciplines might view children and families, or do not have a clue as to how to conceptualize an issue, or disagree with a colleague about the relative importance of a particular mechanism or set of pathways through which behavior is influenced, or am annoyed with a prevailing and usually narrow viewpoint about a topic. I am thankful to have been blessed with high stamina as well as curiosity, since the former has been critical to my development.

At the same time, I have been extremely fortunate to have collaborated with a diverse and wonderful group of scholars. The opportunities afforded by these colleagues have dictated the course of my research and my development as a behavioral scientist. By not saying no, and in the words of Albert Bandura, making the most of fortuitous circumstances, my research has changed in the most unexpected ways. I have been classified as an infancy researcher, an adolescence scholar, a life-course developmentalist, and a policy and evaluation specialist.

On a more negative note, I have been characterized as too eclectic in my tastes to make a contribution to the field of developmental psychology, and too interested in policy, gender, and equity to ever receive tenure, anywhere! I was advised early on that to study reproductive issues (i.e., menarche, menstruation, pregnancy) would never lead to an academic appointment. And I was told not to write the book *He and She: How Children Develop Their Sex Role Identity* with Wendy Matthews for the same reason. The decision to stay in the Research Division at Educational Testing Service for almost two decades was also seen by many as a big mistake. Several of my postdoctoral students have told me that almost all the career decisions that I made went against what they perceived as the pathway to a career in developmental psychology. I never disagreed with them.

Since I never made five-year plans, never received any counseling on managing a behavioral science career, and did not consider my own life course very carefully, the comments made in the first twelve years after receiving my Ph.D. made me somewhat anxious, but obviously did not result in a drastic life change. I figured that as long as the work was exciting, the collaborations were challenging, and a few journals seemed to be interested enough to accept articles, I would never have a career, but would be happy doing behavioral science.

What follows is a reconstruction of the major events that have been instrumental in shaping my research, as well as the theoretical frameworks that I find useful. As is implied above, I believe that the ability to respond to fortuitous events has been critical to my research, collaborations and worldview. And, like many of the authors in this volume, personal experiences also have shaped my research directions (and continue to influence them).

*I*NFANCY: CAN THE SELF IN THE CONTEXT OF THE OTHER BE STUDIED?

I found developmental psychology as an undergraduate and have never left it. The experience of attending a women's college in the 1960s was pivotal in the decision to enter graduate school, and to choose behavioral science rather than law or medicine. Growing up in a small suburb of a midwestern town offered almost no exemplars of college-educated women with a profession. It was a revelation when I met female professionals, women who loved what they were doing. The women who were professors at Connecticut College became my first role models—and I followed in their footsteps, quite literally. Eleanor Rosch came to Connecticut College fresh from her graduate work at Harvard University, and I loved her developmental course. Particularly intriguing was the developmental work on social cognition and social psychology. Meeting Roger Brown and Larry Kohlberg were highlights of my senior year, as was my thesis on social cognition and moral development in elementary school children done under Rosch's tutelage (my thesis was not terrific, but the experience of doing it was). The interest in how the self is experienced vis-à-vis the other and whether or not males and females have different experiences of the self and the self in relation to others has continued since.

After a year at Harvard University in the Graduate School of Education, prompted by meeting Brown and Kohlberg earlier, I moved to the University of Pennsylvania (I also got married, which did limit options, in that I would have gone to the University of Minnesota or Cornell University if my husband and I had not been trying to do graduate work simultaneously). At the University of Pennsylvania, I had the good fortune of working with Sandra Scarr, albeit briefly, before she moved to the University of Minnesota. Assessing infants for a twin study led to an immersion in the then current infancy research as well as the design of a study looking at mother-infant interactions with same-sex and opposite-sex twins. As Scarr was leaving, Michael Lewis came to Pennsylvania and taught an inspiring course on infant development. He funded the twin study (my husband acted as research assistant), and I spent the summer of 1971 as a graduate intern at Educational Testing Service. Lewis's research was flourishing and exciting, and I was pleased that he took me on as a student. We conducted three studies that summer and fall—one on the effect of time spent in a free play session on infant and maternal behavior, and two on social cognition, specifically the development of young children's ability to respond to strangers and to respond to different dimensions of persons.

The rudimentary social cognition work led to my dissertation topic (numerous copies of the dissertation were stashed in strategic locations in case of fire, flood, or some other disaster; I had lost my favorite undergraduate study to a flooded basement)—the development of early knowledge about the self and other, as studied through self-recognition tasks, differentiation of visual dimensions of personhood (gender, age, relationship), early language use attached to social cognition dimensions, and links between the self, emotion, and relationships with others. I have continued to study the interface between self and others ever since, albeit with different age groups and with different questions.

BECOMING A WOMAN: DISCONNECTIONS BETWEEN SELF AND OTHER?

Sometime in the middle of the 1970s while at Educational Testing Service, I met Diane Ruble. In sharing teaching experiences (I was teaching a psychology of women course in the New Women's Studies Program at the University of Pennsylvania and she was teaching a similar course at Princeton University), we discovered that we had similar very annoyed reactions to the writings on women's biology. Our primary focus was on menarche and menstruation, and the fact that the research did not mirror our experiences, nor those of our female students vis-à-vis the universality, the number, or the intensity of cyclic monthly changes. Complaining was only the beginning—we wrote two theoretical and review articles on two reproductive transitions—menarche and menopause, and attended what turned out to be a seminal conference at Smith College on female development run by Jacqueline Eccles. We also conducted a series of research studies on the salience and meaning of reproductive events, especially in terms of definitions of self in the context of reproductive maturity.

Methodological Considerations

In designing and carrying out these studies on menarche, puberty, and transitions into and out of adolescence, many decisions had to be made. Some of the methodological and recruitment issues that were, in my opinion, critical to the research questions under investigation are briefly presented.

Recruitment. Obtaining samples of girls for pubertal studies is extremely difficult. Because our objective has been to chart the course of girls' development, we did not wish to use clinic or medical practice "convenience" samples, but to contact girls within communities. Schools were the obvious choice for young adolescents. But many school administrators were wary about asking questions on pubertal development. The concerns seem to stem from adults' own discomfort discussing puberty and from their belief that teenagers do not discuss such changes. In our menarche studies, conducted in the mid-1970s, principals in two central New Jersey school districts approved our protocol (with two other school districts declining our invitation). To augment the sample, we finally turned to the Central New Jersey Girl Scouts, whose support and enthusiasm were deeply appreciated. Although not the "perfect" sample in terms of representativeness, no discernible differences surfaced between the school and Girl Scout samples.

In the 1980s, we expanded our protocol to include questions on breast and pubic hair development, the growth and weight spurt, feelings about such pubertal changes, and others' responses to such changes. In addition, we needed Tanner ratings of physical development (a well-standardized quantitative assessment of physical development) completed. It was clear that these topics were considered far more sensitive than menarche and the attitudes and feelings associated with it. Indeed, no one even questioned the appropriateness of asking about menarche (either adult attitudes had changed or, given the context, menarche was considered the least sensitive pubertal event in our protocol). Our strategy was as follows: We emphasized the more medically oriented aspects of our research program (made possible by my collaboration with a gynecologist/reproductive endocrinologist and the questions we were asking); provided some (parental) feedback as to the existence of several problems if they occurred (i.e., scoliosis, eating disorders); asked for staff and teacher input in designing questionnaires; gave lecture series at the schools; conducted a summer intern program for seniors from participating schools; provided research reprints to parents and their daughters; and generally made ourselves available to staff at participating schools. We have found that our collaboration with the schools has enriched our research, given the thoughtful comments and suggestions made by the staff.

Several athlete samples were seen to address specific research questions concerning the antecedents and consequences of variations in maturational timing, the emergence of eating problems, and the goodness of fit between a girl's developing body and the athletic context that she has chosen. Most of our early work focused on ballet dancers, but later we included figure skaters and swimmers. Much of this work was conducted with dancers and figure skaters themselves, who were interested in developmental and clinical psychology. We have had dancers in national companies collaborating (and coauthoring papers) with us, as well as graduate students who had stopped dancing because of bone injuries, scoliosis, eating problems, early maturation—all the topics we studied!

Design. The design of the menarche studies was fairly straightforward. In order to examine, on a broad scale, developmental differences in symptom reports and expectations and in attitudes and feelings associated with menarche, a large cross-sectional study was conducted, including late elementary school, junior high, senior high, and college students. To examine change, we also employed longitudinal designs.

Girls' reactions. Given that many adults find puberty to be a sensitive topic, one might expect a similar reluctance in the girls themselves and in their mothers. In the early adolescent studies, we had no one ask to have questions skipped in interviews and very few omitted items on the self-report questionnaire. From a clinical perspective, up to 15 percent of the girls were a bit embarrassed in the Tanner staging examination (quantitative assessment of their physical development). At the same time, they also were pleased when they completed the examination and interview, as many seemed to see it as a major milestone (in that such physical examinations are a part of recommended medical practice). In personal interviews, many girls seemed eager to share their pubertal experiences; given the pervasiveness of such conversations with peers and the meagerness of such talks with parents, having an interested adult woman who is not judgmental may be comforting.

Measurement. Self-reports were used in the cross-sectional studies, augmented with maternal reports for specific topics. For example, several of the schools did not want us to give the girls schematic drawings of the Tanner stages to rate, but felt comfortable having the mothers fill out the Tanner schematics for their daughters (however, girls were asked how much they had developed with regard to breasts, hair, and growth, using a four-point scale for each). We followed up the cross-sectional study with a smaller validity study to see how accurate mothers actually were. Mothers also provided information on their own physical development and reactions to their daughters' development.

In the longitudinal studies, we included structured and semistructured interviews to augment the self-report questionnaires. This has proven to be invaluable for understanding girls' reactions to pubertal events. And we have videotaped mothers and daughters discussing changes, providing a window into family interchanges.

Menarche

In an effort to understand how complicated social, psychological, and physiological factors interacted to influence symptom perceptions, Ruble and I turned to the adolescent experience of menarche as an exemplar. Menarche became the focus of study because it is a discrete event whose experience could be interpreted in terms of previous socialization instead of direct experience. We expected that information gleaned from media sources, the mother, and girlfriends would all be important in explaining the meaning of menarche to individual girls. A series of studies was conducted comparing premenarcheal and postmenarcheal girls with respect to menstrual symptom reports, sources of information about menstruation, and the psychological significance of menarche. Additionally, we examined changes in self-definitions occurring at the time of menarche, specifically aspects related to body image and self-consciousness. Finally, mothers' attitudes about menstruation and menstrual symptoms were examined in an effort to see whether these were associated with the experiences of their daughters.

Reading the literature on menarche was a particularly pivotal experience. In the early 1970s, menarche was perceived as a normative crisis for the pubertal girl (only much later did I start thinking of the effect of menarche on the mother as well as on the daughter). The crisis model was based on retrospective reports of adults' recollections of their pubertal experience, rather than on prospective studies of girls themselves. Additionally, the focus was on negative consequences, not normative aspects, in a sense contradicting the appellation "normative crisis." Perhaps this reflected the psychodynamic, medical, and adult patient perspectives of most of the extant literature. As in the menstrual literature, the primary focus on negative aspects of menarche seemed puzzling. After all, it was an indication of becoming an adult female. Was this necessarily negative? Did all girls resist growing up? Weren't there self-enhancing aspects of becoming mature? We reframed the crisis model into an examination of the *meaning* of menarche to girls, and into a normative transition rather than on a normative crisis framework.

Another set of questions arose for me. Why was puberty seen as negative for girls, but no mention of a similar crisis was found for boys, who, after all, also experience puberty? For boys, puberty was seen as expanding role possibilities into the realm of work and achievement; for girls, roles were believed to be truncated. In Nancy Chodorow's terms, boys are characterized "doing" and girls "being." These distinctions, while believed to exist prior to puberty due to socialization, were thought to become pronounced at puberty, when gender-role divisions became apparent (because of reproductive differences). However, little research existed to substantiate or refute these claims. Does gender intensification occur at puberty, and do girls really redefine themselves primarily in terms of reproductive roles while boys do not? If so, what are the processes underlying such self-definitional changes and how do parents and peers contribute to this redefinition? Much of my subsequent research addresses these sets of questions in one way or another.

Returning to the question of normative crisis, our literature review indicated that the adult psychoanalytic literature most often characterized menarche as anxiety-producing and distressing. Our research, along with that of others, examined how traumatic menarche actually is for girls, rather than relying on retrospective reports from clinical adult samples. Generally, these studies suggest that girls experience an array of feelings— positive, negative, and ambivalent. When we interviewed girls about how they felt right after menarche occurred (within two to three months), 20 percent gave only positive, 20 percent only negative, and 20 percent mixed emotions such as "felt same" or "felt funny." The others experienced a combination of positive and negative feelings. About 60 percent were somewhat scared or upset, although the intensity of these feelings was mild.

Possible ambivalence about menarche also was demonstrated by the fact that, in our longitudinal study, girls were reluctant to tell others for about three to six months after the event that they had begun to menstruate. What we termed the "secretive phase" may indicate either ambivalence, self-consciousness, or both. Indeed, heightened awareness of the body and self-consciousness increase after menarche.

With regard to our initial questions about the emergence of menstrual-related beliefs, we found that girls construct a definition of the menstrual experience from various sources of information, of which direct knowledge of symptoms is only one. Girls' symptom reports are correlated with their own premenarcheal expectations, suggesting that the direct experience of menstruation is interpreted in terms of previously formed expectations. Moreover, individual differences in symptom reports can be predicted from the context in which self-definitions are initially formed. Negative reports of symptoms in postmenarcheal seventh- to twelfth-grade girls are associated with being unprepared for menarche, being early to mature, and receiving information from sources perceived as negative. The definitions established during menarche may be difficult to change; for example, subsequent menstrual experiences are perceived in terms of, and may be instituted by, this definition. Thus, perceptions of and information received about the menstrual experience during menarche and shortly thereafter may have a long-lasting impact, as we saw in our eleventh- and twelfth-grade girls.

In this research, our focus on socialization led to the discovery that comfort discussing menarche was lowest at early adolescence, compared to later adolescence phases. While almost all girls do discuss menarche with their mothers, the content seems focused on practical concerns and symptoms, not feelings. Girls may be more likely to discuss feelings about menarche with girlfriends, a possible concomitant of the rise in same-sex friendships reported for girls during early adolescence. Later on, I returned more specifically to the issue of parent-daughter communication about and during puberty.

Puberty

Given these findings about informational sources and how prepared girls felt for menarche, I initiated discussions with the staff at the Johnson & Johnson Company regarding pubertal health education. It was clear that appropriate and timely information seemed to lessen a girl's negative perception about menarche and menstruation. The vast majority of American girls received such information from pamphlets and films used in health classes and produced by the feminine products industry. The Johnson & Johnson Company funded a conference for those few researchers who were studying menarche. At the conclusion of the conference, it was clear to me (1) that pubertal events other than menarche are imbued with psychological meaning, (2) that these events may also alter self-definitions and expectancies, and (3) that they were virtually overlooked in almost all the developmental research. Indeed, there almost seemed to be a taboo against discussing puberty outside of medical and health education circles. Johnson & Johnson funded a series of seminal conferences on girls at puberty, and used the information to alter their educational materials for girls, as well as to revise their much-used film on menarche.

At the same time, the other highly salient and quite fortuitous event was the introduction of Michelle Warren and me by Louis Cooper, chief of pediatrics at St. Luke's–Roosevelt Hospital Center. As Cooper suspected, Warren, a reproductive endocrinologist at Columbia University, and I had overlapping interests. Here was a highly respected physician who had been studying behavior as well as physical consequences of hormonal dysfunction and was as excited to conduct biobehavioral collaborative research as I was. We set about preparing a research agenda and obtaining funds to initiate it, an endeavor that took almost two years (lest anyone think that new collaborations and projects are quick, all of my new initiatives have taken several years to get off the ground). By 1983 we began the Adolescent Study Program.

The overarching themes of this research program, as it evolved in the first two years, had to do with (1) the biological (hormone changes and the development of secondary sexual characteristics) and environmental contributions to adolescent girls' behavior, (2) the antecedents and consequences of delayed puberty, (3) the emergence of specific forms of developmental psychopathology during adolescence, (4) the formation of gender identity and changes in self-definition, and (5) the meaning and salience of pubertal events. Girls across the adolescent years were drawn both from school populations as well as populations known to have a high incidence of delayed puberty, with ballet dancers as a primary "clinical" comparison group. We initially used the ballet students to examine contextual features influencing behavior. It was a short step to enlarging this paradigm to study (1) the reproductive and social events simultaneously, (2) the interaction of person and environmental characteristics, and (3) the goodness of fit between a child's physical characteristics and aspirations.

Meaning of pubertal events to girls and their parents. In examining the meaning of pubertal events other than menarche, we found that the onset of breast development was associated with enhanced peer relationships, behavioral adjustment, and positive body image, but pubic hair development was not. The reasons for such findings had not been studied previously. However, we hypothesized that these findings were due in part to the social stimulus value of pubertal change to others as well as to the self. Since breast growth is a normative event signaling the onset of maturity, the exhibition of signs of "adulthood" may confer enhanced status to young adolescents. Comparisons with others, while probably covert, are common; fifth- to seventh-grade girls had no difficulty categorizing classmates with regard to their stage of pubertal development. If the onset of puberty is valued by the peer group, which we were positing, physical comparisons that girls make are akin to the processes discussed in the social cognitive and social comparison literature. Girls may initiate more frequent and more positive contacts and will elicit more peer interaction during the onset of pubertal development.

Goodness of fit between physical characteristics and expectations. The importance of contextual features (in this case, early maturation and being unprepared for menarche) upon a girl's self-definition regarding menstruation and body image in the early menarche studies led to a consideration of other contextual features in the Adolescent Study Program.

We wished to see whether the demands of a specific context and individual characteristics predisposed a girl to adapt to that context. In one of our studies we explored how maturation timing relates to adaptation within different social contexts. Specifically, girls in dance company schools were compared with girls in nondance schools in order to examine the goodness of fit between the requirements of a particular social context and a person's physical and behavioral characteristics. With respect to dancers, the demands are clear: Maintain a low body weight in order to conform to professional standards and devote a great deal of time to practice. With regard to maturation, dancers are more likely to be late maturers than are nondancers. Timing of maturation was expected to affect girls in the two contexts differently. Being a late maturer may be particularly advantageous for dancers, even though it is not always so for nondancers. Because dancers are more likely to be late maturers than are girls not participating in dance, being late may be normative in the dance world. In addition, being late may be a positive attribute: Late maturing dancers may be more likely to enter national companies after adolescence than are on-time maturers.

The dance students weighed less and were leaner than the comparison sample and had higher eating problem and lower family relationship scores. The on-time dancers had higher psychopathology, perfection, and bulimia scores, and lower body-image scores than did the later maturing dancers. These findings suggest that the requirements of a particular social context and a person's physical and behavioral characteristics must be considered when interpreting timing effects. Also, they raised questions as to how interactions with parents and peers may be affected by context and maturational timing.

Interaction between environment and physical characteristics. The research just discussed was based on premises about the "goodness of fit," defined as the consequences of certain demands on body size upon girls' adaptation, especially when these demands were difficult to maintain (i.e., caloric expenditure was not high) or were not matched to body type (i.e., being an early maturer when a sport favors the body build associated with late maturation). We broadened this perspective following Urie Bronfenbrenner's view that development is a function of the interaction of person and environmental characteristics.

If behavioral correlates of puberty are studied in different environmental contexts, then it is possible to investigate physical characteristic–environment interactions in at least three ways. First, personal characteristics may influence behavior differently depending on the environment in which they occur, given differences in expectations or demands that characterize a particular social milieu. An example are the findings of Roberta Simmons and Dale Blyth that being an early maturing sixth-grade girl influences body image as a function of attendance at an elementary or middle school. Second, an individual who possesses certain physical characteristics may actively seek or reject a certain social milieu. The work by David Magnusson and his colleagues in Sweden is a case in point. While early maturing girls were more likely to drink and to be sexually active than later maturers, the effect was due to those early maturing girls who had older friends, a phenomenon that was more prevalent in the early than later maturers. Presumably, early maturers actively sought, or were sought by, older adolescents as friends.

Finally, pubertal children may have chosen environmental contexts that become inappropriate as their bodies grow (in contradistinction to the first example where contexts are not actively chosen; i.e., grade in which the transition to middle school occurs). In this instance, the match between individual and environment is altered as a function of changes beyond the control of the individual. The most obvious mismatches involve activities in which body shape and size are critical, as in athletics or modeling. An example is the influence of context and maturation upon dating in seventh-to ninth-grade girls, some of whom were enrolled in national ballet company schools and some who were not. Dating was not related to menarcheal status in nondancers, but was in dancers as premenarcheal dancers dated less than postmenarcheal dancers. It was hypothesized that in a context such as dancing that negatively values a particular characteristic, such as pubertal growth, individuals who develop that characteristic may be more affected than similar individuals who are in a context that does not negatively value a particular characteristic. We wondered whether contexts other than school, peer group, and athletic endeavor, specifically those having to do with family functioning, might also influence behavior differently as a function of puberty. Later on, we had the opportunity to examine this question.

ADOLESCENTS AS DAUGHTERS
Parental Communication Patterns and the Pubertal Experience

The first direct foray into how puberty may influence perceptions of one's parents came from the menarche studies, where we were interested in information transmission and socialization. Girls were more uncomfortable discussing menarche during early adolescence compared to middle and late adolescence and were most uneasy when talking to their fathers. Very few girls, for example, told their fathers about their menarche. About one-half of the girls reported that their mothers told their fathers immediately following menarche. This family openness, as I termed it, may have positive value. Eleventh- and twelfth-grade girls who reported their fathers knew about their menarche early (usually from the mother) had less negative attitudes about their bodies and menstruation than girls whose fathers were reported as not knowing.

These findings, while in retrospect not surprising, led me to speculate on how mothers, fathers, and daughters as a unit might construct the meaning of pubertal events. For example, when girls are asked if they have been teased about breast growth, the most frequently mentioned teasers are parents and the primary feeling reported is anger. We decided to explore girls' perceptions of interactions by using a TAT format. Girls were asked to tell stories about a picture of an adult woman showing a girl and an adult male a bra that she has just taken out of a shopping bag. Fifth- to ninth-grade girls' responses to this picture, the disclosure of the buying of a bra to the father, reflect negative affect and discomfort. Embarrassment about the father's presence and anger at the mother for showing the bra to the father are common. Interestingly, in these stories, the causes of the uneasiness are attributed to the parent, particularly the mother, who is not perceived as being sensitive to the girl's desire for secrecy.

It is my premise that early adolescent girls' communication patterns are altered in large part because of pubertal changes and their feelings about them. Whether this is the stimulus for decreased sharing of other experiences with the mother via self-definitional changes, enhanced realization of separateness from parents in a physical sense, inability to consider one's own sexuality and parental sexuality simultaneously, or other factors, withholding of feelings from parents does not seem to increase thereafter. Thus, discomfort in discussing certain issues could exacerbate distancing and possibly conflict. Indeed, Raymond Montemayor reports that the most frequent response to parent-young adolescent conflict is *not* discussion, but walking away from the situation.

Parental Relationships and Their Effect on Depressive Affect during Puberty

Enlarging upon the theme of parental communication patterns and focusing on the timing and sequencing of events, we have studied the possible effects of social and biological events upon the expression of depressive affect in 120 early adolescent girls. The occurrence of positive and negative events in the family, with peers, and at school was considered separately. Negative family and school events, but not negative friend events, were correlated with depressive affect. Effects of familial disruption upon behavior are well documented. Pubertal changes had no direct effect on problem behavior, but had a mediated effect. Less physically developed girls had lower depressive affect scores than more physically developed girls; however, this was true only in the absence of negative family life events. When undesirable events occurred, the association between physical status and problems was altered; one might go so far as to characterize pubertal growth as a protective factor in the face of negative family events.

Why might this be the case? Although speculative, it is possible that physical maturity, with its high social stimulus value, brings increased internal resources to manage undesirable events. For example, the increases in social maturity, peer prestige, self-esteem, and awareness of the body associated with menarche and breast development may enhance self-definitions in some as of yet unspecified way. At the same time, pubertal growth has high social stimulus value. More physically mature girls may elicit more freedom from parents (and probably request it from them), making it more likely that they will engage in dating, spend more time with girlfriends, and "distance" themselves from their parents. Friends also may respond to the girl's more mature body: Boys may be more likely to ask them out on dates and girls may gravitate toward more mature girlfriends. Finally, friendships may become more intimate during puberty as girls discuss these developments with their best friends. These changes may result in more independence, especially from the family, which may be particularly protective if stressful events involve the family. In brief, a more mature body may facilitate the growth of internal coping skills as well as offer an "arena of comfort" as described by Rhea Simmons and her colleagues. In our study, peers may act as such an arena, being a refuge from stressful events occurring in the family or in school. This aforementioned premise is partially confirmed by the finding that the adolescent's vulnerability to negative events is partially offset by the availability of resources, in this case positive and supportive relationships with peers. Having one arena of comfort may make it easier to negotiate the other anticipated and unanticipated life changes occurring during early adolescence, especially those occurring within the family.

Vulnerability to negative events may in part be due to the unavailability of personal and social resources needed. Indeed, less developed girls may have fewer resources, or may perceive their resources differently. In support of this possibility, premenarcheal girls with less positive parent relationships had higher depressive affect scores than premenarcheal girls with more positive relationships. This association is independent of the occurrence of negative and positive family events, making it unlikely that the relation is due to girls with less positive parent relationships having had more negative events occur. Such findings support the premise that social support may buffer the young person from untoward consequences of the occurrence of negative life events, in this case events occurring in the family.

Parental Relationships and Eating Problems

We also examined the effects of pubertal events and parental relationships upon eating problems. Eating problems are most likely to emerge at the time of the pubertal transition, during the passage toward young adulthood. Ilona Attie and I have hypothesized that the onset of puberty may herald sometimes overwhelming developmental challenges for the vulnerable adolescent, who may have difficulty coping with all the simultaneous changes of early adolescence. One possible factor predisposing the young adolescent toward eating problems is family functioning. Adolescents with eating disorders often live in families characterized by enmeshment, overprotectiveness, rigidity, lack of conflict resolution, and unresolved marital conflict. However, in the absence of controlled prospective and comparative studies of family process, it is difficult to identify predisposing factors, and to distinguish these from those which ensue following the onset of these disorders. Attie's excellent follow-up of about 300 girls from middle to senior high school, gives a partial answer to this question, since any family dysfunction is not due to the existence of a clinical disorder in this school-based sample. In keeping with the clinical literature just cited, low scores on family cohesion, expressiveness, and organization, as reported by mothers, were related to adolescents' self-reported dieting and binging behavior.

Reproductive Events as They Influence Daughter-Mother Relationships

These intriguing findings led me to consider (1) possible changes in family relationships occurring at the time of early adolescence, (2) how such changes might manifest themselves, and (3) what effects upon girls' psychological adaptation such changes might have.

A quick reading of the literature leaves no doubt that parent-child relationships during early adolescence are often characterized as conflictual or as becoming more distant. While relational change has been characterized in terms of renegotiation from unilateral authority to mutuality, or from a more vertical to a more horizontal relationship, research has focused on the distancing of the parent and child from one another and increases in conflict and assertiveness. Only recently has the nature of the conflict been studied as a window onto the salient developmental tasks and the type of renegotiation required as well as the social cognitive processes underlying renegotiations.

Although research has documented the nature of early adolescent relationships, discussion is sparse on actual developmental changes and on the processes underlying such changes. We have begun to think about using a framework stressing the possibility that parent-daughter relationships may be influenced not only by changes in the child (i.e., pubertal events, subsequent self-definitional changes), but that the familial setting or parents themselves also change during adolescence. The larger question being asked has to do with how girls' gender identity formation is influenced by interactions with the mother and how mothers encourage or discourage individuation. These issues are particularly important since the developmental course of girls may be different than boys, with the former being relationally focused and less autonomous.

We have looked at the conflict in order to ask questions about how girls individuate from their mothers and how mothers respond to their development task of promoting individuation and gender-identity development. We found that girls tend to be critical of their mothers and use this criticality as an early means of individuating from her. Ruthellen Josselson describes this early practicing phase of individuation as one in which preadolescents assert a willful autonomy and oppose parental authority while still being dependent on the parent. As such, perhaps this kind of criticality is experienced by mothers as somewhat superficial and as not threatening their control. Mothers of premenarcheal girls exhibit a high level of other-centered recognition of their daughters and do not appear to withhold their recognition when daughters are oppositional.

The research showed evidence of greater conflict between mothers and postmenarcheal seventh-grade daughters, despite the fact that daughters in this phase significantly decrease their criticality of the mother. Daughters in this group begin to claim more autonomy in the sphere of friends and academics and increase their passive resistance to the mother, while mothers increase in projective control and decrease in other-centered recognition of their daughters. This overall pattern may fit descriptively the portrait of ambivalence that clinicians paint of adolescents in the early rapprochement phase. In this phase, as girls demand more autonomy and resist maternal control, their renewed need for the mother's recognition and support may explain their decrease in criticality of the mother. In contrast to premenarcheal girls, these postmenarcheal girls may be perceived by their mothers as beginning to effect their first real separation from the mother. Thus, they may evoke in mothers the tendency to reinforce an undifferentiated closeness by exerting projective control and decreasing the recognition that is so important for daughters in this early phase of rapprochement.

The shift in mothers toward greater projective control of daughters following menarche supports Chodorow's thesis that mothers act to restrict their daughter's individuation in order to maintain the closeness and continuity of the relationship. Thus, maternal projection possibly may be a highly effective form of control of girls. This finding supports Margaret Mahler's and Ruthellen Josselson's positions that argue for the importance of maternal support of adolescent autonomy strivings in order for individuation to be possible.

ADOLESCENTS AS MOTHERS

Adding a focus on pregnancy and parenthood occurred as I began thinking of adolescents both as mothers and daughters and in adopting a more family systems approach. These perspectives originated with the Baltimore Study of Teenage Parenthood. Originally, the Baltimore study was an evaluation of a comprehensive prenatal care program for pregnant adolescents who were primarily black lower- and working-class young women. Frank Furstenberg conducted interviews with both the adolescents and their mothers during the adolescents' pregnancies in 1967. Follow-up interviews were conducted several times over the next five years on a wide range of sexual, social, and family issues. When the five-year follow-up was concluded in 1972, no plans were made for any further contact. However, a decade later, when the children of the teenage mothers began to reach adolescence, the idea of seeing the families again was seriously entertained. In 1983 to 1984, the original teenage mothers and their children were interviewed. Three major findings emerged from the seventeen-year follow-up study: (1) significant variability and improvement in the life circumstances of the original teen mothers, (2) strikingly poor outcomes of their adolescent children, and (3) clear links between changes in the mothers' life courses and the developmental trajectories of their children.

Mothers' Life Course

The results of the five-year follow-up in 1972 suggested that a certain amount of variation in the life courses of the women would be evident in the seventeen-year follow-up. However, the extent of diversity and the degree of improvement seen over time between 1972 and 1984 were totally unexpected. What accounted for the diversity among the Generation II mothers' adaptation to early childbearing? Characteristics of both the teens' families of origin and of the teens themselves were significant predictors of economic success in later life. The important familial factors were educational status of the teenagers' parents, family of origin's size, and welfare status. Teens whose parents had higher levels of education, smaller family sizes, and no welfare assistance were more likely to succeed as adults. In contrast, other familial factors, such as teenagers' mothers' marital or employment status or age, did not relate to the teenagers' long-term outcome.

Three characteristics of the teens themselves predicted economic success in later life: educational attainment and ambition, family size, and marital status. Whether or not the adolescent had repeated a grade by the time of the pregnancy was a powerful determinant of her future economic position. Her educational ambitions also were predictive of later economic outcome, independent of parental education and her own grade repetition.

Both the probability of receiving welfare and of achieving economic security were strongly influenced by the number of additional births that occurred in the five-year period after the birth of the study child. An important additional pathway away from economic dependency for the teen mother was stable marriage. Those women who were married at the time of the five-year follow-up were much more likely to have succeeded economically, presumably because of their husbands' incomes, than those who had never married. In contrast, women who remained with their families of origin for at least five years after their first child was born were less likely to be economically secure and more likely to be on welfare in adulthood. Thus, while living with one's parents for the first year or two promoted school attendance and employment, such an arrangement over the long-term posed obstacles to independence and self-sufficiency in adulthood.

Children's Life Course

The long-term costs of teenage motherhood to the women were considerably less than expected, even given the diversity of outcomes seen at the five-year follow-up. However, the costs to the children were more than we had expected. The complexities of the mothers' lives, as they juggled child care, schooling, jobs, and relationships with men, were mirrored in potentially significant events to their children. One-third of the children had been separated from their mothers at least once for two months or more (excluding summer vacations) during their lives. Many children (40 percent) had another adult as primary caretaker for them during early childhood, as their mothers finished school or worked. The high rate of marital dissolution, the relatively large number of women who never married, and the frequency of short-term cohabitation relationships translated into the fleeting and unpredictable presence of adult men for the children. With the exception of the 9 percent who had never lived with an adult male (father, stepfather, or boyfriend), all of the children had spent some time with a male figure in the household. However, only a handful (16 percent) were living with the biological father as teenagers.

Regarding the academic status of the teenagers, they were characterized by what may only be described as massive school failure. Half the sample had repeated at least one grade during their school career—59 percent of the males and 39 percent of the females. Perhaps the greatest concern of the public and policy makers alike is the spector of "children of children" perpetuating the cycle of early childbearing. In the Baltimore study, 78 percent of the teens were sexually active, with higher rates for boys than girls (84 versus 69 percent). In brief, the mothers' struggle to avoid poverty levied a cost on their children, as measured by academic achievement and management of sexuality. The amount of time the teenage mother had available, the need for complex child care arrangements, the absence of the father, lowered educational attainment, and in some cases, reduced economic circumstances, all are part of the adolescent mothers' experience. Even with the help of family and friends in child rearing, these obstacles could not be totally overcome.

CONCLUSION

I continue to alter and hope to broaden my perspective on how to study the experience of the adolescent in the throes of physical and reproductive growth, of the emergence of initiation of sexual behavior, of the control of fertility, and, sometimes, of the onset of parenthood. How the girls make sense of these events, how they incorporate them into their self-definition as adults (and women), and how they alter their relationships with others are my current primary focus. Additionally, I am interested in (1) how others, especially parents and peers, perceive and respond to these events; (2) what relational changes occur as a consequence of self- and other perspectives; and (3) whether such changes translate into particular modes of adaptation, with a particular interest in those associated with gender-role identity. While not always neat and tidy, my research has always been compelling, fascinating, and fun.

Acknowledgments

The writing of this chapter was supported by all those who have funded my research over the last two decades. I am grateful for their support. Most recent funding has been provided by the National Institutes of Health, the March of Dimes Foundation, the Foundation for Child Development, the W. T. Grant Foundation, The Robert Wood Johnson Foundation, and the Russell Sage Foundation. I would like to thank my two academic homes for being so hospitable—Educational Testing Service and Teachers College, Columbia University. Many thanks to all my collaborators. A special thanks to my office-mate, Pamela Klebanov, who wondered how this piece would end; to my administrative assistant and pal, Rosemary Deibler, who thinks this piece will never end; and to my husband, Robert Gunn, who thinks that this piece is totally inaccurate, missing the more humorous aspects of life as a developmental psychologist.

Portions of this chapter were adapted from the author's chapter "Adolescents as daughters and mothers: A developmental perspective" in I.E. Sigel and G.H. Brody (Eds.), *Methods of family research: Biographies of research projects (Vol. 1: Normal families)*, pp. 213–248, by permission of Lawrence Erlbaum Associates, copyright © 1990.

SUGGESTED READINGS

BROOKS-GUNN, J. (1991). How stressful is the transition to adolescence in girls? In M. E. Colten and S. Gore (Eds.), *Adolescent stress: Causes and consequences* (pp. 131–149). Hawthorne, NY: Aldine de Gruyter.

———— & CHASE-LANSDALE, P. L. (in press). Adolescent parenthood. In M. Bornstein (Ed.), *Handbook of parenting.* Hillsdale, NJ: Erlbaum.

———— & FURSTENBERG, F. F., JR. (1989). Adolescent sexual behavior. *American Psychologist, 44*(2), 249–257.

———— & PETERSEN, A. C. (Eds.). (1983). *Girls at puberty: Biological and psychological perspective.* New York: Plenum Press.

———— & REITER, E. O. (1990). The role of pubertal processes in the early adolescent transition. In S. Feldman and G. Elliott (Eds.), *At the threshold: The developing adolescent* (pp. 16–53). Cambridge, MA: Harvard University Press.

———— & ZAHAYKEVICH, M. (1989). Parent-child relationships in early adolescence: A developmental perspective. In K. Kreppner & R. M. Lerner (Eds.), *Family systems and life-span development.* Hillsdale, NJ: Erlbaum.

FUSTENBERG, F. F., JR., BROOKS-GUNN, J., & MORGAN, P. (1987). *Adolescent mothers in later life.* New York: Cambridge University Press.

GRABER, J. A., & BROOKS-GUNN, J. (in press). Reproductive transitions: The experience of mothers and daughters. In C. D. Ryff & M. M. Seltzer (Eds.), *The parental experience in midlife.* Chicago: University of Chicago Press.

PAIKOFF, R., & BROOKS-GUNN, J. (1991). Do parent-child relationships change during puberty? *Psychological Bulletin, 110*(1), 47–66.

*L*AWRENCE *J*. *W*ALKER (*Ph.D., University of Toronto*) *is Professor of Psychology at the University of British Columbia in Vancouver, Canada. Professor Walker is on the editorial boards of four journals, has served as the Coordinator of the Section on Developmental Psychology of the Canadian Psychological Association, and is currently the president of the Association for Moral Education and the Chairperson of the Board of Carey Theological College. He has numerous publications in the area of moral development, and has received awards for excellence in both his research and university teaching. Dr. Walker is an avid cyclist (even in the Vancouver rain) and enjoys spending time with his wife and two teenagers.*

11

Is One Sex Morally Superior?

❖

"Where did all this come from?" I wondered to myself as the other panelists repeatedly challenged me on the issue of sex differences in moral development and sex bias in theories of morality.[1] Here I was, a beginning academic participating in one of my first scientific conferences, feeling rather surprised and certainly very uncomfortable as my fellow panelists (all women) directed their anger and allegations about sex bias my way. I had been asked to participate in a "conversation hour" at this conference, a time when a number of scholars discuss issues in their area of research before a (hopefully) interested audience. Our conversation hour had an innocuous title like "Issues in Moral Development," and so I was unprepared for the direction our conversation took.

This conference happened rather early in my career, but I had already published several journal articles which had examined the empirical validity of some of Lawrence Kohlberg's claims regarding stages of moral development, and so I was regarded as a "Kohlbergian." This, however, was a label that I resisted because, unlike many researchers in the area, I had neither been trained by Kohlberg nor previously associated with him and I valued the freedom that this independence afforded—freedom to evaluate and comment critically.

---

[1]There is an unresolved controversy in the field regarding the use of the terms *sex* and *gender*. Some authors use the term *sex* to imply that sex differences have a biological origin and use the term *gender* to imply a socialization origin. However, the relative contribution of biological and social factors in this area (and most others, for that matter) has not yet been clearly established and certainly will not be exclusively one or the other. For clarity, I will use the term sex throughout the chapter (without implying biological causality) because the research to be discussed classifies individuals on the basis of their biological sex, not their gender identity.

As it soon became apparent, my fellow panelists had recently read some of Carol Gilligan's work, which argued that males and females have fundamentally different orientations to morality and that dominant theories of moral development (especially Kohlberg's) undervalue or malign this feminine moral orientation. The inevitable result of this bias, Gilligan claimed, was that these theories downscored females' moral reasoning and characterized them as morally deficient. For my fellow panelists, Gilligan's claims had resonated deeply—no wonder they were outraged.

But Gillian's arguments matched neither my personal experience nor my impression of the available empirical evidence. I had grown up in a large, but otherwise traditional middle-class family, and although my parents had taken on predictably different roles in life, I had always regarded them as equally competent and nurturant. Particularly in the area of morality I admired them both as paragons of wisdom, virtue, and action—although as an adolescent I was loath to let them know that. I now realize that their example of moral integrity was a significant impetus for my interest in the processes of moral development. I was also raised in a church that espoused what would be considered conservative theology, except in regards to women, for my denomination had been ordaining women for ministry for over a century and the sexes were regarded as equal in the kingdom of God. So my personal experiences were quite inconsistent with this proffered notion of women's moral inferiority.

Gilligan's claims regarding sex differences in moral development were also inconsistent with my sense of the research literature, having been reading and doing research in the area for several years, beginning with my undergraduate honors thesis. Indeed, I had conducted several studies myself with children and adolescents and never found sex differences in moral reasoning. I was aware of a handful of studies which had reported differences, but I had not noticed any consistent trend. "Perhaps I've been missing something," I thought to myself as the conversation hour drew to a close. I resolved to do some follow-up on the issue, but before sharing those experiences, perhaps it would be helpful to provide a perspective on the field as a whole.

THE PSYCHOLOGY OF MORAL DEVELOPMENT

In my view, morality refers to voluntary actions that have (at least potentially) some social or interpersonal implications and that are governed by some intrapsychic mechanism (that is, some internal cognitive and/or emotive agency). Morality involves one's basic goals and way of life; it prescribes people's activities, regulates their social interactions, and arbitrates conflicts. It is also important to understand the complex and multifaceted nature of actual moral functioning. Of necessity, it entails the interplay of thought, emotion, and behavior. (Try imagining meaningful moral functioning without the involvement of each of these components!) Unfortunately, the various theoretical traditions in moral psychology have obfuscated the interdependent and interactive nature of thought, emotion, and behavior in moral functioning, in that each approach has regarded different aspects of psychological functioning as central to morality.

For example, early in the century, the psychoanalytic approach was dominant in the psychological study of morality. In Freud's psychoanalytic theory, the mechanism for moral development is identification. Depending on child rearing practices, young children were said to identify with their same-sex parent and thereby internalize (that is, adopt as their own) parental values, standards, and behaviors. Once internalization had taken place (early in childhood), powerful emotional consequences (for example, guilt) were said to result from deviating from these values. Thus, the psychoanalytic approach emphasized the emotional aspect of moral development and portrayed moral functioning as a fundamentally irrational process.

The rich theoretical framework of the psychoanalytic approach, however, could not in the end compensate for a major weakness—the difficulty in testing its major concepts—and it eventually was supplanted by behaviorism (and its derivative social learning theory) with its focus on overt behavior. This approach attempts to explain the development of moral behaviors (for example, resistance to temptation) in terms of principles of learning (such as reinforcement, punishment, and modeling). The major limitation of the behavioral approach to moral development was that it ignored individuals' intentions underlying their moral actions (which have always been considered important) and defined morality simply as conformity to social norms. Skinner, of course, regarded our personal sense of morality as simply an illusion. With its behavioral focus, this approach portrayed moral functioning as a fundamentally arational process.

The cognitive revolution that has marked psychology over the last two or three decades affected the study of moral development as well. The influence of Jean Piaget and his cognitive-developmental theory was substantial, but it was Lawrence Kohlberg who brought the field of moral psychology to life. His approach, unlike the others, focused on moral judgment and reasoning, and held that development proceeds through a series of six stages, each stage representing a particular organization of the manner in which people understood the sociomoral world and reasoned about it, and each stage more adequate than the previous one. Because of the focus on judgment and reasoning in this approach, Kohlberg's interest was more on older children and adolescents who could readily verbalize their moral understandings (particularly in school settings). The mechanism for development through the stages was held to be disequilibrium—a state of cognitive conflict that arises from some difficulty in dealing with new information and that induces structural reorganization toward more equilibrated ways of thinking. In this approach, moral functioning is portrayed as a fundamentally rational process. Thus the Kohlbergian moral education paradigm advocated peer discussion of moral dilemmas. Moral education and the provision of other social experiences represented attempts to help children develop in their stage of moral reasoning from a concrete egocentric focus and orientation to authorities to an adolescent concern with interpersonal relationships and social structures and then to a developmentally mature orientation to basic rights and universalizable principles.

SEX BIAS IN THEORIES OF MORALITY

There are three features of Kohlberg's approach that are important to note in the context of this controversy regarding sex differences: One is theoretical, the other two are methodological. Theoretically, Kohlberg explicitly grounded his psychological approach to moral development in a particular tradition of western moral philosophy (relying on philosophers such as Plato, Immanuel Kant, and John Rawls) with justice as its defining principle. Methodologically, Kohlberg relied on responses to classic hypothetical moral dilemmas to assess people's stage of moral reasoning development (for example, "Should a man steal an overpriced drug that he cannot obtain legally in order to save his wife's life?"). Kohlberg believed that such dilemmas were optimal for assessing the limits of moral reasoning competence because most people find them conflictual and they allow reflective thought without interference from preconceived and vested positions. However, some critics argue that because these dilemmas are abstract and seemingly focus on sociolegal issues, they fail to adequately tap aspects of morality other than justice (for example, more everyday concerns regarding relationships). The second notable methodological feature of Kohlberg's approach was that the database (a twenty-year longitudinal project) on which he largely derived and validated his stages of moral development was composed exclusively of males. Late in his life, Kohlberg told me that it was this feature of his research about which he had the most regrets (not surprisingly given the heat he took over it!). He used only males because he was primarily interested in factors that might influence the rate of moral development (and sex was not one of them and including females would have doubled the size of his sample). In the cognitive-developmental view, stage sequences are universal and so it does not really matter whether the sample is male or female, Christian or Hindu, American or Chinese. Nevertheless, these philosophical and methodological features of the approach left the Kohlbergian model vulnerable to allegations of bias.

My reading of Gilligan was that she was making two distinct and separable claims. Her first claim was that there are two sex-related orientations for moral decision making (an ethic of justice which is typical of males and an ethic of care which is typical of females). In the late 1970s and early 1980s, the only evidence relevant to this claim was anecdotal—interview excerpts in Gilligan's writing. She had not yet developed a measure or coding system, so I turned my attention to her second claim, a claim where I thought there was abundant empirical evidence. Gilligan's second claim was that Kohlberg's theory (who incidentally was her former mentor at Harvard), among many other influential theories of human development including those of Freud, Piaget, Erikson, Levinson, and McClelland, was biased against females' "different voice" on morality and downscored their reasoning to lower stages—thereby caricaturing them as morally inferior.

The allegation of sex bias is a serious charge against any theory (and a damning one in the contemporary context). It is even more controversial when made in an obviously value-laden area such as moral development, an area of human functioning that is central to our self-definition. The *minimal* foundation to substantiate such a claim, I believed, would be unequivocal evidence that females score lower on Kohlberg's measure than do males and that there is no other reasonable explanation for this difference. Many critics of Kohlberg's model apparently believe that the finding of sex differences confirms the claim of bias, but I regard that notion as terribly simplistic. I realized, as should be obvious, that a sex difference only indicates bias if it does not accurately reflect reality. For example, males have been found to be taller and heavier than females on average, but that does not necessarily call into question our systems of measurement. A sex difference in moral reasoning may simply be a reflection of a sexist and patriarchal society that oppresses females and restricts their opportunities for growth, not an indication of a biased theory.

It should be noted that the allegations of sex bias against Kohlberg's theory were not made because it predicted or required a sex difference in moral development (unlike Freud who asserted that women lacked moral maturity because of deficiencies in same-sex parental identification and consequent superego formation). Instead, the allegation of sex bias was premised on the view that Kohlberg had inadvertently defined and measured moral maturity in a way that favored males and thus lead to a false conclusion regarding females' moral development.

SEX DIFFERENCES IN STAGES OF MORAL DEVELOPMENT?

Given Gilligan's now well-publicized claims regarding sex differences and sex bias in theories of morality, I undertook to systematically review the research literature regarding this issue. I realized that my subjective assessment simply wouldn't suffice (just as I had been unimpressed by others' selective focusing on some anecdotes and studies). What I needed to do was to find all studies using Kohlberg's measure, in which sex differences were or could be examined. This turned out to be no mean feat! Since

I maintained fairly comprehensive files (my family and friends have been known to joke about my compulsive nature), I began there, carefully going through my records and reprints looking for relevant studies (and checking their reference lists for others). I also wrote to the major researchers in the field asking them for recent studies and any other leads and, of course, I did systematic searches of various databases (such as the *Psychological Abstracts*) so as to omit nothing. Then, I carefully read each of these studies, noting their findings and any complicating or qualifying factors.

I soon realized that there was a major problem in doing such a review, particularly in the area of sex differences—it's known as the "file-drawer problem." It is commonly believed that reviews probably overestimate the magnitude of sex differences given reporting and publication biases. I discovered that many studies failed to report whether or not there were sex differences although subjects of both sexes participated (presumably because researchers found none but did not report that detail since the study focused on other issues). This is a reporting bias. The other aspect of the file-drawer problem is a publication bias, a bias against studies that report nonsignificant findings. It has been shown repeatedly that the publication process in the social sciences is biased toward selecting studies with significant findings. This means that there are probably numerous studies that have examined sex differences but which remain unknown (buried in someone's file drawer) because they found nonsignificant differences (confirming the null hypothesis is usually of minimal interest). Both of these biases lead one to suspect that any review will overestimate sex differences to some extent. I couldn't do anything about the problem of publication bias, but the reporting bias was potentially resolvable. I tried to contact the authors of the studies that involved both sexes but didn't report sex differences, asking them to share with me either the relevant analyses or their raw data (so that I could calculate sex differences myself). To my delight, almost everyone whom I succeeded in tracking down cooperated (sometimes after a gentle reminder).

Finally, then, I had accumulated all the available evidence regarding sex differences in moral reasoning development: The review included 80 studies, with a total of 152 distinct samples, and involved 10,637 participants. I organized these samples developmentally (childhood and early adolescence, late adolescence and youth, and adulthood), but the finding was basically the same regardless of age—the typical pattern was one of nonsignificant sex differences. Overall, the vast majority of the samples (86 percent) reported no differences, with males scoring higher in 9 percent of the samples and females scoring higher in 6 percent (note that a small number of significant differences would be expected simply by chance). There was no consistent evidence to support Gilligan's claim that Kohlberg's theory downscores females' moral reasoning. Incidentally, one of the things I noticed was that most of the (small number of) samples where males scored higher were composed of adults, and further digging revealed a methodological problem. In these samples, the men and women typically differed in educational level and/or occupational status (reflecting our patriarchal society in general)—thus sex and education/occupation were confounded. And in every case where researchers controlled (either methodologically or statistically) for these educational and occupational differences, sex differences in moral reasoning disappeared. This, of course, was not an attempt to "explain away" these significant sex differences (since overall there was no significant pattern to explain) but to simply illustrate Kohlberg's claim that such social experiences are influential in stimulating moral development.

I was pleased that the results of my review were so clear, but then as I shared them with colleagues and at conferences, I began to realize a couple of limitations to what I had done. One limitation was that a traditional narrative review, such as I had done, is rather subjective, susceptible to biases in interpretation (for example, in discounting findings or emphasizing others). A second limitation is that the review procedure is essentially a simple vote-counting means of integrating studies—merely reflecting whether or not a finding was significant. It makes no assessment of the size of the effect. If an effect is weak, then the difference may tend to be nonsignificant in individual studies, but may in fact cumulatively favor a given direction.

Fortunately, in recent years, statistical techniques for combining the results of a series of studies had been developed and shown to be more powerful and objective than simple summary impression. So I set out to learn these meta-analytic techniques and to apply them to the studies in my review. This meant going back to each study and determining the exact one-tailed p value associated with the relevant test of sex differences (often it was necessary to recalculate) and then plugging these statistical values into the appropriate formulas. The meta-analysis turned out to be non-significant and quite unequivocal. The effect size was miniscule—sex explained only 1/20 of 1 percent of the variability in moral reasoning development. There was absolutely no empirical support for the claim that Kohlberg's theory downscores the moral thinking of females. I couldn't help but wonder why the myth of males' moral superiority could have been advanced in the face of so little evidence.

THE CONTROVERSY OVER SEX DIFFERENCES IN MORAL REASONING

I published my review and meta-analysis in 1984, naively thinking that I would unobtrusively make my contribution to the research literature in moral psychology. Was I ever wrong! I was flooded with requests for copies of my article and received numerous invitations to give colloquia and speak at conferences. Obviously, my review had provoked considerable attention—probably because it challenged the well-publicized claims re-garding sex bias. One day I received a phone call inviting me to participate in a major symposium on the topic at the upcoming meeting of the American Psychological Association. I was delighted that the issue would have such an extensive airing and gladly agreed. What I wasn't told and only discovered later was that the chairperson of the symposium (who had invited me to participate) and the two discussants she had arranged for the session had each written critiques of my just-published review. I had been set up perfectly!

As it turned out, the symposium went very well (at least from my perspective)—the session was well-attended (with many people standing despite our being scheduled in a seemingly cavernous room) and our presentations and discussions, although filled with numerous disagreements about both the data and ideology, were reasonably amicable. I had always believed that, given an appropriate understanding of the limitations of psychological science, the best strategy was to let the data speak for themselves. There was one comment from that symposium that I recall quite clearly—because it took me by surprise and was rather troublesome. A woman came up to me in the hallway following the session and blurted out, "I don't care what the data say. I know Gilligan is right." Over the years since then, I have heard this comment or some variant repeatedly. It points both to the real sense of oppression that some women feel and to the significant role that ideology plays in the social sciences.

As I mentioned before, I had become aware of three critiques that had been written to challenge my review and meta-analysis. Such direct, extended criticisms of another's work are relatively rare in psychology. I was pleased that my review had been considered worthy of attention by some eminent scholars, but was understandably nervous about being "under the microscope." These critiques were all submitted to the journal in which I had earlier published my review. Eventually, only one was found acceptable for publication—and I was then asked to prepare a rejoinder to be published along with the critique. My critic argued that my review was flawed in various ways and biased against the finding of differences. We quibbled about issues such as which statistical test was most appropriate for reanalyzing others' data and how to handle researchers' use of different coding systems. In my rejoinder I responded to all of her criticisms and again claimed that I had conducted a dispassionate review, but in order to provide the most liberal test of sex differences in moral reasoning development, I redid my review and recalculated my meta-analysis, yielding to all my critic's demands (just for the sake of argument). The result, nevertheless, was the same—the overall pattern remained one of nonsignificant sex differences. The journal editor pronounced an end to commentaries on the issue.

As a side note, I suspect that part of my critic's motivation for writing her critique was that I had reanalyzed data from one of her studies for my original review—and had reached a different conclusion! In her study, she had reported a significant sex difference in moral reasoning but had used what I believed was an inappropriate statistical test (such tests make certain assumptions which must be met if their use is to be considered valid). So I wrote to her, noting my concern, and asking for her raw data so that I could do a reanalysis. In her reply, she acknowledged that the statistical test she had used was questionable but claimed it had been used for the sake of comparability and ease of presentation. She also sent along data that allowed me to do a reanalysis with a more appropriate test, but the data were for a larger sample. My analysis on this larger data set failed to reveal a significant sex difference and that was what I reported in my review. In her critique, she reanalayzed the data again, using another statistical test, and reported a significant difference, but this time the test was based on still a different sample size. I despaired of ever resolving the statistical significance of that particular finding! It certainly illustrated the point that researchers don't appreciate having their conclusions reversed.

SEX DIFFERENCES IN MORAL ORIENTATIONS?

Having resolved (at least to my satisfaction) the issue of sex differences and sex bias in Kohlberg's theory of moral reasoning development, I turned my attention to what I saw as Gilligan's other claim—that there are two sex-related moral orientations, an ethic of justice and rights that is typical of males and an ethic of care and response that is typical of females. Gilligan was arguing that the sexes typically differ in their basic life orientation, especially in conceptions of self and of morality, that they have distinctive frameworks or perspectives for organizing and understanding the moral domain. In her view, males typically evidence an ethic of justice because of what she believes is their individualistic and separate conception of self, their detached objectivity, their basing of identity on occupation, and their preference for abstract and impartial rules and principles. In boys' early relationships with parents, the experience of inequality is salient and the need for independence and separation is important for self-esteem. On the other hand, females typically evidence an ethic of care because of what Gilligan believes is their perception of the self as connected to and interdependent with others, their basing of identity on intimate relationships, their sensitivity not to endanger or hurt, their concern for the well-being and care of self and others and for harmonious relationships in concrete situations. In girls' early relationships with parents, the experience of attachment, of connecting with others, is central to their self-definition and self-esteem (in contrast to boys' more typical experience of inequality).

Gilligan's original study of moral orientations was limited to a sample of women who had a problem pregnancy, and in her interviews with them she focused on the moral conflicts and issues involved in their abortion decision. A single-sex sample and a single-context dilemma did not strike me as very persuasive evidence for a sex difference in moral orientations. Her 1982 book, *"In a Different Voice,"* although skillfully written and having considerable intuitive appeal, was most frustrating from an empirical point of view since the only evidence presented for her claim of sex-related moral orientations was anecdotal or literary.

I decided to do a more systematic study of sex differences in moral orientations with a reasonably large sample of children, adolescents, and adults. I believed that such a significant psychological claim about the sexes should be subjected to careful empirical evaluation. My original research plans at the time had been to examine the impact of family interactions on children's moral development, but I found it relatively easy to add this additional issue to my design—except for one major problem—I needed a coding manual to score Gilligan's moral orientations. Gilligan, in an unpublished 1982 paper, had referred to the existence of a coding manual and I subsequently learned that it formed part of one of her students' doctoral dissertations. But I had considerable difficulty getting access to this critical document. After several months of prodding and negotiating with both student and supervisor, I eventually obtained a copy of the coding manual.

In our study, we interviewed our participants regarding two types of moral dilemmas: standard hypothetical ones and a real-life dilemma from their personal experience. Up to that point, all the available evidence regarding moral orientations was based on reasoning about idiosyncratic real-life dilemmas that people had generated from their own lives. I believed that if the sex difference in moral orientations was as fundamental and pervasive as argued by Gilligan, then it should also be evident in response to standard stimulus materials such as hypothetical dilemmas. I also suspected that the evidence of sex differences based solely on reasoning about real-life dilemmas might be artifactual; in particular, I wondered whether the orientations people use might be strongly influenced by the type of dilemma they happened to recall from their own lives (and more so than by their sex).

We interviewed a large number of children and adolescents and their parents (the total N was 240) about these two types of moral dilemmas and then followed them longitudinally, doing a retest interview two years later. These individual interviews were conducted in a rather open-ended and clinical format in an attempt to fully tap their moral reasoning. First, a set of three standard hypothetical moral dilemmas were presented, one at a time, each involving some conflict of values (such as the earlier cited one entailing a conflict between obeying the law and saving a life). Participants' reasoning was carefully and systematically probed to reveal how they constructed and understood each problem, what considerations they thought were relevant, and how they believed the problem should be resolved and why. Then, participants were asked to recall a recent real-life moral conflict from their own lives, a personal experience involving right and wrong where they weren't sure what to do. And again they were probed regarding their construction, resolution, and evaluation of the problem. These interviews, typically taking about an hour each, were audio-recorded and transcribed verbatim, yielding several thousand pages of single-spaced transcripts which we carefully and painstakingly scored, sentence by sentence, using the moral orientation coding manual.

My analyses revealed no sex differences in moral orientations on the hypothetical dilemmas. In other words, when the stimulus materials were standardized, sex differences were not evident. I also found no sex differences in moral orientations among our samples of children and adolescents (on either type of moral dilemmas). This contradicted Gilligan's claim that the sex difference is evident across the life span. Thus, the only sex difference revealed in our large-scale study was among the adults when reasoning about a real-life dilemma from their personal experience, and here the sex difference was as Gilligan claimed: The ethic of care was more evident for women than for men.

I submitted a manuscript based on these findings for publication in a psychology journal, suspecting that it might be found somewhat interesting, perhaps even controversial, not only because it challenged some of the empirical claims Gilligan had articulated but also because, by this time, the debate regarding sex bias in Kohlberg's model was in full swing and I was regarded as a major antagonist. My suspicions were confirmed when a total of six reviewers were eventually assigned by the journal editor (in contrast to the usual two or three). Although most of the reviewers were supportive of its publication, they did have some questions and suggestions for improvements. One reviewer's question turned out to be particularly fortuitous. Since the use of real-life moral dilemmas was a relatively new technique, the reviewer was curious to know what types of moral conflicts people actually reported from their everyday experiences.

So in revising our manuscript, I struggled with how best to summarize these very idiosyncratic moral dilemmas. In the end, I developed two content analyses: One was simply descriptive and focused on the type of moral issue that was at the heart of the conflict (for example, theft, substance use, marital fidelity, promises). The other content analysis was more interpretive and focused on the nature of the relationship that each moral conflict entailed (either personal or impersonal). It seemed to me that this was a major dimension in people's dilemmas and potentially relevant to the issue of moral orientations. A personal moral conflict was defined as involving someone with whom the participant had a significant and continuing relationship (examples include whether or not to tell a friend that her husband was having an affair and whether or not to put one's father in a nursing home against his wishes). An impersonal moral conflict was defined as involving acquaintances, strangers, institutions, and so on (examples include whether or not to correct a clerk's error in giving too much change and whether to absorb a business loss as an employer or cut employees' wages).

I wondered whether or not there might be sex differences in the types of real-life moral dilemmas people recalled (not an unreasonable assumption given the fact that the social lives of men and women differ to a considerable extent). I also wondered whether or not moral orientations would be related to dilemma content and, of course, I was particularly interested in determining whether or not the sex difference in moral orientation I had found in adulthood would still be evident within types of dilemma content.

Consistent with my expectations, there was a tendency for women to report real-life dilemmas that were personal in character whereas men were more likely to report impersonal dilemmas. Then I examined the relationship between moral orientation and dilemma content and found a clear pattern—people tended to reason about personal real-life dilemmas in terms of the ethic of care whereas people tended to reason about impersonal dilemmas in terms of justice and rights. Finally, I examined whether or not there were sex differences in moral orientations within types of dilemma content—and found none! Thus, when dilemma content was controlled (either by using standard hypothetical dilemmas or by controlling the content of real-life dilemmas), sex differences in moral orientations were not found although these orientations did vary considerably across types of dilemmas. The orientations also varied considerably within individuals—most people used both orientations to a significant degree with no clear preference or focus. In other words, differences in moral orientations could be better attributed to the type of moral dilemma that people discussed than to their sex. The evidence regarding sex differences in moral orientations had been based on a methodological artifact.

There was a final empirical issue which I realized my data could address. Gilligan had not only argued that Kohlberg's stage model of moral reasoning development was biased against females but that it undervalued and maligned the (feminine) ethic of care. She believed that his model entailed a clear preference for justice and rights reasoning and that it denigrated care and response reasoning to the lower stages. If Gilligan's claim was correct then that meant that people who relied on an ethic of justice should score at the higher stages in Kohlberg's model, whereas those who relied on an ethic of care should score at the lower stages. Such data might point to an ideological or philosophical bias in Kohlberg's approach. I had already coded the interviews for moral orientation, but this hypothesis required a second coding for moral stage, using Kohlberg's scoring manual (which thankfully had always been readily available). Once that was done I examined the relationship between moral stage and moral orientation. On the hypothetical dilemmas, I found no relationship—failing to support Gilligan's claim that Kohlberg's model was biased against the ethic of care. I did find a relationship on the real-life dilemmas, however, but not the one that had been predicted: People who used a care and response orientation scored *higher* in moral stage than those with a justice and rights orientation. If anything, Kohlberg's model favored the ethic of care!

The manuscript was subsequently published as one of the first studies to examine in a comprehensive and systematic way the empirical claims that Gilligan had articulated about morality and the sexes. I concluded, based on my review of the literature and my own research, that there were no data to even suggest that one sex was morally superior nor was there any compelling evidence that the sexes differed in moral reasoning ability. This did not preclude the possibility that the sexes might differ in other aspects of morality, of course, and I suspect that the domain of emotions might be a more profitable area to examine in this regard.

CONCLUDING THOUGHTS

Personally, my involvement in this controversy over the last few years has taught me that almost everyone has a strongly (even passionately) held opinion about the issue of sex differences in the area of morality, and that careful attention to the empirical evidence (including its limitations—there is still a great deal we do not know) goes a long way toward informing the debate. I believe that this topic should be contentious. Whenever we ascribe different moral characteristics and worth to different groups of people we should be clear about what we're claiming and how we know. It should also be realized that this controversy has concerned not just questions regarding sex differences and the form they might take, but also questions regarding conceptions of morality and the philosophy of science—questions that are not so readily resolvable.

I have been disappointed that some people have regarded my challenge of Gilligan's claims regarding sex differences in moral reasoning to imply that I have rejected her theory entirely. Nothing could be further from the truth. Gilligan has made substantial contributions to moral psychology— by helping to broaden our conception of morality (to better include notions of care and interrelatedness, for example), by suggesting alternate means to assess moral reasoning (through the use of real-life conflicts), and by focusing our attention on the need to better represent females' experience in psychological theories of human development.

My involvement in the controversy regarding sex differences in moral development has made it increasingly apparent that there are two quite disparate groups within feminist circles: One group works toward equality between the sexes and minimizes the significance of differences (having what is known as a "beta bias") whereas the other group attempts to discover sex differences and celebrate the previously undervalued female characteristics (having an "alpha bias")—and so it boils down to the questions, "Are these real differences? Are they substantial enough to divide us?" Obviously, there are numerous difficulties with both types of "bias." There is no neutral vantage point in this debate!

Acknowledgments

My program of research in moral development has been funded by the Social Sciences and Humanities Research Council of Canada and facilitated by the supportive environment provided by my department at the University of British Columbia. More personally, I would like to acknowledge my former mentors at the University of New Brunswick, Ann Cameron and Boyd Richards, who taught me, early in my education in psychology, the value of clear conceptualization and careful methodology. And I have been fortunate to have had many excellent graduate students over the past few years who have not only been true collaborators in my research, but also the best of friends.

SUGGESTED READINGS

DAMON, W. (1988). *The moral child: Nurturing children's natural moral growth.* New York: Free Press.

GILLIGAN, C. (1982). *In a different voice: Psychological theory and women's development.* Cambridge, MA: Harvard University Press.

KOHLBERG, L. (1984). *The psychology of moral development.* San Francisco: Harper & Row.

KURTINES, W. M., & GEWIRTZ, J. L. (Eds.). (1991). *Handbook of moral behavior and development* (Vols. 1–3). Hillsdale, NJ: Erlbaum.

WALKER, L. J. (1991). Sex differences in moral reasoning. In W. M. Kurtines & J. L. Gewirtz (Eds.), *Handbook of moral behavior and development* (Vol. 2, pp. 333–364). Hillsdale, NJ: Erlbaum.

*L*AURENCE STEINBERG *(Ph.D., Cornell University) is Professor of Psychology at Temple University. A nationally recognized expert on psychological development and family relations during adolescence, Dr. Steinberg is the author or coauthor of over 100 scholarly articles on growth and development during the teenage years, as well as the books* Adolescence, When Teenagers Work: The Psychological and Social Costs of Adolescent Employment *(with Ellen Greenberger),* You and Your Adolescent: A Parent's Guide for Ages 10 to 20 *(with Ann Levine), and the forthcoming book* Crossing Paths: How Your Child's Adolescence Triggers Your Own Crisis *(with Wendy Steinberg). He serves on the editorial boards of* Child Development *and* Developmental Psychology *and is a fellow of the American Psychological Association.*

12

The Impact of Employment on Adolescent Development

❖

Students often wonder how social scientists come up with their ideas for research projects. One of the best-kept secrets is that most of us stumble upon, rather than carefully select, the most important research questions that drive our careers.

If it hadn't been for Kari Greenberger's interest in earning pocket money, I would never have devoted fifteen years of my career to the study of teenagers and work.

I still can recall the afternoon when Kari's mother, Ellen, and I argued over lunch about whether Kari should be permitted to go ahead and apply for a job selling running shoes at Foot Locker, a national chain with an outlet in one of the local shopping malls. I had recently taken my first teaching position at the University of California, Irvine, where Ellen Greenberger, also a developmental psychologist specializing in adolescence, was on the faculty. We had planned a lunch to discuss our current research interests and the possibility of working on a grant proposal together. Before getting down to business, we chatted about our families. Ellen asked what I thought about the idea of Kari, who was 16, working after school.

My initial reaction was positive. I said that working might help Kari develop a sense of responsibility and learn more about how to manage money. I also suggested that Kari, as the daughter of a university professor, had led a fairly privileged and sheltered life, and that working out in the "real world" might be good for her.

Ellen argued otherwise. After all, Kari was an honors student and an accomplished hurdler on her high school's track team, and she had an active and busy social life. Working would have to take time away from something. Weren't these activities more important than earning money? Moreover, Ellen countered, Kari was an exceedingly responsible teenager; what evidence was there that she "needed" a job in order for her to learn responsibility? Kari was fortunate enough to come from a family that could afford to provide her with all the spending money a teenager really needed. Given that luxury, shouldn't she be taking advantage of the free time and opportunities that adolescence provides? After all, once she reached adulthood, she'd be working for the rest of her life.

While we ate, we continued to debate the merits of employment during adolescence, becoming increasingly amused to discover that two psychologists with expertise in adolescent social development had no idea about whether working during high school was good for teenagers or not. We even made a friendly wager on the subject (dinner at a fancy southern California restaurant): I was in favor of teenagers working; Ellen was skeptical about it.

After lunch, Ellen and I headed over to the university library to see what previous studies of adolescent employment had found. We discovered that, with the exception of a few unscientific anecdotal reports, there was nothing at all in the social science literature on how teenagers were affected by employment. We decided to meet again and determine whether this was something worth pursuing as a research project. Over the next few weeks, I began to become aware of just how many retail stores and restaurants were staffed by teenagers. It was something I had just never noticed before.

Against her mother's better judgment, Kari took the job at Foot Locker.

MAPPING OUT THE STUDY

Stumbling onto a research topic that has no established literature is a mixed blessing. On the positive side, it is relatively easy to bring oneself up to speed intellectually, and, of course, there is the inherent attraction to being the "first" to study something. On the other hand, it is more difficult to design a study when one does not have an obvious starting point, such as a previous piece of research that left one or more specific questions unanswered. And there is always the question of *why* something is unstudied: Just because a question has not been researched doesn't mean that it is worth researching. The question has to be interesting, important, and, of course, researchable. Maybe no one had studied teenage employment for good reason.

Over the next fifteen years, I would come to learn that the question of whether, and how, employment during high school affects adolescent development is, in fact, interesting, important, and researchable. It is *interesting* because it touches on several fundamental questions about the nature of adolescence and the development of competence during the high school years. Put briefly, what sorts of experiences contribute to healthy adolescent development? It is *important* because the question is linked to many issues relevant to social and educational policies potentially affecting millions of American teenagers. For example, are the laws currently governing youth employment adequate? Should work experience be required as a part of youngsters' education? Should schools give academic credit for hours on the job? Whether the question was *researchable* was up to us to decide. That was where our training in applied developmental psychology—and our tolerance for getting our hands dirty doing research out in the real world—would be tested. As you will see, doing research in the field is quite different from running experiments in a university laboratory.

At our first meeting, Ellen and I began to map out the scope of the study in order to clarify our interest and, just as important, to determine whether we would need financial support to conduct the research. At this stage in the development of a research project, it is important to brainstorm and to be open to all sorts of possibilities. Some questions were obvious ones to be asking: Did having a job teach youngsters responsibility? Did it teach them "the meaning of a dollar"? Did working interfere with school responsibilities? Some questions were less obvious: Did working affect youngsters' mental and physical health? Did having a job change teenagers' family and peer relations? Were some jobs "better" than others? What did we mean by "better"? And some questions came to us over a period of weeks, as the study began to take shape: What activities did youngsters engage in at work? How did variations in activities on the job affect variations in adolescent development?

We realized immediately that in order to even begin to answer these questions, we were going to have to employ a longitudinal, or over-time, design. A cross-sectional study, in which one simply contrasted workers and nonworkers, or adolescents who worked a lot with those who worked only a little, at one point in time, might tell us if working were correlated with adolescent responsibility or school performance, but such a correlation would be open to multiple interpretations. We might find, for example, that students who work are more responsible, but we would not be able to tell whether working *made* them more responsible, whether youngsters who were more responsible to begin with were simply more likely to work, or whether some third factor (for example, intelligence) was correlated with both working and responsibility, thus making the two only *appear* to be related to each other. The only way around this problem was to follow a sample of adolescents over time to see how they changed as a function of working. That was the only way we could begin to separate cause and effect.

The next decision we faced had to do with drawing a sample. Our first inclination was to contact local employers of adolescents and begin there, but we realized that this would not enable us to draw a sample of non-workers easily, which we needed as a comparison group. If we simply followed a group of workers over time, we could not tell whether any changes we observed in their adjustment were due to working or merely to the passage of time. We concluded that a more sensible approach would be to begin with a large sample of adolescents who had never worked and track them over time, because over a one-year period, some would take on jobs and others would not. In order to do this, we decided that we probably should begin with a sample drawn from a school population.

Although we realized that the study ultimately would need to be longitudinal, we recognized that there was much to be gained by collecting cross-sectional data along the way. In this phase of the research, we would contrast workers with nonworkers, knowing full well that we could not draw any conclusions about cause and effect, but hoping that the cross-sectional comparisons would generate hypotheses that we could test with longitudinal data. Ultimately, we planned a study that would occupy two years. During the first year, we would compare a sample of nonworkers with a sample of first-time workers. During the second year, we would follow up the students who had been nonworkers at the beginning of the research and compare those who entered the labor force with those who did not.

Once we decided to draw our sample from one or more schools, we needed to determine how many subjects we would need to recruit to begin our study. We knew we wanted to end up with a sample of students on whom we had longitudinal data, some of whom had entered the labor force during the one-year interval and others who had not. We took two factors into account in making our calculations. First, we knew that over time, a certain percentage of research participants would drop out of the study, either because they moved out of the area or simply were tired of participating, so that we would have to take into account attrition over the course of the study. Second, we knew that out of an initial pool of non-workers, only a certain percentage (perhaps as few as 40 percent) would take jobs during the next year. We needed to make sure that, when the data collection was complete, we would have enough subjects in this critical group to conduct our statistical analyses. Working backward, we decided that we needed to begin the study with about 500 students—about 200 first-time workers and about 300 nonworkers (we needed more nonworkers to begin with because we were following this group over time). This would permit us to make our first year cross-sectional comparisons and to have enough students in a longitudinal sample to compare those who entered the labor force with those who did not.

We knew from the previous research each of us had done that about 70 percent of high school students will participate in research if they are asked to, so we estimated that we needed to ask about 725 students to be in the study to end up with a sample of 500. But, remember, we were only interested in two groups of students: Those who had never worked and those who were in their first jobs. Unfortunately, we knew from published government statistics that the majority of students would not fall into one of these groups. This meant that we would need to do an initial survey in order to screen out students who did not meet our participation criteria. We also realized that we could not study high school seniors (since they would be hard to follow up the next year, after graduation) nor could we study freshmen (since we knew from government employment statistics that very few of them would enter the labor force between ninth and tenth grades). Based on our estimates of how many students would be ineligible, we realized that we were going to have to screen something like 3,000 students just to arrive at a reasonable sample!

By now, I was beginning to get a little nervous. I was a new assistant professor, fresh out of graduate school. My graduate training at Cornell had not prepared me for taking on a study of this magnitude. The previous research I had worked on involved thirty families studied in a structured experimental situation. Now I was facing the possibility of having to collect data from 3,000 respondents out in the field. Although to a certain extent, many of the basic principles of sound research apply across all types of studies, doing large-sample, nonexperimental field research is quite different from working on controlled experiments.

It was at this point that I learned the value of collaborating with someone who was more experienced. Before coming to Irvine, Ellen had directed a large-scale study of adolescents that involved thousands of respondents. She knew the ins and outs of securing outside funding, developing a workable budget, negotiating with schools about access to student populations, managing data so that one didn't drown in it, handling crises that erupted in the field, and coordinating a large staff of research assistants. I considered myself well-trained, but I had learned none of this in graduate school. As it turned out, I would call upon the skills I acquired during this project again and again throughout my career. When I look back on it, I think of my involvement in this project as perhaps the most important component of my training as a social scientist. I am not sure whether we could do a better job of teaching these sorts of skills in our graduate programs, but I can say with certainty that knowing how to interest school officials in participating in a research study and knowing how to supervise a large staff is just as important a part of being a skilled researcher as is knowing how to analyze data or conduct an observation of a child.

Ellen and I soon realized that we were going to have to apply for some source of outside funding if we were going to do the research as we had designed it. We contacted some colleagues we knew at the National Institute of Education (this was in the late 1970s, before there was a U.S. Department of Education), who were very encouraging. At the time, many educators were excited about the possibility of using nonschool settings as educational environments, and there was enthusiasm for research that might show that students learned important skills from their jobs. However, finding out what students learned on their jobs required that we actually go into the workplace and study what adolescents really did at work, which was going to be complicated and time-consuming. We decided to press ahead anyway, and developed a full grant proposal.

When we had finished, we had designed an enormous study. In 1978, the National Institute of Education approved our grant and, with additional funding from the Spencer Foundation and the Ford Foundation, we launched our project. Of the first five high schools we approached, four agreed to participate.

We assembled a large staff of graduate and undergraduate students and a small, paid staff of professional and technical workers. The students were trained in questionnaire administration, interviewing techniques, and behavioral observations. Ellen and I were eager to get started. We each wanted to see whose intuition about the pros and cons of working was correct. And besides, we had a bet riding on the outcome.

THE RESEARCH DESIGN

We began by administering a screening questionnaire to all the tenth and eleventh graders at four public high schools. This questionnaire, which was completed by approximately 3,100 students, asked youngsters questions about their employment history, current employment status, and background (including their ethnicity, social class, and household composition). This screening survey would provide us with the necessary information to draw our samples of youngsters who had never worked and youngsters who were in their first paid jobs. The background information was necessary in order to ascertain whether the workers and nonworkers came from markedly different backgrounds, which would have made interpreting any differences between them quite difficult. Fortunately, the groups turned out to be comparable.

One important step in survey research that students overlook involves what we called "cleaning" the questionnaires. When a survey is administered to a large population, there are always some individuals who misunderstand questions (for instance, although we asked about "paid employment only" some students listed unpaid, volunteer experiences in their work histories), some who give responses that do not fit in our predetermined categories (for example, someone who reported her salary in terms of her weekly take-home pay, rather than in terms of hourly wages, as the questionnaire requested), and some whose responses clearly show that they do not take the research seriously (some students wrote profanities on the questionnaire, while others wrote joke answers). As a result, all questionnaires need to be examined and, if possible, cleaned (e.g., converting weekly pay into hourly wages, erasing volunteer work from someone's work history, or throwing out joke questionnaires), before the data are entered into the computer. It took a staff of about a dozen undergraduates several weeks to get the screening questionnaires ready for analysis.

While we were waiting for the cleaning to be concluded, we continued to work on developing our first-year questionnaire battery. This battery included measures of school performance (e.g., grade-point average, time spent on homework, class attendance, etc.), psychosocial development (e.g., self-esteem, self-reliance, achievement motivation), mental health (e.g., anxiety, depression, psychosomatic complaints), problem behaviors (e.g., drug and alcohol use, school misconduct, delinquency), attitudes toward work and money (e.g., materialism, cynicism about work), and social relations (e.g., closeness to parents, closeness to peers). We also developed a multiple-choice test of what we called "practical knowledge," which measured students' understanding of business, money management, and consumer awareness. We needed such a test in order to examine the hypothesis that students would learn about the "real world" by holding a job. After using the screening survey to select our sample, we returned to the schools and administered our battery to 300 nonworkers and 200 first-time workers. This administration provided the basis for our cross-sectional analyses.

Although most of our hypotheses could be tested using questionnaire data, Ellen and I believed that we should supplement these data with information from other sources. We therefore selected a subsample of 100 of the first-time workers employed in different sorts of jobs for further study. This subsample was interviewed and observed at work, and we interviewed their parents at home, as well. The adolescent interview focused on their reasons for working, their experiences on the job, and what they thought they were getting out of the experience. The parent interview asked about the role parents played in their youngster's decision to work and job search, how much control parents exerted over their adolescent's earnings, and how working had affected their family life. As I described later, the observations were conducted in order to examine the actual behaviors youngsters engaged in at work.

One year later, we returned to the schools again and readministered our questionnaire battery to the 300 students who had been nonworkers at the time the study began. Because some of these students had remained nonworkers and others had not, we were able to compare students who had remained nonemployed with those who had entered the labor force. This was the basis for our longitudinal analyses.

I don't think I've ever been involved in a research project that was so full of surprises from the outset. For starters, our screening questionnaire had revealed something quite unexpected: A very high proportion of students—well over half the tenth and eleventh graders we surveyed—held jobs, and many of these workers were employed over twenty hours each week. There were students in our sample who were working over thirty hours each week! Some had had three or four different jobs by the time they had reached their junior year. Although social scientists had not paid close attention, it was clear that working had become a significant part of American teenagers' lives.

Now we were going to try to learn how it was affecting them.

SURPRISING FINDINGS

Once the first year of data collection was completed, we began our cross-sectional comparisons of the nonworkers and first-time workers. Again, we were surprised: By virtually all our measures, it appeared as if the non-workers, not the workers, were better off. Students who didn't have jobs were performing better in school (in terms of grades, time spent on homework, and school attendance), scoring higher on measures of positive family relations (e.g., they reported feeling closer to their parents and spending more time with their families), and reporting less delinquency and alcohol, drug, and cigarette use. Moreover, we could find little evidence that the workers were more responsible, based on our measures of things like self-reliance or work motivation. If anything, it looked as if work was promoting *irresponsibility*. Compared to nonworkers, the workers were more cynical about the value of hard work and more tolerant of unethical business practices. They also reported surprisingly high rates of questionable conduct at work—stealing money or property from their employer, overstating their work hours on their time cards, or working while drunk or "stoned." Indeed, after nine months on the job, more than 60 percent of the workers had done something unethical or illegal, and one-quarter of the workers were frequent offenders.

These findings flew in the face of common sense and conventional wisdom. Wasn't working supposed to be "character-building"? Wasn't having a job supposed to teach responsibility? Provide opportunities for learning? Why would working be associated with poorer school performance and more frequent drug and alcohol use? We decided to look more closely at our students' jobs. We put our questionnaire data aside for a moment and turned to the results of our behavioral observations.

The observations were a unique and especially interesting part of the study, because they involved extensive field work. Each of 100 workers was observed for a minimum of two hours on the job, during which time our observer recorded, using an elaborate numerical code and a portable computer, every single activity and interaction that occurred on the job. We had categories for various types of manual work (e.g., cleaning, lifting, or moving objects), various types of social activities (e.g., greeting customers, answering questions, receiving instruction), various types of "thinking" activities (performing calculations, reading, writing) and so forth. (Try to imagine yourself standing next to a fast food worker, office janitor, or supermarket cashier recording every behavior and utterance. One of our observers even followed a hot dog vendor up and down the steps of Anaheim Stadium during an Angels' baseball game and another accompanied a boating assistant on a fishing trip off the coast of Newport Beach.) At the end of an observational shift, the observer would return to the university and hook the portable computer up to the mainframe computer and transfer the day's observational data to our large computer account.

Our data analysts then took these observational data—several thousand entries for each worker—and tabulated them to give us a sense of what the teenage workers were actually doing. We were shocked at the results: Much of the average worker's time was spent in two specific activities—cleaning things and carrying things. In contrast, almost no time on the job was spent in reading, writing, or arithmetic computation, and even less time was spent in activities that permitted decision making or higher-order thinking. No matter what type of job the teenager worked at, the typical worker spent his or her shift doing one or two low-level tasks over and over again. Teenagers' jobs were highly routinized, very repetitive, and intellectually unchallenging. No wonder adolescent workers seemed to be learning so little from their jobs.

The fact that teenagers' jobs were so dreary helped explain why working did not seem to have the benefits that many adults presumed it did. But why did it have so many apparent costs? Why was working associated with diminished school performance, increased drug and alcohol use, and higher levels of delinquency? We returned to the issue of weekly hours of work.

We began a series of analyses in which we looked at *how much*, not whether, a student was working. These analyses proved to be very informative, for they indicated that it was not working, but rather, working long hours, that was associated with the adverse outcomes. In general, students who worked fewer than ten hours per week looked no different from those who did not work at all on our measures of schooling, behavior, and mental health. Students who worked more than twenty hours each week were at the greatest risk. Working long hours interfered with other activities (like school), provided students with a large amount of discretionary income (some of which went to drugs and alcohol), and placed students under a lot of stress (which adversely affected their mental health).

Because these findings were cross-sectional, we could not be sure about cause and effect. Perhaps it was the poorer students who chose to work. Perhaps students who were already using drugs and alcohol were more inclined to work in order to make money. Before concluding that working led to poor school performance and more delinquency and drug use, we needed to clarify the direction of effects. We attempted to do this in two ways. First, we compared nonworking students who said they wanted to work with those who said that they did not. This would let us see whether students who chose to work were different from their peers to begin with—that is, before they ever entered the labor force.

Second, we turned to our longitudinal data. We took our two groups of nonworkers (those who became workers and those who did not), statistically matched them on their initial adjustment scores, and looked to see whether the groups differed over time. If they did, this would suggest that working was actually having an effect. If they did not, we would conclude that the correlation we observed between working and poor adjustment was due to the fact that students who choose to work are different from those who do not before they enter the labor force.

For the most part, these analyses confirmed our suspicion that working was actually leading to the adverse consequences we were observing. Far from being beneficial, it looked as if working long hours was taking its toll on teenagers' health and education.

Ellen had won the bet. I bought dinner.

THE MEDIA BLITZ

Although I was surprised by the results of the research, I never could have anticipated what would happen next. I began the next phase of my "postgraduate" training as a social scientist: Dealing with the press.

Because they depend on public monies, universities have a lot invested in making sure that the public hears about all the important research going on within their hallowed halls. For that reason, Ellen and I were happy to share the results of our research with a writer from the university's press office, who was interested in doing a release on our research. We met with the writer and worked to make sure the release was accurate. After we approved each and every word, the release went out to local media.

Within days, we were deluged with calls from reporters.

An article in the *Los Angeles Times* led to one in *The Wall Street Journal*, which led to *The New York Times*, *The Washington Post*, and *The Boston Globe*. *Newsweek* wanted to do a story. So did *Time*, *Fortune*, and the *Ladies Home Journal*. For a phenomenon that no one had paid much attention to, our work was generating an awful lot of attention.

No one believed our findings, however. Questioning the value of having teenagers work was like criticizing motherhood and apple pie. We received angry letters from parents telling us to come out of the "ivory tower" and recognize that adolescents were learning about the real world from their jobs. Vocational and career educators perceived our study as a threat. The fast food industry, worried about negative publicity, began funding research designed to show that their jobs were not harmful to teenagers.

Each of us was pressed to defend our findings and the design of our study over and over again.

I had to make a decision at that point whether I was going to be the type of social scientist who would be accessible to the media or whether, like many of my colleagues, I would avoid reporters like the plague. I decided to try to work with the press in disseminating the results of our research to the public. I reasoned that the public had, in essence, paid for the research (remember that much of our funding had come from the federal government) and that it had a right to know what had come of its expenditure. Moreover, I knew that our work was going to be reported, whether I cooperated or not. If I tried to be helpful, at least I could play some role in making sure that the reports were accurate. If I refused to be interviewed, I ran the risk that our research would be misrepresented. Ellen and I continued to work with the press in making sure that the results of our research were published in popular outlets. We also continued to write up our research for publication in scholarly outlets.

About a year later, we discovered that our work was potentially as important as it was interesting. The Reagan administration, under pressure from the restaurant and retail industries, had made a proposal to Congress to relax a number of federal child labor laws so that adolescents would be able to work longer hours during the school year. The legislators wanted to know how this change might affect teenagers' well-being. Ellen was asked to present our research findings in testimony before a subcommittee of the U.S. Congress. We argued that more work was something that American adolescents did not need, and that relaxing the existing laws was not in children's best interest. With the help of other experts, we were able to persuade the administration to withdraw its proposal.

Based on the public reaction to our work, Ellen and I realized that our research was potentially of interest to a wide audience of parents, educators, and policy makers. We decided to write it up in book form, in which we could take the time and space we needed to really flesh out the issues in detail. In 1986, we published *When Teenagers Work*, which was, to my knowledge, the first systematic analysis of the costs and benefits to adolescents and to society of work during the school year. Another round of publicity followed, and Ellen and I each spoke with dozens of reporters and appeared on several of the national television morning news shows to discuss the issue. By now, we had become seasoned professionals in dealing with the media.

After several months of this sort of attention, the excitement of being in the media spotlight started to fade. I began to dread receiving calls from reporters, who would all ask the same questions. To tell you the truth, I was getting pretty sick of the topic of teenagers and work. I hadn't planned on becoming quite so specialized.

Although I tried to distance myself from the topic of adolescent employment, however, I had become labeled as an expert on the subject. There seemed no way to extricate myself from the issue. Shortly after the publication of our book, Ellen and I each started receiving calls from state and federal policy makers asking us for advice on issues related to child labor. As a result of our work, several states were considering legislation that would restrict the number of hours teenagers could work during the school year. I was asked to testify before the National Commission on Children. I even received a call from the White House asking for a copy of one of our reports.

In 1988 I began a new study of adolescents, this time focusing on family, peer, and extracurricular influences on adjustment and on engagement and achievement in school. We were planning on conducting annual surveys of more than 10,000 high school students in Wisconsin and northern California. (I was no longer fearful of getting involved in large-scale survey research.) One of my collaborators suggested that we include in our survey a few questions about teenage employment.

I couldn't resist.

This time, though, I was no longer sailing in uncharted waters. The work that I had done with Ellen ten years earlier set the stage for a more focused series of questions on the relation between hours of employment and various indicators of adolescent well-being. This time, I could test these hypotheses in a much larger and more diverse sample of students.

To my surprise, our new analyses replicated the findings Ellen and I had reported in our initial studies. In 1991 we published a report showing that working long hours was associated with disengagement from school, higher rates of drug and alcohol use, more delinquency, and weakened ties to parents. In 1993, we published a follow-up report showing that working actually led to these consequences. Once again a press release was issued reporting our findings.

Reporters called, but this time their tone was different. Most of their stories were on how adults were rethinking the role of work in the lives of adolescents. One reporter, who worked for the Associated Press, said that our findings weren't very surprising and didn't warrant news coverage. Another, after interviewing me, said that the research was old news. After all, she said, everyone "knows" that working can be harmful to teenagers. Hadn't some researchers even written a book several years ago on the subject?

As I hung the phone up, I thought to myself that it was really quite amazing how much public opinion about teenage employment had shifted. It felt both satisfying and strange to think that a research project I had helped design had actually had some social impact.

I suppose you're wondering what happened to Kari and her job at Foot Locker. She lasted less than a month. She said that it was tiring, boring, and that it interfered with school. After graduating from high school, Kari completed college and graduate school, and she became a psychology professor.

*S*UGGESTED READINGS

GREENBERGER, E., & STEINBERG, L. (1986). *When teenagers work: The psychological and social costs of adolescent employment.* New York: Basic Books.

STEINBERG, L., & DORNBUSCH, S. (1991). Negative correlates of part-time work in adolescence: Republication and elaboration. *Developmental Psychology, 27,* 304–313.

——— FEGLEY, S., & DORNBUSCH, S. (1993). Negative impact of part-time work on adolescent adjustment: Evidence from a longitudinal study. *Developmental Psychology, 29,* 171–180.

——— GREENBERGER, E., GARDUQUE, L., RUGGIERO, M., & VAUX, A. (1982). Effects of working on adolescent development. *Developmental Psychology, 18,* 385–395.

*J*ACQUELINE *V. LERNER (Ph.D., Pennsylvania State University) is Professor of Psychology at Michigan State University. She has served on the editorial board of* Infant Behavior and Development *and is a reviewer for various child and adolescent journals. She publishes in the area of temperament, adolescent transitions, family relations, and maternal employment. She has coedited several books including* Employed Mothers and Their Children *(with N. Galambos) and has just finished a book titled* Working Women and Their Families. *When she is not busy with work or family demands you will find her exercising, skiing, or reading Stephen King.*

13

The Contextual History of My Research on Adolescent Temperament

❖

INTRODUCTION

My desire to pursue a career in psychology stems from my high school days. I was doing well in both academics and gymnastics, but decided that a career in gymnastics was not realistic. I had been brought up to believe that I could achieve anything if I tried hard enough, and during my junior year I took a psychology class. I became intrigued at the prospect of discovering the causes of human behavior, and decided that year, at the age of 16, that I would pursue a Ph.D. in psychology. Nine years later, I realized my goal. During my college years at St. John's University, I was interested in clinical psychology and I pictured myself as a therapist. It was the most popularized field of psychology, and I was excited about it.

After college I began a master's program in clinical psychology at Eastern Michigan University. It was during that year that I met Richard Lerner, a developmental psychologist (whom I later married), and was introduced to the research world of developmental psychology. I decided to pursue a research rather than a clinical degree, and we began to collaborate on research involving the influences that children's characteristics (physical, behavioral) have on their development. Much of Richard's research had been done on the role that children's physical attractiveness plays in the feedback they receive from others, and how this "feedback"

203

further influences their development. For example, two children of equal intelligence may differ in their physical attractiveness. For the child who is attractive, the interactions he or she has with others will most likely be pleasant, encouraging, and approaching. This is not merely an opinion, research has shown that from infancy through adult life, attractive people are responded to more positively by others in their contexts (their family, their teachers, and their peers) than are unattractive people.

It seemed unfair to me that this was the case, that attractiveness gave people an "edge." The research of social psychologists Ellen Berscheid and Karen Dion on the role of physical attractiveness substantiated this unfairness. Through their research they discovered that teachers, for example, tend to think that attractive children are smarter and are more well-behaved than unattractive children. Imagine how this would play itself out in the classroom. Unattractive children could receive less attention or more negative attention from teachers, and could become less motivated to do well, even though they may be equal in intelligence to their attractive peers. After some time of being ignored, unmotivated, and suffering from a lowered self-concept, unattractive children could begin to fail in school. Thus, after beginning elementary school with the same potential for success as attractive children, unattractive children may be on a much different developmental pathway. The feedback they receive from the others in their context influences how they think about themselves and their abilities, and it affects their performance—and their future development.

CIRCULAR FUNCTIONS

Psychologists call the following cycle—children's characteristics influencing others in their context—then children receiving feedback from the context (positive, negative, or neutral)—and the feedback influencing the children's future behavior and development, a "circular function" or a "circular feedback cycle." More specifically, the children develop certain individual physical and behavioral characteristics as a result of both maturation and experience. The children then act on their environment, providing stimuli for the environment to react to. The children's behavior may stimulate other children, their parents, or even themselves. This stimulation evokes responses which will become part of their experience and shape further development. Therefore, children, through their individual characteristics, become sources of their own development.

My master's thesis supported part of the process that I just described. In a sample of fourth- and sixth-grade children, those who were more attractive (as rated by 100 adults who viewed slides of the children) were doing better in academics regardless of their intellectual potential, were rated more positively by their teachers and peers, and had higher levels of self-esteem. Although long-term assessment of the same children would be necessary to test the entire circular feedback cycle, the study did support the idea that children differing in physical attractiveness were receiving different feedback from others in their environment. This research further supported my interest in pursuing how children's characteristics influence their development.

TURNING TO TEMPERAMENT AND LIFE SPAN DEVELOPMENT

My interest in physical attractiveness never dwindled, but I was eager to test the notion of child-context interactions with another organismic characteristic—temperament. First, let me detail some of the events that led to this interest. After my master's work at Eastern Michigan University, I entered the doctoral program in educational psychology at Penn State University. I was becoming more and more fascinated with how we interact with our contexts, how the contexts in which we interact shape our development, and how, through our individuality, we are all active producers of our own development. My belief was that development occurs as the result of an interaction between people and their contexts, and without studying both it would be impossible to determine the processes that underlie development and human behavior.

THE LIFE SPAN PERSPECTIVE AND TEMPERAMENT

Using an interactionist framework, I study both the person and the context because I believe that they are inextricably tied to each other, affecting each other constantly. Another perspective that guides my thinking and my research is the "life span perspective," which has been written about by psychologists such as Paul Baltes, Hayne Reese, Lewis Lipsitt, Sherry Willis, and Richard Lerner. The major assumption of this view is that development can occur at all points of the life span, from conception to death, as opposed to the more traditional views of development which assert that growth and maturation take place during infancy, childhood, and adolescence, that there is stability in adulthood, and decline and degeneration during old age.

Another attribute of this perspective is that each portion of the life span is seen as just one part of the entire life span. Life span developmentalists focus on three tasks: description, explanation, and optimization. They wish to describe the changes that occur throughout development, to explain the processes that underlie these changes, and to prevent unhealthy development and foster change and healthy development.

In 1979 I was introduced to the two psychiatrists who founded the New York Longitudinal Study (NYLS). The NYLS is a "life span" study begun in 1956 that traces (I say traces because it is still going on) the development of 133 Caucasian children from birth. Drs. Alexander Thomas and Stella Chess had begun this work as a study of behavioral individuality. They were convinced that all children had their own individual behavioral styles, or "how" they acted and reacted. They had noticed in their private practices that parents noticed their children's individuality, had expectations for their children's behavior, and reacted differently to different characteristics.

For example, some parents were extremely distressed by their children's irregularity of sleep or feeding cycles, and were finding parenting difficult. Others were distressed by how sensitive their infants were to sounds, lights, and movement. This sensitivity made it difficult for their children to get to sleep or to stay asleep in some situations. Others complained about their children's reactions to new situations, new people, or new foods. Some children's adjustment to any changes in their environment was slow or difficult, while others seemed to approach and adjust to new things with ease.

WHAT IS TEMPERAMENT?

Thomas and Chess realized that these differences in behavioral style (later they also refer to it as temperament) were responded to differently by parents, and that these behavioral style characteristics were influencing the interactions between parent and child. After several years of collecting interview data on behaviors, they delineated nine attributes that they felt were behavioral styles or temperamental attributes. These are activity level, rhythmicity or regularity of functions such as sleep and eating, approach or withdrawal, adaptability or adjustment to new situations, intensity of reaction or the strength of a response, threshold of responsiveness or the energy necessary to evoke a response, quality of mood (positive, negative, or neutral), distractibility, and attention span/persistence. These characteristics all refer to the "how" of behavior. Not "what" children do, but how they go about doing the behaviors they engage in, with a lot or a little activity, with a positive or negative mood, etc.

From an interactional perspective, children's development would be affected either negatively or positively, depending on how the context reacted to their temperamental attributes, and how this "feedback" was processed by them. At the same time, children are also affecting their parents' development.

I decided that the work of Thomas and Chess on temperament in children was important for the framework of my own research. I began to read their writings, and learned more about their ideas regarding temperamental individuality. Temperament, as an organismic characteristic, played a role in children's development in a similar way to physical attractiveness. Temperament, however, because it involves behaviors, is more of an active influence. I thought that it would be an interesting way to test the circular functions notion that I believed to be operating and influencing development. The work of Thomas and Chess intrigued me for another reason. In their writings they discussed a concept called "goodness-of-fit." In their goodness-of-fit model they specified what they believed the process was that influenced children's development. All parents have certain demands or expectations for their children's behaviors—these demands are based on their values, stereotypes, or on the parents' own behaviors. For example, parents may believe that there are gender differences, and thus expect that their daughter should not be as active as their son because she is female. If she is extremely active, she may receive negative feedback from them, and if she does not change her behavior or if the parents do not eventually tolerate her activity level, then the persistent negativity she receives can adversely influence her development.

On the other hand, children whose characteristics meet the demands of their parents will be easier to care for and interact with, and thus parent-child interactions should be more enjoyable. These positive interactions should contribute to a more positive adjustment for these children. This can be further seen in the classroom, where children who are able to meet the demands of the classroom setting and the teacher are more likely to be viewed positively, may therefore feel better about their abilities, may try harder, and may end up being more successful in school than children who cannot meet the contextual demands of the classroom.

All of this made intuitive sense to me, and I viewed it as the most appropriate way of thinking about the interaction between people, their characteristics, and the contexts in which they interact. I decided to investigate the role of both temperament and the goodness-of-fit model in my dissertation. Using the nine dimensions of temperament described by Thomas and Chess and found in the NYLS, I developed a questionnaire of demands for teachers and students. For each characteristic of temperament, the questionnaire assessed what degree of that characteristic they "expected or demanded" from their students. For example, for the characteristic of activity level, the item for teachers would be "I expect my students to have a (low, moderate, or high) activity level."

Although Thomas and Chess had discussed the goodness-of-fit model in all their writings that I had read, they had never actually measured the demands that parents held for temperament. They used their clinical skills to detect that parents had different demands for child temperament, and from what they could see of the development of the children that they were studying, these demands, in interaction with the children's temperaments, were influencing parenting and child development.

The NYLS sample was collected by snowballing—they asked their friends and colleagues who were having children to participate, then these participants would recommend others. This process led to a sample that was largely upper middle class, professional, Caucasian, and Jewish. They labeled this sample the "core" sample. Knowing that they could not generalize their findings to other groups, they set out to collect data on a sample of lower-income, Puerto Rican children. They used a similar framework—parent interviews to obtain information about the infants' temperaments, their parenting, and the children's overall adjustment.

This sample is known as a cross-validation sample—a sample used to determine whether findings from one sample will hold up for other groups. What they found in the sample of Puerto Ricans was really fascinating. It was, in my opinion, the strongest support they had for the goodness-of-fit model. Their first realization was that the Puerto Rican parents did not have the same set of demands for temperament as did the Caucasian parents. For example, Caucasian parents desired high rhythmicity, or regularity, from their children. If they could not get their children on a predictable eating and sleeping schedule, it was extremely disturbing for them. After all, most mothers from this sample were employed and went back to work a few months after their babies were born. An irregular child would not allow these busy working parents to get enough sleep, and difficulties in parenting arose. Parents complained about the characteristics of low rhythmicity, negative mood, and high intensity, to name a few.

Interestingly, it was the children who did not meet the expectations of the parents in the core sample who were also having problems in behavioral adjustment later on. Now they were onto something. Thomas and Chess had identified a cluster of temperamental attributes—low rhythmicity, negative mood, high intensity, frequent withdrawal, and slow adaptability—that they labeled "the difficult child" cluster. They called it difficult because these were the attributes that did not fit with parental demands, and it was these children, the difficult ones, that were more likely to have behavioral problems. They decided that this finding needed to be cross-validated with the Puerto Rican sample. They were surprised at what they found. The children in the Puerto Rican sample who were identified as difficult according to the core sample attributes, were not the ones that seemed to be more behavior disordered, nor were parents complaining about the same attributes. For example, rhythmicity was not an issue for these parents. Most of them did not have jobs, so *when* the children went to bed at night or awoke in the morning did not concern them.

Negative mood did not bother them either; parents explained that their children needed to be "bad" in order to survive on the streets of Spanish Harlem. One characteristic that did bother these parents that was not an issue with the core sample was that of high activity. The children in the core sample lived in nice neighborhoods, in large apartments, with safe playgrounds nearby. If children had high activity levels, there were plenty of outlets available. On the other hand, the Puerto Rican children lived in small apartments, with many family members, and without safe playgrounds nearby. High activity level for these children definitely did not "fit" with parental or physical demands.

By evaluating which children in the Puerto Rican sample did not fit the parental demands for temperament, they noticed that it was the children with high activity level who were more likely to have difficulties in parent-child relations and overall adjustment. Thomas and Chess realized that their goodness-of-fit model was indeed operating, but that you could not generalize the demands of one set of parents to a different group of parents. Another finding supporting this model was that although sleep arrhythmicity was not a problem when the Puerto Rican children were preschoolers, it did become a problem when these children had to adjust to the demands of the school setting, which required waking early in the morning.

Thus, using the ideas of Thomas and Chess, I launched into my dissertation research. As I said above, I studied the temperament of junior high school students, and the contextual demands for temperament of their teachers and peers. I also collected information on their peer relationships, through a peer nomination technique, and their academic functioning. Overall, the goodness-of-fit model was supported. Those children who better fit with the demands held by their teachers and peers were more likely to be more adjusted (as measured by their self-esteem, popularity, and academic achievement) than were children who were not as fit.

*I*NHERITING THE NYLS

At the same time that I was completing my dissertation research, Alex Thomas and Stella Chess contacted Richard and me because they wanted to make us heirs to their NYLS data set. They were approaching age 70 at the time, and they had visited their lawyer to update their wills. He noted that everything was in order except that they had not "willed" their data to anyone. He asked if they had thought about it and what would happen to it after they were gone. They approached us and told us that they would like to "will" us the data, so that it could be kept active and alive. They gave us the data that year, even though they were still actively collecting follow-up information on the sample. We obtained a three-year grant from the MacArthur Foundation to archive the data and make it available to the scientific community. We received this grant in 1981. I had received my Ph.D. in 1980 and had had my first child, Justin.

We had spent the 1980–1981 academic year at Stanford University. Richard was asked to be a fellow at the Center for Advanced Study in the Behavioral Sciences—a social science think tank. I spent that year writing, working part-time on a research project at Stanford, and as a visiting scholar at the Center for Research on Women. The flexibility of that year gave me the opportunity to spend a lot of time with Justin, getting used to my new role as a mother.

The grant from the MacArthur Foundation began in 1981, when we returned to Penn State. I did not have a formal job there, but was able to pay myself a salary from the grant. The department head of Human Development and Family Studies gave me a temporary appointment as an assistant professor for the duration of the grant period. I also began teaching in the department, although my first priority was to archive the NYLS. It was a huge job; the study had been going on for twenty-five years and every piece of paper had to be copied and microfilmed. A three-hour interview had been conducted when the NYLS participants were three years old— and that had to be duplicated and transcribed. We had a staff of secretaries working on clerical tasks, and our graduate students were busy doing an inventory.

An inventory was essential to this project because, although Thomas and Chess had published a great deal on the negative and positive aspects of the development of these children, there was an enormous amount of interview data that was never analyzed.

The inventory took an enormous amount of time. Detailed parental interviews were conducted every three months for the first five years of each child's life. These were supplemented by nursery school observations, teacher interviews, and IQ assessments. The children themselves were interviewed during adolescence, their early twenties, and their late twenties/early thirties. At each age, parents were also interviewed. During their development, extensive information was collected from their schools, and if at any point in their development they developed problems they were seen in therapy by Stella Chess. Therefore, if any of the participants were seen in therapy, extensive data exists on their problems and the course of the therapy. Overall, about fifty of the participants had been seen in therapy at some point—these were known as the "clinical cases."

One very interesting point about the NYLS is that over the course of the thirty-eight years of the study, only two participants dropped out. At some of the interview points, several of the participants were unavailable; for example, some were in the service for years. However, when they returned, they were interviewed, so that there exists continuous data for most of the life spans of these people. This has been due to the commitment of Thomas and Chess, who dedicated their careers to the participants, their families, and to the quality of the study. They conducted interviews in airports, hospitals, and traveled the country many times to catch up with participants who were unable to be in the New York area. Some interviews had to be conducted by phone, and an attempt was always made to also interview the parents. You see, from the bidirectional perspective that was described above, it was essential to obtain information on the significant people in the context, people who were influencing and being influenced by the participants of the NYLS.

The inventory took about three years to complete and make available to others in the scientific community. We had many scholars come to Penn State to work with the data and conduct analyses on interesting issues.

Thomas and Chess continue to work with the "clinical" sample, and they write prolifically about other issues in life span development. After all, they have been able to chronicle the life spans of 133 people. Some of the areas that I have investigated using NYLS data are the influences of maternal employment on child development, the precursors of drug and alcohol use, the correlates of negative emotional and behavioral characteristics, and sibling similarities and differences. While I probably will be analyzing and publishing NYLS data throughout the rest of my life span, in 1984 another research opportunity emerged.

E*ARLY ADOLESCENT TRANSITIONS*

Although I have always characterized myself as a *child* developmentalist, in the early 1980s there was a surge of interest in the adolescent period, particularly early adolescence. Adolescence had not always been viewed as a period of development in its own right, and researchers began to realize that it needed to be viewed as a stage with its own unique issues and characteristics, and not just an extension of childhood. As a life span developmentalist, I asserted that one needs to understand what precedes a period of development before one can understand the period under investigation. Therefore, my expertise in child development prepared me for an investigation of early adolescent development.

With a large grant from the W. T. Grant Foundation, Richard and I began an investigation of early adolescent transitions. We called it the Pennsylvania Early Adolescent Transitions Study (PEATS). The purpose of the project was to study a group of elementary school students during their last year of elementary school, and then continue to study them after they made the transition to junior high school. A major interest in early adolescent research is on transitions, since during this period transitions occur in children's physical, intellectual, social, sexual, and academic development. To undergo multiple transitions is thought to put some children at risk for problems. Some early adolescents will handle these transitions with ease, some will have problems in some areas, and others will be plagued by multiple problems. The point is that the popular notion that adolescence is a period of "storm and stress" had never really been supported by research.

Surely, there are adolescents who are rebellious, have incredible problems, and appear to be going through the most difficult time of their lives. But for these youngsters, it is likely that they were always experiencing problems, and the challenges of adolescence exacerbated whatever issues were already present. Even for adolescents who may have sailed through childhood, a move to a new school when they are already experiencing multiple transitions can be risky. With our view about the need to evaluate development within the context of the person, it was our belief that we could learn more about how children go through these transitions if we paid attention to their characteristics, and the characteristics of their family, peer, and school contexts.

We set out on a longitudinal investigation of approximately 150 sixth graders in northwestern Pennsylvania. We assessed all the characteristics we believed would play a role in their development: Temperament, physical attractiveness, intelligence, pubertal level, social relations, family relations, family makeup, self-esteem, adjustment, to name a few. We asked their teachers, parents, and peers about their demands for temperament, so that we were able to assess goodness-of-fit. We were interested in finding out what personal, family, school, and peer characteristics would be related to early adolescents' ability to make the transitions of that period smoothly. We believed that adolescence was not a universal period of storm and stress and that if we could evaluate which characteristics were linked to healthy or poor adjustment, then we could educate others about this period. This knowledge could also be used to help parents, teachers, and adolescents themselves understand more about this period. And perhaps the knowledge could also be used to identify children "at risk" for problems.

We were able to find out a great deal about this period of life. For example, the goodness-of-fit model was supported. Those adolescents whose characteristics of temperament fit with the demands of their parents, teachers, and peers, were doing well on several indices of adjustment. For example, parents wanted children who were moderately distractible and had moderate activity levels, and peers wanted friends who had positive moods. Adolescents who fit these demands reported higher levels of self-esteem, peer relations, family relations, grades, etc. In addition, several temperamental characteristics themselves were linked to better functioning. Positive mood was a characteristic that indicated better peer relations, and low distractibility was linked to better grades. Physical attractiveness was also indicative of high levels of self-competence and scholastic competence.

We believed that the PEATS had been an extremely useful study in our investigation of early adolescent development, but we felt the need to cross-validate our findings. We were funded by the National Institute for Child Health and Human Development to conduct a four-year investigation of the same sorts of issues we had investigated in the PEATS. This cross-validation and replication study was called the REPEATS—the Replication and Extension of the Pennsylvania Early Adolescent Transitions Study. The REPEATS was more extensive. We were not able to obtain a sample to study as they made the transition into middle school, but we were able to study two groups of sixth graders as they went through middle school (sixth, seventh, and eighth grades for group 1, and sixth and seventh grades for group 2).

Although these children had already made the transition to middle school, they were by no means finished making transitions. They varied in pubertal level, as well as in their social and cognitive development. We were interested in studying how these children were adjusting to middle school, and evaluating which personal, family, peer, and physical characteristics were associated with a positive adjustment and which characteristics were associated with a negative adjustment. We have finished our data collection and are in the process of evaluating our results. Some of our findings support those that we found with the PEATS sample and others extend our knowledge about this period of development. For example, in the REPEATS we examined the coping styles of the adolescents and found that both the temperament of the child and the degree of peer support experienced during a problem situation were related to coping style. In this case, when the adolescent had a tendency toward a negative mood and experienced low levels of peer support he or she was more likely to exhibit a negative coping style when faced with a problem. Thus, we were able to show the interplay among an organismic characteristic (temperamental negative mood), a contextual characteristic (peer support), and the adolescent's reaction to a stressor.

In another analysis involving pubertal change and aggression, preliminary results have revealed that the onset of puberty may result in heightened levels of aggression toward adults and peers for girls but not for boys. While these analyses are in the early stages, we will continue to investigate whether early maturation may be a risk factor for the development of negative behaviors. For example, it could be that the girls in the REPEATS who are making the transition to puberty are also experiencing other transitions or difficulties. Further analyses and research will make it possible to examine the individual and contextual factors that lead to aggression and other behavior problems.

I am hoping that by demonstrating how development is a function of both the person and the context that we can better understand the adolescent period and help both adolescents and their parents have a better understanding of this time of life. I now have three data sets that I will be evaluating and analyzing for many years to come. My interest in temperament has filtered into other projects that I am involved in because I believe it is an integral part of how people interact with the world, how others treat them, and how they eventually develop. I will probably follow up the NYLS sample when they are in their forties. I will look at their temperaments, their career developments, and their relationships, with a particular interest in stability and change. It is rare to be able to evaluate a sample of individuals across the entire life span.

I have gone through several of my own transitions. I now have three children (Justin, Blair, and Jarrett), and have moved from Penn State to Michigan State where I am a professor of psychology. I have become involved in several other projects, most of which have to do with the same issues I have always studied. My knowledge about adolescent transitions and development has helped me understand my son Justin, who is now 14, and my work in maternal employment helps me wrestle with the daily combination of work and family. My work in temperamental individuality helps me understand myself, my family, and others. I have been influenced by and continue to influence the contexts I live in, and I will continue to be intrigued by the processes that underlie development.

Acknowledgment

The research reported in this chapter was supported in part by Grant #HD 23229 from the National Institute of Child Health and Human Development (NICHD) to Richard M. Lerner, Jacqueline V. Lerner, and Alexander von Eye.

SUGGESTED READINGS

LERNER, J. V., & LERNER, R. M. (Eds.) (1986). *Temperament and psychosocial interaction in infancy and childhood: New directions for child development.* San Francisco: Jossey-Bass.

LERNER, R. M., LERNER, J. V., & TUBMAN, J. G. (1989). Organismic and contextual bases of development in adolescence: A developmental contextual model. In G. R. Adams, R. Montemayor, & J. Gullotta (Eds.), *Biology of adolescent behavior and development* (Vol. 1, pp. 11–37). Beverly Hills, CA: Sage.

*C*AMERON J. CAMP *(Ph.D, University of Houston) is a Research Professor of Psychology at the University of New Orleans, in New Orleans, Louisiana. Dr. Camp is on the editorial boards of the journals* Adult Development *and* Experimental Aging Research, *is on the advisory board of the New Orleans Chapter of the Alzheimer's Association, chairs the Greenwalt Alzheimer's Care and Research Center Advisory Board, and is on the Board of Directors of Citizens for Quality Nursing Home Care in New Orleans. He is currently coauthoring a college textbook on adult development and aging with Dianne Papalia-Finley and Ruth Feldman, and has won departmental awards for teaching. He is kept busy conducting research in applied developmental psychology, focusing on designing interventions for persons with dementia. When not working, he reads fiction and writes tidbits such as the very short story at the beginning of the chapter.*

14

The Return of Sherlock Holmes: A Pilgrim's Progress in Memory and Aging Research

❖

A SWEET POTATO TALE

Visiting in-laws at Christmas ensures a steady supply of soap operas on the TV. Retreat or redress during bad weather is almost impossible, except for reading a book (or these days, playing a battery-powered Game Boy). Still, the dialogue intrudes. Thus, I was struck with wonder when I heard what seemed to be a sublimely surreal exchange. A young man at the door had just told a couple:

"I've come to smell your Christmas yams."

All my attention was intently focused on what would be said next. The couple on the screen looked at the Dadaesque character as if they were unsure of what had just happened. They glanced at each other, then said,

"What?"

I had to relay my own response to the TV's audience in the room.

"This is great! What a line! 'I've come to smell your Christmas yams.' True genius."

This in turn drew looks from in-laws as if I had just grown a yam in the middle of my head. Someone said,

"What?"

"Wonderful!" was my reply. "Life imitates art."

At that moment my wife informed me that the young man's line was, "I've come to tell you about LuAnn."

It was time to play the Game Boy again. But one must never lose the chance to find magic, under whatever guise, even when we are the true magicians.

A few years ago I was working with a client at an adult day care center who exhibited dementia. A research team from my lab was training him to remember the name of a staff member at the center. The technique we used is called spaced retrieval. It is a shaping paradigm applied to memory. In essence, it consists of asking a person to recall information at successively longer intervals.

In this case, a group of us were sitting around a table engaged in conversation. The group included the client, my research team, and the staff member in question. I asked the client to name the staffer. When he could not, I let him know that her name was "Ann" and asked him to repeat it. He did, then I asked the question again five seconds later. He said the staffer was "Ann." He kept succeeding at successive recall trials, each of which was longer: ten seconds, 20 seconds, 40 seconds, 60 seconds, 90 seconds, 120 seconds, etc.

At the 210-second trial, something strange happened. When asked to name the staffer he said "Sherlock Holmes." We were a bit perplexed, then he looked us over and laughed. "Gotchya!" he said. "Her name is really Ann." We admired his wit, then waited for 240 seconds (4 minutes) and asked him to name the staffer. He replied: "Sherlock Holmes—Gotchya! Her name is really Ann." This happened on each of the next two trials, then we called it a day. As we were leaving the center, my students looked at me and asked "What just happened?" The answer to that question, and the implications it has for interventions in dementia, constitute a major theme of this chapter. But first, let me explain how I arrived at this juncture in my career.

THE CAVE OR THE COUCH

Unlike most of my colleagues, I knew that I wanted to become a psychologist at the early age of 14. I came to this conclusion because I wanted to study people as a full-time vocation, and the choices available for this career path seemed to be: (1) become a salesman (definitely out, since my father was one), (2) become a hermit (the contemplative aspect was enticing, but the pay was a bit too low), or (3) become a psychologist. After due and painful deliberation, I chose the latter path. From then on, most of the important choices in my life were determined by totally serendipitous events.

My professional development has been largely unplanned, but an openness to discovery and change has led it in some interesting directions. Looking forward, I can only hope that the future will remain whimsically unpredictable. Looking back, I would not change a thing.

ANYTHING BUT A LONGHORN

My high school counselor (I lived in Tyler, a town east of Dallas) advised me that only the University of Texas at Austin and the University of Houston had programs approved by the American Psychological Association. I hated the University of Texas due to growing up in Oklahoma (the Texas/OU rivalry was and is very fierce on and off the football field), so my mind was made up. Oddly enough, I did not understand what the counselor meant when he said that these two schools had CLINICAL programs approved by the APA. This was odd because the one thing I did *not* want to do was to become a clinical psychologist. I had heard that training in this area required students to undergo psychoanalysis themselves. This would mean revealing the hidden, darker, abnormal, perverted, or (you fill in the blank) aspects of my true self, and so was not for me.

My choice of higher educational programs was initially limited by funds—I had none. During a high school career day tour of the local junior college, a counselor from that institution answered my question, "What is epistemology?" with, "I think it is the study of the Epistles." As a result, I warily enrolled there after leaving high school, and earned two years worth of courses as a psychology major. None of these courses had anything to do with psychology, for I was saving those credit hours for my training in Houston. It seemed prudent to temporarily delay my study of psychology until I could get to the big city. The years in junior college did allow me to get through the grind of freshman-level courses with levels of faculty advice, guidance, and tolerance which would not have been found elsewhere. Overall, things worked out well for all concerned.

While attending junior college I worked thirty to thirty-five hours a week as a cook at a hamburger joint. Cooks at the establishment had to take all orders from memory. This involved simultaneously remembering three groups of orders, with eight patties in each group. For example, the cook would take one order (two regular patties, two with cheese, one regular, one cheese, one double pattie [two patties on one bun] with cheese). After starting this batch, the next group of orders would be taken (three regular, two with cheese, three regular). After starting the second group of patties, the cook would give buns to the sandwich makers (the first set of patties were now cooked, and had to be placed on buns along with lettuce, pickles, etc.), repeat the first order to them, and then take the third order from a new group of customers, starting the cycle over again. All this had to be done without writing anything down and without error, eight to ten hours a day. This did interesting things to my memory, and I learned that I did not have to take extensive notes in college in order to remember what was said in lecture. (I could also recite endless strings of hamburger orders in correct sequence, but why bother?) Such was my introduction to memory training, though I did not recognize it as such at the time. It was just part of the job.

*I*F *I HAD A HAMMER*

Getting to the big city, I was faced with the problem of how to become a psychologist while avoiding psychotherapy. The answer lay in experimental psychology. I took MANY psychology courses as an undergraduate at U of H. I spoke to graduate students. I listened, I learned, and I thought I was getting a pretty good handle on the field and my next step (graduate school). I was wrong.

My graduate application was submitted on an out-of-date form. In addition, I had written an incomprehensible letter of intent (something about fusing the works of Piaget and B. F. Skinner). This caused my file to be put into a "special student" category (aka "WHAT?????"). Fortunately, I checked to see if my file was complete and was told that it was missing. Having worked my way through school, I had acquired some "street smarts." It was obvious that the true sources of power and competence in any department were the secretaries. I had already made their acquaintance, often bearing gifts, and one of them tracked my file to the desk of the graduate coordinator. She asked if I would like to meet with him, and not knowing about faculty protocol (perhaps one should try to make an appointment to discuss matters regarding one's life and career), I said "Yes." Not caring about faculty protocol, she took me by the arm and led me to his desk. "Mr. Camp is here to see you," she announced, and then left, closing the door behind her.

Looking me over with a somewhat jaundiced eye (I found out later that he liked to avoid contact with undergraduates when possible), he asked "Who are you?" I replied that he had my folder on his desk. Upon glancing over my letter of intent he emitted a sound which conveyed disheartened disbelief. He then asked "Do you know carpentry?" I did not. "Photography? Electronics? Computer programming? Metal work? Digital switching circuitry and Boolean algebra?" My answers were "No," "No," "No," "No," and "What?" At that point he sighed and asked "Well what do you know?" My answer was that I had forty-six hours of psychology. He responded "That is not worth very much. You are useless in a lab." But when all seemed lost, I had an inspiration. Gathering my courage, I said "I do have two elective courses left to fill this summer." This interested him, and he said "Would you take courses in Fortran programming and digital switching circuits?" Stifling the first response in my mouth, I said "Sure.

I'll take anything. I'll do whatever it takes." This last comment clinched it, and I left with his promise that he'd see what he could do. The next thing I knew, I was admitted into the graduate program at the University of Houston. I was a "special student" in a program called "Cognitive Education." This was OK, though I did not know what that meant. At least I was in a doctoral program and I would not be going into therapy anytime soon. I was also going to study cognitive psychology, which I had yet to encounter in forty-six hours of course work.

WORLD KNOWLEDGE (OR "WHAT PAPER DO YOU WORK FOR?")

My days as a cognitive educational psychologist were numbered (approximately ninety-five). Before the first semester was completed, I was visited in my graduate cubby by my adviser (a cubby is, in essence, a shallow cave with a prayer mat). He said "You are now in aging. You will study aging. It will be good for you." My reply, as usual, was "Sure! Sounds great." That was fourteen years ago, and my career has involved the study of aging ever since. My research has focused on cognition in aging: first, the study of memory for information acquired in the course of living, then research involving improvement of memory in normal adults of different ages, and finally ways to help older adults suffering from memory problems associated with dementia.

In Houston during the mid-1970s, our lab was investigating knowledge about the real world in people of different ages. My adviser and his wife (actually, my coadvisers) had the good (or bad) luck to antedate hot trends in psychological research by five to ten years. We were interested in how well people of different ages recalled information available in their long-term memories. Creating a set of questions similar to those now asked in trivia board games, we asked subjects to recall the answers to these items. (For example, "What is the capitol of Cambodia?" [Phnom Penn]). Questions which could not be freely recalled were presented a second time in a multiple-choice format. The number of items recalled plus the number of items answered correctly in multiple-choice form served as an index of how much world knowledge was available (i.e., total knowledge). The percentage of this total knowledge which was answered in recall format was an index of the efficiency of retrieval from the world knowledge base of a subject (i.e., = the number of items recalled/total knowledge). What we found was that the size of total knowledge increased with age in adults, while the efficiency of retrieval remained constant. In 1977, this was relatively novel research, and my advisers allowed me to present their findings at a national conference.

After giving the talk, a man with a "Press" badge asked me for an interview. This was my first conference (hell, it was my first airplane ride), and of course I was more than happy to be interviewed. However, I kept my head and gave all credit for the work to my mentor. As the tape recorder was being turned off, I had a flash of clear thinking and asked "What paper do you work for?" When he gave me the name of a tabloid distributed at the checkout lines of supermarkets, I froze. Then he was gone, but I was secure in the knowledge that the research was too boring to make it past his editor. Two months later, however, a department secretary informed me that she had read about the work we were doing while getting her hair done at the beauty parlor. My adviser called me in for a talk soon afterward, reminding me that even the best of news magazines can misquote scientists, and that I might want to act with a bit more discretion in the future.

THE PLANET VULCAN (OR, BEER AND FRIED ZUCCHINI)

My coadviser (my mentor's wife, who is now a corporate lawyer, but that's another story) was brilliant at both creating and answering the questions used in our research. Once, she came across the question "What was the name of the mythical planet which was supposed to be between Mercury and the Sun?" She thought for a moment, and then said "Vulcan."

I was amazed that she had remembered such a fact, much less ever learned it. Reading my mind, she stated "I did not get the answer from memory, I created it. I knew it would be a Roman god, something to do with fire since it was near the sun, and Vulcan seemed the best choice." Thinking this over a bit more, she wondered out loud how often that could happen in our trivia test. Looking in my direction again, she said "Cameron, why don't you find out." Thus was the idea for my master's thesis born, and I was soon busy creating questions whose answers I had never seen before. This was done so that I could study how people make inferences based upon their world knowledge.

The questions used to force people to start "inferencing" were an odd lot. They included items such as, "Which domestic animal continually wears manufactured apparel?" (horse; due to horse shoes). "What common, natural cooking ingredient does not come from a living organism?" (salt). "What fire-making instrument cannot usually be used at midnight?" (magnifying glass). "What horror movie character could starve to death in northern Sweden in the summer?" (Dracula). Over the course of several studies, I found that older adults generally answered such questions as well as younger adults, though more slowly. The lone exception was when many alternatives to an answer were given in a multiple-choice format. In such a case, I speculated, the short-term or working memory capacity of older adults became more overwhelmed by choices than was the case for younger adults. Older adults answered trivia questions which only demanded the recall of facts (without making inferences) as well as or better than young adults.

What was most interesting was that older adults believed that they had become better at "figuring out" (aka inferring) answers to questions as they had grown older, and had become worse at remembering facts. Thus, stereotypes regarding failing memory and increased wisdom with age may have influenced the way older adults felt about their answers to world knowledge questions.

I also learned better ways to come up with inference questions. The best I discovered after taking my first academic job out of graduate school. I was now an assistant professor of psychology at Fort Hays State University in Hays, Kansas. My lab members would meet at a bar across from the campus and order pitchers of beer and fried zucchini. We would put the names of objects into a hat, and randomly draw two names. We would then try to find a connection between the two which could serve as the basis of a question. This led to items such as "What piece of fruit would you want aboard a canoe if it tipped over?" (a watermelon—it floats) and "What western hero would the wolf man fear the most?" (the Lone Ranger—he only shoots silver bullets; I suppose today the question would be phrased "What beer does the wolf man fear most?"—Coors Lite). I think the beer and food may have helped.

THE CORNS AND BUNIONS EFFECT (OR, FOOTWORK)

At Fort Hays State I was introduced to the concept of "workshops." These were courses for students drawn from the general public. These classes were taught on weekends, lasted all day, and generated extra credit hours for the university (a public university needs all the credit hours on its books it can get). Since these workshops were aimed at "nontraditional" students, the topics had to have at least a semblance of relevance to everyday life. I was informed that my background made me immanently qualified to teach a workshop in "memory improvement." This meant that I had to memorize the contents of several books and articles just in advance of my first workshop. Fortunately, since the books taught me how to memorize stuff, this was an easier task than I had anticipated. After serving my time in this way, I became interested in the idea of teaching memory improvement to normal older adults. I gave this project to a student of mine named Lucy Anschutz, and we went out to apartment complexes for older adults to recruit subjects. I had asked for research funds from the graduate council at Fort Hays, and received about $500, all of which was used to pay subjects.

We trained five older adults in each of two apartment complexes in the use of a memory technique called the method of loci. This involves using mental images of different locations, and "putting" things you want to remember in these locations in your mind's eye. My work in Houston had shaped my preference for using meaningful, real-world stimuli. Thus, we trained our subjects to memorize a grocery list made up of items of their own selection. Our subjects were then driven to a grocery store, and were to put items from the list into their grocery carts. The dependent measure in this study was the number of items which went through the checkout line. Participants were paid based on the number of items remembered, and this money was used to pay for the groceries. So, we went through a series of adventures driving people to the store, following them up and down isles with clipboards, and then driving them home to put away the groceries. Our participants also became local celebrities in their apartment complexes, and lines of well-wishers would send them off to the store with cheers (it must have been like this as the Crusaders were leaving for the Holy Land).

Our studies turned up some useful findings. Older adults were able to learn and utilize their memory training, but after a month some of them began to abandon the strategy we had trained. When interviewed later, one person said that it was easier for her to try to remember items in the order she would encounter them in the store. Our way made her have to back-track too much (having learned the items in a specific order of the experimenter's choosing in advance). This, in turn, caused her corns and bunions to ache too much after the shopping trip. Applied psychology can be an enlightening and humbling experience.

LIFE IN THE BIG EASY

After about four years in Hays, I saw an ad for a job at the University of New Orleans. The department was recruiting a person in applied gerontology for a position in their new doctoral program in applied psychology. I answered the ad, ate some gumbo, interviewed, and moved south in the fall of 1983.

At the University of New Orleans we have doctoral programs in applied developmental psychology and applied biopsychology. The work in my lab stands at the interface of these two programs. Most of our data are collected in people's houses, adult day care centers, or nursing homes. Much of our current research deals with discovering or developing interventions for older adults, many of whom are cognitively impaired. Our work, as is often the case with applied psychology, serves two functions. First, it seeks to apply the theoretical ideas and research outcomes from the lab (or work with other clinical populations) to solving problems of older adults in their everyday environments. Second, it serves as a testing ground and feedback loop for such theories and research.

In the spring of 1985 I attended a conference on Cape Cod dealing with memory and aging. I presented a paper summarizing research on world knowledge and aging. In addition, I heard several speakers from England present research on memory interventions in normal and impaired elderly populations. I had begun to have contact with adult day care centers in New Orleans, and had been requested to suggest interventions for clients suffering from dementia, especially dementia associated with Alzheimer's disease. I had quickly found that the techniques for memory improvement used with normal older adults were of little value in working with these problems. The speakers from England at the memory conference had some interesting suggestions, which they elaborated over cocktails one evening. The design of behavioral and cognitive interventions for demented populations has been the focus of most of my research since that time. Recent theoretical and research developments in cognitive aging have guided work in my lab and help explain our success.

For example, Daniel Schacter has described two types of memory: explicit and implicit. Explicit memory involves conscious retrieval of previous life experiences. It is this system which is particularly devastated early in the course of Alzheimer's disease (AD) and other dementias, especially retrieval of very recent life episodes. Explicit memory is also the source of memory differences seen when comparing normal older and younger adults. Darlene Howard speculates that most attempts to improve memory in older populations have required the use of explicit memory. She suggests that the use of alternative types of memory should be the basis for memory improvement techniques with older adults. One such memory system is called "implicit memory."

Schacter has defined implicit memory as a form of memory that does not require conscious recollection of specific personal episodes. David Mitchell states that tests of implicit memory demonstrate that it starts functioning effectively early in life, and remains stable from at least ages 3 to 83. Lars Bäckman in Stockholm says that implicit memory may remain relatively intact in Alzheimer's disease, at least in its early stages. As a result, Leslie McKitrick (my student) and I have suggested that implicit memory appears to be a logical basis on which to attempt interventions in AD, but what form might such interventions take?

Larry Squire has listed a series of memory abilities under the heading nondeclarative (implicit) memory [Squire included the parenthetical "implicit" label]. Among these are conditioning and priming. Working from his model, we have attempted to design interventions for persons with dementia making use of abilities which Squire suggests should be accessing implicit memory. Here is an example of the use of conditioning with dementia. An example of priming will follow that.

I LOVE THIS GUY!

Staff at an adult day care center came to us with a problem. A group of older women, all suffering from dementia, were insulting a new client. The client was an African-American man, also suffering from dementia. His feelings were being hurt, and he was becoming depressed and withdrawn. Attempts to talk to the women, all of whom were Caucasian, did not alter their behavior. First, they believed themselves justified because of their socialization in a more prejudiced time. Second, they would forget such conversations almost as soon as they were over.

We took a different approach. We asked the staff to let this man become the person who distributed all prizes or rewards given out at the center to other clients. In a short while, the attitudes of the women changed and they quit insulting the man. They could not remember having insulted him in the past, nor could they explain why they liked him now. Thus, even though the declarative memory system was impaired in these women, they were able to learn a new set of responses toward this man. In addition, the social status of the gentleman rose and he eventually became the official greeter of guest speakers for the center.

Nelson Butters has shown that motor priming may be less impaired in Alzheimer's disease than other forms of priming. We make use of this. We also make use of another finding from the neuropsychological literature—the ability to read printed words is retained far into the course of Alzheimer's disease. The problem we attack is that clients at day care centers ask repetitive questions about who will pick them up, when will they be going home, etc. If staff tell them the answer, the information is quickly lost and the question is repeated . . . and repeated . . . and repeated . . . and—you get the picture.

We place bulletin boards in day care centers with messages for specific clients, e.g., *Mrs. Smith, your son Corey will pick you up today at 4:30.* These are written with felt pens on a slick surface. (Pinning a note on a board results in clients taking the note down, putting it in their pockets, and forgetting where they put it.) When staff are asked a question, they respond by saying "Let's go find out" and walk with the client to the bulletin board. They then ask the client to read the message out loud and explain it. The client is reassured, and goes back to his or her class or other activity in the center. This procedure is repeated when the question is asked again. Soon, staff start a fading paradigm by simply telling the client to go over and read the message. Giving the client motoric practice at going to the bulletin board makes it easier for the client to find it. In addition, we are setting up another conditioning paradigm. When the anxiety level of the client rises to the point where he or she would normally ask a repetitive question, the client becomes conditioned to go to the board instead. The alleviation of anxiety acquired by reading the message further enhances the conditioning. The process becomes a self-regulating system, with staff no longer required in order for the anxiety of the client to be reduced.

At this point, our bulletin boards contain messages for several clients. Each client's message is in a different color ink so as to make it distinctive. In addition, we change the wording of the messages each day. We have found that with repeated readings, clients begin to recognize when a message is "old" and complain that the message is no longer valid. Here is an example of verbal priming. This also illustrates two important points. The first is that memory loss is not an "all-or-none" phenomenon in dementia. Some new learning may take place (even when we wish it would not). The second is that it may be useful, on occasion, to circumvent higher levels of functioning to create effective interventions. Here is an illustration.

I was visiting Lars Bäckman's lab a year ago and went to an Alzheimer's day care center in the suburbs of Stockholm. Staff there were trying to get a male client to lay out coffee cups and spoons for the nine clients. (Adult day care centers in New Orleans have forty to sixty clients, many of whom have dementia.) The man started counting place mats at the table. He got to seven, lost count, and quickly forgot the original task. One of Lars' staff taught the man to stop counting and instead to simply put one cup on each place mat. When the client used the simpler or more concrete approach, he was successful.

DAYS OF OUR LIVES

In our labs, we have been training persons with AD to learn a strategy, "Look at the calendar to remember what to do." The strategy is trained using the spaced-retrieval technique. Spaced-retrieval is a method of learning and retaining information by recalling that information over increasingly longer periods of time. It is, in essence, a shaping paradigm applied to memory. When a retrieval is successful, the interval preceding the next recall test is increased. If a recall failure occurs, the participant is told the correct response and asked to repeat it. Then the following interval length returns to the last one at which retrieval was successful.

We have recently engaged in a series of studies training demented older adults to remember specific pieces of information using the spaced-retrieval method. These include names of common objects, a prospective memory task (remembering to perform a future action), face-name associations, object-location associations, as well as the strategy "Look at the calendar" for using an external memory aid—a calendar. The external memory aid of the calendar enables caregivers and AD patients to change calendar content daily, thus giving great flexibility to the tasks which can be remembered when the strategy is implemented. A researcher in my lab, Alan Stevens, was testing to see if a subject had learned the training strategy. He asked a gentleman with AD, "How will you remember what to do?" The subject answered "I can't remember. That's why I have to look at the calendar!"

The spaced-retrieval technique has several aspects that make it especially applicable to AD subjects and their caregivers. The intervals between recall trials can be filled with conversation, playing games, looking over photo albums, etc. Thus, the intervention takes on the form of a social visit or pleasant social interaction rather than a "testing" or "training" session. Due to the use of shaping procedures, individuals with AD experience high rates of successful recall with spaced-retrieval training. This success contrasts sharply with most other attempts to remember recent information. Finally, the learning seems to take place with little or no expenditure of cognitive effort on the part of the learner.

*P*UT IT ON!

There are other occasions when former skills or abilities can be utilized as the basis for intervention. A client at a day care center began to periodically take off her clothes in the afternoons. Staff asked her to stop, and she would apologize, then do it again. We were asked to help with this problem. The first thing we asked was "What was her former occupation?" The client had been a seamstress, and staff said that she liked to touch their clothes and tell them about the material they were made of. We then asked if there had been any unusual behaviors exhibited by the client before taking off her clothes. Staff responded that she had been a model citizen for fourteen months, but that a week before stripping she had started to take off her shoes and roll down her anklets, which they had stopped.

At that point we suggested that staff get a big purse or bag and put the client's name on it in big letters (the client could read; big letters help with poor vision). Staff were to find squares or swatches of different types of cloth and put them in the bag. In the afternoons, staff were to give the bag to the client and tell her they had a new game. The client was to close her eyes, put her hand in the bag, feel a swatch of cloth, and try to guess what type of cloth it was. Then the client was to remove the cloth and see if her guess was correct.

The client loved the game, was good at guessing the cloth types, and (incidentally) quit taking off her clothes. We had hypothesized that the client might have engaged in self-stimulation as a result of stimulus deprivation. We therefore attempted to find an activity which would utilize past experiences and skills in an alternative behavior which was more socially appropriate.

A SOLUTION TO THE MYSTERY

This leads us back to the case of the return of Sherlock Holmes, and its solution. The client who kept saying "Sherlock Holmes" was a literate, witty man who understood socially appropriate behavior. He knew that you could not tell the same joke twice to the same people, but he also had a devastated explicit memory system. As a result, he could not remember that he had told the joke before. The name of the staffer was being learned through spaced-retrieval, but this form of priming is a context-free type of learning. Finally, since the same context was involved when the client was asked to recall the staffer's name, it is not surprising that a similar "joke association" was elicited. We were, in essence, priming the joke along with the name of the staffer. Thus, in this case, we see the unique dynamics of memory in dementia—access to long-term memory, impaired explicit memory, and access to new learning through implicit memory. It is only by considering memory in dementia as a dynamic system that such cases can be solved and intervention be made most effective.

AS MY WHIMSY TAKES ME

For the student reading this chapter, my hope is that this brief description of my professional life will bring a bit of comfort. If your future is uncertain, fear not. Perhaps Einstein was wrong and God does role dice. Whimsy seems to permeate the fabric of the universe. Looking back on the road that led to this moment, the choice points seem clear and the outcomes obvious. I guarantee that this did not seem the case at the time they were unfolding. Even now, the future is murky, though bright (like an oncoming light seen in a fog?). But as an apostle of Toynbee, I would like to suggest to the gentle reader that it is just this uncertainty that makes the future worth waiting for, and the day worth embracing. The only guarantee in my research is that surprises will abound. That is what makes the job so very, very worth waking up for each morning.

Acknowledgments

I would like to express my appreciation to my parents, my mentors at the University of Houston (Roy and Janet Lachman), my mentor at Fort Hays State University (Robert Markley), Nick Moffat (who introduced me to spaced-retrieval), and my editorial assistant at the University of New Orleans, Catherine Gaumer. A special thanks to the staff and clients of the Kenner Adult Day Health Care Center and the New Directions Adult Day Care Center, where much of the recent work reported in this chapter has been conducted.

SUGGESTED READINGS

ABRAHAMS, J. P., & CAMP, C. J. (1993). Maintenance and generalization of object naming training in anomia associated with degenerative dementia. *Clinical Gerontologist, 12*, 57–72.

BJORK, R. A. (1988). Retrieval practice and the maintenance of knowledge. In M. M.

Gruneberg, P. Morris, & R. Sykes (Eds.), *Practical aspects of memory* (Vol. 2, pp. 396–401). London: Academic Press.

CAMP, C. J. (1989). Facilitation of new learning in Alzheimer's disease. In G. Gilmore, P. Whitehouse, & M. Wykle (Eds.), *Memory and aging: Theory, research, and practice* (pp. 212–225). New York: Springer.

———— & McKITRICK, L. A. (1992). Memory interventions in Alzheimer's-type dementia populations: Methodological and theoretical issues. In R. L. West & J. D. Sinnott (Eds.), *Everyday memory and aging: Current research and methodology* (pp. 155–172). New York: Springer-Verlag.

———— & SCHALLER, J. R. (1989). Epilogue: Spaced-retrieval memory training in an adult day-care center. *Educational Gerontology, 15,* 641–648.

———— & STEVENS, A. B. (1990). Spaced-retrieval: A memory intervention for dementia of the Alzheimer's type (DAT). *Clinical Gerontologist, 10,* 58–61.

LANDAUER, T. K., & BJORK, R. A. (1978). Optimal rehearsal patterns and name learning. In M. M. Gruneberg, P. Morris, & R. Sykes (Eds.), *Practical aspects of memory* (pp. 625–632). London: Academic Press.

McKITRICK, L. A., & CAMP, C. J. (in press). Caregiver participation in word-retrieval training with anomic Alzheimer's disease patients. *Clinical Gerontologist.*

———— & BLACK, F. W. (1992). Prospective memory intervention in Alzheimer's disease. *Journal of Gerontology: Psychological Sciences, 47*(5), 337–343.

STEVENS, A. B., O'HANLON, A. M., & CAMP, C. J. (1993). Strategy training using the spaced-retrieval method: A case study. *Clinical Gerontologist, 13,* 106–109.

K. WARNER SCHAIE *(Ph.D., University of Washington) is Evan Pugh Professor of Human Development and Psychology in the Department of Human Development and Family Studies and Director of the Gerontology Center at Pennsylvania State University in University Park, Pennsylvania. He also holds an appointment as Affiliate Professor of Psychiatry and Behavioral Sciences at the University of Washington in Seattle. Dr. Schaie has received the Kleemeier Award for distinguished scientific contributions from the Gerontological Association of America and the 1992 Distinguished Scientific Contributions Award of the American Psychological Association. He has served as president of the Division of Adult Development and Aging of APA and as editor of the* Journal of Gerontology: Psychological Sciences. *Dr. Schaie is married to Sherry L. Willis, who is also a developmental psychologist. They spend the academic year in University Park, Pennsylvania, and summers at their research field site in Seattle, Washington.*

15

The Natural History of a Longitudinal Study

--- ❖ ---

In this chapter I will describe how I became intrigued with the study of psychological development from young adulthood to advanced old age, how I came to be a "gerontologist," and how my career became interwoven with a program of scientific inquiry conducted by me, my associates, and my students over the past thirty-five years that has come to be known as the Seattle Longitudinal Study (SLS).

SOME BRIEF BIOGRAPHICAL NOTES

I was born in the city of Stettin, which was then the capital of the German province of Pommerania, in 1928. My parents belonged to the Jewish middle class; my father and mother ran a small outfitters store for the then rapidly growing crowd of motor bikers. We lived in a three-room apartment in one of those dreary tenement blocks that had become common in most German towns by the turn of the century. Our apartment fronted the street and at least had a balcony that my mother kept covered with flowers during the warmer months, of which there are few on the shores of the Baltic. My native town was a sleepy, provincial city of about 150,000 inhabitants involved primarily in the garment industry, ship building, and fish processing. It also had a terminal for transferring grain and coal from the river barges to freighters that went to Scandinavia, Russia, and beyond. The big excitement was a visit to Berlin, which was an hour's train ride away. Today, Stettin is Poland's westernmost port city, and I confuse people by telling them that I was born in Poland, but have never lived there! Both statements are technically correct, since during my childhood, Poland was somewhere way off in the east and as a child I never knew anyone who spoke Polish!

233

Shortly after I was born the great depression hit Europe; hence I remained an only child. And not very long thereafter the unemployment lines lengthened, the Weimar Republic went on a self-destruct course, and Hitler and his Nazis took over. When I turned 6 years old, the time came to start elementary school, and I attended a private school that had hastily been formed by the local Jewish community to protect its children from the daily harassment experienced in the public schools. I attended that school through the middle of Fifth grade, learning enough basic skills so that I can still converse in German and write grammatically correct prose in that language, although studded with archaic colloquialisms that were common in the 1930s.

In the middle of Fifth grade came "Crystal Night" (November 9, 1938), the systematic destruction of Jewish synagogues and stores by Nazi hooligans, and the incarceration of most Jewish men in concentration camps. My father was able to avoid the latter by going into hiding. He desperately tried to find a way for our family to leave Germany, since the likely consequences of our remaining had become convincingly clear. By that time hardly any country was willing to accept Jewish refugees from Germany; thus the question was primarily one of how to get out, regardless of where one might wind up going. My father discovered that it was possible to book passage on an Italian cruise ship that plied a route through the Suez Canal and around India and Malaysia ending up in the Chinese port city of Shanghai. In June 1939 my parents and I took the train from Stettin to Trieste (the two anchor points in Winston Churchill's famous iron curtain speech!) and embarked not really knowing where we would go. After several futile attempts to go ashore along the way, we finally were allowed to enter Shanghai. At the time, Shanghai was still an international settlement governed by the consular representatives of seventeen nations that were signatories to the so-called "unequal treaties" that during the nineteenth century had forced foreign concessions upon Chinese soil that were not subject to Chinese law. Thus, the reason we were allowed to land was primarily because the amorphous local government had not been able to get its act together to keep us out!

To an 11-year-old, the trip to the Far East and the bustling and exotic streets of Shanghai seemed high adventure, and I gave little thought to the uncertain future facing my family. There was a large foreign population in Shanghai, with a substantial Jewish community that arrived either during the expansion of western trade in China or after the Bolshevik Revolution in Russia after World War I. Some of these people had even acquired great wealth, and they formed charitable organizations that attempted to provide shelter and food for all and education for the young. I attended a school for refugee children for about two years, acquiring English language competence, and completing an educational program that would approximate that of an American junior high school. Then came Pearl Harbor. My English and American teachers were interned by the Japanese authorities, and I became an involuntary high school dropout at age 14!

After a few months at a private business school where I learned some typing, shorthand, and bookkeeping skills, I spent the next three years at various jobs as a clerk and telephone receptionist. After the Japanese authorities made all the refugees relocate to a ghetto area, vocational options became even more restricted. I was lucky to find a job as an apprentice in a small print shop. When the war ended in 1945 and the local English language newspaper reopened, I managed to get in their print shop and learned how to use a linotype machine and to typeset newspaper advertisements. During my final months in Shanghai I also had the opportunity to work as an untrained social worker with the American Joint Distribution Committee helping people about to resettle in the United States. Thus, in 1947, after my father's death, I decided it was time to resettle myself and my mother to the United States. We arrived in San Francisco in December of that year.

My printing experience served me well in finding a job, but as a newspaper printer this typically meant night work, with little to occupy my days. One day, while making up a newspaper page, I noticed a story on a high school program for adults at the local community college, and on the spur of the moment decided that it might not hurt me to have a high school diploma. I enrolled at City College of San Francisco and was able to test out of most requirements and obtained my diploma. Having gotten used to and liking the college setting, I decided to go on. I built my program of studies primarily around those courses that were offered in the afternoon, since I needed to sleep in the morning following my night shift as a printer. Since most science labs were offered in the morning, this meant that I was destined to concentrate on social science topics.

The California higher-education system allowed automatic transfer to the state university system upon graduation from junior college, and in the spring of 1950 I entered Berkeley as a psychology major. The first question my adviser asked was whether I intended to go on to graduate school, since she did not want to waste her time with me otherwise. I had not given much thought to graduate school, but since I wanted to retain my adviser, I agreed on the spot that this was what I intended to do. My casual decision was reinforced by the outbreak of the Korean war. Realizing that my student status would provide draft deferral as long as I remained in school, my decision to go to graduate school became the obvious choice.

During my first semester at Berkeley I took an excellent tests and measurement course from Read Tuddenham, who became my adviser during my second semester. Once again having trouble building a full schedule confined to the afternoons, I asked to do a directed study with him. Discussing various possibilities, I idly mentioned that I had thought his class discussion of Thurstone's (1938) primary mental abilities (PMA) work was interesting, and I wondered whether there had been any research on the PMA in adults. As a good teacher, Tuddenham told me to go to the library and find out.

In the 1930s Thurstone had analyzed more than sixty measures of mental ability with large samples of children and adolescents in Chicago. Applying his new method of centroid factor analysis he discovered that individual differences on these measures could be accounted for by no more than ten factors, which he thought of as the "building blocks of the mind." Thurstone published a formal test of the five most important of these ability factors. They were verbal meaning (a measure of recognition vocabulary), space (a measure of being able to rotate abstract figures in two-dimensional space), reasoning (a measure of the ability to induce rules from common features of an activity), number (a measure of addition skill), and word fluency (a measure of word recall).

After a thorough search it turned out that there were lots of data on children and adolescents but nothing on adults. Hence, I proposed a directed study to determine whether the low correlations between different abilities reported in childhood could be replicated in adulthood.

But where does an undergraduate find adult subjects beyond college age? As serendipity would have it, I was still being treated for the consequences of malnutrition during my Shanghai years. As it turned out, my family physician, Robert M. Perlman, was interested in geriatric practice. When I mentioned my subject problem to him, he offered to provide me with testing space and allowed me to recruit subjects in his waiting room. He also introduced me to Florence Vickery, the director of the San Francisco Senior Citizens Center, one of the first to be established in the United States. She also allowed me to recruit and test subjects at her facility. My first aging study was on the way. I was able to test several dozen subjects ranging from the twenties to the seventies. I found that the PMA remained distinct in adulthood, but that age differences were not identical for all abilities. As compared to the normative data for adolescents, it turned out that young adults and those in early middle age, on average, did better than the high school students. There were significant age differences thereafter, and older adults in particular did less well on space and reasoning than they did on their verbal and numeric skills. Administering the test to a subset of study participants in an untimed condition showed that the age difference patterns were even more pronounced when the speed restriction was removed.

Soon thereafter Dr. Perlman received an announcement that the Second International Congress of Gerontology was to be held in St. Louis, Missouri. Perhaps to ensure a tax-deductible trip, he suggested that I submit my findings as a convention paper with him as a coauthor. The paper was accepted, but in order to report respectable statistics, I now had to recruit a friend, Fred Rosenthal, who was a semester ahead of me, to run the tests that I had not yet mastered. Thus, in August of 1951, I mounted the Greyhound bus for my first long American trip: St. Louis. Gerontology was still a very small group; the congress had about 200 registrants, two-thirds of whom were Americans. Perhaps no more than thirty were psychologists. I met many of the founders of geropsychology, including James Birren, Robert Kleemeier, Irving Lorge, and Robert Havighurst. This was very heady stuff for a college junior, and I was even more excited when the editor of the *Journal of Gerontology*, John Esben Kirk, invited me to submit my paper, entitled "Differential Deterioration of Factorially 'Pure' Mental Abilities," as a journal article and promptly accepted it. My entry into the field of adult developmental psychology and gerontology was obviously determined by these events!

During my last semester at Berkeley, I did some more reading on individual differences and became interested in the concepts of behavioral rigidity and perseveration, as studied by psychologists such as Kurt Lewin, Abraham Luchins, Jacob Kounin, and Charles Spearman. They suggested that the boundaries between different domains of behavior would rigidify with age, and that there would be increasing interference in shifting away from old and no longer appropriate strategies to the adoption of new and more appropriate problem-solving strategies. If this was the case, I thought that age differences in the PMA might well be explained by progressive reduction in cognitive functions for those who were more rigid to begin with or who became less flexible as they aged.

The article in press probably helped my acceptance into the clinical psychology program at the University of Washington. What was more important, in contrast to most of my classmates, I found an intellectual niche and I had a set of research objectives at the very beginning of my graduate training. In addition to obtaining the necessary clinical training to become an academic clinical psychologist, I wanted to focus my research on the interesting puzzle of why it is that some people maintain their intellectual powers into old age while others begin to decline at an early adult stage. I didn't realize it at the time, but I was posing a challenge, the response to which would occupy my entire career.

My first year as a graduate student was spent working my way through the various background courses needed to eventually pass the comprehensive examination. Having had excellent preparation in the conventional statistical methods at Berkeley, in a combined experimental and statistics course (taught by Warner Brown, Rheem Jarret, and Donald Riley), I was able to skip the usual first-year methods sequence, and dive directly into multivariate analysis and factor analysis (Paul Horst) as well as scaling methods (Allen Edwards) courses. Thus, I was ready to begin the development of an instrument to measure the rigidity-flexibility concept that I had become interested in at Berkeley. I thought this might have explanatory value for individual differences in cognitive aging. I identified a set of ten potentially appropriate measures from the literature that I adapted for use with a population ranging in age from young adulthood to old age. Subjects were recruited from presentations given on various topics on personality in adulthood to church and fraternal groups as well as to adult education classes. I was able to test about 300 subjects over several months, and was ready to conduct a multiple group factor analysis (on a Monroe calculator, a device on which an analysis now requiring a few minutes of computer time then took several weeks of full-time work), in which I identified that the different measures could be represented as three dimensions of rigidity-flexibility. These factors were a *motor-cognitive rigidity* factor, representing difficulty in shifting problem-solving strategies on motor-cognitive tasks; an *attitudinal rigidity* factor, involving questionnaire responses that represented unwillingness to shift established behavior factors in favor of new and more appropriate behaviors, and a *psychomotor speed* factor, consisting of the ability to perform psychomotor tasks rapidly. I replicated the factor solution on another sample, and eventually published this material as the *Test of Behavioral Rigidity*. This work was accepted in early 1953 as my M.S. thesis (directed by Charles Strother, Paul Horst, and Sidney Bijou).

It is important to note here that no one on the Washington psychology faculty was particularly interested in adult development or aging. It was necessary, therefore, to create my own academic support system. I discovered that there was a latent interest in gerontology in a number of other departments, and I was able to convince the dean of the graduate school to sponsor a Committee on Gerontology. Of course, the committee needed an executive secretary; consequently, in the fall of 1953, I was finally able to give up working nights as a newspaper printer, since I was given fellowship support in return for staffing the new committee as well as pursuing my own research on aging.

As the first activity of the new committee, I proposed an intensive study of a group of well-functioning elders that would encompass not only psychological variables, but also include an examination of health status, physical activities, and environmental contexts. A small grant from the University of Washington research council to Charles Strother permitted the recruitment of twenty-five men and twenty-five women over the age of 70 years who had completed a college degree or beyond. Most participants came from the membership of the retired faculty association, supplemented by others living close to the university. Not surprisingly, this advantaged group still maintained high levels of functioning and activity on virtually all our measures. Several reports emerged from this study, the first was presented at the 1955 American Psychological Association meeting in San Francisco.

*O*RIGINS OF THE SEATTLE LONGITUDINAL STUDY

Having passed my comprehensive examinations, it was time to propose a dissertation project. I was now ready to put together my pilot work on rigidity-flexibility and intelligence. As serendipity would have it, Charles Strother, my adviser, had just been named chair of the board of trustees of the Group Health Cooperative of Puget Sound, one of America's first (and now, one of the largest) health maintenance organizations (HMO). The HMO was interested in doing a consumer satisfaction survey, but had neither staff nor financial resources to allocate. A deal was struck. I was allowed to collect my dissertation data on a random sample of the adult HMO members with the condition that I conduct the consumer satisfaction survey at the same time. This arrangement worked out well, because it allowed me to recruit subjects with the formula—"we wanted to learn about the characteristics and opinions of a random sample of the HMO membership"—rather than having to recruit directly for a psychological experiment.

I randomly selected about 3,000 persons, ranging in age from 22 to 70 years. I administered the PMA and my rigidity-flexibility test (the TBR— test of behavioral rigidity) until I had assessed twenty-five men and twenty-five women in each five-year interval. As it turned out, I was able to replicate my earlier findings on differential patterns of age differences in intelligence as well as show that peak ages of performance had risen (thirties or older) since the earlier work by Wechsler and others. Substantial significant correlations were also found between rigidity-flexibility and the ability measures, but I did not find the predicted causal relationship; that, as it turned out, required longitudinal data.

When I obtained my doctoral degree in 1956 there were no employment opportunities for someone specializing in gerontology. Consequently, my mentor advised me to strengthen my clinical skills through a year of postdoctoral study and then seek employment as an academic clinician. I obtained an appointment as a fellow in medical psychology at Washington University in St. Louis, gaining skills in the assessment of psychopathology and in behaviorally oriented psychotherapy under the supervision of Ivan Mensh, Laverne Johnson, and Jack Hafner. I also had the opportunity to do some research with James Weiss, a psychiatrist who directed the Washington University Psychiatric Outpatient Clinic, to develop a Q-sort instrument for assessing the attributes of the complaints that brought older patients to the clinic, reinforcing my interest in older populations.

In the summer of 1957, I was offered an appointment as assistant professor at the University of Nebraska to teach adult cognitive and personality assessment and to supervise students in the clinical program. Consequently, my interests turned to the development of an unobtrusive method for objective personality assessment via the relation of color and personality. In this context, I studied school children as well as mentally retarded and mentally ill persons in state institutions, and almost abandoned my interests in human aging.

CONVERTING A CROSS-SECTIONAL TO A LONGITUDINAL STUDY

In my fourth year at Nebraska, I was asked to teach the developmental section of the departmental proseminar. In preparing for that seminar, I was confronted with addressing the discrepancies between cross-sectional and longitudinal findings in the study of adult intellectual development. I soon became convinced that this issue needed to be addressed by following a structured cross-sectional sample such as the one I had collected for my dissertation. Subsequently, I designed a follow-up study that converted my original cross-sectional study of cognitive aging into a series of short-term longitudinal studies, each extending over the same seven-year period. I received funding for this study from the National Institute of Mental Health, and with the continuing cooperation of the HMO I went into the field in 1963 to conduct this follow-up. Additionally, I drew a new random sample from the HMO membership that permitted comparison of panels tested at the same age but at different times (known as "Schaie's most efficient design"). Thus the Seattle Longitudinal Study (SLS) was now in place! The first longitudinal follow-up provided some answers but it also raised sufficient methodological and substantive questions that have led to a continuing program of studies (including six major and several collateral data collections) that is still in progress. The basic design has been to retest participants every seven years, and to draw a new random sample—ranging in age from 22 to 84 years—on each test administration. Since our sample is located in Seattle, we established temporary field offices for each of the individual cycles. As more collateral studies have been added to keep us busy during the seven-year cycles, we now maintain a permanent Seattle field office. The longitudinal research program has been continuously supported by the National Institute on Aging since 1970, and has just recently been refunded to continue through 1998.

SOME FURTHER BIOGRAPHICAL DATA

Throughout the course of our longitudinal study, my own professional development continued as well. I left my first academic position at the University of Nebraska in 1964 in order to organize a clinical training program at West Virginia University. Then, in 1965, I was asked to be the founding director of a Human Resources Research Institute whose mission was to provide intellectual linkages between a new College of Human Resources and Education and the traditional social science disciplines in the College of Arts and Sciences. In the context of this institute I supervised research on the effects of the community action programs sponsored by Lyndon Johnson's "war on poverty," as well as statewide evaluations of the effects of early "headstart" programs. I was also able to conceptualize and receive funding for one of the first institutional training grants awarded by the National Institute on Child and Human Development to develop the concept of training in life span developmental psychology. Under this grant I initiated the series of conferences and monographs known as the West Virginia Lifespan Series. In 1968, I was prevailed upon to "simplify" my life by becoming chair of the Department of Psychology, a role I served in until 1973.

My old friend James Birren had founded the Andrus Gerontology Center at the University of Southern California in 1965. In 1973, I joined him as associate director for research (later director of the Gerontology Research Institute) and as professor of psychology. At USC I directed the interdisciplinary doctoral training program in aging and was instrumental in developing and overseeing a number of project-program efforts, trying to focus the skills of scientists in the biological, behavioral, and social sciences on major issues in the aging process. I also started a new longitudinal study of cognitive aging (including memory functioning) that I followed over a three-year period. It is now being continued by one of my former students, Elizabeth Zelinski.

Several years earlier I met Sherry Willis who taught at Pennsylvania State University. As our personal and professional interests began to merge, we decided that we should be at the same institution. I therefore left USC at the end of 1981 to accept an appointment as Professor of Human Development and Psychology at Penn State, and to marry Sherry. Since 1985, I have directed the Penn State Gerontology Center and in 1986 I was honored by the university with an appointment as the Evan Pugh Professor of Human Development and Psychology.

*T*HIRTY-FIVE YEARS OF LONGITUDINAL STUDIES

The second cross-sectional study (1963) essentially replicated the findings of the base study. The short-term longitudinal study, however, disclosed substantially different information about peak levels and rate of decline. Publication of results was therefore delayed until a theoretical model could be built that accounted for the discrepancy between the longitudinal and cross-sectional data. These analyses suggested that comparisons of age group means needed to be conducted for the repeatedly measured samples as well as for successive independent samples drawn from the same cohort.

Results were reported that called attention to substantial cohort differences; that is, differences in level of functioning between groups tested at the same age but at successive points in time (e.g., 25-year-olds in 1984 and 1991). These findings questioned the universality and significance of intellectual decrement with advancing age in community-dwelling persons. To be specific, we found that because of increases in educational attainment and other favorable environmental and lifestyle changes over the past half century, successive cohorts will perform on many variables at a higher level than did their earlier predecessors at the same age. On the other hand, if some widely practiced skill is given less attention, there may be reductions in level of performance over successive cohorts. When cohort changes are positive, older persons look like they have declined, when, in actuality, they may have remained stable but at a lower level of attainment than their younger peers. On the other hand, when cohort changes are negative (that is, earlier-born cohorts attained a higher level than later-born cohorts), older persons may look like they have remained stable even though they have declined, because they compare favorably to younger peers who attained a lower peak performance in their youth. The first phenomenon was observed for reasoning, space, and verbal meaning, while the latter phenomenon occurred for number skills and word fluency.

While the cross-sectional data implied peaks in early adulthood with decline beginning in middle age and becoming severe in the sixties, the longitudinal data, by contrast, suggested little age-related decline prior to the sixties, and only modest decline during the decade of the seventies.

It soon became evident that conclusions based on data covering a single seven-year interval required further replication, if only because two occasions of measurement permit the examination of cross-sectional, but not of longitudinal sequences; the latter requires a minimum of three measurement occasions. Only longitudinal sequences allow designs that permit contrasting age and cohort effects. Hence, plans were made for a third data collection, which was conducted in 1970. In that cycle, as many persons as possible examined on the first two test occasions were retested, and a third random sample was drawn from the residual members of the base population.

The results from the third data collection seemed rather definitive in replicating the short-term longitudinal findings, but a number of questions remained. Discrepancies between findings in the repeated-measurement and independent-sampling studies suggested the need for a replication of the fourteen-year longitudinal sequences, and it also seemed useful to follow the original sample over twenty-one years. A fourth data collection was therefore conducted in 1977, again retesting the previous samples and adding a new random sample, this time from an expanded population frame. Continuous funding also made it possible to address a number of bothersome questions. These included analyses of the consequences of shifting from a sampling without replacement model to a sampling with replacement paradigm, an analysis of the effects of monetary incentives upon participant characteristics, an examination of the aging of the tests, as well as causal analyses of health and environmental factors upon change or maintenance of adult intellectual performance.

From the beginning of the study we followed what was then the conventional wisdom of assessing each primary ability with that observable marker variable which was thought to be the most reliable and valid measure of a particular ability. With the widespread introduction of modern methods of factor analysis, it became obvious that we needed to extend our concern with changes in level of intellectual functioning in adulthood to the assessment of structural relationships within the ability domain. In a factor analysis one begins with a larger number of measures and seeks to obtain a solution which allows one to organize these multiple measures in the smallest possible set of distinct basic dimensions. This concern argued for collecting further data with a much expanded battery.

The fifth (1984) SLS cycle was the beginning of a major role for Sherry Willis, who brought her skills in designing and implementing cognitive training paradigms. A major part of the fifth cycle was therefore devoted to the implementation of a cognitive training study with our long-term participants aged 64 years or older. This study was designed to determine whether cognitive training in the elderly remediates cognitive decline or whether it increases the level of skill beyond those attained at earlier ages. The cognitive training programs involve teaching participants more effective strategies and providing immediate feedback. In this study we found that almost two-thirds of all subjects benefited significantly from a five-hour cognitive training program, and that 40 percent of those who had reliably declined could be brought back to the performance level they had shown fourteen years earlier. The cognitive training program was also shown to remove the "reliably demonstrated" gender difference on the spatial orientation measure.

The database available through the fifth cycle also made it possible to update the normative data on age changes and cohort differences. In addition, these data made it possible to control for the effects of subject dropout and practice from repeated test administrations. Finally, this cycle displayed the introduction of new measures, such as practical intelligence, analyses of marital assortativity using data on married couples over as long as twenty-one years, and development of actuarial tables that allow the prediction of risk of cognitive decline and of the age at which decline is to be expected for a particular individual.

The most recent (1991) study cycle included a set of four related studies. First, in collaboration with Robert Plomin, we took advantage of the longitudinal data to begin a study of cognitive family resemblance in adulthood. Although family similarity in cognition has been previously documented in young children and their parents, we have not known whether this similarity also remains throughout adulthood. We did this by recruiting a large number of adult offspring and siblings of our longitudinal panel members. Interestingly enough, family similarity in cognitive functions remains about as strong throughout adulthood as previously demonstrated for young parents and their children. Second, we abstracted health histories on our panel members and conducted more detailed investigations of the relationship between health and maintenance of intellectual functioning. These studies show both the influence of chronic disease on maintenance of intellectual functioning, as well as the importance of intellectual competence in postponing the onset of chronic disease. Third, we conducted a seven-year follow-up on the cognitive training study, showing continuing effects of the training intervention, and have replicated the initial findings with a more recent cohort of older persons. Fourth, with the first longitudinal replication of our expanded test battery, we were able to conduct longitudinal analyses of cognitive ability structures, demonstrating the greater stability of longitudinal data, and further update our normative data.

CONTRIBUTIONS OF THE SEATTLE LONGITUDINAL STUDY

The SLS has charted the course of selected psychometric abilities from young adulthood through old age. It has investigated individual differences and differential patterns of change, and has described the differential magnitude and relative importance of the observed age differences and age changes. These efforts have corrected previously held popular stereotypes about the universality of cognitive declines with advancing age. An important feature of the study has been the detection of substantial generational differences in intellectual performance. We have identified a number of contextual health and personality variables that offer explanations for differential change and that provide a basis for possible interventions. Cognitive interventions were designed that have been successful in remediating carefully documented declines and that have improved the cognitive functions of those older persons who have remained stable. We have also studied changes in cognitive ability structures across age and different cohorts, conducted analyses of the relative effects of age decline and training gain on speed and accuracy, investigated the relevance of cognitive training to real-life tasks, and studied parent/offspring and sibling similarity in adult cognitive performance.

Throughout the history of the SLS, now covering more than thirty-five years, I have focused on five major questions which I have attempted to ask with greater clarity and increasingly more sophisticated methodology at each successive stage of the study. These questions are the following:

1. *What is the differential life course of intellectual abilities?* Our studies have shown that there is no uniform pattern of age-related changes across all intellectual abilities. Hence, studies using an overall index of intellectual ability (IQ) are of only limited use for an understanding of age changes and age differences in intellectual functioning whether in individuals or in groups. Our data do lend limited support to the notion advanced by John Horn and Raymond Cattell that active or fluid abilities tend to decline earlier than passive or crystallized abilities. However, gender difference trends suggest that women decline earlier on the active abilities, while men do so on the passive abilities. Although fluid abilities begin to decline earlier, crystallized abilities show steeper decrements once the late seventies are reached.

   Cohort-related differences in the rate and magnitude of age changes in intelligence remained quite linear for cohorts that entered old age during the first three cycles of our study. However, in the more recent cycles, it was found that rates of decremental age change have abated, while at the same time, negative cohort trends are observed as we begin to study members of the baby-boom generation. It is becoming apparent that patterns of socialization that are unique to a given sex role within a specific historical period may be major determinants for the pattern of change in abilities.

2. *At what age can we observe a reliable decline in intellectual abilities and how large is the decline?* Our general finding has been that reliable average decline in mental abilities does not occur before age 60 for any ability, but that reliable average decline may be found for all abilities by age 74. However, detailed analyses of individual differences in intellectual change demonstrate that even at age 81 less than half of all observed individuals experienced reliable decline over the preceding seven years. Up to age 60, individual changes, when found, are almost trivially small. But, by age 81, average decrement rises to approximately one population standard deviation (a rather substantial change) for most abilities.

   The findings from the SLS provide a normative base that can help determine at what ages declines reach practical significant levels of importance for public policy; related to such issues as mandatory retirement, age discrimination in employment, or the determination of the population that can live independently in the community. These bases will shift over time, as we have demonstrated in the SLS: Both level of performance and rate of decline show significant shifts across successive generations.

3. *How do successive generations differ in intellectual performance?* The SLS has conclusively demonstrated the prevalence of substantial generational (cohort) differences in psychometric abilities. These cohort trends differ in magnitude and direction by ability and, therefore, cannot be determined from composite IQ measures. One conclusion of these findings is that when cross-sectional data are used as a first estimate of age changes within individuals, they will overestimate age changes before the sixties for those abilities that show negative cohort gradients, and underestimate age changes for those abilities with positive cohort gradients.

    Our past studies of generational shifts in abilities have been conducted with random samples from arbitrarily defined birth cohorts. A supplemental and even more powerful demonstration of generational shifts was provided by our recent family studies which compare performance levels for individuals and their adult children.

4. *What are the causes of individual differences in age-related ability change in adulthood?* The most unique contribution of a longitudinal study of adult development stems from the fact that only longitudinal data allow us to investigate individual differences in antecedent variables that lead to early decline for some persons and maintenance of high levels of functioning for others well into very advanced age. In our study we have been able to implicate several factors that account for these individual differences, some of which are amenable to experimental intervention. The variables that we have identified as being important in reducing the risk of cognitive decline include: (a) the absence of cardiovascular and other chronic diseases; (b) a favorable environment that is often a consequence of high socioeconomic status; (c) involvement in a complex and intellectually stimulating environment; (d) flexible personality style at midlife; (e) marrying an intelligent spouse; and (f) maintaining high levels of perceptual processing speed.

5. *Can age-related intellectual decline be reversed through educational intervention?* Findings from the cognitive training studies conducted with our longitudinal subjects (under the primary direction of Sherry Willis) suggest that intellectual decline observed in many community-dwelling older people is likely to be a function of disuse and is therefore reversible for many persons. In our study, approximately two-thirds of the experimental subjects showed significant improvement, and about 40 percent of those who had

declined significantly over fourteen years were returned to their predecline level of functioning on the ability on which they were trained.

The dialectic process between data collection and model building that has been characteristic of the SLS, in addition to the increase in our knowledge base, has a number of methodological advances to the design and analysis of studies of human development and aging. In addition, the study has provided baselines for clinical assessment, and has made contributions relevant to education, basic instruction in geropsychology, and a variety of public policy issues.

WHAT LIES AHEAD?

Life as a professional gerontologist encourages one to believe that scientific productivity can be maintained well into advanced old age. Consequently, since mandatory retirement for academics finally ended this year, my future plans do not include formal professional retirement. Work in my laboratory has just started examining the role of health behaviors in the maintenance of physical health and high levels of cognitive functioning. We are busy with the secondary data analyses following our last study cycle, and we are branching out into studies of qualitative changes in word fluency over age. We expect to continue exploring the relation between psychometric intelligence and competency in the instrumental tasks of daily living, and we are committed to studying rate of intellectual aging in families and conducting a seventh study cycle beginning with a further follow-up on the effects of cognitive training in 1997. Finally, we hope to work on the relationship between our screening measures of cognitive behavior and neuropsychological assessment methods to explore the possibility of earlier identification of risks for dementia. If our subjects will allow us to conduct a postmortem, we might even be able to study anatomical and cellular features of the normal aging brain and their relations to cognitive behavior. Longitudinal studies have a life of their own; they involve multiple generations of students and investigators. For me it has been, and continues to be, an intellectually exciting and professionally rewarding odyssey.

Acknowledgments

A lifelong program of research such as the one characterizing my career, depends greatly on the influences of many teachers, colleagues, and students too numerous to list here. However, I wish to acknowledge my particular gratitude for the seminal contributions of my wife and colleague Sherry L. Willis; my mentors Read D. Tuddenham, Paul Horst, and Charles R. Strother; and my colleagues, and former and present students, Paul B. Baltes, Theresa M. Cooney, Ranjana Dutta, Kathy Gribbin, Ann Gruber-Baldini, Christopher Hertzog, Gisela Labouvie-Vief, Ann O'Hanlon, Scott B. Maitland, and Iris A. Parham. I am also greatly indebted to the members and staff of the Group Health Cooperative of Puget Sound, for their enthusiastic support. Extensive documentation of the studies that are briefly reviewed here are found in *Intellectual Development in Adulthood: The Seattle Longitudinal Study*, published by Cambridge University Press. This program of research has been supported since 1963 by various grants from the National Institute of Mental Health and the National Institute on Aging. It is currently supported by Research Grant R37 AG08055 from the National Institute on Aging.

SUGGESTED READINGS

SCHAIE, K. W. (1955). A test of behavioral rigidity. *Journal of Abnormal and Social Psychology, 51*, 604–610.

——— (1965). A general model for the study of developmental problems. *Psychological Bulletin, 64*, 91–107.

——— (1983). The Seattle Longitudinal Study: A twenty-one year exploration of psychometric intelligence in adulthood. In K. W. Schaie (Ed.), *Longitudinal studies of adult psychological development* (pp. 64–135). New York: Guilford Press.

——— (1989). The hazards of cognitive aging. *Gerontologist, 29*, 484–493.

——— (1990). Intellectual development in adulthood. In J. E. Birren & K. W. Schaie (Eds.), *Handbook of the psychology of aging* (3d ed., pp. 292–310). New York: Academic Press.

——— (1994). The course of adult intellectual development. *American Psychologist, 49* (4), 304–313.

——— (1995). *Intellectual development in adulthood: The Seattle Longitudinal Study.* New York: Cambridge University Press.

——— & HERTZOG, C. (1986). Toward a comprehensive model of adult intellectual development: Contributions of the Seattle Longitudinal Study. In R. J. Sternberg (Ed.), *Advances in human intelligence* (Vol. 3, pp. 79–118). Hillsdale, NJ: Erlbaum.

——— PLOMIN, R., WILLIS, S. L., GRUBER-BALDINI, A., & DUTTA, R. (1992). Natural cohorts: Family similarity in adult cognition. In T. Sonderegger (Ed.), *Psychology and aging.* Nebraska Symposium on Motivation, 1991 (pp. 205–243). Lincoln: University of Nebraska Press.

——— & Willis, S. L. (1986). Can intellectual decline in the elderly be reversed? *Developmental Psychology, 22*, 223–232.

——— & Willis, S. L. (1991). *Adult development and aging* (3d ed.). New York: HarperCollins.

WILLIS, S. L., & SCHAIE, K. W. (1986). Practical intelligence in later adulthood. In R. J. Sternberg & R. K. Wagner (Eds.), *Practical intelligence: Origins of competence in the everyday world* (pp. 236–268). Cambridge, New York: Cambridge University Press.

——— & ——— (1994). Cognitive training in the normal elderly. In F. Forette, Y. Christen, & F. Boller (Eds.), *Plasticité cérébrale et stimulation cognitive*: pp. 91–113. Paris: Foundation National de Gerontologie.

*L*AURA **L.** CARSTENSEN *(Ph.D., West Virginia University) is Associate Professor of Psychology at Stanford University. She has been president of the Society for a Science of Clinical Psychology, visiting fellow at the Max Planck Institute for Human Development, and recipient of the Kalish Innovative Publication Award from the Gerontological Society of America. She also was the recipient of a FIRST Award from the National Institute on Aging and has served on the editorial boards of five professional journals. She is pictured here with her son, David Pagano.*

16

Socioemotional Selectivity: A Life Span Developmental Account of Social Behavior

--- ❖ ---

OVERVIEW OF PSYCHOLOGY AND AGING

At the turn of the century, the average life expectancy in western countries was 45 years and roughly half of all children born died before they reached age 5. Today, the vast majority of children born in industrialized countries can expect to live into their eighties.[1] This dramatic change in survival rates is producing a profound shift in the age distribution of the population. By the year 2020, close to a quarter of the U.S. population will be over 65 years of age. Yet, we know less about the last thirty years of life than we know about the first five.

Against this demographic and scientific backdrop, there has been an acceleration in empirical research on aging. And even though much of the early research has been purely descriptive, it has held its surprises—many initial assumptions based on widely held stereotypes have proven wrong. Whereas the mission of early research was seemingly to document the direness of problems that await

---

[1]Note that this shift in age distribution is not occurring in underdeveloped countries, where mortality rates continue to be comparable to rates in the late 1800s.

aging individuals and aging societies, empirical findings have painted a more heartening picture. In the social and personality arenas, in particular, it appears that older people are generally doing quite well. They are not sad and dejected, and neither are they mentally incompetent nor socially isolated. Certainly, there are psychological losses that occur with age; however, these turn out to be rather small, and are often offset by psychological gains.

In fact, the study of old age, albeit in its infancy, has presented us with a central paradox: Although age is associated with many losses, including loss of power, social partners, physical health, cognitive efficiency, and, eventually, life itself—and although this list of losses encompasses the very things that younger people typically equate with happiness—research suggests that older people are at least as satisfied with their lives as their younger counterparts. Such findings raise intriguing questions for social and personality psychologists: Why, given these losses, are older people relatively happy, and not depressed? How do older people maintain a strong sense of self when so many external sources of self-esteem and support have disappeared? How is it that older people can have fewer social contacts, yet describe social relationships that are better than ever before?

Although answers to such questions promise to enhance our understanding of old age, in my view, research on aging has a much broader potential. Rather than viewing old age as an insular stage of life—separate from all that comes before—I believe that old age is best viewed as part of a continuum of adult development. Considered in this light, studies of aging offer the potential to illuminate basic psychological processes that operate throughout adulthood, particularly those human qualities that develop slowly over the entire lifetime. By including older people in our studies, we can come to a fuller understanding of a number of processes and phenomena including the experience of complex and poignant emotional states, the refinement of the ability to manage strong emotions, the nature of social interaction in long-term relationships, and the cumulative effects of adaptive or maladaptive dispositional styles. Even studying the physical frailty and cognitive inefficiency that characterize the oldest of the old may help to elucidate the processes, mechanisms, and coping strategies that begin to appear decades earlier, when people begin to cope with the inexorable physical and mental changes that come with age.

I believe that we are on the threshold of the most exciting period ever in the psychology of aging. Much of the essential descriptive work has been done. The time for major theory-building is upon us and it must be based on the integration of research findings on aging with findings from other areas of psychology as well as those from other disciplines. Aging may be a journey driven in no small part by biology, but the tremendous variability in aging, even in identical twins, makes it clear that environmental influences, mediated by emotion, cognition, and behavior, help to steer the course.

OVERVIEW OF MY RESEARCH PROGRAM

People often ask me how I became interested in the study of old age. It seems to surprise people that a relatively young researcher would be interested in very late life. Sometimes people assume that I "just like" old people, which is mildly amusing because this has little to do with my interest in the topic. I do like many old people. I dislike some. For me, the hook was intellectual.

My interest in aging actually precedes my interest in psychology. It was neither a college course nor meeting a particularly fascinating older person. The path that lead me to aging was the silver lining of a very dark cloud. When I was in my early twenties, a serious automobile accident left me with multiple injuries, primarily broken bones, requiring many months of orthopedic traction and years of rehabilitation. Predictions about my recovery were far from optimistic, but I repeatedly beat the odds and recovered faster and more fully than I or they expected.

To make a long story short, my very compassionate father, who is also a university professor, suggested that I take a college course while I was in the hospital. I disliked high school and had not planned to go to college, but at that point I was very bored and open to any suggestions about ways to pass the time. He offered to approach the instructor of whatever course interested me and request to have the class lectures taped. The plan was that my father would bring the tapes to the hospital and I would study on my own. I decided to take introductory psychology. As planned, I listened to the lectures on tape and read the textbook while I was confined to bed in a four-patient room of an orthopedic ward.

The setting was important. There is a bimodal age distribution on hospital orthopedic units. Essentially these hospital wings house very young people who have been in motor vehicle accidents and very old people who have suffered falls. In my case, the nurses had decided to take advantage of the fact that I was alert, rather friendly, and terribly bored, to help keep older patients oriented during their hospital stays. They regularly roomed older people with me; consequently, I was surrounded mostly by elderly women during a four-month hospital stay in which I became acquainted with psychology.

That period in my life marked the beginning of my passion for social science. I talked incessantly about psychology to my visitors and older roommates. And I observed people. I watched the hospital staff, who were wonderful people, rehabilitate me. And I watched those same wonderful people ignore the older women in my room. It was so clear that I was being rehabilitated for some nebulous future aim and my roommates were being made comfortable, as if for them the future did not exist. I also noticed how I changed once other people assumed so much responsibility for my care. I remember one day being furious when a nurse forgot to open a milk carton left on a lunch tray and realized that I could do it myself. I recall the realization that life goals change when life itself is genuinely threatened. I began to wonder how much of the aging process was determined by biology and how much was determined by social and psychological processes about which most people are not even aware.

Of course, I am grossly oversimplifying the process in the telling of this story. My hospitalization did not result in a scientific conversion, but it definitely did mark the beginning of a shift in life paths. As an undergraduate I considered different professions that would allow me to study aging, but decided early on that psychology, more than any other discipline, would best integrate the multifaceted nature of aging. I had an "idea" or a "sense" about aging early on but it was not until graduate school that I began to really think like a scientist.

In graduate school, I was trained in both life span developmental and clinical psychology. Very likely this diversity in my training led to my interest in the interface between normal adult development and individual differences in adaptive outcomes. Very old cohorts include among them the wisest people in society as well as the most mentally incompetent. I became intrigued with the entire spectrum of outcomes associated with age, including these dramatic extremes and those more moderate outcomes that fall in between. Although I maintain active interests in psychopathology in old age, including depression, schizophrenia, and dementia, my primary interest in recent years has been in understanding how normal older people actively construct their social worlds in ways that lead to *successful* aging.

At this point, I think of old age as providing a set of circumstances that compel changes in behavioral, cognitive, and emotional goals. Studying adults ranging from the very young to the very old, I have focused on emotions, social patterns, social preferences, and social choices. In this work, I have attempted to document where age differences occur and where they do not. But, more important, I have attempted to identify the processes that underlie these age differences. I like the saying that "nobody ever died of old age," because it conveys the message that age itself doesn't cause much of anything. I believe that some of my most interesting and important findings are ones showing that changes once thought to be inevitable and immutable consequences of aging are, in reality, quite variable and even malleable—and, thus, are not *caused* by age. It has been these findings that have suggested the nature of more fundamental psychological and socioemotional processes, the true agents of change.

Conceptually, my approach has been to focus on psychological mechanisms such as thoughts and preferences, rather than macrolevel influences such as retirement or reductions in social network size. Empirically, my approach has encompassed both laboratory and field studies. I have attempted to describe social patterns as they occur in the natural environment and to elaborate psychological processes in experimental tests of specific hypotheses. Below I describe the basic issues that I have studied, briefly summarize the theory of socioemotional selectivity that I have formulated, and review the empirical path that led to this theory.

THE ISSUES

The most pronounced change associated with aging involves slowing in virtually all aspects of functioning, from the reactivity of internal organ systems to the rate of social contact. It is this latter reduction in social behavior, considered to be the most reliable finding in social gerontology, that captured my scientific attention years ago and continues to motivate most of my research. Because human beings are inherently social creatures, reduced social contact raises concern about the very well-being of older people. Under many conditions the absence of social contact is indicative of a deterioration in the quality of social relationships and emotional experience. Subsequently, if in old age a reduction in social contact is *prototypical*, either it suggests a diminution in the quality of life *or* raises fundamental questions about the function and meaning of social contact.

PRIOR THEORIES

When I began working in this area, reduction in interpersonal contact with age was a central feature of the two prevailing theories of social aging: *activity theory* and *disengagement theory*. Activity theory, which has been the dominant paradigm in social gerontology, views inactivity as a societally induced *problem*. Proponents of this view argue that the causes of inactivity are rooted in social ills, such as mandatory retirement, which more diffusely reflect an indigenous ageism in our sociopolitical structures. According to activity theory, active people are happy people; thus, whatever can be done to encourage increased social activity in old age should be done. Stressing that societal change is needed to remedy the problem, advocates of this view have exerted great influence on social programs and federal policies. I suspect that the widespread influence this model has exerted is fueled in part by its congruence with American ideals about activity and productivity.

Disengagement theory is diametrically opposed to activity theory. According to this theory, a preconscious awareness of the eminence of death instigates social withdrawal. Grounded in psychodynamic ideas about conflict and defenses, in this view social inactivity represents a normal adaptive process. Thus, emotional quiescence, pensive self-reflection, and a turning away from the social world are considered to be a natural part of aging. Carl Jung captures the view well in the following excerpt from *The Stages of Life*: "[a child's psychic processes] are not as difficult to discern as those of a very old person who has plunged again into the unconscious, and who progressively vanishes within it" [1933, p. 131].

Dominant as these theories have been, they are certainly not without their critics. For example, social exchange theorists have argued that age robs people of their capacity to engage in the reciprocal give-and-take that is the hallmark of social relationships, and thus weakens their attachment to others. Though obviously distinct in many ways, virtually all previous theories seem to share the view that reduction in social contact is uniquely a late-life phenomenon. Furthermore, these theories have tacitly (or explicitly) assumed that the principle organizer of changed social patterns in old age is loss.

At the time that I undertook my program of research, there was widespread recognition in the field that none of these models really captured the essence of social aging. But there were no alternative models that did. Initially, my research was aimed at clarifying the picture, that is, finding evidence supporting or disconfirming existing theories. As the data accumulated, however, I began to evolve a new model of social aging.

SOCIOEMOTIONAL SELECTIVITY THEORY

Socioemotional selectivity theory focuses on psychological processes that mediate observed changes in social preferences and social behavior. According to this theory, social contact is motivated by a variety of goals. Specific goals or functions of interaction range from basic survival (such as protection from physical danger) to psychological goals (such as development of self-concept and regulation of emotion). The theory holds that a similar set of social goals operates throughout life, but that the salience of specific goals fluctuates depending on one's place in the life cycle. In particular, the regulation of emotion becomes increasingly salient over the life course, while the acquisition of information and the desire to affiliate with unfamiliar people decreases.

This reorganization of the goal hierarchy results in a change in preferences for social partners. This can be illustrated by contrasting the goals of emotion regulation and information seeking. When emotion regulation is the goal, people are highly selective in their choice of social partners, nearly always preferring social partners who are familiar to them. Infancy and old age are the two life stages that probably represent the peak emphasis on emotion regulation. Babies turn to their mothers whereas very old people turn increasingly to their adult children for emotional comfort.

When information seeking is the goal, by contrast, novel, unfamiliar people are often the best sources. Thus, when a person is exploring the world, trying to understand how it works, what the culture is like, how he or she compares to other people, and what other people are like, interactions with novel social partners have greater potential than familiar ones to fulfill such goals. The period from adolescence to young adulthood likely represents the peak emphasis on the goal of information seeking and, consistent with the theory, it is a time when people are establishing their in-

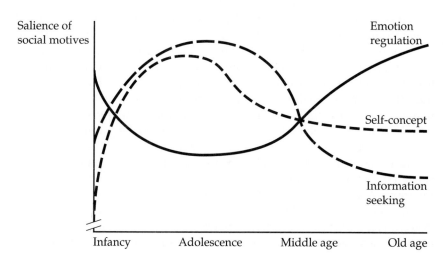

FIGURE 16-1
Idealized illustration of life span trajectory.

dependence from long-time friends and family and seeking out new social relationships.

Figure 16-1 provides an idealized illustration of the life span trajectory, as postulated in socioemotional selectivity theory, of three primary social motives: Emotion regulation, the development and maintenance of self-concept, and the seeking of information. The theory acknowledges the presence of each motive throughout life; it is the *relative* salience that changes.

Accumulated experience, for which age serves as a reasonable proxy, accounts for some of the apparent changes in social motives. As people establish what Robert Kahn and Toni Antonucci call "social convoys," i.e., select groups of people who serve as reliable sources of emotional and instrumental support, emotion regulation through social contact is greatly facilitated. People come to know with whom and how to interact in order to modulate emotion states. Accumulated experience influences information seeking quite differently. As individuals' expertise increases, fewer social partners can provide novel information and, moreover, familiarity with social partners is often inversely correlated with their information potential. Thus, social interaction in the service of obtaining novel information becomes less effective over time, while the regulation of emotion becomes more effective.

According to socioemotional selectivity theory, however, experience provides only part of the story. The salience of specific social motives is also influenced by the construal of the future, for which chronological age is also a good index. When the future is perceived as limited, attention shifts to the present. Immediate needs, such as emotional states, become most salient. When the future is perceived as largely open-ended, long-term goals assume greater importance. Thus, early in adulthood, much social behavior is geared toward the acquisition of information, even to the neglect of emotional states. The ambitious graduate student tolerates the crotchety professor because the long-term gains outweigh the short-term losses. In contrast, in late life, emotion regulation assumes primacy, in part, due to the implicit irrelevance of the future that age imposes. The theory predicts that, relative to younger people, older people will be less motivated to engage in emotionally meaningless (but perhaps otherwise functional) social contact, and will make social choices based on the potential for emotional rewards derived from social interactions. Thus, when that same graduate student is a 90-year-old chemist, such trade-offs will no longer be tolerated; the crotchety neighbor will be avoided even if he or she is a former professor who is highly knowledgeable about some subject. Although inconsistent with traditional models of social aging, the view that reductions in social contacts are adaptive is wholly consistent with life span theory, especially notions about the nonlinearity of development and the importance of social context.

Socioemotional selectivity theory leads to a number of testable postulates. For one, it suggests that the age-related reduction in social contact does not begin suddenly in old age, but rather represents a gradual (perhaps lifelong) phenomenon. Second, it suggests that conditions other than old age, such as the prospects of geographic relocation or other externally imposed social endings, will also influence the salience of different goals and, subsequently, the choice of social partners. If true, when younger people hold similar expectations about the immediate future, they should make the same kinds of social choices as those typically made by older people. Third, it suggests—in stark contrast to disengagement theory—that emotional concerns will become more important, not less so, in old age and whenever the future is limited. To state it most simply, socioemotional selectivity theory argues that the social changes that are seen reliably in late life are not determined by a set of biological constraints unique to old age, but rather reflect cognitive and motivational processes that have their roots early in development and operate to influence social behavior during all stages of life.

THE NATURE AND MALLEABILITY OF SOCIAL BEHAVIOR IN OLD AGE

When I started studying social behavior in the aged about ten years ago, much of the research in gerontology was being conducted in nursing homes. Although limits to generalizability are considerable, these settings held a certain appeal, namely, ready access to large samples of elderly people, relative homogeneity of the environment, and stability in community structure. Moreover about one-third of all U.S citizens will live in nursing homes at some point during their lives, so knowledge about these settings is clearly important. Because nursing homes are notorious for low rates of social interaction, a number of intervention programs were being tested in which the goal was to increase social interaction among residents. Looking back on this period, my beliefs reflected the current zeitgeist that something unique about old age changed social interaction. Setting out to isolate (and ultimately to modify) the ostensibly negative effects of social inactivity, I conducted several observational studies of socially active and inactive nursing home residents. I expected that differences in social activity would predict well-being, with socially active older people being the most psychologically and physically healthy. Reality, as it turned out, starkly contradicted this widely held view.

A series of studies, in which trained observers recorded social behavior of subjects at random times over periods of up to thirty days, revealed that the amount of social interaction was quite unrelated to indices of psychological well-being such as depression and loneliness. With the exception of the grossest of impairment, cognitive status was also unrelated to social interaction. Perhaps most tellingly, in a study in which neuropsychological functioning was carefully measured, social activity was reliably predicted by only two things: spatial memory and general intelligence. Contrary to all prevailing views, people with *deficits* in spatial memory were the most socially active while the most intelligent people spent the most time alone in their rooms.

With these surprising findings in hand, I began to wonder about the many interventions aimed at increasing social interaction that had been reported in the literature. Researchers had shown repeatedly that the *quantity* of interaction could be increased, but no one had demonstrated that the *quality* of interaction improved or any other psychological benefits occurred along with such an increase. Rebecca Erickson, a former undergraduate honors student who is currently a professor at Ohio State University, and I implemented an intervention in which the experimental manipulation was the presence or absence of a social hour. We used an ABAB withdrawal design. Subjects were observed during four conditions. First, they were observed during a baseline period in order to establish the natural flow of behavior. Next, the intervention (a social hour) was implemented. Third, the intervention was withdrawn and, fourth, the intervention was reinstated. This type of design is very useful for addressing causality in natural settings. This very intervention had been used previously by other researchers and was shown to increase social interaction among nursing home residents.

Our question was slightly different. Erickson and I wanted to know about the nature of those social interactions. So in addition to recording how many social interactions occurred, we also recorded, transcribed, and coded *what* people said to each other. Our findings, illustrated in the Figure 16-2, replicated those of others, showing that the intervention (viz., providing refreshments during a social hour) produced a marked increase in the amount of social contact. If you consider increased rates of contact a positive outcome, the intervention was surely a success.

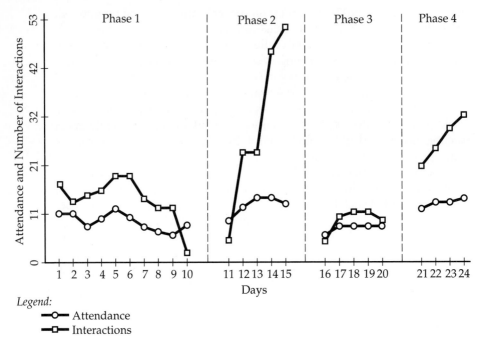

FIGURE 16-2
Impact of social hour on interaction.

Analysis of the verbal data, however, was sobering. All the verbal data had been classified into one of several categories: positive vocals, negative vocals, questions/requests, offer services, statements of fact, greetings, singing, or ineffective communication. Ineffective communication was the category that we created to classify verbalizations that did not make any sense to us. In order to be conservative, however, we decided that in order to be classified as ineffective a verbalization had to meet two criteria: (1) it had to be incomprehensible to us, the coders, and (2) it had to be "ineffective" in that it did not elicit a response from the person to whom it was directed. Thus, if two people were exchanging nonsense words and responding to one another, we categorized it as neutral verbalization. If one person was saying something that was nonsensical (as interpreted by the coders) and the person to whom it was directed also ignored it, we categorized it as ineffective communication.

It turns out that most of the increase in social interaction was accounted for by the ineffective communication category, viz., verbalizations reflecting disorientation and confusion. Figures 16-3 and 16-4 depict the breakdown of different types of verbalizations as they occurred during the baseline period and during the intervention. My students came to refer to this study as the "Babble Study." Once again, social contact and high-level functioning proved to be anything but synonymous and, once again, I

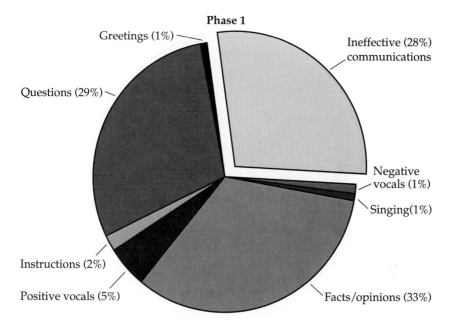

FIGURE 16-3
Breakdown of verbalizations during baseline.

could not help but question the goal of increasing the quantity of social activity for its own sake.

At this point, it was becoming clear to me that prevailing notions about social activity were overly simplistic, if not altogether wrong. Findings from my research were pointing to the possibility that social withdrawal, at least in this context, was adaptive for it was the highest-functioning nursing home residents who articulated and displayed the most active social avoidance. Further, my conversations with high-functioning subjects revealed that although they were not at all interested in pursuing new relationships, they were not seeking social isolation. The people they knew well remained extremely important to them, yet possibilities of new friendships were not appealing. Residents who sometimes did not know their roommates names looked forward eagerly to family visits.

*T*ESTING SOCIOEMOTIONAL SELECTIVITY THEORY

The Integrity of the Emotion System in Old Age

The most controversial tenet of socioemotional selectivity theory concerns the increasing importance of emotion in late life. As indicated above, prior theories (e.g., disengagement theory) had viewed old age as being charac-

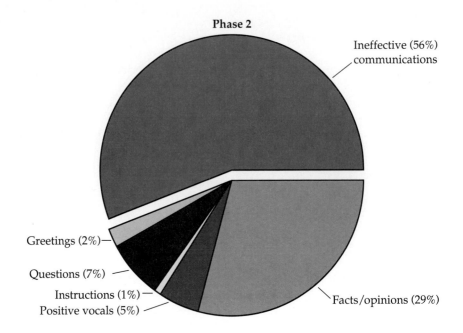

FIGURE 16-4
Breakdown of verbalizations during intervention.

terized by dampened affective states. According to these views, reductions in social behavior likely resulted from this lessened emotionality. Given findings that the reactivity of the central and autonomic nervous systems diminishes with age, it was certainly feasible that age would take a similar toll on emotion. However, there had been few prior studies that had directly examined any of the fundamental aspects of emotion in older people (e.g., subjective experience, expressive behavior, physiology, modes of activation). What data did exist were tangential, based on such things as age-related admission rates to psychiatric hospitals.

Probably the single best aspect of academic life is having colleagues and students to talk with about ideas. Occasionally a group joins forces and works together on a project that might never be done if each individual researcher worked alone. With Robert Levenson (UC–Berkeley), Wallace Friesen (University of Kentucky), and Paul Ekman (UC–San Francisco), I was able to conduct such a study. Levenson is a psychophysiologist who studies the biological underpinnings of subjective feeling states; Ekman and Friesen are experts in the study of facial expression and emotion. Together we designed a study in which we directly explored the emotional responses of older people when emotions were activated in two ways, through cognition (recalling emotional memories) and by muscular activity (posing emotional facial expressions). Subjects come to the laboratory, electrodes that measure physiological states, such as heart rate and galvanic skin response, are attached, and subjects interact with an experimenter over an intercom system while a videocamera records their facial expressions during the procedures. In the emotional recall condition, subjects are asked to recollect an event from their past that made them experience very strongly one of several different emotions (e.g., sadness, anger, happiness). After gathering information about the event, subjects are asked to reexperience the targeted emotion, to try to feel the emotion as strongly as they did when the event occurred. Of course, only rarely can a subject experience an emotion that intensely, but the instructions communicate our wish that they attempt to regenerate the emotional state that they had originally. In the facial posing condition, subjects are instructed by an experimenter to move specific facial muscles that correspond to the natural expressions of specific emotions. In this condition, emotions are not discussed at all.

Findings from this study cleared up a major theoretical issue. Older adults can and do experience emotions as intensely as younger adults and the integration among subjective, expressive, and autonomic subsystems remains intact. Findings about the physiological response did provide limited evidence for the proposition that emotions are dampened with age. Compared to younger subjects, the magnitude of autonomic arousal during emotional experience was, in fact, slightly diminished in older subjects. However, this was the only difference. In terms of facial expressions, the distinctness of autonomic patterning associated with specific emotions, and, perhaps most interesting, the *intensity* of reported subjective experience, older subjects were no different from younger subjects. Since then Levenson and I—in collaboration with Jeanne Tsai, a graduate student of Levenson's at UC–Berkeley—replicated the finding with both Caucasian- and Chinese-Americans using films to elicit emotions.

The Onset and Pervasiveness of Reduced Social Interaction

Socioemotional selectivity theory envisions the narrowing of social contacts as a gradual process that begins long before old age, with the low rates of social contact in late life representing the culmination of a lifelong process characterized by an increasing tendency to limit social contacts to those people who have the most positive affective potential.

Ideally, this notion should be tested in a longitudinal study that allows for charting the course of changes in individuals' social networks over time, rather than relying exclusively upon extrapolations from cross-sectional comparisons. Several years ago, I had the good fortune of being invited to use a longitudinal data set housed at the Institute for Human Development at the University of California at Berkeley. I should say a word or two here about the value of longitudinal research. There are many psychological questions that can be answered only by following lives through time. When researchers are interested in changes that occur over an entire lifetime, the task is ominous indeed. The financial and personal costs of conducting longitudinal research are overwhelming. And no single individual researcher can conduct more than one such study in a career. The fact of the matter is that they nearly always reflect the combined efforts of groups of researchers. The findings that I describe below are based on a study undertaken by Jean Mcfarlane in 1933. The subjects, at that time, were approximately 18-months-old. Today they are in their sixties. They were interviewed and observed many times during childhood. In adulthood they were interviewed four times, at 17 or 18, 30, 40, and 50 years of age.

Specifically, I predicted that, throughout adulthood, people would become more selective in their choice of social partners, devoting increasingly more time to the most emotionally rewarding relationships and less time to less rewarding ones. Thus, reductions in social contacts should be most evident in peripheral relationships, whereas contacts in the most important and intimate relationships would be relatively unchanged. To test these ideas, I examined the frequency of contact, relationship satisfaction, and emotional closeness in six types of relationships (acquaintances, siblings, parents, spouses, children, and close friends).

The variables of interest had not been asked directly of subjects in the longitudinal study, so I relied on transcripts of interviews. Psychologists had interviewed the subjects extensively each time they were evaluated. They were asked about their friendships and love relationships, personal ambitions, and likes and dislikes. I trained two undergraduate research assistants to reliably rate the contact, satisfaction, and closeness variables after reviewing the transcripts.

Coding of the interviews conducted with subjects at different stages of life generally supported my hypotheses. Contact with acquaintances declined over time. In more intimate relationships, both the rates of interactions and the sense of emotional closeness remained stable or increased. It appeared that people were carefully choosing social partners, investing in the most important and discarding less important ones.

Cross-sectional examination of old and very old age. Even in research on aging, the oldest old are rarely studied. One year I had a marvelous opportunity to study a very old group of people in another country, which afforded me the opportunity to examine the generalizability of my earlier findings. I was invited to be a visiting fellow at the Max Planck Institute, the premier research institution in Germany, and to work with a group of researchers who had just completed a comprehensive study of a representative sample of people aged 75 to 102. Social networks had been assessed thoroughly as part of an extensive battery of tests including measures of physical health, cognition, and psychological well-being. Frieder Lang, one of the Max Planck scientists, and I reasoned that if, on the one hand, drops in social contacts were due exclusively to deaths or other bar-

riers to contact, they would occur evenly across different types of relationships. If, on the other hand, older people played a role in limiting contact to their closest social partners, reductions would be unevenly distributed. Thus, we hypothesized that the size of social networks would be
significantly smaller for people in their nineties compared to people in
their eighties. However, we also hypothesized that, consistent with socioemotional selectivity theory, reductions would occur primarily in more
peripheral relationships. The data supported our hypotheses. Although the
oldest people had far fewer acquaintances in their social networks, they had
roughly the same number of emotionally close social partners as their
younger counterparts. Just as I had shown in the American longitudinal
sample, diminishing social network size with age was accounted for primarily by having fewer acquaintances, not fewer confidants.

These two studies, one longitudinal and one cross-sectional, supported principle tenets of socioemotional selectivity theory. First, it is increasingly clear that social selectivity is not unique to old age. Second, decreases in social contact are not uniform across all types of social partners,
but are selective, with the reduction seen primarily in nonemotional relationships. These findings suggest that, rather than being hapless victims
of biology, older people appear to take an active role in shaping their social worlds.

Affective Salience: A Possible Basis for the Selection of Social Partners

Charting the longitudinal course of a phenomenon such as social selection
can only hint at the underlying mechanisms responsible for observed
changes. According to socioemotional selectivity theory, affective characteristics of social partners become increasingly important with age. However,
in order to test this postulate, I needed to know how people *think* about other
people. As people age, are their mental representations of social partners
more likely to become organized around affective dimensions? If people do
actively construct their social worlds, do they do so on the basis of affective
criteria? Do the changes that are observed reflect people's *preferences*, for example, or are these changes the result of external factors over which individuals have little control? These were not easy questions to answer; if people are merely asked if they have taken an active role in constructing their
social environments, demand characteristics and cognitive dissonance might
conspire to cause them to say "Yes." Moreover, even if people do take an active role in social selection, they might not be aware of this activity.

Dimensional underpinnings of social selection. In collaboration with
Barbara Fredrickson, one of my former doctoral students who is now on
the faculty at Duke University, I developed a procedure aimed at eluci-

dating the psychological underpinnings of social selection. Rather than ask subjects directly, we adopted a similarity paradigm to assess mental representations of social partners. If older people categorized social partners in terms of affect, we would expect to see evidence of this in their grouping of social partners.

In our first experiment, we studied teenagers, middle-aged adults, healthy older adults, and frail older adults. Subjects were shown a series of cards with brief descriptions of a variety of potential social partners (e.g., the author of a book you have read, your sibling, a close friend, a sales representative, a clergy person). Subjects were asked to sort the cards into piles based on how similarly they would feel about interacting with the person described. The data were analyzed using multidimensional scaling.

The final scaling solution produced three dimensions that accounted for most of the variance: anticipated affect, future possibilities, and information seeking. *Anticipated affect* represents the positive-negative valence of the prospective interaction. *Future possibilities* represents the potential for continued contact; and *information seeking* represents the degree to which the prospective social partners could provide new information.

As predicted, the four subgroups differed in their relative weightings of the three dimensions. Compared to their younger counterparts, healthy older subjects, and especially frail older subjects, weighted the affective dimension most heavily. For younger subjects, the weightings afforded to the future possibilities and information-seeking dimensions were greater. In a simpler, more direct test, we asked subjects to tell us which of the people described on cards they would like to get to know better. Whereas the majority of teenagers included novel social partners among their choices, far fewer healthy older people did. Among frail older people, only 5 percent included any unfamiliar social partners in their selections.

We recently replicated the dimensional findings derived from this study in a larger, more representative sample, which included equal numbers of males and females, both blue-collar and white-collar workers, and a large number of African-Americans. Findings provided strong support for the reliability of the phenomenon.

Memory for emotional information. Since we had relied on the card-sort procedure in the preceding studies, I felt it was important to examine age-related changes in emotional salience in another way. In collaboration with Susan Turk-Charles—then an undergraduate honors student, now a graduate student at the University of Southern California—I conducted a study using an implicit memory paradigm[2] with subjects who ranged in

---

[2] An implicit memory paradigm is one where subjects are not told ahead of time their memory will be tested, but are asked at one point during the experiment to recall information that was presented earlier. The advantage of this type of experimental paradigm is that it avoids demand characteristics and closely mimics memory in everyday life, i.e., rarely does someone instruct you to remember something, you simply do or do not.

age from 20 to 83. Subjects were asked to read a narrative that featured comparable amounts of emotionally laden and emotionally neutral information. At the end of a one-hour experimental session, they were asked to indicate what they remembered from the story. We operationalized "emotional salience" as the proportion of emotional versus neutral phrases that were recalled. Consistent with the previous studies, the proportion of emotional memories recalled increased linearly with age as illustrated in Figure 16-1. Further, analyzing the total number of memories recalled, the recall of neutral memories showed decrements with age, while the recall of emotional memories was well preserved.

These studies provided support for socioemotional selectivity theory's notion that emotional aspects of social relationships loom increasingly larger with age. Further, and perhaps most interestingly, they suggest that the oft-observed memory decrements associated with age may not apply to information that has emotional significance.

It was also clear that age was not the *only* determining factor in the salience afforded to emotion. The fact that the affective weighting was greater in infirm 80-year-olds than in healthy 80-year-olds, despite the equivalence of age, suggested something else was involved. Given differences in health status, the two older groups had very different life expectancies, and it was clear from talking to them that they were very aware of the time they had left. In fact, infirm subjects often commented that they had "no time for those people" (referring to unfamiliar social partners). I began to think that construal of the future—generally correlated with age, but potentially independent—might be a major influence on the socioemotional selectivity phenomenon we had been studying.

The Role of Expected Futures

If the tendency to weight emotional factors more heavily in selecting social partners resulted, in part, from construing the future as limited, then a bias toward choosing emotionally close social partners should be observable in younger people under conditions where opportunities for future contact were foreshortened. Moreover, by studying younger people, I could manipulate futures independent of health status, ruling out the possibility that preferences change simply because of poor health.

Experimentally limited futures. To test this hypothesis, Fredrickson and I conducted a telephone interview with people between the ages of 11 and 92 who were randomly selected from telephone listings. There were two conditions. In the *normal-future* condition, we asked subjects what they would do if they had thirty minutes free, wanted to engage in social contact, and could select among three prospective social partners. One prospective partner was familiar, "a member of your immediate family," and two were less familiar, namely, "the author of a book you've just read" and "a recent acquaintance with whom you seem to have much in common." In the *limited-future* condition, we asked subjects to choose among the same three alternatives imagining that they were about to move across the country by themselves, but had thirty minutes free before they left and wanted to spend time with another person.

Our basic prediction involved an age by future interaction. Because age itself imposes a shorter future, we expected that regardless of the condition, older people would be more likely than younger people to select a familiar social partner. In contrast, we expected that younger people, tacitly unaware of limitations on the future, would choose a novel social partner under the normal-future condition, but in the limited-future condition, we expected that younger people would choose a familiar social partner. Results provided strong support for our predictions.

Experimentally expanded futures. Working with Amy Lutz, another former undergraduate honors student, currently a research assistant, I recently revised the conditions slightly and replicated the study with a sample of subjects aged 8 to 93. The *normal-future* condition was identical to that of the original study. However, in the second condition, instead of limiting the future, we presented a scenario that entailed an *extended future*, asking subjects to imagine that they just learned from their physician about a new medical advance that ensured they would live in relatively good health for at least twenty years longer than they expected. Once again, under the normal-future condition, older people demonstrated a bias for familiar over novel social partners. In the extended-future condition, the bias disappeared. In other words, even in old age, it appears that expectations have a powerful influence on the choice of social partners, which would imply that modification of these expectations would change age-related patterns of social selectivity.

Future limited by disease. Our first two studies of the impact of perceived futures on social selection required subjects to "imagine" conditions of altered futures. To test the generalizability of these findings I sought a naturalistic context to assess the role of the expected future.

Fredrickson and I recently completed a third study, working with young men living with the human immunodeficiency virus (HIV), a group of people whose futures have been greatly foreshortened by the seemingly inescapable fatal consequences of the virus. We recruited three subsamples: (1) healthy gay men; (2) HIV-positive, asymptomatic gay men; and (3) HIV-positive, symptomatic gay men. The comparison group was a sample of young, middle-aged, and old subjects recruited by the survey research company to represent the general population of the Bay area. We used the paradigm described earlier in which subjects sorted descriptions of various kinds of people into piles based on how similarly they would feel about interacting with the person described.

As we hypothesized, the social preferences of healthy gay men were similar to those of an age-matched sample of young men sampled from the general population, with comparable salience placed on the three primary dimensions. Responses of HIV-positive, asymptomatic men mimicked those of our middle-aged subjects, and responses of HIV-positive, symptomatic men displayed choices strikingly similar to those of our oldest subjects; that is, the closer the men were to the end of their lives, the greater weight they placed on affective qualities of prospective social partners. In short, changes in social preferences appear to be altered in much the same way when futures are limited by age as when futures are limited by disease.

Findings from these last three studies indicate that the kinds of social partners that are chosen, as well as the underlying dimensions that form the basis for evaluating social partners, are affected similarly when people face more limited futures, regardless of whether those futures are shortened by age, disease, or experimentally induced changes in context. As futures become increasingly limited, people become increasingly prone to choose familiar over novel partners and give greater weight to the affective qualities of a prospective social contact.

In terms of the changes in social networks that have often been observed to vary with age, it may be more parsimonious to explain these in terms of the length of expected futures than in terms of chronological age. Stated differently, social preferences that have long been associated with old age may have less to do with years from birth than years until death.

At a broader level, these studies provide strong evidence for the powerful influence that expectations and beliefs can exert in the social domain. Rather than viewing age-related changes in biology as destiny, these findings suggest a true dialectic between mind and body, with older people (like younger people) playing an active role in determining the nature and qualities of their lives.

CONCLUSION

Together, findings from this program of research paint a picture of emotion, social interaction, and social relationships in later life that is quite optimistic. Age-related reduction in social contact appears to be highly selective—and dictated by relatively rational calculations of self-interest rather than by a deterioration of capacity. People seem to play an active role in molding their social environments such that they retain emotionally close social relationships and detach from relationships that are not emotionally meaningful. Importantly, the selection process appears to be driven in large part by expectations for the future. When the future is perceived as limited, emotional goals become more salient than others and social relationships are selected or rejected according to emotional criteria.

I suspect that limiting interaction to those persons who are most familiar functions as an excellent strategy for regulating emotion, particularly in old age, when time and social energy need to be invested wisely.

I also expect that continued study of the second half of life holds tremendous promise to inform us about the entire life course. I leave you with a favorite quote from *The Second Half of Life*, written by Simone de Beauvior:

> The whole meaning of our lives is in question. If we do not know what we are going to be, we cannot know what we are. Let us recognize ourselves in this old man or in that old woman. It must be done if we are to take upon ourselves the entirety of our human state. [Simone de Beauvoir, 1972, p. 12]

SUGGESTED READINGS

ANTONUCCI, T. C. (1985). Personal characteristics, social support, and social behavior. In R. H. Binstock & E. Shanas (Eds.), *Handbook of aging and the social sciences* (2d ed., pp. 94–128). New York: Van Nostrand Reinhold.

———— (1991). Attachment, social support, and coping with negative life events in mature adulthood. In E. M. Cummings, A. L. Greene, & K. H. Karraker (Eds.), *Life-span developmental psychology: Perspectives on stress and coping* (pp. 261–276). Hillsdale, NJ: Erlbaum.

BALTES, P. B., MAYER, K. U., HELMCHEN, H., STEINHAGEN-THIESSEN, E. (1993). The Berlin Aging Study (BASE): Overview and design. *Aging and Society, 13,* 483–515.

CARSTENSEN, L. L. (1992). Social and emotional patterns in adulthood: Support for socioemotional selectivity theory. *Psychology and Aging, 7,* 331–338.

———— (1993). Motivation for social contact across the life span: A theory of socioemotional selectivity. In J. Jacobs (Ed.), *Nebraska Symposium on Motivation: 1992, Developmental Perspectives on Motivation* (Vol. 40, pp. 209–254). Lincoln: University of Nebraska Press.

———— & Erickson, R. E. (1986). Enhancing the social environments of elderly nursing home residents: Are high rates of interaction enough? *Journal of Applied Behavior Analysis, 19,* 349–355.

———— & Turk-Charles, S. (1994). The salience of emotion across the adult life course. *Psychology and Aging, 9,* 259–264.

CUMMING, E., & HENRY, W. E. (1961). *Growing old: The process of disengagement.* New York: Basic Books.

DE BEAUVOIR, S. (1972). *The coming of age.* New York: Putnam.

FREDRICKSON, B. L., & CARSTENSEN, L. L. (1990). Choosing social partners: How old age and anticipated endings make people more selective. *Psychology and Aging, 5,* 335–347.

HAVIGHURST, R. J. (1961). Successful aging. *Gerontologist, 1,* 8–13.

JUNG, C. G. (1933). *Modern man in search of a soul.* New York: Harcourt, Brace & World.

KAHN, R. L., & ANTONUCCI, T. C. (1980). Convoys over the life course: Attachment, roles and social support. In P. B. Baltes & O. G. Brim (Eds.), *Life-span development and behavior* (pp. 254–283). New York: Academic Press.

LANG, F. R., & CARSTENSEN, L. L. (1994). Close emotional relationships in late life: Further support for proactive aging in the social domain. *Psychology and Aging, 9,* 315–324.

LEVENSON, R. W., CARSTENSEN, L. L., FRIESEN, W. V., & EKMAN, P. (1991). Emotion, physiology, and expression in old age. *Psychology and Aging, 6(1),* 28–35.

MADDOX, G. L. (1963). Activity and morale: A longitudinal study of selected elderly subjects. *Social Forces, 42,* 195–204.

DAVID **A.** C*HIRIBOGA (Ph.D., University of Chicago) is Professor and Chair, Department of Health Promotion and Gerontology, School of Allied Health Sciences, University of Texas Medical Branch, Galveston. A fellow in both the Gerontological Society of America and the American Psychological Association, he is past president of APA's Division 20 (Adulthood and Aging) and currently serves on the Division 38 (Health Psychology) Aging Committee. On the editorial board of the* Journal of Aging and Health, *he is a member of the new NIMH Health Behavior and Prevention study section. His research interests center on stress exposure, transitions, and adaptation; he has recently become more active in the studies of Hispanic aging. Recognizing the merits of age irreverency, he is the well-exercised father of two advanced-belt karate sons (ages 7 and 8); his wife, psychologist Barbara Wai Kinn Yee, specializes in the problems faced by minority elderly such as her husband.*

17

Stress and Adaptation in Adulthood

*P*RELUDE

There is an understanding among psychologists that we are often drawn to fields of specialization that hold personal relevance. Among fellow gerontologists, I have noticed many with unusual bonds to a "skip generation" family member. Several were raised by grandparents, for example, and a number of others were either late arrivals to their families or the products of late marriages. In my own case, my father was singularly off schedule when he married at the age of 45. Moreover, as an immigrant with a very low paying job, he (and the rest of us) had trouble fitting in with the affluent lifestyle of the New England town where we lived. Perhaps it was not entirely coincidental, then, that my entire academic life has been spent studying the two topics of aging and stress!

While background experiences may have set the stage, the actual decision to become a gerontologist came about in 1963, while I was taking an upper-division class entitled "Contemporary Trends in Psychology" at Boston University. Freda Rebelsky, a developmental psychologist, taught the course. Freda asked each of us to select a topic, and to illustrate her intent she listed some examples, including "gerontology." I had no idea what gerontology was all about, but as a relatively new area with few established leaders, it sounded like just the ticket for someone at the beginning of a career in psychology. "Imagine," I thought to myself, "a field that is wide open, where, with hard work, you actually might become recognized for your own accomplishments rather than for adding a footnote to some 'great leader's' work." With that thought came a decision not only to investigate the status of gerontology as my class assignment, but also to start preparing for a career in the field.

Rebelsky's class provided the defining moment in my choice of career and in several other ways helped shape my career. For instance, I gained my first experience in professional collaboration, an integral feature of much gerontological research due to the breadth and complexity of the subject. I shared my excitement about this "new" field with a fellow student, Stan Levinson. Stan was more interested in the biological issues related to aging, and I was more interested in the psychosocial factors. We decided to work together on a more comprehensive review than either of us could have done alone.

My paper for the course also provided a focus to my interest in aging. While reviewing the literature, I discovered many descriptive reports of age differences in personality and well-being, but few attempts at explanation. One article, written by Robert Butler in 1963, did offer a suggestion. Butler presented the intriguing idea that social and personal conditions may prompt a reorganization of personality, although he concluded that with respect to psychological processes:

> The relationships of changed functions to aging per se and to diseases, psychosocial crises, and personality remain obscure. [p. 74]

For some reason this passage sparked my interest in psychosocial crises, or stressors, as a dynamic force in adult development. Another critical article, by Raymond Kuhlen, also emphasized the interplay between external and internal factors but added a fascinating point about age and identity: older people who identify themselves as old may be less adjusted than those who see themselves as middle-aged. At that stage in my education, the cross-age group relationship of identity to adjustment seemed paradoxical, since my training had led me to believe that people who are more reality-oriented are better adjusted. This seeming paradox provided an intellectual challenge that made me want to know more about the aging process.

Graduate School and a New Identity

Being the child of an immigrant family, the entire issue of what it meant to be a professional, and how one got to that point, was beyond my comprehension. My first act after being accepted by the Committee on Human Development at the University of Chicago was to take a bus trip there. I left Newton, Massachusetts, my hometown, in the late afternoon, and remember waking up during the night as we were passing through what seemed like a scene from Dante's Inferno: fire belched forth across the entire landscape. Only later did I learn we were passing the steel mills of Gary, Indiana. I arrived, took the elevated train to 55th and Garfield, hopped on a bus, spent about half an hour at the university, and left, satisfied: The place actually existed! But for years I pondered the symbolism of having to go through hell to get to Chicago.

Of my graduate education, probably the less said the better. However, three bits of acquired knowledge still guide my work. First, if left to their own devices, interviewers will probably spend more time asking questions about things that interest them, not you. This I learned from my first real job: conducting a content analysis of in-depth interviews with middle-aged men and women for a grant headed up by Bernice Neugarten and James Birren. I noticed that certain domains, notably sex and death, were invariably longer if done by specific interviewers; questioning revealed these domains were the very ones in which the interviewers were themselves interested.

Second, I learned the fine art of revising manuscripts. My tutor was my adviser, Bernice Neugarten. Bernice was—and at age 80 still is—the best editor I have ever encountered. She never hesitated to write "Awk" (trans: awkward) or "Logic?" and other daunting expressions all over my manuscripts, but often took the further step of providing rewrites to illustrate her point. To this day, when reviewing a draft, I can hear Bernice's voice commenting on its logic, point, and style.

And third, I learned, painfully, the distinctions between interdisciplinary, multidisciplinary, and unidisciplinary training and research. I say "painfully" because while the faculty in the Human Development program generally endorsed the value of interdisciplinary research, in practice, many of them totally ignored anything outside their own narrow specialties. I remember, for example, having to beg and cajole an eminent faculty member into letting me write a paper about the roles of the elderly in agrarian societies: A specialist in child development, he seriously doubted there was anything worth saying about the elderly. Generally, it was left to the student to figure out what interdisciplinary research was all about, and whether in fact it was even possible. In the end I concluded that the best one can usually hope for is multidisciplinary research, where a group focuses on the same topic from multiple perspectives but at least shares those perspectives with each other from time to time!

Cross-disciplinary fertilizing. In working on my doctoral thesis I discovered the value of exploring how separate disciplines view the same phenomenon. I put together a proposal to study predictors of mortality and morbidity that were common to three very different groups of older persons, all of whom were being forced to relocate. One group consisted of forty-five military widows who were to be moved from a beautiful mansion to a barrackslike campus facility, a second group was composed of eighty-five Jewish men and women about to move into sectarian long-term housing, and a third consisted of eighty-two men and women who were being relocated from a rural, custodial institution into community facilities.

The thesis focused specifically upon relocation stress, about which there was an extensive literature by the early 1970s. To my surprise, however, studies of relocation experiences of older adults rarely if ever considered relocation as a specific instance of the more general domain of stress research, and rarely if ever referenced the literature on the latter. Thus it was only by painful fits and starts that relocation research acquired something resembling a stress paradigm.

Consider for example the stages of relocation. According to Mort Lieberman, there are three stages: anticipation, impact, and long-term adaptation. In the series of relocation projects that Lieberman and Shelly Tobin headed up, and which formed the basis of my doctoral work, the anticipation stage was operationally defined as lasting up to three months, and long-term adaptation as status one year following the actual relocation. On the other hand, in the research of Richard Lazarus, a leading stress researcher who at the time dealt primarily with laboratory experiments, anticipation was operationalized in terms of seconds, and long-term adaptation in terms of minutes. Both approaches worked, and defined critical aspects of the stress phenomena under study! More interesting to me is that neither investigator was apparently aware of the other's research.

My sense is that this reliance upon discipline-specific knowledge continues even today. During the present decade of the 1990s, for example, there has been a tremendous growth of research on caregiving to dependent elderly. One of the most vigorous concepts to appear in this research deals with caregiver burden—and yet as far back as the 1960s, J. Hoenig and Marion Hamilton, among others, were developing sophisticated perspectives on the burden of families caring for dependent children and young adults, and had emphasized the distinction between objective and subjective burden. Years later, gerontologists have more or less rediscovered the same distinction. We now include assessments of cognitive deficits and functional limitations of the patient, and how much time is spent in the provision of care, in addition to asking what the caregiver perceives to be the level of burden.

Working on a stress model. Among the findings of my doctoral thesis was that perceptions of the stressor and one's control over the situation helped predict both short- and long-term morbidity and mortality. The perceived control phenomenon clearly illustrated the differences between objective and subjective truths: For most if not all subjects there was in reality no control over their relocation. But what they lacked in reality they made up for with their personal interpretations of the way things were. The data showed that if people thought they were involved, in some way, with the relocation, they fared better. This involvement varied from something as seemingly minor as participating in decisions about what day they would be moved, to what floor, room, or even what place they would be moving.

*F*IRST JOB AND ALL THAT STUFF

Hardly had I completed the first frequency runs for my thesis when I got a job offer that proved hard to resist: working with a multidisciplinary team of researchers at UC–San Francisco on a recently funded longitudinal study of transitions. My role was to develop the more psychological instruments and to oversee development of stress indices. Despite the obvious problems in leaving graduate school before completing one's dissertation, I yielded to temptation and accepted—a decision that led to the expected delay in completing my thesis, but on the whole was probably the right one.

A Study of Normative Transitions

Perhaps my first impression of my new colleagues in California was that they all had well-developed hobbies and great parties! In California, so it seemed, nearly everyone had a carefully developed avocation or hobby to which they devoted large amounts of time. One of my new friends flew gliders in Napa Valley, another raced pigeons, others raced sailboats. Instead of staying within a circumscribed geographic region (e.g., Hyde Park, in Chicago), people lived and played all over the place. And, in contrast to Chicago, where parties provided a context for demonstration of intellectual prowess, parties in California were predicated on fun and fancy.

Parties and hobbies did not diminish the team's commitment to solid research and hard work. The study for which I was recruited in late 1968 was a life span study of what happens to average, community-dwelling people over time. One rather unique feature of the study was that we sampled according to where people stood in relation to one of four normative and, therefore, predictable life transitions, instead of selecting subjects according to age. Two of the respondent groups were in the early stages of adulthood: (1) high school seniors who were facing graduation and entry into adult status, and (2) men and women whose first marriage was less than one year old and who would presumably be dealing with issues of parenting within the next few years. We also included persons at earlier and later stages of middle age: (3) men and women whose youngest child was a high school senior and who therefore were likely to face the proverbial "empty nest," and (4) men and women who either were expecting to retire within five years or who had a spouse about to retire.

A study of ordinary people with ordinary lives. One goal of the research was to study ordinary people, since many longitudinal studies have been based on relatively elite sample populations. In order to simplify the sampling design, we began by selecting the most homogeneous district of one west coast city: San Francisco. The district we selected was composed primarily of lower-middle-class and blue-collar workers of Caucasian descent.

From school records, fifty-two high school seniors who were the youngest members of their families were identified; the same process also identified fifty-four parents whose youngest child was about to graduate from high school. For both groups, names were drawn at random; with one exception, this procedure generated high school and parent subjects who were unrelated. Using public vital statistics, fifty newlyweds (for all, this was their first marriage) were located, with at least one of each pair living or having lived in this district. The oldest group, consisting of sixty men and women who planned to retire within two to three years, was located through records of firms or agencies in the area, or suggested by people in the other three groups.

The five contacts. The first interviews began in 1968, and usually required a total of from six to eight hours to complete. Each of the four remaining interviews was designed to fit within a single three-hour session and took place at two- to three-year intervals. The fifth and final set of interviews was completed between April and August, 1980. Over the twelve years, the sample was reduced in size to 168 persons—78 percent of the original sample. Not unexpectedly some respondents had died, eighteen in all; most were middle aged and older.

We ended up with a sample generally representative of traditional blue-collar workers. Being for the most part upwardly mobile, their ways of living resembled those of the middle and lower middle classes. The primary concern for most lay with the family, both nuclear and extended. Aside from those who were high school seniors at the first interview, the majority had some technical or general education beyond high school—few had completed college. Not surprisingly, the newlyweds were better-educated than the middle-aged, who in turn had more schooling than the pre-retirees. Also reflecting national trends, the oldest respondents were likely to have more siblings, but they themselves had an average of two to three children. Most acknowledged some religious affiliation, with more women than men attending services; many parents who did not participate themselves sent their children to Sunday school or synagogue. More than three-fourths of the women had jobs, frequently on a part-time basis.

Development of a Life Span Orientation to Stress

The transitions study provided a near-ideal platform from which to launch a series of investigations into the life span implications of stress exposure. One reason is that even in the baseline interviews we were able to incorporate questions that addressed stressors from Thomas Holmes and Richard Rahe's "life events" perspective. Due to concerns about whether the Holmes and Rahe Schedule of Recent Events (SRE) contained sufficient items appropriate for older age groups, we did not include the latter instrument in our initial interviews. Instead we asked multiple questions, using approaches ranging from the open-ended to very structured, in an effort to identify sources of distress that should be included in more structured inventories at follow-up.

Another unique aspect of the study was the opportunity to study transitions and stress exposure on a prospective basis. Generally stress researchers are forced to identify persons only after they have experienced the stress condition of interest. For example, one generally studies the bereaved after the death of a loved one because it is so difficult to identify those who are facing bereavement and who are willing to be interviewed. Here, on the other hand, we identified persons who could be anticipated to experience a major normative transition within a few years and who would be followed during those years.

A less obvious but perhaps more critical resource was the intellectual environment. The San Francisco area provided an exceptionally rich environment for those of us interested in stress. In Berkeley there was Richard Lazarus, one of the pioneers in the field of stress research. At UC–San Francisco we had Mardi Horowitz, an innovative and gifted psychiatrist, and at Stanford there was Rudolf Moos, one of the pioneers in the study and assessment of coping.

During the years of the project I was fortunate in being able to work collaboratively with most of these researchers, especially Horowitz, whose Center for the Study of Neuroses brought in hundreds of persons suffering from stress-related disorders. Mardi had extensive data on his center's clinical caseload of past years, data that allowed him to identify the most frequently mentioned life events. Combining his data with that from the baseline transitions interviews allowed us to create a comprehensive instrument that contained events relevant to older as well as younger adults. For example, in addition to items about parenting and work, there were items concerning grandchildren, retirement of one's spouse, and relatives moving in with the respondent. To help in the final revision, Mardi brought in Richard Rahe, codeveloper of the original life events schedule. The result really consisted of two instruments that shared a common pool of 136 items. The version adopted by Mardi included a weighting system based on averaged ratings by psychiatrists on the clinical implications of each event. The strategy I elected, based on findings from my doctoral thesis on the importance of perceptions, as well as Lazarus' work on cognitive appraisal, was to have subjects rate each experienced event on a simple four-point scale. They were asked whether the event had made them feel very unhappy to very happy. I also included another rating: whether at the present time they still thought about the event a lot, sometimes, or never.

In later years I added a two-wave panel study of a nonnormative transition as a companion to the normative study of transitions. Using county clerk records as a framework for random sampling, 333 men and women recently separated from spouses were interviewed shortly after marital separation, and then again some 3.5 years later. Other studies that helped establish my sense of stress and adaptation included a study of 550 medical, surgical, and intensive care nurses and a study of 385 adult children and their parents. Working with Kyriakos Markides, I am now looking at stress and adaptation in a longitudinal study of Mexican-American families that covers three generations within each family, and a two-wave epidemiological study of 3,060 Mexican-American elderly.

Each of these studies has incorporated the basic stress paradigm, and developed or refined one or more components. In the study of divorce, for example, I added a version of Richard Lazarus and Susan Folkman's original Ways of Coping instrument that substituted a three-point rating system for the original's binary code, and also a hassles scale. Incidentally, I was sometimes able to get instruments from the divorce study incorporated into the transitions study follow-ups and sometimes not. Since the rest of the team felt that I was much too quantitative, and already had more than my fair share of interview time, I generally had a lot of negotiating to do!

STRESS AND ITS IMPLICATIONS FOR WELL-BEING

What then have I learned from studying stress over a period of some twenty-five years? Most simply, I have learned three things. First, stress conditions are only part of the picture. Second, stressors come in many shapes and sizes that bear a complex relationship to each other. And third, stressors not only influence adaptation in the short run but have implications for the long term as well.

Stressors: Only Part of the Picture

Obviously, stress exposure is completely unrelated to many aspects of life. Perhaps not so obvious is that stress exposure often does not have a direct relationship to outcomes. As a health/developmental psychologist, my interest has generally been on health-related outcomes and I have used stress as one means of trying to better understand the mental health and adaptation of people at different stages of life. At the time I was getting started, the widely acclaimed model proposed by Holmes and Rahe was quite simple: The more life changes, the greater the risk of physical and mental health problems. On the whole this model seemed to present only part of the picture.

In contrast, current stress paradigms will usually consider one or more variables within three basic components: stressors, mediators, and responses. The idea is not that the stress process is a mechanical and preordained relationship, but rather that stressors work through a variety of mediators, such as social supports, self-esteem, and coping strategies. The stressors are impinging agents, including life events as well as the more ephemeral conditions that last seconds or minutes and the more durable that may last for years. Stressors include both positive and negative situations, since both are associated with change. Responses are reactions to the stressors. Most investigators consider the negative consequences: either some physical health response, such as stroke or hypertension or the common cold, or psychological responses such as anxiety or depression. A few investigators also study positive responses, such as morale, since in the long run even a negative stressor may lead to psychological growth and development. The mediators orchestrate the relationship of stressor to response, with the most commonly studied mediators being social supports and coping strategies.

The Many Shapes and Sizes of Stressors

Most social scientists are familiar with the previously mentioned Schedule of Recent Events and its impressive impact on stress research. From the mid-1970s onward, a number of instruments have been developed as replacements for the SRE. As mentioned earlier, my first objective in the transitions study was to develop a 136-item stress inventory more sensitive to the range of events that might be experienced by a life span sample. The next step was to compare the correlates of the standardized weighting systems used by Holmes and Rahe, as well as by Horowitz, with weights established on the basis of subject perceptions of the experience. Using stress inventory data from the five-year follow-up, I found that both types of standardized weights correlated significantly with a variety of outcome variables but did so at about the same level as a score obtained by simply adding together the total number of stressors reported. On the other hand, when each subject's own perceptions were used to subdivide stressors into positive and negative categories, and more or less positive or negative within each category, significant increases in variance could be gained. My conclusion was that: (1) standardized weights ignore individual perceptions and (2) individual perceptions are the key to understanding how and why people respond to life events and other stressors.

With an instrument that provided reasonable data on life events, some of the transitions team felt that the stress domain was now sufficiently developed. On the other hand, our own research had suggested that life events were not the only kind of stressor to affect people's lives. Open-ended responses to baseline questions revealed a host of stressors, including chronic strains, anticipated stressors, stressors affecting close family members, stressors affecting the community and even positive events that were expected but didn't occur, such as marriage or the birth of a child. As a way of obtaining an overview of these diverse types of stressors, I grouped them into categories: micro, mezzo, and macro.

The microlevel. At what can be called the microlevel, the focus is on the stressors of everyday life. Examples include getting caught in a traffic jam, mislaying your social security check, or even not being able to find your favorite dress just when you're heading off to dinner. By far the most commonly experienced stressors, until recently, they were the least studied. My approach to microstressors was to develop an eleven-item hassles scale that traces its heritage conceptually, but not in terms of content, to the 115-item version developed by Lazarus in 1984. Hassle scores have proved to be useful supplements to information provided by the life events inventory.

The mezzolevel. The most studied of the three levels, mezzo stressors deal with situations that are less frequent than microstressors, but which generally are more memorable and hold implications for personal health. The well-known life events type of research falls into this category, as do studies of the more chronic, or durable stressors.

Using the life events questionnaire, I found that events could predict psychological well-being over periods of five and even twelve years. I also became intrigued by the fact that life events, as viewed at one point in time, can also correlate significantly with events experienced several years later. As an example, a total or summary score for negative stress exposure reported at the seven-year follow-up correlated .51 with negative stress reported at the twelfth year. Positive events correlated at .53 for the same time period. Such findings indicate both that life events are not necessarily random and that they may chain forward in time.

The macrolevel. Stressors at the macrolevel are those that impact first on society at large. War in the Middle East, bad economic news, a flurry of near-misses in the air lanes, or a spill of environmentally hazardous materials not only make the headlines but can create anxiety and a generally heightened sense of distress on the part of the populace. Perhaps the earliest study of macrolevel events was conducted inadvertently. In the United States, Norman Bradburn and his colleague David Caplovitz were testing a new morale measure in a series of national probability studies that happened to take place before and after the assassination of President John Kennedy. They found a national increase in the experiencing of negative emotions in the wake of the murder.

Given such evidence, it seemed important to develop a systematic approach to assessing macrostressors. In the transitions study we actually included a macrolevel stress inventory from the beginning. Called the Social Change Scale, it was administered at all contacts. As originally developed, the Social Change Scale consisted of the self-reported impact of ten items. Five were events of the past (the great depression, etc.) and five were for the present. The five present conditions consisted of (1) new ways of doing things at work, (2) changing roles of women, (3) changes in rights of minorities, (4) crime in the streets, and (5) changes in the economy and employment. At the last session, three new items were added: The international situation, danger at nuclear plants, and new lifestyles.

When we looked at scores from the Social Change Scale, we found that they were significantly associated, among older adults, with psychological symptoms and the ratio of positive to negative emotions. The kinds of items endorsed also were of interest. For example, at the fourth contact, somewhat less than a third of the youngest men, now aged 20 to the mid-thirties, cited changes in rights of minorities and about the same proportion were concerned about new roles for women. Youngest women were equally concerned about new roles and crime in the streets. Newlywed men worried about new ways at work and changes in the economy. Their female counterparts cited changing roles of women as well as the economy. The four older groups were less varied in their response: Crime in the streets was the big problem, and the proportion singling that item out ranged from two-fifths of the oldest women to two-thirds of the middle-aged men.

Two years later, changes in the economy and employment were foremost in the minds of the young, ranging from a third or more of the youngest people to well over half the newlyweds of both sexes. All the four oldest groups had become even more worried about crime. For example, while two-fifths of the oldest women cited crime at the fourth interview, four-fifths of them did so at the last one. In fact, most of these women had become more worried in all content areas.

Beyond life events. Letting go of the SRE as the standard "tool" of the trade has had the advantage of freeing researchers to explore more innovative and diverse approaches to stress measurement. The active pursuit of alternatives to life event methodologies has generated a wealth of concepts and instruments designed to assess stressors. One challenge that now must be addressed is the relationships that exist among these various kinds of stressors, as well as the role of factors such as personality and environment in determining the kinds and levels of stressors experienced. For example, is it appropriate to consider as "life events" those which are strongly associated with the occurrence of past and/or future events, or to personality? Another challenge is to develop a standard, comprehensive battery of stress indicators.

Stressors and Adaptation

As we looked at the impact of all these stressors on people's lives, we began to identify some important characteristics of stress conditions. One characteristic of importance from a developmental perspective is that stress exposure was associated with psychosocial functioning not only in the present but up to twelve years in the future. In several studies, negative life events predicted subsequent adaptation at higher levels than positive events, but still remained only part of the equation: Hassles, anticipations of stress, and macrolevel stressors add significantly to what is known. Finally, stress exposure seems to influence changes over time not only in mental health factors but in areas as diverse as morale, goals, ability to project into the future, and levels of leisure activity. Relating back to my early interest in why older people who retained their identity as middle-aged were more adapted, there is evidence that a positive self-concept can be maintained well into later life if life circumstances do not include continual exposure to high stress loads.

Going beyond the specifics. In trying to better understand the linkages between stress and adaptation, I have become interested in the idea that health researchers often are very absorbed in some specific health-related condition and tend to focus their attention nearly exclusively on factors specific to a specific problem. In my research with people going through the process of divorce, a serendipitous finding was that general instruments of stress and well-being provided data just as informative as instruments tapping conditions specific to divorce.

What I learned from the divorce findings is really very simple: Just because something particularly stressful is going on in people's lives does not mean that other aspects of life should be disregarded. For one thing, there can be a contagion effect that spreads into many areas of life. In the case of divorcing subjects, during the period immediately following marital separation they reported significantly higher levels of stress than age-matched transitions subjects, not just in the marital area but across most of the eleven content areas covered by the life events questionnaire. On the other hand, some 3.5 years later the two groups were virtually indistinguishable in terms of event exposure. This last finding suggested that researchers should keep in mind that the stress condition of interest to them is just one aspect of the individual's life.

Drawing upon the idea that people's lives are influenced by multiple conditions, when I investigated the stress conditions involved in caregiving I was careful to include indices sensitive to the specific situation in which subjects found themselves, but also to include general indicators of stress and well-being. The two-wave panel study included 385 adult children and 200 parents with Alzheimer's disease.

In order to assess stress from a broad perspective, the caregiver study included measures of general life events and hassles, but caregiver items were added to the hassles inventory, and other indices tapped caregiver perceptions of stress loads, and factors I thought to represent stressors more specific to caregiving. For the latter information, a geriatric nurse practitioner rated parents on levels of behavioral dependency, cognitive impairment, depression, and other physical and mental health conditions. For outcome information, I included not only measures of caregiver burden, anticipated problems of the future, and how much care each caregiver provided, but also general indices of depression, anxiety, and psychological well-being.

The results were more or less as I anticipated. For example, the general indices of stress were most effective in predicting general levels of well-being, while the caregiver-related stressors were most effective in predicting burden and other characteristics of caregivers linked to the caregiving context.

On the other hand, the situation with their parents did predict depressive symptoms. Especially when caregivers felt burdened by a combination of guilt and uncertainty, or when they felt embarrassed in public by their parents' behavior, depression was more likely. Moreover, caregivers who felt their parents made unreasonable demands were less depressed. One explanation may be that perceiving parents to be unreasonably demanding makes it easier for caregivers to distance themselves from the situation. Overall though, findings from the caregiver study reinforce what Robert Butler and Raymond Kuhlen suggested many years ago: that one should always keep in mind that multiple factors influence the individual.

*C*ONCLUDING THOUGHTS

As is probably true of anyone who has worked in a field for twenty-five or so years, I have witnessed multiple changes that affected my professional career. I have also been fortunate to have witnessed a period of dramatic growth in the field of gerontology. In 1964, when I attended my first meeting of the Gerontology Society, this was a small and closely knit group of approximately 500 members. Because few people knew of the field and there was no established funding source, people seemed to work together with common cause: to promote the study of aging. Subsequently and as the field achieved recognition, a larger membership, and greater funding, multiple and often competing agendas emerged. Today the Gerontological Society of America has over 6,000 members and there are a number of additional professional societies at the regional as well as national and international levels. Ironically, gerontology is still seen by many as being a dynamic "new" field of study!

Reflecting evolution in the field of gerontology, during its approximately fourteen years of funding, the transitions team was forced to seek funding from three different federal agencies. The first was the National Institute on Child and Human Development, through which the study was originally funded because NICHD had been officially designated as the site for aging grants. Conveniently for us, they seemed to define aging as involving studies of people over the age of 21! Some four years later, the Institute on Aging was in operation and we were next funded through that body. However, as the priorities of the latter institute evolved, the transitions study received criticism because it was not a study solely of older persons. After several rejections by the NIA, we capitalized on our growing focus on stress and mental health by turning to the National Institute on Mental Health, which had established its own center for the study of aging in the 1970s.

The field of stress research has also evolved substantially over the past few years, with each change creating its own challenges and opportunities in order to remain on the cutting edge. To use a life-cycle analogy, over the past twenty-five or so years, there seem to have been three generations of stress research. Each building upon the accomplishments of its predecessor, the three generations can be categorized as (1) catastrophe research, where a potentially devastating situation, such as internment in a concentration camp or forced institutionalization, is the focus of attention; (2) life event research, where inventories of more commonly experienced situations with a definable onset are studied; and (3) research on the stressors of everyday life, such as day-to-day hassles, or chronic strain in the family or work situation. We may even be on the verge of developing a fourth, and more integrative model that incorporates properties of the catastrophe, life event, and everyday life models that have preceded it.

Each of these generations had its own advantages and disadvantages, and I learned from each. For example, an advantage of the catastrophe approach is the capability of selecting persons who have experienced a crisis that most would agree is devastating. My doctoral work on involuntary relocation of older persons exemplifies the catastrophe model, and it provides useful information on how people cope with adversity. On the other hand, a weakness of the catastrophe model is the frequent assumption that everyone is equally stressed and that the critical issue is how they cope. To the contrary, my thesis suggests that there is great variation in how people perceive apparently similar stress conditions, and that these variations in perception influence coping behaviors and outcomes. In my later studies, I have often selected samples on the basis of some shared stress condition, but have been careful to include multiple assessments of perceptions as well as both broad and context-specific events, hassles, and chronic stressors.

From There to Here: Coping with the Life Course

As I advance through the different stages of my own life course, other forces of change are also apparent. I have begun to realize, for example, that a commitment to longitudinal research places certain restrictions on the number of studies one can complete over one's own life course. There are only so many twelve-year studies that one can participate in!

For personally obscure reasons I have also felt an obligation to pay attention to my ethnic roots and in consequence my current research is now taking on more of a Hispanic flavor. Working still in the area of stress experiences, I am now collaborating with Kyriakos ("Kokos") Markides in a two-wave panel study of Mexican-Americans aged 65+. The study is closely modeled after existing Established Populations for Epidemiological Studies of the Elderly (EPESE) research and includes most EPESE instruments. Home interviews have just been completed with a representative sample drawn from five southwestern states. Stress indices included twenty acute (eleven health-related and nine general) and four chronic (all economic) items. As anticipated, the oldest old (85+) were most likely to report changes related to personal health, but no age differences are apparent in general life events. Persons born in Mexico were more likely to report financial problems, while the American-born were more likely to report both general and health-related events. As is true in most stress studies, women generally reported more events than men, but no gender differences were found for chronic economic strains. Such preliminary findings are exciting, and I am now eager to consider whether models of stress developed from mainstream samples are applicable to minority populations.

SUGGESTED READINGS

Butler, R. (1963). The life review: An interpretation of reminiscence in the aged. *Psychiatry*, 26(1), 65–76.

Chiriboga, D. A., & Bailey, J. T. (1989). Burnout and coping among hospital nurses: Research and guidelines for action. In B. Riegel & D. Ehrenreich (Eds.), *Psychological aspects of critical care nursing* (pp. 295–321). Rockville, MD: Aspen Publications.

——— Catron, L. S., & Associates. (1991). *Divorce: Crisis, challenge or relief?* New York: New York University Press.

——— Yee, B. W. K., & Weiler, P. G. (1992). Stress and coping in the context of caring. In L. Montada, S-H. Filipp, & M. L. Lerner (Eds.), *Life crisis and experiences of loss in adulthood* (pp. 95–118). Hillsdale, NJ: Erlbaum.

Fiske, M., & Chiriboga, D. A. (1990). *Change and continuity in adult life.* San Francisco: Jossey-Bass.

Hoenig, J., & Hamilton, M. W. (1966). The schizophrenic patient in the community and his effect on the household. *International Journal of Social Psychiatry*, 12(3), 165–176.

Lazarus, R. S. (1993). Why we should think of stress as a subset of emotion. In L. Goldberger & S. Breznitz (Eds.), *Handbook of stress* (2d ed., pp. 21–39). New York: Free Press.

Lowenthal, M. F., Thurnher, M., & Chiriboga, D. A. (1975). *Four stages of life.* San Francisco: Jossey-Bass.

R OBERT KASTENBAUM *(Ph.D., University of Southern California) is Profes-sor of Communication at Arizona State University. He studies life span de-velopment with an emphasis on the later adult years. His frontline experi-ence includes serving as director of a hospital for the aged and cofounder of the National Caucus for the Black Aged. Dr. Kastenbaum is editor of* The International Journal of Aging and Human Development *and* Omega, Journal of Death and Dying, *as well as* The Encyclopedia of Death *(with Beatrice Kastenbaum) and* The Encyclopedia of Adult Development. *His own books include* The Psy-chology of Death *and* Defining Acts: Aging as Drama. *Dr. Kastenbaum's work reached a new stage in 1995 with the premier of the opera* Dorian, *based on Oscar Wilde's novel of a youth who refuses to age (music by Herbert Deutsch).*

18

The Cave at the End of the World: How the Unknowing Studied the Unknowable

---❖---

The Living Dead (1965)

They were back again. The young people, a woman and two men, had visited this ward (and others) twice a day for two weeks. Today would be a little different. First they repeated their usual observations. All three observed the man in the bed directly before them for a period of two minutes, then made independent assessments on a form that had been developed through a pilot study. The assessments matched perfectly. This man had not altered position, gestured, spoken, moaned, or exhibited any discernible action. He was therefore still in the bottom category of the Low-Level Behavior Syndrome, the category that had come to be known informally as "the living dead."

The members of the ward staff took up positions where they could observe the observers. The staffers were beset by conflicting feelings of resentment and curiosity. This ward was their turf; visitors often were perceived as invaders. Because this particular invasion was part of an approved research project, the staff could

289

not simply shoo them away. But it was also special and slightly mysterious to have this trio of college students come by and go through their little rituals. Somebody must think something is happening on this ward that is worth attention.

Now it was finally time for the "experimental intervention." One of the visitors stepped forward and approached a pale old man who looked like a cold wax doll between the clean, crisp sheets of his bed. Standing at bedside, the student leaned forward and called the man by name. He also placed a hand gently on the man's forearm and patted several times. "Mr. Arnold . . . Mr. Arnold . . . may I please speak with you?"

The Bottom Line (1967)

Miss Eggerton had sent for me, just as she had sent for several others with whom she sensed some connection. She was one of the few patients to have her own room. This privilege supposedly was in deference to her age—at 94 a senior among seniors—and to her fading health. It was obvious, though, that Miss Eggerton had emerged as a special person among the more than 600 residents of this geriatric institution and would not be denied whatever small comforts might be available. What made her special? She had once defined herself to me as "a tough old spinster—and don't you forget it!" We had all been impressed by her dignity and charmed by her crusty, imperial manner.

"I'm dying," she informed me as soon as I had both feet inside her room. "You probably want to ask me some questions for your study!" "Tell me your answers," I proposed, "and I'll make up the questions later." Miss Eggerton explained that death should be taken seriously. "It affects your plans!" She herself was acknowledging the approach of death by altering her behavior pattern. Her strategy was to reduce the amount of territory she had to defend. Times Square (the social center of the hospital) would have to do without her, even though this meant missing the movies, the rumors, and the passing scene. Patients and staff throughout the hospital complex would have to solve (or create) their problems without her advice. Now she kept to this room which "is all that death and myself need." Within this constricted space Miss Eggerton had managed to preserve her integrity and control—an intense mind within a frail body within a small room. "This is your last chance, young man. Any questions?"

"Yes, I do have a question now. Two questions actually: What are you embroidering on those panties, and why?"

And One for the Road (1976)

The Captain's Chair was doing great business. Perhaps this was not so surprising because the drinks, snacks, and gossip were free. The surprise was that The Captain's Chair actually existed. The hospital had long outlived its expected use and was competing with its residents in rate of physical decline. It was absurd even to consider building and operating a cosy tavern within a facility that should have been razed to the ground years ago and which had to function within a spartan state budget. However, the project seemed a little less peculiar when it was described as a "geriatric socialization chamber" and bolstered with several published studies. Our research had legitimized this island of adult satisfaction in the depths of a state-run institution, although some feathers had been seriously ruffled in the process.

This afternoon marked a special occasion (although the resourceful hostess, a former charge nurse, found a way to make almost every day special). Mr. Zella would have his 100th birthday properly celebrated. This birthday had come and gone several weeks ago, but he was feeling poorly at the time. It was his own idea that the celebration be postponed until he felt more like himself.

Staff as well as patients had so crowded The Captain's Chair that the hostess had asked some revelers to wait for a second sitting. There were two focal points: the tiered birthday cake with its two candles (one for the first century, the other for the next) and Mr. Zella's much admired moustache. Ordinarily moustaches comprise an endangered species in a hospital environment. Nurses were only too eager to shave them off at the first excuse. None could bring themselves to deprive Mr. Zella of his moustache, however, so both had survived his most recent skirmish with death.

At 100+ he was an impressive figure, his face ennobled rather than ravaged by age. Mr. Zella was silent as he was serenaded by the "Happy Birthday" chorus and offered gifts. He brushed away requests to make a wish and blow out the candles. Was he not enjoying the party? People were growing uneasy. Finally, he spoke.

DEVELOPMENTAL PSYCHOLOGY IN A GERIATRIC HOSPITAL

These episodes were among the many that I experienced while serving first as a psychologist and then as director of a hospital for the aged. My colleagues and I conducted several research projects that attempted to bring the experiences of aged men and women into the compass of a life span developmental psychology. This was regarded as a peculiar enterprise at the time: "developmental" meant "children" and perhaps "adolescents." Few behavioral or social scientists were concerning themselves with the entire life span, and fewer still were hanging around with aged men and women in a public institution. So what was I doing there?

Like almost all new Ph.D.'s circa 1959, I had received essentially no academic education pertaining either to elderly adults or to dying/death/

grief. In five years of graduate study I had never been exposed to a lecture nor assigned a reading on any of these topics. I was not without curiosity, however. From early childhood I had wondered about all that was beyond me—the night sky sprinkled with stars, the places I had never been, the people and books who knew so much more than I did. Several years' experience as a newspaper reporter and editor had honed my ability to ask questions and not necessarily take the answers at face value. Zipping along the corridors of a massive warehouse as a skating messenger (it paid better than editing a community newspaper!) had heightened my appreciation for the ever-present danger of being blindsided. Dabbling in the playpen of philosophy had not only resulted in some enduring friendships (Plato, Hume, Nietzsche, James, Pierce, and all the gang), but, amazingly, had also resulted in the offer of a graduate scholarship that made it possible to go on for the doctorate at the University of Southern California. Somehow I wandered off into psychology and was admitted to the Veterans Administration's Clinical Training Program. There I did meet many an elderly veteran and perhaps did not do them too much harm, though it is doubtful I did them much good either.

After a couple of years, it seemed as though I had been in school forever. Had there been a life before graduate school? Was the afterlife only a rumor? I became acutely aware of time. Hmmm: *time!* With the journalist's and skating messenger's sense of urgency and the philosopher's infatuation with theory I came up with a framework for considering time as the key to understanding development, aging, death, and creativity. This framework was vague and unfounded, of course. No doubt it said more about my own feeling of being trapped in the corridors of academe than it did about consensual reality. And yet there was something here that felt authentic and propulsive.

Psychology (in the 1950s) did not seem to appreciate "raw time." We had estimated time perception, reaction time, and all the other times that experimenters, professors, and administrators kept within their control. But we seldom allowed ourselves to notice time in its most vital and elusive form—that indefinable shiver of being that gives all and then takes it all away. It is raw time that offers us moment after moment of immediate experience, a fantastic gift that only animals, children, and lovers seemed to appreciate. Yet time is also connective tissue, a woven tapestry, a garment that one dons in childhood and does not doff until age exhales its last breath. What we call the future is time at its most alluring and most terrifying. *Everything we hope to be, experience, and achieve has its locus in the future—but so does every fear of failure, catastrophe, and the unknown, as well as the prospect of aging and death.* This statement is not as fanciful and arbitrary as it might sound. It was one of the conclusions from my doctoral study. A sample of high school students portrayed themselves as rushing toward a future that was both fiercely desired and desperately feared. The "goodies" were all out there, all right, and perhaps just around the corner. But there was also a sense of peril: One could lose everything at any time. Furthermore, the later years of life (from about age 30 onward) were generally viewed with dread.

These findings emerged with remarkable clarity from a battery of procedures I had assembled from various sources and supplemented with a few new techniques. ("Beginner's luck" is the cliché that seems most applicable: In most of my later studies the findings have been more complex and elusive.) Here are a few examples of how the overall pattern of results derived from specific measures:

- The high school students showed a marked preference for images of time that emphasized rapid movement. On the Time Metaphor Test [Knapp & Garbutt, 1958], they would choose statements such as "Time is like a galloping horseman" to statements such as ". . . like a string of beads."

- When asked to select the "most important years" of their lives (past, present, and future), they rarely projected beyond their mid-twenties.

- Similarly, when asked to make a number of predictions about their own future, the "density" (number and detail) of anticipated events was thick for the next few years, but thinned out rapidly thereafter. Most respondents had little to say about what would happen throughout their adult lives; and the few events that were predicted were of negative or aversive character (e.g., "I get myself killed"). Predictions became increasingly negative as the teens moved from the near to the more distant future. Converging results were found in the use of futurity in four stories they were asked to write from the "story roots" (opening sentence) provided to them: Their stories showed a strong impulse to go out and do something, but an uncertain, anxious, and aversive attitude toward what will happen just after the next turn of the plot.

- I used a then-popular technique known as "the projective question." Respondents were asked to give as many answers as they could to the query, "Who am I?" I added two related questions: "Who was I?" and "Who will I be?" Their responses were decisive: "Who was I?" attracted relatively few responses, and these overwhelmingly negative (e.g., "A kid everybody bossed around"). "Who am I?" attracted many responses, including neutral/factual, positive, and negative. "Who will I be?" attracted the most positive responses when the "will be" time frame was within the next five years. It attracted the most negative responses, however, when the "will be" time frame included the middle and later adult years.

- In responding to a semantic differential-type procedure, the teens distanced "myself" from the remote future and death. Their adult lives were also conceived as incompatible with the idea of the "real."

However we sliced it, the results came out the same way: "I feel like I am rushing into the future. It's going to be great—for a while. After that: don't ask! I don't think I want to know!" These findings jolted me a little. I had been trying to keep up with the outpouring of research from Jean Piaget and his colleagues on the development of cognitive processes—this was new stuff to most of us in the late 1950s and early 1960s. Piaget had concluded that the ability to use the highest level of cognition ("formal operations," in his terminology) comes into play during the adolescent years. High school students should be able to "think about thought" and conceptualize alternative future scenarios. My data did not dispute the proposition that teens *could* think about the future in a resourceful way. It seemed, however, that most of the respondents chose not to do so. I was ready to tell Piaget that just because young men and women could project possible futures did not necessarily mean that they wanted to expose themselves to the associated anxieties. Cognitive potential might not be enough. Alas, Piaget never did ask me!

From what I could observe in general, beyond this study as such, it seemed hard to live with or without time. "Heavy" time was a burden and a bore. This was time that people did not feel they could use for their own purposes, time that had no intrinsic connection to their being. For youth, heavy time often took the form of "hanging out," excess snoozing, or glazed captivity in the classroom. Life was much more exciting with lightfooted time. On the high school campus, for example, there was usually a lot of scuttling about, animated flitting from one station or throng to another. A parallel pattern could be discerned in their thought patterns: the impulse to move on, move on, move on, fly with time. Where they were going and why was often inarticulated, however, and apparently not guided by a coherent controlling purpose.

A COLLECTING HOUSE FOR TIME

And now I was in a position to learn something about time in human experience at the other end of the age spectrum. Cushing Hospital was a kind of collecting house for time. There were more than 600 residents, almost all of whom would end their lives in this institution. The average age was about 84. This amounts to something over 50,000 years of lived experience, and the years represent more than 18 million days. How many hours of triumph and failure, crisis and comfort, work and play had comprised those days! How many moments of terror, joy, discovery, wonder, and doubt?

So here is where past time came to settle! It settled in the aging bones and the aging bricks. Occasionally, visiting children would run through the corridors just for the pleasure of running. Time for them was immediacy, this moment, and activity its own purpose. Staff would compel themselves to walk the corridors yet again. Time was a closed system and a repeating cycle. Shift after shift they fulfilled their obligations, time a harness. At the end of one's shift, there would be a double sigh: "Ahhh, this day is done," followed by a weariness borrowed from the future: "Ahhh, tomorrow—same thing!" Meanwhile, the old people stayed where they were. Where was there to go? Furthermore, the sparkle of the moment and the rounds of duty were no longer their concern.

Each was a hermit. Each was a hermit living with, through, and off his or her own time. Each was a hermit clutching and clutched by a sack of used time. Each treasured and lamented this possession within a cave that was sunk deep into a crevice of the community's undermind. The busy and often hard-pressed people at the surface had enough on their minds without having to be faced with age and death. They had more important things to do than to listen to old people and adjust their lives to accommodate the needs of their elders. The authorities agreed. It would not only be a kindness to frail and vulnerable elders but also a cost-effective procedure to "place" them. That's how the powers-to-be were thinking about society's elders as we moved into the 1960s. It's the way many decision makers still think.

This plan had something else going for it. If the aged could be hidden, then so could death. Remember, please, that these arrangements were made before the term "hospice" became generally known. It would still be some years before the first death education courses would be offered (sociologist Robert Fulton, psychologist Edwin S. Shneidman and myself independently introduced such courses in the mid-1960s and are all still at it).

Peer support groups for survivors (e.g., Widow-to-Widow) or for people actively coping with life-threatening conditions (e.g., One Day At A Time) were only ideas in the minds of a few people. A tactful and responsible person would not even use such words as "dying" or "death." As a society we were fascinated by violent death, but took evasive actions whenever called on to face our natural mortality.

Old men and women offended us by reminding us of that unpalatable truth. So—put them away, put them away, bury them alive, bury them alive in the cave. Call the cave a hospital. Build a high fence all around. Keep the military guardhouse at the entrance. Allow the city dump to continue functioning across the street, as though one facility were the extension of the other. Pay for it. Show a little respect. Stay away. Close the gates to protect the community from these disturbing figures who seem to personify our own anxieties. Open the gates to allow new admissions. Close the gates again.

The bricked cave with its numbing tunnels might have served as the poor neighborhood in one of the visions of the underworld that flourished in ancient Crete, Babylon, Egypt, and the Greek city-states. The physical set-apartness of the hospital matched well with its psychological function. Age and death could remain buried deep in our metal vaults because those who seemed most to embody these anxieties had been properly entombed.

All of this, however, did not reckon with the embers of life that continued to glow within the cave and which at times roared up in protest or even danced in exultation.

Entering the Cave

My first visit was at the invitation of Peter Comalli, a real faculty member (not a nebulous postdoctoral fellow like myself) whose cubicle adjoined mine. He knew that I was studying psychological aspects of time, change, and death. Wouldn't I like to meet a lot of old people who would probably enjoy participation in this study? Sure, Peter, show me the way. He would do better than that: He would drive me to the hospital, up the road a few minutes on the Boston side of Worcester. Oh—by the way—would I give him a hand with a bit of equipment? As it turned out, Comalli had been studying perceptual illusions in children and adults and for this purpose had cobbled together several bulky pieces of equipment. I fell right into his little trap.

For several visits I would help Comalli lug his equipment about and then wander about the facility, chatting with anybody who seemed chattable. I then decided to try out my current research interview procedure with residents who were willing to spend a few hours responding to ridiculous questions from a stranger. I had been interviewing "the usual suspects" (college students) regarding their views of time, change, and death. This was a pilot study intended to come up with observations that could be incorporated into a formal research project concerning the processes people use to conceptualize the nearly unconceptualizable (i.e., the nature and meaning of time, change, life, and death).

The Cushing Hospital interviews were memorable and illuminating encounters for me. The interviewees took the interviews seriously and seemed to welcome the opportunity to reflect on their lives and share some of their thoughts and experiences.

Here is one excerpt from an interview that has never lost its hold on me:

It was the last of three formal interviews with Mr. Svenholm, a man in his late eighties who had outlived his closest friends and relations. He was essentially alone in the world, despite passing each day in the company of hundreds of other elders and the staff. Mr. Svenholm was a quiet and rather deliberate person. One had the impression that he had developed an exceptional self-discipline over the years that was helping him to retain his dignity under trying circumstances.

Near the end of this interview I presented him with the magic time machine proposition. "There is this machine—suppose. It is a machine that makes time, time that can add to our lives. The machine can be set to make any amount of time for us. Because *it* is a machine, however, we have to make a precise setting, instruct it just how much time we want. How would you set this machine, Mr. Svenholm?"

He said nothing. Time passed in what for me was an increasingly uncomfortable silence. I had overtaxed his patience. He had withdrawn, perhaps in anger, perhaps in fatigue, or even dementia. Just when I figured that I would have to bring the interview to the most satisfactory conclusion possible under the circumstances, Mr. Svenholm sat forward a bit in his chair and answered the question that he apparently had been pondering all that time.

"Don't bother. I could not use the time. Not even a day. I am all used up."

This response immediately recalled to mind an episode from our first meeting. As part of the first session I introduced a time-estimation procedure. There had been conflicting reports in the literature about the subject of estimation of time in older as compared with younger people, and I thought it might be useful to include such a measure. I had no special equipment available other than a stopwatch, so I would simply rap the table and have the respondent rap back when he or she estimated that twenty seconds had passed. I rapped. The return rap was sounded about seven seconds later. I was surprised by this unusually large overestimation of the elapsed time, so I suggested that we try it again. Same result. Mr. Svenholm noticed the funny expression on my face, and offered his own explanation:

"I was fast. Of course. Could not help it. At my age time eats you alive."

In recalling this previous episode, I could not help but be struck by the old man's predicament. He felt devoured by time, yet also felt he could not make use of additional time. Not enough time and too much time—at the same time. This seemed to me a distinctly human dilemma, and one that could not be understood in terms of reductionistic theoretical models. From a personal standpoint, I was touched by his candor and his despair. It suddenly struck me, however, that the dilemma had not been created by Mr. Svenholm himself. A person with his intelligence and perspective would seem to have a lot to offer the world as well as to interest his own life with meaning. No, much of the despair had been generated by this cave into which the community had emptied its anxieties and sealed them with fences, denial, and neglect. What could a person *do* here? What could a person *be* here?

I was given a chance to follow up these questions and concerns sooner than I expected. A few days later I was strolling through the main corridor (fantasizing my long-lost roller skates) when a hand seized my arm. The capture had been effected by a wiry man in a dark suit. He had something of the executioner's look about him. "Are you a psychologist?" "Yes," I replied, "Sort of. They gave me a degree." "You've been talking to the patients?" "Yes, sort of. They don't seem to mind." (What laws had I violated, or whose turf had I invaded? Was this the arm of the law or of our friendly local Mafioso?) "Come with me," the dark suit insisted, having not relinquished his grip on my arm. "Boss wants to see you."

For the first time I ascended the stairs to the management suite and was brought into the office of the executive officer (known for obscure historical reasons as "superintendent"). Boss was a stocky, balding individual who fixed me in the most intense glare I had been subjected to since a certain disturbance on the back staircase in P.S. 35 (The Bronx, circa 1939). He looked like the Lord of the Owls deciding whether this humble prey was worth the shredding. Boss and Executioner exchanged conspiratorial glances as the questioning proceeded.

After a few minutes Boss explained that he had just taken over this place and did not much care for the idea of running what we called a "premortuary establishment." He wanted Cushing Hospital to be a place where there was always something going on—research and uproar. "The psychologists I know best are born troublemakers. I would make the mischief myself, but I can't do that and run this damn place. We need somebody to make this place interesting for everybody." Years before *The Godfather*, I had been made an offer I did not feel inclined to refuse.

THE RESEARCH PROJECTS

The Boss Owl had proved to be J. Sanbourne Bockoven, M.D. He had the manner of a down-home, no-nonsense country doctor, driving his horse and buggy along earthen paths in nineteenth-century New England. The interior man was as sly and sophisticated as they come, a fiery advocate of human rights, and a distinguished historian of psychiatry. He was a whole education unto himself and became my first real mentor. The Executioner had proved to be a free-spirited sociologist who would soon make his international reputation with the book, *The Pursuit of Loneliness*. He was "cool" incarnate. I would also learn much from Phil Slater, ranging from the nitty-gritty of setting up a complex research project to the almost infinite universe of prankstering that awaited one's less responsible moments.

My first office as director of psychology was a reformed broom closet one door down from the hospital morgue. This turned out to be a useful location. One would not be sought out by those who merely had their own time and mine to waste. And, yes, the neighbors were quiet. The location was also a dependable stimulus for reflection. The interesting old fellow I had visited with on the ward two days ago was now making a horizontal journey down the hall to the morgue. I even attended a few autopsies and learned a few lessons about terminal anatomy and philosophy from the consulting pathologist.

The first real task, as I came to realize, was to help create an atmosphere in which psychology and psychologists would be welcome. The everyday

functioning of the hospital depended primarily on the efforts of the nursing personnel. The medical staff was also important, but doctors were far
less numerous than nurses and generally just went about their own business. I tried to make myself useful and visible. After seeing enough "problem patients," participating in enough staff meetings, and losing ping-
pong games in Times Square, I had enough of the strangeness rubbed off
me to receive partial and conditional acceptance by the nursing staff. There
was still an elevated level of suspicion, though: What did psychologists really do? Staff who seemed to have come to the hospital with the first load
of bricks were not that keen about having a new type of person walking
their corridors and speaking with their patients.

The first research project was opportunistic: Bockoven was in a position to know that very little work had been done to evaluate the effect of
psychotropic drugs (mainly tranquilizers and stimulants) on elderly patients. This meant that physicians were more or less in the dark when making decisions on medications and dosage. There was a practical need to
study drug effects in the steadily increasing population of elderly patients
throughout the nation. I knew almost nothing about psychotropic drugs at
that point and did not see much of theoretical interest in such a project, but
it did look like a way to get started. The Owl and the Executioner did know
something about drugs, and I was steeped in methological fervor from my
recent graduate studies travail. The proposal was funded, and for three
years or so I served as codirector of what was then the most systematic and
refined study of its type.

This study proved more interesting than I expected both in process and
outcomes. It also established a fairly solid working relationship between
researchers and service providers. We respected each other and saved our
frustrations and aggressions for the touch football games that had sprung
up on the hospital campus after many a taunt and jeer. The drug study
proved to be but prologue, however, to the major project.

TRAINING FOR WORK WITH ELDERLY DYING PATIENTS

We were very fortunate. The feds approved and funded our proposal for
a demonstration project that would help nurses and other service providers
care more adequately for elderly dying patients and reduce their own stress
in doing so. It was remarkable, almost without precedent, that the government was willing to spend money on aged patients and their caregivers,
especially when the focus was on death and dying, topics that were beyond
the pale of clinical practice and science. Our credentials were modest, but
even modest credentials were something in those days. We did have a facility that was willing to lend itself to such a project. We did have the drug
study as a token of our ability to do presentably what we said we would

do. And we did have my own handful of publications on various aspects of dying and death. As it came out eventually, several influential people in the social sciences and health care fields had judged that the time had come to make up for a history of neglect. It was not acceptable for our oldest men and women to die in isolation, anxiety, and despair, nor for their caregivers to labor without support and appreciation. Years later, I appreciate even more the unusual combination of circumstances that opened the way for this project. Although I have subsequently participated in even larger research projects, never again did I sense that behind the funding decision was the authentic desire to improve the quality of life as death approaches.

The project had many facets and continued to evolve over its seven-year span. One procedure became particularly important not only for its own contributions but also for its continuing spin-offs. The *psychological autopsy* originated as a method for investigating deaths whose causes were difficult to determine. The main interest was in learning whether a particular death was suicidal, homicidal, accidental, or "natural." Psychological autopsies were developed by an interdisciplinary team in Los Angeles and became an enduring feature of the pioneering suicide prevention center in that city. Psychologists Edwin Shneidman and Norman Farberow were the major innovators and directors of the first psychological autopsy series, working alongside pathologists, social workers, police officers, and other specialists. I had known Shneidman and Farberow and became acquainted with their work as I moved through a Veterans Administration clinical psychology traineeship.

We modified the psychological autopsy procedure for use in a hospital setting. The original psychological autopsy method emphasized detective work with the hope of discovering the cause of death. We, too, were interested in cause, but more interested in reconstructing the entire final phase of the deceased person's life. At this time (the mid-1960s) very little was known about the intrapersonal and interpersonal experiences of terminally ill people. All those who would be included in our psychological autopsy series were aged people with a variety of physical afflictions. They were in Cushing Hospital because they needed care and shelter they could not find elsewhere in the community, and their residency with us was almost always terminated by death. This meant that it was not the fact of death but the circumstances and meanings that were most in need of explication. Accordingly, we set out to reconstruct as best we could the terminal phase of life for recently deceased patients.

I was fortunate to enlist the consultant services of a very wise man. Actually, he spells his name Avery Weisman, and it is followed by an M.D. Weisman is an existentially oriented psychiatrist with a rare combination of sensitivity, compassion, and tough-mindedness along with a world-class wit. Together we worked out a basic conceptual orientation for the entire project as well as for the psychological autopsy:

During every phase of the life span, people are potentially vulnerable to medical illness and psychological disturbance. Obviously, this fact does not mean that the entire life span or any particular segment of it is intrinsically pathological. Yet there is a strong tendency to define a person as pathological simply because he is dying. In contrast with this view, the investigators hold that the dying process is as "natural" as any other phase of life—as natural as childbirth, for example. A particular dying person may be suffering physical or mental anguish, but the dying process itself is not automatically equivalent to personal pathology, even though it may be accompanied by somatic illness and deterioration. [Weisman & Kastenbaum, 1968, p. 2]

This was a rather new approach at the time. It also included the idea that "there is a preterminal period that may be regarded as a developmental phase . . . (although) generally ignored by psychiatrists and developmental psychologists." We also emphasized the need "to disentangle observations from implicit value judgments." Much of what people thought they knew about dying and the experiential life of elderly people was in the realm of value judgments and assumptions rather than verified fact.

The psychological autopsy procedure started with the view of all deaths that had occurred in the hospital within the previous ten days. A preliminary review was made of charts and records for each of the deceased patients; these documents were sometimes quite voluminous, going back for years. In selecting a patient for psychological autopsy study we used a two-track system: (1) Some deaths virtually "asked" to be studied for various reasons, e.g., a sudden, unexpected death, a death that particularly disturbed the staff, a death that perhaps might have been prevented or delayed, or the death of a patient who was "famous" in the hospital. (2) Random selection. By selecting salient deaths we tapped into the staff's collective nervous system: They had feelings about these deaths and would be interested to know more about them. By also selecting cases on a random basis we obtained a more representative sample over time. Our eventual sample of 120 psychological autopsy cases included many people who had lived and died obscurely in the hospital as well as those whose exit had created a stir.

There was much work to be done once a case was selected. We would abstract the most significant information from the records and summarize it on forms we had devised. A series of interviews would be conducted with those who had known the deceased person in various capacities—the ward staff, certainly, a physician or two, a chaplain, social workers, occupational and physical therapists, volunteers, etc. Depending on the circumstances, we might also contact people outside the hospital for further information. We were especially interested in detailed descriptions of specific interactions that the interviewees had with the deceased. For example, precisely what did the patient say and do when his family did not show up for their expected visit on his birthday? What exactly did the patient do that morning that led staff to assume that she was "confused"? We continued to press for specific information grounded in particular experiences and events, distinguished from generalized attributions.

The psychological autopsy proper was an interdisciplinary conference involving somewhere between fifteen and twenty participants. A medical review of the case was followed by a far-ranging discussion of the deceased person's life and death, drawing upon the experiences of those present as well as upon the information previously collected. Everybody was encouraged to raise questions as well as provide answers: this included staff members whose knowledge and opinions were seldom sought, notably, the licensed practical nurses (LPN's) who worked under the supervision of registered nurses (RN's).

As the psychological autopsy series proceeded it became evident that we were making two types of discovery—about the patients and about ourselves. Regarding the dying elderly person, for example, we found that most people remained mentally alert and capable of communication until the very end or close to the end. (This finding no doubt owed something to the medical staff's enlightened policy of not "snowing" patients with drugs that would dull their mentation.) We also learned that their language and actions often had a symbolic quality. In retrospect we could see that giving away a personal possession or talking about plans to "meet the boss" were ways of saying farewell.

Most important, however, was what the hospital learned about itself. At first wary and uptight with the psychological autopsy, the staff gradually entered into the spirit of open and egalitarian sharing. I remember one sixtyish LPN remaining in her chair after a session had concluded. "Are you all right?" I inquired (for the discussion had been intense and, at times, stormy). "I'm too stunned to move," she replied. "I opened my mouth and a roomful of doctors and nurses listened to me!" It was true. People actually listened to each other (at least, sometimes). Rank and status became less important when staff entered that room for a psychological autopsy session: What a person knew and what a person could contribute through an incisive question or a challenging suggestion were the important considerations.

As a spin-off of the psychological autopsy, the staff of several wards organized their own peer support groups. They had all found tears in their eyes at autopsy sessions, and realized how much stress and tension they had been enduring without the opportunity for sharing. Over a period of several years, the staff gradually abandoned the "see-no-death-speak-no-death" attitude that was so prevalent at the time. Anger, frustration, and what was coming to be known as "burnout" diminished as staff members decided it was acceptable to express their feelings and useful to provide mutual support. The project staff strongly encouraged this process and offered help at various points.

The self-discovery process went deeper for many individuals. All this attention to dying, death, and grief started to connect with their own unresolved personal experiences. As time went on, project staff spent an increasing amount of its time counseling with staff members who could, for the first time, weep or rage over the long-ago death of a parent or child. Project staff were not excluded from this process of emotional self-discovery. Psychologists were no longer perceived as outsiders. We were seen as a somewhat disturbing and destabilizing influence (just as the Owl had hoped), but also as colleagues who could help them make valuable connections between their own personal lives and the challenges they encountered in each day's work.

There were other spin-offs in the spheres of staff communication, patient care, and research, all involving the efforts of many people beyond the members of the project team. Visiting clinicians and researchers from hither, thither, and yon would come by to see what we were doing, and take away a few ideas they could apply in their own settings. Nevertheless, the project had a bumpy ride all the way along. We could not help but stir up controversy just by taking an interest in something and asking a few questions. Furthermore, our ability to discredit mistaken assumptions and identify neglected problems far exceeded our ability to offer firm new propositions and solve problems. As they say on the greasepaint circuit, we played to mixed reviews.

We return to one of the small research spin-offs from the psychological autopsy series: *the living dead*.

"Mr. Arnold . . . Mr. Arnold . . . may I please speak with you?"

No response. The young research assistant patted the man's forearm again and repeated his salutation.

Slowly, the cold wax doll turned toward the voice. Its eyes opened. The empty gaze achieved focus after a moment.

"Mr. Arnold. I am so glad to see you."

"Son—get me a glass of water."

Admittedly, this was one of the most dramatic encounters, but it was not the only occasion on which a person locked into the lowest of the Low-Level Behavior Syndromes had responded to this simple "experimental intervention." Nearly half the "living dead" responded to touch and personal salutation in a manner that could be detected by all three observers. Closed eyes would open and seek the eyes of the speaker, the head would turn, the lips would attempt to form words, a human expression would take shape on the masklike face. There had to be some clearly discernible response on the part of the patient and it had to be observed independently by all members of the research team. A few of the "living dead" proved capable of engaging in coherent conversation. This does not mean that they were entirely aware of their surroundings or that they had full access to memory and higher cognitive processes. However, it does mean that they were able to engage in some kind of dialogue with another human—although supposedly incapable of doing so.

In this study we had identified those patients throughout the hospital with the lowest frequency of behaviors and interactions: men and women who, literally, seemed to do nothing. Their "behavior output" was so meager that an observer could encompass all their actions and interactions with just a few simple statements, e.g., "taps fingers of right hand on available surfaces in short bursts of rhythmic action." To be classified in the lowest level (the living dead), a person would have shown *no* orienting, vocal, gestural, or self-adjusting behavior when observed twice a day by three research assistants over a period of two weeks. They did not seem to exist as persons.

This small study had a blockbuster effect on the intensive care unit. Ward staff could appreciate better than anyone else what they were seeing with their own eyes. Those planks of wood, those effigies, those unburied corpses—why, they still had something of the human spirit. Staff behavior toward patients of this type changed immediately. There was now more contact with patients who seemed unresponsive—more speaking, more touching, more time spent with them. The ward atmosphere also became more relaxed and natural. The staff had been experiencing more tension than they realized in dealing with the "living dead." Now the staff could behave in a more normal manner. Nobody would think them foolish for treating a nonresponsive patient as though there was "still somebody home." The project staff did not have to do anything to bring about this change, other than having provided unresponsive patients with the opportunity to respond. The lesson we all learned went far beyond a couple of wards in one hospital. Service providers in many other settings heard about this experience (often through word of mouth) and made their own similar discoveries.

Our project as a whole was exploratory and flawed. It could hardly have been otherwise. Perhaps the most systematic source of difficulty was the fact that we were trying to conduct formal research into complex human experiences and interactions in a "real-life" setting where other priorities dominated. Cushing Hospital did not exist as a sort of "data farm": It had the challenging function of trying to provide care and comfort for some of society's most vulnerable and impaired members. Often it was not feasible to introduce the methodology we might have preferred on scientific grounds because of the extra burden it might place on staff or patients. Ethical concerns were ongoing. At one extreme, we could ask ourselves: Did we have *any* right to conduct research in this setting? At the other extreme was the question: How can the staff fulfill its responsibilities and the government spend its funds wisely if there is not a careful effort to evaluate and improve the services? In short, the project could never be put "on automatic." Every step had to be considered and negotiated in a responsible way with concern for the well-being of patients and staff as well as for learning potential. Prior to these projects, I had no educational or applied experience in conducting research in such a complex real-life (and real-death) setting. I learned, but not without making at least my share of mistakes, probably more. Overall, though, I think all the participants can feel good about their role in increasing sensitivity to the possibility of continued or reawakened mental life in unresponsive patients.

As long as we are touring the corridors of memory again, let us complete our visit with Miss Eggerton:

"What are you embroidering on those panties, and why?"

This question would have been out of place with most of our other residents, and, in fact, I have never had the occasion to try it again. But Miss Eggerton (a fictitious name for a real person, as is the case with the others) was the one who invited my questions and the one who was indeed embroidering something on a pair of pink panties while otherwise occupied with dying. And the question did not faze her in the slightest.

She raised her handiwork for my inspection. The backside of the panties bore an inscription in valentine-red lettering: "Egger." "It will be Eggerton before I am finished. You know the hospital laundry. Clothes wind up anywhere, on any body. When I am gone this will be covering somebody else's rear end. I want them to know whose they were."

Miss Eggerton was not unusual in being skeptical about an afterlife. Many of our other residents, though brought up in the Christian church, did not place much stock in visions of heavenly bliss. (This had been one of many surprises for us as our assumptions about older adults, dying, and death were confronted with the realities.) During this last conversation together she succeeded in compressing her philosophy into one sentence: "One damned life is enough!" Even so . . . even so! Her leathery face allowed itself the hint of a smile. "My panties may go on forever!" Her laugh broke through.

My colleagues and I learned that we could go only so far with sharply articulated hypotheses and quantitative analyses. The experience of aging, dying, and yet somehow still living in this cave at the end of the world was too complex, too nuanced, too dynamic to be reduced to number-crunching. As Miss Eggerton and many others allowed us access to their private worlds we realize anew that one could not really understand "aging" or "dying" as though separate and pristine variables. We needed to understand the inner world of the individual, and the situation with which the individual had to contend. More, we needed to understand the all too unknowing minds that we ourselves brought to this enterprise as researchers and clinicians. One of the lessons from Miss Eggerton was the hint to look for the subtle ways by which a person can symbolically transcend his or her approaching mortal limits.

*B*EER, WINE, AND MUTUAL GRATIFICATION

The drug study made it possible to head off in another research direction as well. Text-books and lectures had drilled the proper sequence of research development into my head. There was supposed to be a theoretical model from which well-honed hypotheses would be deduced after an exhaustive literature review, and before devising methodology and research design that would force "Bravos!" from the most erudite professors. I had labored to bring this kind of academic thinking to the planning of the drug study, and still believed that was the only proper way to go about research.

Perhaps I would still think that way if Rosalie had not put a Pacific Gas and Electric newsletter under my nose. Project colleague Rosalie Rosenfelt owned a few shares of stock in PG&E, which was not of itself especially entertaining. But she was amused and pleased by a photograph in their latest newsletter. As I recall, the photo showed a new mother sitting up in her hospital bed and sipping a glass of wine, perhaps with her husband. Apparently some doctors were finding that a little wine could be relaxing and reduce the need for other medications. Rosalie thought that was neat. So did I. I noticed the caption said something about the California Wine Advisory Board (CWAB).

In a surprisingly short time, we had a signed contract. The medical director of the CWAB immediately thought it was a great idea to see if a little wine might also be helpful to elderly men and women in institutional settings. The CWAB would provide the wine as well as some money for research assistants and related small expenses. I had not done much homework for this project. There was not much literature to review, and I had feelings more than hypotheses. The feelings went something like this:

- Here we are, contributing to the use of tranquilizers and stimulants by studying their effects. Doesn't this mean that we are also contributing to keeping older people locked into their roles as medical patients?
- Why not treat these men and women as we would our friends and ourselves? We would not invite friends over for a phenothiazine tablet, but for a taste of the best wine we could afford and for the good conversation that might flourish.
- Is it possible that wine could function as a symbol of self-esteem and good companionship? Perhaps institutionalized elders would call upon the confidence, competence, and social skills that seemed to have deserted them in the rather depressing congregate setting.

We set up a study on the ward that housed the most physically and mentally intact male patients. Despite their semi-independent functioning, these men generally had a forlorn appearance. Each had his little personal routines and engaged in minimal social interactions. These men would make it down to Times Square for movies and special events, and might have a favorite staff member or fellow patient to chat with. Essentially, however, they had a drifting and alienated, nonpurposeful lifestyle within the institution, pretty much dragging themselves along from day to day.

Medical clearance was obtained for including all the residents of this ward in the study. Fortunately, the chief of the medical staff was open to the idea and aware that many elderly patients could make moderate use of alcohol without risk. Actual participation was up to residents themselves. Those who cared to participate would wander down to their own day room (the ward was divided into north and south units) in the middle of the afternoon to find several young research assistants and a beverage table. For the first three weeks, Unit A featured a red wine, and Unit B grape juice. This arrangement was reversed for the second three weeks. Both beverages were served in handsome goblets (having resisted the staff's insistence that paper cups would do nicely). In the seventh week all residents had their choice of either beverage.

That wine was preferred over grape juice probably does not qualify as a news bulletin. Other findings, though, were more evocative. When wine was available, social interaction was more extensive, persistent, and varied (as measured by eye contact, spontaneous comments addressed by one resident to another, duration of stay in the day room area, etc.). This effect became more pronounced as time went on. Mr. Powell, for example, would at first protect his goblet with both hands, turn away from the gathering, down his drink, and scurry away. Within a week, he was lingering over the wine and competing with Mr. Flaherty as the dominant storyteller.

More impressive still was the overall change in the pattern of communication and behavior in the ward area. Staff members were drawn to these "wine socials" like a magnet (although limited to grape juice as their own refreshment). These daily events had become the liveliest "goings-on," and nobody wanted to miss the stories, the teasings, the unexpected revelations as the old men (and sometimes the staff) expressed themselves with remarkable pungency and zest. We could not measure all these changes quantitatively, but it was possible, for example, to note an increase in staff members calling patients by their actual names, as distinguished from generic salutations such as "honey." Furthermore, there was general agreement that the men had become more independent and self-motivated. Everybody wanted to have some adventure, joke, secret, or rumor to contribute to the socials. It was also clear that the men were behaving in more individual ways, letting their distinctive personalities come through rather than enacting the generalized role of a geriatric patient. Staff and patients also seemed to have developed stronger bonds and could be observed plotting mischief together. Unfortunately, we had not thought to document length of staff-patient interactions prior to the experiment, but the supervisors and directors of nursing independently reported that ward nurses were spending more of their time interacting with the patients: Why not, the patients by now had become more interesting people.

The ward atmosphere had changed so much that steps had to be taken to protect the unit from being overrun by visitors both from within the institution and the outside world. No doubt much of this was generated by the staff's boasting and bragging, but it remained credible because visitors could see for themselves that the residents were much more purposeful and enlivened than in former days, and that an exciting air of "What will happen today?" stirred through the ward.

Two further developments sealed the success: (1) Residents and staff alike were insistent that the wine socials continue beyond the set limits of the study; (2) physicians and nurses on other wards rushed upon us with the demands that we do something of a similar nature in their provinces. This response was almost without precedent. Institutional staff tend to feel imposed on by research projects. Now instead of merely dutiful cooperation we had colleagues in medicine and nursing actually twisting our arms to do more research. In a sense, this was not so surprising, because the results had been positive and easy to see even apart from the statistics. Staff members were delighted to see residents showing a greater involvement in life, and this also made their own work more rewarding. We were able to conduct several other studies within the institution (some involving beer as well as wine), and to keep the wine flowing in its original domain. Not long afterward, we were able to do spin-off projects on the physiological and psychosocial effects of moderate wine use in other institutions and with community-dwelling elders.

The Captain's Chair eventually came into being as a permanent home for a bit of tippling and a lot of socialization. By this time we had a somewhat more developed theoretical model. This included the concept of mutual gratification: People can exercise a kind of power by giving each other pleasure. A person need not be young, strong, agile, politically connected, or affluent to be a source of mutual gratification power. A frail aged person with many physical problems and disabilities could be a charming host in The Captain's Chair—and the residents, as a group, could wield collective power through their control of a "pleasure system." (We also had quite a different theoretical model that focused on the serenity-inducing effects of certain constituents of wine.) Moreover, the sense of power from pleasure might contribute to a more general increase in self-efficacy. The formation of a Patient's Advisory Council was one indication that at least some residents now felt more empowered to influence the conditions of their everyday life. Positive changes such as these remained vulnerable to many forces, including illness and mortality among the patients, staff turnover, and budgetary pressures. Nevertheless, staff who had the perspective to judge "before" and "after" felt that the institution had become a livelier, warmer, and more interesting place as a result of the wine projects.

Looking back over a distance of years, I can see that we all needed something like wine adventures and The Captain's Chair to balance somewhat the unremitting effects of physical deterioration and the certainty of loss. No matter how diligent and competent the staff, they would seldom be able to return a patient to independent status in the community and never restore lost youth and lost loves. We all had to accommodate ourselves, in one way or another, to the limits of knowledge, the limits of therapy, the limits of control. Mr. Zella said it pretty well at his 100th birthday party:

> "I am one old guy!" (laughter and applause). "But what the hell can I do about it?" (pause). "One thing we can do about it. Everybody sing! Everybody drink!" (and so they did).

CONCLUDING THOUGHTS

These were a few of my experiences in my immediate postdoctoral years. Some good things have happened since then. The hospice movement is providing a welcome alternative for terminally ill people and their families. Many peer support groups exist through which people help each other cope with dying, death, and grief. A growing number of educators and counselors provide opportunities for people of all ages to share their feelings and develop their competencies when dealing with death-related issues. Topics that once could not be mentioned are now discussed and debated by society at large, e.g., the right to die and assisted suicide. Many negative assumptions about older adults have proven to be unfounded and are gradually being replaced with a more positive outlook. Furthermore, those who are interested in learning more about aging and the aged can find more teachers, books, and other resources to guide their path so perhaps they will make fewer errors than I did.

The cave persists, however. It will continue to persist as long as we find it necessary to bury our anxieties about aging, death, and the unknown. Unfortunately, we also continue to pay dearly for this luxury. Those who remain clouded by their dedication to unknowing are most at risk for finding themselves trapped in a cave partly of their own making. And yet this need not be. The study of human development—with aging and death left in—can provide us with a clearer vision. Wait up, Mr. Zella: We're on our way!

BIBLIOGRAPHIC NOTE

For a sampling of reports regarding the research experiences mentioned here, one might read the Weisman and Kastenbaum (1972) monograph on the psychological autopsy, and several chapters in the Mishara and Kastenbaum (1980) book, *Alcohol and Old Age*. For an overview of studies on time perspective in the later adult years, try Kastenbaum (1982). During my return tour of duty at Cushing Hospital (as director), we attempted a therapeutic program with some of the most impaired and inaccessible patients. This is reported in *Old, Sick, and Helpless: Where Therapy Begins* (Kastenbaum et al., 1981). My more recent writings include *The Psychology of Death* (rev.

ed., 1992), *Death, Society, and Human Experience* (4th ed., 1991), and a couple of encyclopedias: *The Encyclopedia of Death* (1989) and *The Encyclopedia of Adult Development* (1993). The first of these was done in the hope of learning how to spell encyclopedia reliably, but after two tries, I still hesitate. The newest book is something of a departure. *Defining Acts: Aging as Drama* (1993) presents a set of plays that I have written in which older people figure prominently. Perhaps it's just my way of continuing to enjoy the company of men and women who have lived long, eventful, and somewhat mysterious lives.

*S*UGGESTED READINGS

KASTENBAUM, R. (1982). Time course and time perspective in later life. In C. Eisdorfer (Ed.), *Annual review of gerontology and geriatrics* (Vol. 3, pp. 80–101). New York: Springer.

———— (1992). *The psychology of death* (rev. ed.). New York: Springer.

———— (1993). *Death, society, and human experience* (5th ed.). Boston: Allyn and Bacon.

———— (1993). *Defining acts: Aging as drama*. New York: Baywood.

———— (Ed.). (1993). *The encyclopedia of adult development*. Phoenix: Oryx Press.

———— (1995). *Dorian, graying: Is youth the only thing worth having?* New York: Baywood.

———— BARBER, T. X., WILSON, S. G., RYDER, B. L., & HATHAWAY, L. B. (1981). *Old, sick, and helpless: Where therapy begins*. Cambridge, MA: Ballinger.

———— & KASTENBAUM, B. K. (Ed.) (1989). *The encyclopedia of death*. Phoenix: Oryx Press.

KNAPP, R. H., & GARBUTT, J. T. (1958). Time imaginary and the achievement motive. *Journal of Personality, 26,* 426–434.

MISHARA, B. L., & KASTENBAUM, R. (1980). *Alcohol and old age*. New York: Grune & Stratton.

WEISMAN, A. D., & KASTENBAUM, R. (1968). *The psychological autopsy: A study of the terminal phase of life*. Community Mental Health Journal Monograph No. 4.

Epilogue

———— ❖ ————

After reading *The Developmental Psychologists: Research Adventures across the Life Span*, we hope that you feel the excitement that characterizes the exploration of important issues in developmental psychology. More important, though, we trust that you have gained insight into the psychological research process and the people who engage in that process.

We have devoted a great deal of energy to the preparation of this book and would appreciate your feedback. If you have any comments or suggestions for improvement, we would like to hear from you. Please forward your comments to us at the Department of Psychology, State University of New York at Plattsburgh, Plattsburgh, NY 12901.

Thanks.
Matthew R. Merrens
Gary G. Brannigan